Positive Psychology in Business Ethics and Corporate Responsibility

A volume in
Ethics in Practice
Robert A. Giacalone and Carole L. Jurkiewicz, *Series Editors*

Positive Psychology in Business Ethics and Corporate Responsibility

Edited by

Robert A. Giacalone

Fox School of Business Administration and Management
Temple University

Carole L. Jurkiewicz

Public Administration Institute
Louisiana State University

and

Craig Dunn

San Diego State University

INFORMATION AGE
PUBLISHING

80 Mason Street • Greenwich, Connecticut 06830 • www.infoagepub.com

Library of Congress Cataloging-in-Publication Data

Positive psychology in business ethics and corporate responsibility /
edited by Robert A. Giacalone, Carole L. Jurkiewicz, and Craig Dunn.
    p. cm. – (Ethics and the environment)
  Includes bibliographical references.
  ISBN 1-59311-322-6 (pbk.) – ISBN 1-59311-323-4 (hardcover)
  1. Business ethics–Psychological aspects. 2. Social responsibility
of business–Psychological aspects. 3. Positive psychology. I.
Giacalone, Robert A. II. Jurkiewicz, Carole L., 1958- III. Dunn, Craig.
IV. Series.
  HF5387.P66 2005
  174'.4'019–dc22

                                                    2005001683

Printed in the United States of America

LIST OF CONTRIBUTORS

Roy F. Baumeister	Florida State University
Jack W. Berry	Virginia Commonwealth University
Evan Browstein	George Mason University
Judith A. Clair	Department of Organization Studies Boston College
Ronald L. Dufresne	Department of Organization Studies Boston College
Craig Dunn	San Diego State University
Pacey C. Foster	Carroll School of Management Boston College
Louis W. Fry	Tarleton State University–Central Texas
Matthew T. Gailiot	Florida State University
Robert A. Giacalone	Fox School of Business Administration and Management Temple University
Carole A. Jurkiewicz	Public Administration Institute Louisiana State University
Jeanne M. Logsdon	University of New Mexico
Fred Luthans	Department of Management University of Nebraska–Lincoln
Marcia P. Miceli	Georgetown University
Barry M. Mitnick	Katz Graduate School of Management University of Pittsburgh
Janet P. Near	Indiana University
James O. Pawelski	Department of Human and Organizational Development Vanderbilt University
Isaac Prilleltensky	Department of Human and Organizational Development Vanderbilt University
Kevin L. Rand	University of Kansas–Lawrence
Ronald E. Riggio	Claremont McKenna College
Robert S. Rubin	DePaul University
Victoria A. Shivy	Virginia Commonwealth University
Hal S. Shorey	University of Kansas–Lawrence
C.R. Snyder	University of Kansas–Lawrence
William R. Torbert	Carroll School of Management Boston College
Everett L. Worthington, Jr.	Virginia Commonwealth University
Sandra Waddock	Carroll School of Management Boston College
John E. Young	University of New Mexico
Carolyn M. Youssef	Department of Management University of Nebraska–Lincoln

CONTENTS

FOREWORD

What constitutes aberrant human behavior? To this question every psychologist and most lay persons could provide an answer with confidence, and all are likely to be in part at least, correct. The discipline of psychology has skillfully focused its scientific inquisitiveness toward chronicling and analyzing that which is unhealthy in the human psyche, toward the end of healing it, making the person better, restoring them to a state of mental health. No one questions the value of such inquiry, nor should they. Profound advances have been made through research conducted within this paradigm.

Yet when we strive to restore mental health, what is it, exactly, that we hope to attain? How will we know when we get there? Is it simply the absence of pathology or negative psychological states that define mental health? Is this enough? Should there something, some level of psychological engagement beyond just the absence of problems that defines a positive psychological state? Without such a belief, does the discipline of psychology then relegate mental health to a default state of what's left when the problems have been resolved?

The authors in this book maintain this is not enough. Since its development in the 1990s, the field of positive psychology continues to grow in research volume and recognized utility, strengthening the integrity of this new paradigmatic shift in the psychological sciences. In essence, positive psychology has sought to shift attention away from a strict focus on pathologies and deficits, toward identifying attributes and traits that constitute psychological strengths and individual qualities that give life meaning and purpose, and through which individuals experience heightened opportunities for growth and satisfaction (Seligman, 1999a,b; Seligman & Csikszentmihalyi, 2000).

Positive psychology addresses a variety of different behaviors, including those with emotional foci such as flow (Nakamura & Csikszentmihalyi, 2001) and emotional intelligence (Salovey, Mayer, & Caruso, 2001); cogni-

Positive Psychology in Business Ethics and Corporate Responsibility, pages ix–xiii
Copyright © 2005 by Information Age Publishing

tive foci such as hope (Snyder, Rand, & Sigmon, 2001); interpersonal foci such as gratitude (Emmons & Shelton, 2001); and transcendent foci such as spirituality (Giacalone & Jurkiewicz, 2003b; Pargament & Mahoney, 2001). This paradigm has been articulated in a handful of seminal works. Lopez and Snyder (2003) and Snyder and Lopez (2002) offer a psychological perspective, Giacalone and Jurkiewicz (2003a) set forth the workplace spirituality argument, Cameron, Dutton, and Quinn (2003), Luthans (2002), and others contributed the organizational viewpoint, and other concept areas such as hope and generativity are covered by Snyder (2000a,b) and McAdams and de St. Aubin (1998), respectively.

At its essence, positive psychology seeks to understand the human strengths that make life worth living and, in organizational research in particular, to demonstrate a direct link between these positive psychological dispositions, business ethics, and social responsibility; the literature in this area is sparse. A few studies have attempted to link positive psychological domains such as spirituality (Cavanagh & Bandsuch, 2002; Epstein, 2002; Giacalone & Jurkiewicz, 2003a,b; Jackson, 1999; Jurkiewicz & Giacalone, 2004), corporate character (Stoll, 2002), and minimizing self-interest (Carson, 2003) to business ethics, but in the aggregate, it is clear that our understanding of the relationship between positive psychological attributes, business ethics, and social responsibility is only in the earliest stages of development.

The goal of this volume is to begin to create those critical linkages between positive psychological attributes and relevant research areas. Undoubtedly, there are many topics in positive psychology that could not be covered in just one volume, and many more topical linkages to business ethics and social responsibility that need to be made. While much research yet needs to be done in this nascent area, we hope that much as other volumes on positive psychology served as an impetus for research in social psychology (see Snyder & Lopez, 2002) and organizational behavior (Cameron, Dutton, & Quinn, 2003), this volume will ignite scientific interest in the role positive psychology plays in key areas such as ethics and social responsibility. As the study of positive psychology continues to emerge more fully, it may well help us to better comprehend the impact of this paradigm on predicting ethical decision making, organizational citizenship, and social responsibility toward the end of creating more positive and productive workplaces in general.

—Robert A. Giacalone
Temple University

Carole L. Jurkiewicz
Louisiana State University

Craig Dunn
San Diego State University

REFERENCES

Babyak, M., Snyder, C.R., & Yoshinobu, L. (1993). Psychometric properties of the Hope Scale: A confirmatory factor analysis. *Journal of Research in Personality, 27,* 154–169.

Cameron, K.S., Dutton, J.E., & Quinn, R.E. (2003). *Positive organizational scholarship.* San Francisco: Berrett-Koehler.

Campbell, D.G., & Kwon, P. (2001). Domain specific hope and personal style: Toward an integrative understanding of dysphoria. *Journal of Social and Clinical Psychology, 20,* 498–520.

Carson, T.L. (2003). Self–interest and business ethics: Some lessons of the recent corporate scandals. *Journal of Business Ethics, 43,* 389–394.

Cavanagh, G.F., & Bandsuch, M.R. (2002). Virtue as a benchmark for spirituality in business. *Journal of Business Ethics, 38,* 109–117.Chang, E.C. (1998) Hope, problem-solving ability, and coping in a college student population: Some implications for theory and practice. *Journal of Clinical Psychology, 54*(7), 953–962.

DiPadova, L.N. (1998). The paradox of spiritual management: Cultivating individual and community leadership in the Dilbert age. *Journal Of Management Systems, 10,* 31–46.

Emmons, R.A. (2003). Acts of gratitude in organizations. In K.S. Cameron, J.E. Dutton, & R.E. Quinn (Eds.), *Positive organizational scholarship: Foundations of a new discipline.* San Francisco: Berrett-Koelher.Emmons, R.A., & McCullough, M.E. (in press). Counting blessings versus burdens: An experimental investigation of gratitude and subjective well-being in daily life. *Journal of Personality and Social Psychology.*

Emmons, R.A., & Shelton, C.M. (2001). Gratitude and the science of positive psychology. In C. R. Snyder & S.J. Lopez (Eds.), *Handbook of positive psychology.* New York: Oxford.

Epstein , E.M. (2002). Religion and business—The critical role of religious traditions in management education. *Journal of Business Ethics, 38,* 91–96.

Giacalone, R.A., & Jurkiewicz, C. (Eds.). (2003a). *Handbook of workplace spirituality and organizational performance.* Armonk, NY: M.E. Sharpe.

Giacalone, R.A., & Jurkiewicz , C.L. (2003b). Right from wrong: The influence of spirituality on perceptions of unethical business activities. *Journal of Business Ethics, 46,* 85–97.

Hart, H.M., McAdams, D.P., Hirsch, B.J , & Bauer, J.J. (2001). Generativity and social involvement among African Americans and white adults. *Journal of Research in Personality, 35,* 208–230

Hatfield, E., Cacioppo, J.T., & Rapson, R.L. (1993). Emotional contagion. *Current Directions in Psychological Science, 2,* 96–99

Jurkiewicz, C.L., & Giacalone, R.A. (2004). A values framework for measuring the impact of workplace spirituality on organizational performance. *Journal of Business Ethics, 49,* 129–142.

Luthans, F. (2002). The need for and meaning of positive organizational behavior. *Journal of Organizational Behavior, 26,* 695–706.

MacDermid, S.M., Franz, C.E., & De Reus, L.A. (1998). Generativity: At the crossroads of social roles and Personality. In D.P. McAdams & E. de St. Aubin

(Eds.), *Generativity and adult development: How and why we care for the next genera-tion.* (pp. 311–333). Washington, DC: American Psychological Association.

McAdams, D. (1993). *The stories we live by.* New York: Morrow.

McAdams, D.P., & de St. Aubin, E. (1992). A theory of generativity and its assess-ment through self-report, behavioral acts, and narrative themes in autobiogra-phy. *Journal of Personality and Social Psychology, 62,* 10031015.

McAdams, D.P., & de St. Aubin, E. (Eds.). (1998). *Generativity and adult development: How and why we care for the next generation.* Washington, DC: American Psycho-logical Association.

McAdams, D.P., de St. Aubin, E., & Logan, R.L. (1993). Generativity among young, midlife, and older adults. *Psychology and Aging, 8,* 221230.

McAdams, D.P., Hart, H.M., & Maruna, H. (1998). The anatomy of generativity. In McAdams, D. P., & de St. Aubin, E. (Eds.), *Generativity and adult development: How and why we care for the next generation.* Washington, DC: American Psycho-logical Association.

McCullough, M.E., Emmons, R.A., & Tsang, J. (2002). The grateful disposition: A conceptual and empirical topography. *Journal of Personality and Social Psychology, 82,* 112–127.

McCullough, M.E., Kirkpatrick, S., Emmons, R.A., & Larson, D. (2001). Is gratitude a moral affect? *Psychological Bulletin, 127,* 249–266.

Nakamura, J., & Csikszentmihalyi, M. (2001). The concept of flow. In C.R. Snyder & S.J. Lopez (Eds.), *Handbook of positive psychology.* New York: Oxford.

Pargament, K.I., & Mahoney, A. (2001). Spirituality: Discovering and conserving the sacred. In C.R. Snyder & S.J. Lopez (Eds.), *Handbook of positive psychology.* New York: Oxford.

Ray, P.H. (1996). *The integral culture survey: A study of transformational values in Amer-ica.* Sausalito, CA Institute of Noetic Sciences.

Ray, P., & Anderson, S.R. (2001). *The cultural creatives.* New York: Three Rivers Press.

Seligman, M.E.P. (1999b). *Positive psychology: Network concept paper.* Accessed from the World Wide Web, 14th September, 1999: http://psych.upenn.edu/selig-man/pospsy.htm

Seligman, M.E.P., & Csikszentmihalyi, M. (2000). Positive psychology: An introduc-tion. *American Psychologist, 55,* 5–14.

Snyder, C.R. (1994). Hope and optimism. In V.S. Ramachandran (Ed.), *Encyclopedia of human behavior* (Vol. 2, pp. 535–542). San Diego, CA: Academic Press.

Snyder, C.R. (2000a). A new model of hope. In C.R. Snyder (Ed.), *Handbook of hope: Theory, measurement, and interventions.* New York: Academic Press.

Snyder, C.R. (Ed.). (2000b). *Handbook of hope: Theory, measurement, and interventions.* New York: Academic Press.

Snyder, C.R., Cheavens, J., & Sympson, S.C. (1997). Hope: An individual motive for social commerce. *Group Dynamics: Theory, Research, and Practice, 2,* 107–118.

Snyder, C.R., Harris, C., Anderson, J.R., Holleran, S.A., Irving, L.M., Sigmon, S.T., Yoshinobu, L., Gibb, J., Langelle, C., & Harney, P. (1991). The will and the ways: Development and validation of an individual differences measure of hope. *Journal of Personality and Social Psychology, 60,* 570–585.

Snyder, C.R., Irving, L.M., & Anderson, J.R. (1991). Hope and health: Measuring the will and the ways. In C.R. Snyder & D.R. Forsyth (Eds.), *The handbook of social and clinical psychology: The health perspective* (pp. 285–307). Elmsford, NY: Pergamon Press.

Snyder, C.R., & Lopez, S.J. (Eds.). (2002). *Handbook of positive psychology*. New York: Oxford University Press.

Snyder, C.R., Sympson, S.C., Ybasco, F.C., Borders, T.F., Babyak, M.A., & Higgins, R.L. (1996). Development and validation of the State Hope Scale. *Journal of Personality and Social Psychology, 2,* 321–335.

Snyder, C.R., Rand, K., & Sigmon, D. (2001). Hope theory: A member of the positive psychology Family. In C.R. Snyder & S.J. Lopez (Eds.), *Handbook of positive psychology*. New York: Oxford.

Spohn, W.C. (1997). Spirituality and ethics: Exploring the connections. *Theological Studies, 58,* 109–124.

CHAPTER 1

A POSITIVE ORGANIZATIONAL BEHAVIOR APPROACH TO ETHICAL PERFORMANCE

Carolyn M. Youssef and Fred Luthans

INTRODUCTION

As the turn of the new millennium marked the emergence of positive psychology, there is now a similar shift away from negativity and dysfunctional behavior, and toward human strengths and moral values and ethics in the field of organizational behavior. In this post 9-11 era, and especially in light of the ramifications of corporate scandals, both academics and practitioners have become fed up with "gloom and doom" and what is wrong with people, and now yearn for the positive, what is good, worthwhile, sustainable, and authentic. This craving for positivity is evidenced by the bulging sales of feel-good, self-improvement, airport-type books, most of which have little or no theoretical grounding nor empirical research support. Organizational leaders and other stakeholders, public policy makers, and even lay observers have become constantly on the watch for positive, innovative, and morally sound approaches for developing and managing

Positive Psychology in Business Ethics and Corporate Responsibility, pages 1–22
Copyright © 2005 by Information Age Publishing

1

for ethical performance at the self/individual, unit/group, and organizational levels.

Drawing from the positive psychology movement (Seligman, 1998b; Seligman & Csikzentmihalyi, 2000; Sheldon & King, 2001; Snyder & Lopez, 2002) and the environmental context for today's organizations, we have recently introduced positive organizational behavior, or simply POB, as "the study and application of positively-oriented human resource strengths and psychological capacities that can be measured, developed, and effectively managed for performance improvement in today's workplace" (Luthans, 2002b, p. 59). Using this definition as a point of departure, in addition to being positive and strength-based, POB capacities must be based on theory and research (thus differentiating from the popular self-help, positive literature), be somewhat unique (thus differentiating from traditional organizational behavior constructs such as positive affectivity or even humor), and, most important, state-like, open to development, change, and performance improvement (thus differentiating from trait-like, relatively fixed dispositional personality and motivational constructs found in most of positive psychology and organizational behavior). The positive psychological constructs that best meet these POB inclusion criteria include confidence/self-efficacy, hope, optimism and resiliency (Luthans, 2002a,b). Stajkovic (2003) has integrated these four into a latent core confidence factor for work motivation and we have combined them into a higher order factor we call "positive psychological capital" (Luthans, Luthans, & Luthans, 2004; Luthans & Youssef, 2004). We propose that these POB states and positive psychological capital perspectives may be the type of innovative approach to help meet the challenge of ethical performance in today's organizations.

In the current environment, organizational leaders can no longer afford to be constantly in a problem-solving mode, putting out fires and reacting to ethical breakdowns after they have turned into full-blown crises. Remedial approaches, which may have worked to a degree in the past, are not sufficient for the proactivity and creativity that today's ethical dilemmas and corporate social responsibility standards demand. Even the development and management of human and social capital, although important, are now deemed to be insufficient for effective performance (Luthans et al., 2004; Luthans & Youssef, 2004; Youssef & Luthans, 2003b) and moral, authentic leadership (Luthans & Avolio, 2003; May, Chan, Hodges, & Avolio, 2003). On the other hand, the positive organizational behavior approach, through the psychological states of self-efficacy, hope, optimism, and resiliency, or in combination as positive psychological capital, may be an alternative to the prevailing preoccupation with negatively oriented approaches and help with the ethical performance challenge facing today's organizational leaders.

Since the case has been made that investing in positive psychological capital can lead to the return of competitive advantage (see Luthans & Youssef, 2004), the argument could be made that it does not assure that this or other outcomes will be attained in an ethical manner. In other words, positivity does not equal ethicality, but neither do other proposed approaches nor guidelines. We would argue that our recently proposed POB and positive psychological capital approach to competitive advantage also has potential application to morality and business ethics. Specifically, the purpose of this chapter is to introduce the newly emerging POB states of self-efficacy, hope, optimism, and resiliency as possible contributions to meeting the challenge of ethical performance at the self/individual and, cumulatively, at the unit/group and organizational levels.

ETHICAL EFFICACY: THE CONFIDENCE IN ONE'S MORAL AND ETHICAL CAPACITY

Grounded in social cognitive theory (Bandura, 1986), self-efficacy is "one's belief about his or her ability to mobilize the motivation, cognitive resources, and courses of action necessary to execute a specific action within a given context" (Stajkovic & Luthans, 1998b, p. 66). Self-efficacy encompasses an enabling confidence that allows challenges to be perceived as achievable, efforts as conducive to accomplishment, and obstacles as surmountable. In other words, self-efficacy supports people with the power to dream, and the motivated effort to accomplish their dreams. A meta-analysis has shown that self-efficacy is strongly related to work performance (Stajkovic & Luthans, 1998a). However, since self-efficacy is domain-specific (Bandura, 1997), it is not necessarily generalizable across realms of life. However, most relevant for positive organizational behavior, self-efficacy is a trainable, developable state. Established approaches to building self-efficacy in a particular domain include mastery and successful experiences, vicarious learning and modeling, social persuasion, and physiological and psychological arousal (Bandura, 1997).

Self-Efficacy and Workplace Domains

Recent studies have shown the importance of self-efficacy in various workplace domains, such as creative self-efficacy (Tierney & Farmer, 2002), test-taking self-efficacy of job applicants (Truxillo, Bauer, Campion, & Paronto, 2002), computer self-efficacy (Thatcher & Perrewé, 2002), job change self-efficacy (Cunningham et al., 2002), participation efficacy (Lam, Chen, & Schaubroeck, 2002), career decision-making self-efficacy

(Nilsson, Schmidt, & Meek, 2002), learning self-efficacy (Ramakrishna, 2002), and entrepreneurial self-efficacy (Drnovsek & Glas, 2002). We propose that in the same way self-efficacy can predict performance in these workplace domains, "ethical efficacy" can be a helpful antecedent for self/individual ethical performance.

Bandura (1997) offers that self-efficacy regarding a particular domain should be measured on two dimensions: magnitude and strength. The magnitude of self-efficacy assesses the level of task difficulty in which a person expects to be able to perform. The strength of self-efficacy refers to the degree of certainty that a person possesses about the ability to perform at each level of difficulty (Bandura, 1997; Locke, Frederick, Lee, & Bobko, 1984; Stajkovic & Luthans, 1998b). Moreover, according to Bandura's (1997) theory-building, self-efficacy is founded in the cognitive processes of symbolizing, forethought, observation, self-regulation, and self-reflection. With this brief theoretical overview of self-efficacy as a point of departure, we now propose the conceptual linkages between self-efficacy and ethical performance.

Self-Efficacy and Ethical Performance

A widely recognized academic stream of business ethics literature can be traced back to Kohlberg's (1976, 1981, 1984) model, in which he discusses six stages of moral reasoning and development. The most basic of these stages are the two pre-conventional stages: obedience to avoid punishment (stage one), and in self-interest issues with an instrumental outcome of an exchange value (stage two). Moving to the conventional level, a step above the pre-conventional level, there is the idea of interpersonal accord and conformity to others' expectations of how a "good person" should act (stage three). Moreover, there is social accord and system maintenance, i.e., fulfillment of perceived duties and responsibilities as part of a functional institutional framework (stage four). At the highest level that very few achieve, the post-conventional level, ethics can be viewed as part of a social contract, and moral principles can be viewed as either universal rules or self-chosen ideals (stages five and six).

In addition to Kohlberg's stages of moral development, Rest's (1986) seminal theory building and subsequent research supports that ethical behavior is the outcome of a process that starts with moral recognition, followed by moral evaluations, moral intentions, and finally actions. According to Jones (1991), each of these steps is influenced by the moral intensity of the moral dilemma at hand. The dimensions of moral intensity include: the magnitude of the consequences, temporal immediacy, proximity, probability of effects, social consensus, and concentration of effect.

Although Kohlberg's work is not without criticism (e.g., see Gilligan, 1987; Noddings, 1984), clear parallels can be drawn between the magnitude dimension of self-efficacy and Kohlberg's stages of moral development, as well as between the magnitude of the consequences and probability of effects of moral intensity, and the magnitude and strength dimensions of self-efficacy. In other words, to the extent that moral reasoning can be developed, moving individuals toward higher stages of moral development, ethical efficacy can be enhanced. Moreover, the more the moral intensity of ethical dilemmas can be increased through enhancing the perceived magnitude of consequences and probability of effects, the more likely decision makers are to perceive the possibility for and extent of difference that their ethical decisions can make, further enhancing their ethical efficacy. In fact, research shows that the magnitude of consequences is the most influential dimension of moral intensity (Davis, Johnson, & Ohmer, 1998; Frey, 2000). The question is: can moral reasoning be developed resulting in ethical efficacy and ethical performance?

A Social Cognitive Approach to Developing Ethical Efficacy

Empirical support exists for the developmental nature of moral reasoning (see Rest, 1986 for a comprehensive review of 500 studies that outline factors such as education and general life experiences, and interventions that impact moral development beyond individual differences and dispositional traits). Also, there is evidence that the various steps of the ethical decision making process are developmental. For example, frequent exposure to moral issues has been found to enhance moral issue schema development, which facilitates moral recognition (Gautschi & Jones, 1998). This is in line with the findings of research that self-efficacy can be developed in a particular domain through mastery experiences (practice and performance attainments), observation of relevant role models, or even imaginal experiences, in which oneself is imagined successfully dealing with challenging situations (Maddux, 2002).

Repeated wrestling with ethical dilemmas is likely to provide opportunities for actual and imaginal experiences that can enhance ethical efficacy. In fact, one of the recent developments in the business ethics literature is the construct of "moral imagination" (Werhane, 1999). Moral imagination is the awareness of and ability to understand various dimensions of a particular context. It broadens decision makers' reasoning skills, and thus enhances their moral recognition and evaluations. Acquiring such an ability may be more effective than commonly used ethical sensitivity training programs. Commonly used ethical sensitivity training programs assume that managers act unethically out of greed or self-interest, which is not necessarily the case. Moreover, managers who act as role models when dealing with ethical issues, and who involve their associates in the ethical decision making process, are providing vicarious, as well as guided mastery experiences, and thus building their employees' ethical efficacy. The capacity of symbolizing, an integral component of social cognitive theory, seems to be particularly relevant here, as ethical situations and decisions are integrated into abstract cognitive models that can guide future (hopefully ethical) decision making and actions.

Kohlberg's model is one of several approaches to moral evaluations. For example, May and Pauli (2002) integrated two approaches to moral evaluation into Jones' (1991) ethical decision-making model. The first views evaluation as either deontological (the inherent rightness or wrongness of behavior based on personal values or rules of behavior) or teleological (a utilitarian approach based on the desirability and probability of consequences, in which alternatives that offer the greatest good for the largest numbers are selected). The second approach comes from the organizational justice literature, and classifies evaluation concerns into those of procedural justice (the fairness of allocation processes), and distributive justice (equitability of outcome distribution).

We propose that the forethought capacity from social cognitive theory is integral for moral evaluations, and to building ethical self-efficacy. If managers and employees cannot accurately estimate the future implications of their decisions and actions, many unethical consequences may be overlooked, leading to distorted justice evaluations and consequently larger-than-expected damage. On the other hand, the richer the forethought capacities of organizational members, the more they will be able to take into account the depth and breadth of the positive consequences of their ethical actions. This is likely to make ethical decisions appear more attractive and worthwhile, even in light of today's tight budgets and the prevalence of teleological evaluations.

Intentions are one of the strongest predictors of behavior (Ajzen, 1991). Therefore, if ethical intentions can be developed, ethical behavior and resulting performance are more likely to follow. Motivational aspects that moderate the process include vicarious rewards and the development of outcome expectancies (Treviño & Youngblood, 1990), which are supported in the social cognition literature. The capacity of self-regulation allows managers and employees to build and elevate their own internal standards based on their self-set ethical performance aspirations. This holds even by today's suboptimal, relativistic ethical standards that they may rank adequately. Self-regulation allows for progressive ethical standards to guide ethical intentions, even in the lack or deficiency of explicit expectations. As higher standards are met, the self-reflective social cognitive capacity is the key for ethical efficacy to be built through experienced success and accomplishment.

The Role of Social Support in Ethical Efficacy

Ethical behavior does not take place in vacuum. It impacts and is impacted by the social context within which it occurs. In today's organizations, goals are mostly shared and accomplished through the collaborative thinking, decision making, and effort of groups and teams, rather than isolated individuals. Maddux (2002) highlights the importance of collective efficacy in complementing self-efficacy. While individual abilities have limits, collective efficacy allows a group of individuals to tap each other's abilities and achieve common goals. Ethical efficacy is unlikely to develop in an organizational culture that thwarts or ridicules ethical efforts. Such a culture may numb the ethical sensitivity of some, swallow others into its public image development propaganda, and alienate the persistent few who may eventually give up or leave the organization for more ethical, socially responsible competitors.

Ethical behavior is challenging. Ethical decision making is wrapped with a lot of uncertainty, as many ethical dilemmas can at best be portrayed in shades of grey. Ethical efficacy can only be developed in contexts that are rich in social and emotional support, communication, interaction, and collective efforts. In such environments, ethical team mental models are developed, the moral intensity dimensions of ethical issues are elaborated, and the ethical decision making process is prioritized and refined, as organizational members discuss, interact, and share their experiences and perspectives regarding ethical dilemmas. Ethical decisions are made along with, not in spite of effective strategic, tactical and operational decisions.

HOPE: THE WILLINGNESS AND THE ABILITY TO ACT ETHICALLY

Based on the extensive theory-building and research of C. Rick Snyder, hope is "a positive motivational state that is based on an interactively derived sense of successful (1) agency (goal-directed energy) and (2) pathways (planning to meet goals)" (Snyder, Irving, & Anderson, 1991, p. 287). Agency thoughts are developed when the person views him/herself as the "author of causal chains of events," and incorporate the willpower, investment and energy toward goal achievement. Pathway thoughts develop when the person can predict and explain events that are related in time and logical sequence, through the systematic observation of correlation and causality (Snyder, Rand, & Sigmon, 2002, p. 259). In other words, pathways, or waypower, incorporate the ability to generate alternative ways to achieve goals, even when the original ones have been blocked. Hope is related to success in various life domains (Snyder, 2000), including the workplace (Peterson & Luthans, 2003). Snyder's research supports that hope can be both a dispositional trait and a developmental state.

Hope and Ethical Performance

We have all come across people (and organizations) that seem to be determined to act ethically, regardless of the circumstances and pressures. Such willpower is a necessary ingredient of hope. We also read about individuals, business units, and whole companies that find creative ways to achieve their goals while still maintaining their ethical standards, or even extending a helping hand through socially responsible philanthropic actions. Such ability constitutes the pathways or waypower component of hope. We propose that without such willpower and waypower, organizations and their members are likely to be trapped in their traditional ways of doing things, and would lack the drive or the innovative ability to sustain uniqueness and competitiveness.

Another chapter of this book presents a detailed discussion of hope in ethical decision making. In this chapter, we briefly outline some of the approaches to developing hope that are of particular relevance to ethical performance (see Luthans & Jensen, 2002 and Snyder, 2000 for more detailed coverage of approaches to hope development). For the willpower and waypower components of hope to develop in organizational members, they need to be targeted at specific, measurable, and achievable goals. However, for those goals to also be strategically and ethically sound for an organization, rather than just self-serving for its members, that organization needs to align individual ambitions and dreams with business unit and organizational goals (Rampersad, 2003). A clear mission and a vision from which goals and objectives emerge are very likely to serve that purpose. Such a vision should incorporate the organization's ethical goals and standards as an integral component of its strategic orientation and what it aspires to be. For example, in today's post-Enron environment, ethics have been recently proposed as one of the most effective risk management and reputation preservation strategies (Francis & Armstrong, 2003). Moreover, Reynolds (2003) has recently proposed a single ethical-strategic framework, in which the tension between the ethical dilemmas of justice versus caring is aligned with the strategic imperatives of integration and responsiveness.

Guidelines for Developing Hope for Ethical Performance

Organizations today need to have a clear approach to handling ethical dilemmas that is properly designed and communicated. Otherwise it cannot expect business unit and department managers, supervisors and associates to consistently act in an ethical manner regarding workplace ethical dilemmas because they do not have a clear ethical framework within which to operate. An even more proactive approach would be ethical goal-setting and management by ethical objectives. Such an approach is more likely to bring ethical expectations into focus, as they become part of the specific, agreed upon performance expectations, with clear, measurable performance criteria and reward/ advancement implications.

Mentoring is another, less formal, approach for those who need help in setting their ethical goals and priorities. Mentoring can also be a very effective approach to enhancing organizational members' perceptions of moral intensity. Mentors can help their protégés enrich their cognitive frames for moral recognition and moral evaluations, and guide them through more systematic and fruitful ethical planning and decision making efforts. The result hopefully translates moral intentions into ethical behaviors and performance. Such mentoring requires a huge time investment, as well as a sincere recognition on the part of the organization of the importance of helping people to learn how to perceive ethical dilemmas and set ethical goals. However, we believe that the role-modeling aspect of mentoring is indispensable for employees to buy into the organization's ethical goals and strategies for at least two reasons. First, ethical mentoring is likely to create a dialogue between managers and associates regarding ethical issues, highlighting the priority that the organization in general, as well as the manager in particular, places on ethical behavior. Second, this continuous dialogue is likely to mitigate the fear and hesitation that are usually associated with speaking about ethical concerns out loud, being the bearer of bad news regarding unethical behavior that may be underway, or even whistle-blowing if necessary.

Participative decision-making can be another very useful approach for creating open communication channels and gaining more buy-in regarding the ethical goals of an organization or a business unit. Although complex, research over the years has generally found that employees are more likely to internalize goals if they have participated in setting those goals, which increases the likelihood of goal commitment (Locke & Latham, 2002). Moreover, employees are more likely to voice their personal values and interests into those goals, which allows organizational values and ethical assumptions to be frequently challenged, put to the test, and refined when necessary.

For managers and employees to have the willpower component of hope toward ethical goals and objectives, motivation tools are necessary. Importantly, such motivation need not be financially-based. If ethical goals are attractive enough, they can generate the motivational desire and determination to achieve them through simple encouragement and recognition. This is where the importance of effective leadership comes into play. However, setting goals that are too high or idealistic is likely to reduce the sense of agency, as well as the sense of waypower, i.e., hope is diminished. People lose hope if they do not possess the means to design pathways toward the goals. On the other hand, "stretch goals" and "stepping" are established approaches for building the agency component of hope (Snyder, 2000). Stretch goals allow for new, more challenging but achievable goals to be targeted and accomplished, while "stepping" allows for difficult but important goals to be broken down into smaller, more manageable subgoals. Ethical goals are no exception. Stretching employees regarding ethical goals and standards communicates the message that ethical behavior is not the realm of saints and "do-gooders," but rather an expectation that every employee could and should measure up to. Stepping and recognition of the accomplishment of ethical milestones allows employees to gradually accept and espouse organizational values regarding ethical conduct.

One of the ways of increasing the waypower component of hope is providing managers and employees with enough resources to achieve goals. Just like rewards, resources need not always be financial. Educational and training resources are necessary for expanding managers' and employees' potential. Training need not be just directly focused on ethics and moral education in order to enhance ethical behavior (Rest, 1986). For example, problem solving and decision-making training equips organizational members with systematic approaches for designing and evaluating alternative courses of action, i.e., hope pathways. Social support and open communication channels are also resources that can facilitate the ethical decision making process leading to ethical performance. Contingency planning is another important approach for creating the perception and the reality of having alternative pathways. It creates a hope culture within the organization, where organizational members can count on the organization's preparedness for surprises as a buffer when making ethical decisions and facing the uncertainties associated with ethical dilemmas.

OPTIMISM: A POSITIVE EXPLANATORY STYLE
FOR TODAY'S ETHICAL DILEMMAS

Drawing from attribution theory and the recognized father of positive psychology, Martin Seligman's (1998a) substantial research, an optimistic explanatory style entails attributing favorable events to personal, permanent, and pervasive causes, and unfavorable events to external, temporary, and situation-specific ones. On the other hand, a pessimistic explanatory style has the opposite—externalizing positive events and attributing them to temporary, situation-specific causes, while internalizing negative events, and attributing them to permanent and pervasive causes. As is the case with the POB states of self-efficacy and hope, Seligman (1998a) emphasizes that optimism is a learnable and developable state. He presents empirical research evidence from various life domains, including work, education, sports, politics, and health.

An indiscriminant, across-the-board optimistic explanatory style can be unrealistic, and possibly irresponsible. If a person consistently takes credit for all the positive events in life, then one's talents, skills and abilities can be overestimated. If this overly optimistic person also externalizes all negative events, then responsibility for poor choices can be evaded. This is why Seligman, as well as other researchers in the area of optimism (e.g., Schneider, 2001), highlight the importance of "realistic optimism," which does not take an extreme in internalizing good events and externalizing negative ones. Seligman and others (e.g., Peterson, 2000) also recommend "flexible optimism," which is the ability to use both optimistic and pessimistic explanatory styles, and the adaptive capacity that allows for the use of alternative explanatory styles depending on the situation.

Optimism, Values, and Beliefs

According to Seligman (1998a, p. 282), the main sources of depression and learned helplessness (the opposite of learned optimism) in people's lives today are "the waxing of the self and the waning of the commons." In the past, life's meaning was drawn from a general framework of values and beliefs, which provided people with a context that is larger than themselves (Seligman calls this context "the commons"). When setbacks hit, people used to pause and reflect on their "spiritual furniture," such as their beliefs in their country, religion, family, or purposes that are beyond themselves. Besides being rich with meaning and sustainable value that helped provide stability in times of uncertainty, such beliefs reinforced in people's minds the perception, understanding, and most importantly acceptance that there are things in this life that are uncontrollable. This allowed them to legitimately externalize problems caused by external factors.

However, today much of these sources of meaning have tended to fade away due to divorce, mobility, erosion of national and religious commitment, which Seligman refers to as "the waning of the commons." Moreover, individualism and the immense increase in choices and personal control, as evidenced, for example, by the wide range of products and brands in the consumer market, have resulted in too much emphasis and investment toward pleasing and exalting the self. Consequently, the values and beliefs that gave life a meaning beyond the self may become lost, leading to an extreme personalization of positive, as well as negative events. In the search for meaning, Seligman (1998a) suggests there has been an exponential increase in experiences of helplessness as people continuously strive to expand their personal control over domains that they cannot possibly control.

Optimism and Ethical Performance

If humankind in general, and managers and employees in particular, are in a constant search for stable sources of meaning that are beyond their own selves, then it follows that an organization that builds a context of meaning and reinforces in its members the values, goals and behaviors that are targeted toward the common good are likely to have an optimistic workforce. We propose that organizations that have ethical visions, missions, values, and strategies, are more likely to capture their members' yearning for meaning, enhancing their optimism, and consequently their ethical performance. For example, the well-known mission statement of Medtronic—"to restore people to fuller lives"—has, according to the former CEO, had a reverberating effect on the ethical performance of this medical technology firm's tremendous success (George, 2003). Also, organizations that get involved, and encourage their shareholders' and employees' involvement in socially responsible decisions, programs and actions, have a better chance of winning their identification with and commitment to organizational goals and objectives, an aim that many purely profit-oriented organizations struggle to achieve. The increasing popularity and worldwide expansion of socially responsible investment (SRI) is an excellent example of the manifestation of this idea (e.g., McCann, Solomon, & Solomon, 2003; Schueth, 2003).

As organizational members find meaning and "practice" their ethical skills in a favorable ethical organizational climate, they are likely to perceive themselves as making a real difference beyond just numbers on financial statements, padding investors' portfolios, or even boosting their own paychecks and promotion opportunities (although clearly these are not mutually exclusive). In such a meaningful context, managers and employees are not only likely to build their optimism, but also their ethical efficacy and hope, since they can start regarding themselves as proactive change agents, capable of initiating and implementing ethical decisions that contribute to their organization's reputation, as well as to the well-being of overall society. An optimistic explanatory style is likely to be reinforced as organizational members successfully participate in and internalize the favorable outcomes of their ethical actions, as well as the organizational values that represent the stable (permanent), general (pervasive) foundations that guide future ethical decision making and resulting performance.

Besides optimism per se, we believe that organizations have the moral obligation to instill in their members the "realism" aspect of "realistic optimism." As noted, an optimistic explanatory style can be a double-edged sword. In order for managers and employees to steer clear of unethical behaviors, they need to be able to recognize the negative ramifications that their own behaviors can inflict on other parties. Unrealistically optimistic individuals who always externalize negative events are likely to lack this capacity, and to underestimate these ramifications. On the other hand, realistically optimistic organizational members are likely to be responsible individuals who strive toward ethically sound endeavors, rather than just blame others or use situations as excuses for their unethical pursuits.

Guidelines for Developing Realistic Optimism for Ethical Performance

Among the practical recommendations for developing realistic optimism that are particularly relevant for ethical decision making and performance are "leniency for the past," "appreciation for the present," and "opportunity-seeking for the future" (Schneider, 2001). This approach can be effective for individuals and organizations that may have previously been involved in "questionable" actions, but that are proactively trying to become more ethical and socially responsible. Leniency for the past may be the necessary "healing" process in which relevant individuals, as well as their organizations, forgive themselves and each other for past unethical decisions. Organizational members need to be able to reframe and accept their past failings, giving themselves and their organizations the benefit of the doubt, in order to perceive the present as a turning point, and to believe that the future holds second chances. Appreciation for the present is the contentment and gratitude about the positive aspects of the current situation, such as the awakening and recognition that resulted in pursuing more ethical, socially responsible actions and deeds. Opportunity-seeking for the future involves daring and courage to introduce change and the willingness to take the necessary risks and challenges associated with being different, but hopefully more ethically sound and socially responsible.

RESILIENCY: THE POWER TO STAY ON TRACK DESPITE ADVERSITY OR SETBACKS

As individuals and organizations pursue ethical decision making and performance, there are likely to be many obstacles and setbacks. For example, in most situations, ethical dilemmas bear more than one 'right' answer, and rarely does an answer hold an equal distribution of benefits and harms to all those involved. In free enterprise, making ethical choices may also involve sacrificing short-term profitability, which may be a necessity, not a luxury, for the very survival of some smaller or troubled organizations, especially in adverse economic conditions or declining industries. In such situations, resiliency is a vital capacity that can keep ethical organizations, managers and employees on track despite severe challenges.

Drawing from its legacy in developmental psychotherapy, resiliency as a POB state can be defined as "the positive psychological capacity to rebound, to 'bounce back' from adversity, uncertainty, conflict, failure or even positive change, progress and increased responsibility" (Luthans, 2002a, p. 702). Unlike self-efficacy, hope and optimism, resiliency is reactive, rather than proactive in nature. Based on the established research of positive psychologist Ann Masten and her colleagues (e.g., Masten, 2001; Masten & Reed, 2002), resiliency can be viewed as a group of phenomena that is characterized by patterns of positive adaptation in response to adversity or risk. Resiliency is influenced by three sets of factors: assets, risks and adaptational processes. Assets include knowledge, skills, abilities, social relationships, and material resources that can enhance chances of success and adaptation despite setbacks. Risk factors include adversities such as unemployment, divorce, loss of loved ones, and physical illness, as well as the lack of essential assets. Adaptational processes include coping, stress management, problem solving, and goal setting strategies. These adaptational processes may contribute more resiliency than the presence of assets or the lack of risk factors (Cowan, Cowan, & Schulz, 1996).

According to Coutu (2002, p. 48), the elements of resiliency include: "a staunch acceptance of reality; a deep belief, often buttressed by strongly held values, that life is meaningful; and an uncanny ability to improvise." Moreover, resiliency is not a magical capacity that only a few have been endowed with (Masten, 2001). It is a developable, trainable state. It is a life-long, interactive learning process, rather than just a desirable outcome or a trait that enhances chances of success (Egeland, Carlson, & Sroufe, 1993). Recently emerging literature emphasizes the importance of resiliency for employees (e.g., LaMarch, 1997; Luthans, 2002a; Luthans & Youssef, 2004; Youssef & Luthans, 2003a), managers and leaders (e.g., Luthans & Avolio, 2003; Luthans, Luthans, Hodgetts, & Luthans, 2001; Zunz, 1998), work motivation (Stajkovic, 2003), organizations (e.g., Horne & Orr, 1998; Klarreich, 1998; Ortiz, 2002; Sutcliffe & Vogus, 2003; Worline et al., 2002) and even countries (e.g., Fay & Nordhaug, 2002; Youssef & Luthans, 2003b), especially in light of the recent events and the related socioeconomic and geopolitical turbulence.

Resiliency and Ethical Performance

Managers and employees may successfully build their ethical efficacy, develop their hopeful willpower and ethical pathways, and build a realistically optimistic explanatory style regarding ethical dilemmas and decisions. However, developing and engaging in such proactive POB states by no means exempt today's managers and employees from facing adversities, or even failing to behave ethically. For example, many highly ethical managers and employees may face various pressures that may lead them to act unethically, including peer pressures, financial pressures, or even supervisory and organizational pressures (e.g., reward and promotional structures that justify ends at the expense of means). Without resiliency, such employees are unlikely to return to their ethical paths after committing questionable or unethical actions. Even when managers and employees act ethically, they may still face setbacks. For example, even when whistle-blowers and peer-reporters are protected by organizational policies, they tend to be disliked by their peers (Treviño & Victor, 1992). Without being able to consistently bounce back from such adversities and setbacks, managers' and employees' ethical efficacy, hope and optimism are likely to fade away over time.

Moreover, it is not enough that managers and employees bounce back to their previous level of ethical performance, efficacy, hope and optimism after a moral setback. As they face ever more challenging situations and counter-pressures, organizational decision makers at all levels need to be continuously able to rise up to the occasion and endure in order for the organization's ethical vision, mission, strategy, and goals to materialize and be accomplished. Resiliency is not a zero-sum, remedial approach. It allows people not only to overcome, steer through, and bounce back, but also to thrive and flourish in times of difficulty, reaching out and committing themselves to the pursuit of new challenges and to finding meaning in their lives and their relationships with others (Luthans & Youssef, 2004; Reivich & Shatte, 2002; Ryff & Singer, 2003; Sutcliffe & Vogus, 2003). When such a persistent positive perspective spreads across and trickles down an organization, it can create a culture of resiliency, enabling that organization to consistently perform ethically and meet its social responsibilities (Youssef & Luthans, 2003a).

Developing Ethically Resilient Organizations and Employees

In line with Seligman's (1998a) emphasis on the importance of stable values in providing a source of meaning and building realistic optimism, Coutu (2002) highlights the importance of realism and value-based beliefs in building resiliency. However, Coutu (2002) also warns that stable values and beliefs need not be ethical in order to contribute to the resiliency development process. For example, the "survival" values that have been held by the "fittest" and most resilient individuals in previous eras may have not been ethical (e.g., the early capitalist "robber barrons"), although they were effective in maintaining their existence and growth. That is why it is not enough to build resilient organizations and develop resilient employees. Ethical resiliency is a necessary factor in ensuring that organizations and their members thrive and flourish through sustainable, morally sound means.

Luthans and Avolio's (2003) authentic leadership model highlights the importance of the organizational context in creating leaders who are not only self-efficacious, hopeful, optimistic, and resilient, but also ethical, genuine, and transparent. Through an organizational vision and culture that emphasizes ethical strategies and approaches and capitalizes on people's talents and strengths, leaders are likely to develop self-awareness, as well as self-regulation. Self-awareness develops as leaders accurately perceive their areas of strength, as well as their areas of vulnerability. Self-regulation equips them with the capacity to adapt and adjust their approaches so that they can authentically and ethically react to challenges and gray areas. This enhances leaders' ability to build their own, as well as their associates' ethical resiliency.

In contrast to instances of ethical behavior (which may be short-lived) or to just have resilient behavior at any cost (which may be unethical), our proposed version of ethically resilient behavior allows for sustainable, morally sound performance. The realism component of resiliency (Coutu, 2002) allows organizational members to unfortunately avoid ethical, idealistic strategies and perfectionist tendencies that may defy implementation in survival-oriented profit-centered contexts. However, if they act ethically even in the face of adversity, managers and employees are likely to find personal meaning in holding onto consistent values and beliefs, and therefore to build their moral resiliency (May et al., 2003). The adaptability and ability to improvise that resiliency equips organizational decision makers with, enhances their capacity to create and evaluate alternative courses of action (pathways) when faced with ethical dilemmas. Combined with their determination (willpower) to act ethically and the confidence (self-efficacy) in their ability to do so, managers and employees can develop a calm, flexible and responsive approach (i.e., resiliency) in dealing with ethically challenging situations.

Some of the research-based approaches to developing resiliency include asset-focused, risk-focused, and process-focused strategies (Masten, 2001). In the context of ethical decision making and performance, asset-focused strategies may include leveraging managers' and employees' abilities and moral capacities through effective training and development, modeling ethical and authentic leaders, social support, and adequate material and financial resources. Accurate information, open communication, a culture of trust and transparency, and realistic performance expectations are also likely to enhance ethical resiliency through mitigating the risk factors of fear and insecurity. Together with process-focused strategies such as ethical organizational strategic planning, feedback, reward and promotional systems that emphasize ethical behavior, and consistently held organizational value systems, organizational members are more likely to develop ethical resiliency.

CONCLUSION

In today's environment, ethical behavior is finally recognized as indispensable for long-term success and effectiveness. As Bill George (2003, p. 1) recently exclaimed: "Thank you, Enron and Arthur Anderson. The depth of your misconduct shocked the world and awakened us to the reality that the business world was on the wrong track, worshiping the wrong idols, and headed for self-destruction." Ethics are no longer just the domain of philosophers, regulators, or law enforcers. Customers, shareholders and employees are becoming increasingly aware of the importance of corporate ethics and social responsibility for the sustainability of their organizations' performance, and are continuously making all decisions accordingly. Organizations, as well as their leaders and associates from top to bottom, need to equip themselves with the capacity to act ethically if they aim to meet or exceed the expectations of today's very scrutinizing stakeholders.

We have proposed the developable and manageable positive organizational behavior (POB) states of self-efficacy, hope, optimism, and resiliency that can effectively be applied to and enhance ethical decision making and consequently effective, sustainable performance at the self/individual, unit/group and organizational levels. These POB states do not replace, but rather further employ, complement, and instill deeper meaning to established approaches such as envisioning, culture-building, role-modeling, moral development, innovation, and adaptation.

Our primary purpose, like the other contributors to this volume, is to introduce an alternative framework or lens within which ethical dilemmas, as well as the approaches to dealing with them, can be viewed. Instead of emphasizing a negative, remedial approach, which views humans as predominantly unethical and solely motivated by self-interest, as part of the positive psychology movement and our recent application to organizational behavior (POB), we choose to focus our lens on managers' and employees' strengths, as powerful, responsible actors and decision makers.

Specifically, we propose that through a positive approach and the development of POB states, today's managers can:

- be ethically *efficacious and confident* of their capacities to act ethically, even in the most difficult situations.
- be *hopeful* change agents who are determined and have the will to act ethically, and who possess the creativity to continuously invent and reinvent their own and their organizations' pathways to doing things so that newer, uncertain situations can be handled in a competitive and morally sound manner.
- have a *realistically optimistic* explanatory style, which allows them to accurately assess their power and personal control over ethical situations, as well as their responsibilities, and even their areas of vulnerability.
- Have a *resiliency* to bounce back and flourish under pressures, adversities and setbacks, and are instrumental for creating and sustaining ethical cultures and response mechanisms in their own areas of responsibility and the overall organization.

The impact of this positive organizational behavior approach still needs basic and applied research to substantiate the above points, but the considerable theory and related research findings to date outlined in this chapter, suggest that it can make meaningful inroads in the complex mosaic of ethical performance.

REFERENCES

Ajzen, I. (1991). The theory of planned behavior. *Organizational Behavior and Human Decision Processes, 50,* 179–211.

Bandura, A. (1986). *Social foundations of thought and action.* Englewood Cliffs, NJ: Prentice-Hall.

Bandura, A. (1997). *Self-efficacy: The exercise of control.* New York: Freeman.

Coutu, D.L. (2002). How resilience works. *Harvard Business Review, 80*(5), 46–55.

Cowan, P., Cowan, C., & Schulz, M. (1996). Thinking about risk and resilience in families. In E. Hetherington & A. Blechman (Eds.), *Stress, coping, and resiliency in children and families* (pp. 1–38). Mahwah, NJ: L. Erlbaum.

Cunningham, C., Woodward, C., Shannon, H., Macintosh, J., Lendrum, B., Rosenbloom, D., & Brown, J. (2002). Readiness for organizational change: A longitudinal study of workplace, psychological and behavioral correlates. *Journal of Occupational and Organizational Psychology, 75,* 377–352.

Davis, M., Johnson, N., & Ohmer, D. (1998). Issue-contingent effects on ethical decision making: A cross-cultural comparison. *Journal of Business Ethics, 17,* 373–379.

Drnovsek, M., & Glas, M. (2002). The entrepreneurial self-efficacy of nascent entrepreneurs: The case of two economies in transition. *Journal of Enterprising Culture, 10,* 107–131.

Egeland, B., Carlson, E., & Stroufe, L. A. (1993). Resilience as a process. *Development and Psychopathology, 5,* 517–528.

Fay, C., & Nordhaug, K. (2002). Why are there differences in the resilience of Malaysia and Taiwan to financial crisis? *The European Journal of Development Research, 14*(1), 77–100.

Francis, R., & Armstrong, A. (2003). Ethics as a risk management strategy: The Australian experience. *Journal of Business Ethics, 45,* 375–385.

Frey, B. (2000). The impact of moral intensity on decision making in a business context. *Journal of Business Ethics, 26,* 181–195.

Gautschi, F., & Jones, T. (1998). Enhancing the ability of business students to recognize ethical issues: An empirical assessment. *Journal of Business Ethics, 17,* 205–216.

George, B. (2003). *Authentic leadership.* San Francisco: Jossey-Bass.

Gilligan, C. (1987). Moral orientation and moral development. In E.F. Kittay & D.T. Meyers (Eds.), *Women and moral theory.* Savage, MD: Rowman and Littlefield.

Horne III, J., & Orr, J. (1998). Assessing behaviors that create resilient organizations. *Employment Relations Today, 24*(4), 29–39.

Jones, T. (1991). Ethical decision-making by individuals in organizations: An issue-contingent model. *Academy of Management Review, 16,* 363–375.

Klarreich, S. (1998). Resiliency: The skills needed to move forward in a changing environment. In S. Klarreich (Ed.), *Handbook of organizational health psychology: Programs to make the workplace healthier* (pp. 219–238). Madison, CT: Psychosocial Press.

Kohlberg, L. (1976). Moral stages and moralization: The cognitive- developmental approach. In T. Lickona (Ed.), *Moral development and behavior* (pp. 31–53). New York: Holt, Reinhart & Winston.

Kohlberg, L. (1981). *The philosophy of moral development: Moral stages and the idea of justice.* San Francisco: Harper & Row.

Kohlberg, L. (1984). *The psychology of moral development: The nature and validity of moral stages.* San Francisco: Harper & Row.

Lam, S., Chen, X., & Schaubroeck, J. (2002). Participative decision making and employee performance in different cultures: The moderating effects of allocentrism/idiocentrism and efficacy. *Academy of Management Journal, 45,* 905–914.

LaMarch, J. (1997). The resilient worker: Employees who can cope with change. *Hospital Material Management Quarterly, 19*(2), 54–58.

Locke, E., Frederick, E., Lee, C., & Bobko, P. (1984). Effects of self-efficacy, goals and task strategies on task performance. *Journal of Applied Psychology, 69,* 241–251.

Locke, E., & Latham, G. (2002). Building a practically useful theory of goal setting and task motivation. *American Psychologist, 57,* 705–717.

Luthans, F. (2002a). The need for and meaning of positive organizational behavior. *Journal of Organizational Behavior, 23,* 695–706.

Luthans, F. (2002b). Positive organizational behavior: Developing and managing psychological strengths. *Academy of Management Executive, 16,* 57–72.

Luthans, F., & Avolio, B. (2003). Authentic leadership development. In K.S. Cameron, J.E. Dutton, & R.E. Quinn (Eds.), *Positive organizational scholarship* (pp. 241–258). San Francisco: Berrett-Koehler.

Luthans, F., & Jensen, S. M. (2002). Hope: A new positive strength for human resource development. *Human Resource Development Review, 1,* 304–322.

Luthans, F., Luthans, K., Hodgetts, R., & Luthans, B. (2001). Positive approach to leadership (PAL): Implications for today's organizations. *The Journal of Leadership Studies, 8*(2), 3–20.

Luthans, F., Luthans, K., & Luthans, B. (2004). Positive psychological capital: Going beyond human and social capital. *Business Horizons, 47*(1), 45–50.

Luthans, F., & Youssef, C. (2004). Human, social, and now positive psychological capital management: Investing in people for competitive advantage. *Organizational Dynamics, 33*(2), 143–161.

Maddux, J. E. (2002). Self-efficacy: The power of believing you can. In C.R. Snyder & S. Lopez (Eds.), *Handbook of positive psychology* (pp. 257–276). Oxford: Oxford University Press.

Masten, A.S. (2001). Ordinary magic: Resilience process in development. *American Psychologist, 56,* 227–239.

Masten, A.S., & Reed, M.J. (2002). Resilience in development. In C.R. Snyder & S. Lopez (Eds.), *Handbook of positive psychology* (pp. 74–88). Oxford: Oxford University Press.

May, D., & Pauli, K. (2002). The role of moral intensity in ethical decision making: A review and investigation of moral recognition, evaluation and intention. *Business and Society, 41,* 85–118.

May, D., Chan, A., Hodges, T., & Avolio, B. (2003). Developing the moral component of authentic leadership. *Organizational Dynamics, 32,* 247–260.

McCann, L., Solomon, A., & Solomon, J. (2003). Explaining the growth in UK socially responsible investment. *Journal of General Management, 28 (4),* 15–36.

Nilsson, J., Schmidt, C., & Meek, W. (2002). Reliability generalization: An examination of the career decision-making self-efficacy scale. *Educational and Psychological Measurement, 62*(4), 647–658.

Noddings, N. (1984). *Caring: A feminine approach to ethics and moral education.* Berkeley: University of California Press.

Ortiz, L. (2002). The resilience of a company-level system of industrial relations: Union responses to teamwork in Renault's Spanish subsidiary. *European Journal of Industrial Relations, 8,* 277–299.

Peterson, C. (2000). The future of optimism. *American Psychologist, 55,* 44–55.

Peterson, S., & Luthans, F. (2003). The positive impact and development of hopeful leaders. *Leadership and Organization Development Journal, 24,* 26–31.

Ramakrishna, H. (2002). The moderating role of updating climate perceptions in the relationship between goal orientation, self-efficacy, and job performance. *Human Performance, 15*, 275–297.

Rampersad, H. (2003). Linking self-knowledge with business ethics and strategy development. *Business Ethics: A European Review, 12*, 246–257.

Reivich, K., & Shatte, A. (2002). *The resilience factor: 7 essential skills for overcoming life's inevitable obstacles.* New York: Random House.

Rest, J. (1986). *Moral development: Advances in research and theory.* New York: Praeger.

Reynolds, S. (2003). A single framework for strategic and ethical behavior in the international context. *Business Ethics Quarterly, 13*, 361–379.

Ryff, C., & Singer, B. (2003). Flourishing under fire: Resilience as a prototype of challenged thriving. In C. Keyes & J. Haidt (Eds.), *Flourishing: Positive psychology and the life well-lived* (pp. 15–36). Washington, DC: American Psychological Association.

Schneider, S. (2001). In search of realistic optimism. *American Psychologist, 56*, 250–263.

Schueth, S. (2003). Socially responsible investing in the United States. *Journal of Business Ethics, 43*, 189–194.

Seligman, M. (1998a). *Learned optimism.* New York: Pocket Books.

Seligman, M. (1998b). Positive social science. *APA Monitor, 29*(2), 5.

Seligman, M., & Csikszentmihalyi, M. (2000). Positive psychology. *American Psychologist, 55*, 5–14.

Sheldon, K., & King, L. (2001). Why positive psychology is necessary. *American Psychologist, 56*, 216–217.

Snyder, C.R. (Ed.). (2000). *Handbook of hope.* San Diego, CA: Academic Press.

Snyder, C.R., & Lopez, S. (Eds.), (2002). *The handbook of positive psychology.* Oxford: Oxford University Press.

Snyder, C.R., Irving, L., & Anderson, J. (1991). Hope and health: Measuring the will and the ways. In C.R. Snyder & D.R. Forsyth (Eds.), *Handbook of social and clinical psychology* (pp. 285–305). Elmsford, NY: Pergamon.

Snyder, C.R., Rand, K., & Sigmon, D. (2002). Hope theory. In C.R. Snyder & S. Lopez (Eds.), *Handbook of positive psychology* (pp. 257–276). Oxford, UK: Oxford University Press.

Stajkovic, A.D. (2003). *Introducing positive psychology to work motivation: Development of a core confidence model.* Paper presented at the Academy of Management, Organizational Behavior Division, national meeting. Seattle, WA.

Stajkovic, A.D., & Luthans, F. (1998a). Self-efficacy and work-related performance: A meta-analysis. *Psychological Bulletin, 124*, 240–261.

Stajkovic, A.D., & Luthans, F. (1998b). Social cognitive theory and self-efficacy: Going beyond traditional motivational and behavioral approaches. *Organizational Dynamics, 26*, 62–74.

Sutcliffe, K.M., & Vogus, T. (2003). Organizing for resilience. In K.S. Cameron, J.E. Dutton, & R.E. Quinn (Eds.). *Positive organizational scholarship* (pp. 94–110). San Francisco: Berrett-Koehler.

Thatcher, J., & Perrewe, P. (2002). An empirical examination of individual traits as antecedents to computer anxiety and computer self-efficacy. *MIS Quarterly, 26*, 381–396.

Tierney, P., & Farmer, S. (2002). Creative self-efficacy: Its potential antecedents and relationship to creative performance. *Academy of Management Journal, 45,* 1137–1148.

Treviño, L., & Victor, B. (1992). Peer reporting of unethical behavior: A social context perspective. *Academy of Management Journal, 35,* 38–64.

Treviño, L., & Youngblood, S. (1990). Bad apples in bad barrels: A causal analysis of ethical decision-making behavior. *Journal of Applied Psychology, 75,* 378–385.

Truxillo, D., Bauer, T., Campion, M., & Paronto, M. (2002). Selection fairness information and applicant reactions: A longitudinal field study. *Journal of Applied Psychology, 87,* 1020–1031.

Werhane, P. (1999). *Moral imagination and management decision making.* New York: Oxford University Press.

Worline, M. C., Dutton, J. E., Frost, P. J., Kanov, J., & Maitlis, S. (2002). *Creating fertile soil: The organizing dynamics of resilience.* Paper presented at the Academy of Management, Organizational Behavior Division, national meeting. Denver, CO.

Youssef, C., & Luthans, F. (2003a). *Developing resilient organizations and leaders.* Paper presented at the Academy of Management, Organizational Development and Change Division, national meeting. Seattle, WA.

Youssef, C., & Luthans, F. (2003b). Immigrant psychological capital: Contribution to the war for talent and competitive advantage. *Singapore Nanyang Business Review, 2*(2), 1–14.

Zunz, S. (1998). Resiliency and burnout: Protective factors for human service managers. *Administration in Social Work, 22*(3), 39–54.

CHAPTER 2

POSITIVE PSYCHOLOGY OF LEADING CORPORATE CITIZENSHIP[1]

Sandra Waddock

Wage Peace
By Mary Oliver

Wage peace with your breath.
Breathe in firemen and rubble, breathe out whole buildings and flocks of redwing blackbirds.
Breathe in terrorists and breathe out sleeping children and freshly mown fields.

Breath in confusion and breathe out maple trees.
Breathe in the fallen and breathe out lifelong friendships intact.
Wage peace with your listening; hearing sirens,
pray loud.

Remember your tools: flower seeds, clothes pins, clean rivers.
Make soup.
Play music, learn the word for thank you in three languages.
Learn to knit and make a hat.

Positive Psychology in Business Ethics and Corporate Responsibility, pages 23–45
Copyright © 2005 by Information Age Publishing
All rights of reproduction in any form reserved.

23

Think of chaos as dancing raspberries,
imagine grief as the outbreath of beauty or the gesture of fish.
Swim for the other side.

Wage peace.
Never has the world seemed so fresh and precious.
Have a cup of tea and rejoice.

Act as if armistice has already arrived.

Don't wait another minute.

From the realities of corporate life and the globalized world that we live in today to a world in which companies behave as leading corporate citizens seems a remote trip to a distant village. Corporate life seems more like a war than cooperative attempts to build healthy and sustainable societies among humankind. Can we imagine a world in which community—local-ness—and globalization peacefully coexist, where the diversity of life, the integrity of markets and of organization, are honored and celebrated, where we breed peace and cooperation instead of competitiveness? A world in which true wealth is recognized in the diversity and quality of life, in the relationships that generate peace rather than violence, a world where integrity matters at every level—individual, organizational, societal? A world where the capacity of every person to live up to her fullest potential and realize his dreams, is what matters, not just in material goods and dollar signs but in connection, sustainability, and inspiration? Can we imagine a world of companies that in Mary Oliver's words 'wage peace,' that cooperate *and* compete in an effort to create services and products for a sustainable world, that show respect and provide dignity for the stakeholders with whom they interact, who respect the resources of the natural environment and the diversity of life, whose vision and values reflect their capacity to actually build the better world so many people dream of? That is the promise or at least the hope of applying positive organizational psychology to corporate citizenship.

Any vision of positive corporate citizenship is a promise far from realization in today's hyper-competitive (D'Aveni, 1994), dominator culture (Eisler, 1988) world, where might makes right and material wealth trumps other values. After all, we face an institutional world in which failures of integrity may be one of the most consistent features. The litany of poor corporate (institutional) citizenship seems endless: from corrupt governments (see Transparency International's annual corruption index at http://www.transparency.org/) to the sexual and (not incidentally) power abuses by priests in the Catholic Church, and the lack of transparency associated with hiding those abuses (Post, 2003). From the seeming incapacity of the accounting industry to live up to its public responsibilities for financial assurance, to the rampant corporate scandals that hit the airwaves and the front pages with the collapse of Enron, the misdealings and overt greed of WorldCom, Adelphia, and Tyco executive (to mention only a few of the most visible), to problems within health care, pharmaceutical, educational, and formerly respected financial institutions, including banks, brokerage firms, and investment bankers. Even respected social service institutions like the Red Cross and United Way in the United States have been hard hit by scandal. Add in what linguist William Lutz (1988–89) calls 'doublespeak' for corporate language that attempts to obfuscate, and no wonder that trust of companies (not to mention other large institutions) is at an all time low.

Protesters call for changes in the globalization policies of companies that have adversely affected their communities, cultures, and even local laws (see Cavanagh et al., 2003). Activists on issues like human rights, labor, environment, corruption, and social cohesion challenge the current view that profit is all and suggest that there may be human values more important than money. Business leaders presumably wish no harm to their stakeholders. Indeed, many corporations are actively engaged with stakeholders (Svendsen, 1998), are instituting systems for managing responsibility (Waddock, Bodwell, & Graves, 2002; Waddock & Bodwell, 2002), and have active philanthropic and community relations programs (Burke, 1999) to demonstrate their commitments to improving society. Some progressive firms are actively attempting to develop reputations as good corporate citizens, monitoring supply chain activities to ensure that standards are met, and attempting to transform themselves into sustainable companies at the ecological, community, and business levels (see, e.g., Mirvis, 2000; Mirvis, Ayas, & Roth, 2003). Many companies' leaders, positioning their companies as progressive, join efforts like the UN Global Compact, the Global Reporting Initiative, or the Fair Labor Association, or use accountability standards like AA 1000, labor standards like SA8000, or environmental management standards like ISO 14000 to demonstrate their corporate citizenship. Despite all of these initiatives (and there are many more), public trust that companies, particularly large and powerful ones, will do the right thing seems scarce.

Companies and their leaders arguably need a positive and aspirational vision of what it means to be a leading corporate citizen, just as people need inspiration, role models, exemplars, and personal aspirations that inspire achievement, creativity, and personal integrity. This is what a concept of positive corporate citizenship could provide, a way or path forward, not to perfection but to a journey that speaks of foundational values, respect for stakeholders and nature, mutuality and engagement, and active involvement in working for the common good—as defined by those who share in that good, not just individual or company gain at the expense of others.

As the special issue of *American Psychologist* on positive psychology highlights, several characteristics describe about what is currently known about individual level positive psychology (Seligman & Csikszentmihalyi, 2000). First, is a focus on happiness, optimism, subjective well-being, and self-determination, instead of unhappiness, pessimism, and subjective negativity. The second thread is that positive psychology emphasizes "human beings as self-organizing, self-directive, adaptive entities,' while the third is the recognition of the important role of social context in human happiness and well-being (Seligman & Csikszentmihalyi, 2000, p. 93). Topics related to positive psychology include relational as well as individual strengths, including the emphasis of development of wisdom, which combines individual strengths with a sense of collective good (Aspinwall & Staudinger, 2003), suggesting a link for positive psychology to levels of analysis beyond individual, including group, community, and organization.

Positive psychology deliberately turns attention away from the almost exclusive study by psychologists of mental illness toward the study of mental health at the individual level. By focusing on human strengths and individual characteristics such as "hope, wisdom, creativity, future mindedness, courage, spirituality, responsibility, and perseverance," positive psychology focuses attention on issues like autonomy and self-regulation, optimism, and self-efficacy, i.e., how happy, healthy, confident, and self-determining individuals live their lives (Seligman & Csikszentmihalyi, 2000, p. 5). With roots in humanistic psychology (Warmoth, Resnick, & Serlin, ca. 2003), the field developed after Martin Seligman issued a "call" for positive psychology in his presidential address to the American Psychological Association in 1998. At the individual level, Seligman (2000) argued that by focusing on predominantly mental illness rather than mental health, psychology was in some fundamental way failing the majority of reasonably healthy people who hoped to live even better lives. Similarly, scholars of corporate citizenship and corporate responsibility have largely emphasized the negative, unethical, and even fraudulent practices that get companies into trouble and make the front pages of daily newspapers. They have focused on bad corporate behaviors in the hope that those activities could be corrected, while providing too few insights into the ways that positive aspirations (vision), sound values, and integrity in implementation can result in positive relationships with stakeholders and even possibly value added.

POSITIVE CORPORATE CITIZENSHIP

What might this concept of positive corporate citizenship be? Can we uncover at the company- and stakeholder-relationship level what Seligman (2000, 2002) and others have begun to do at the individual level and others have begun with respect to organizational scholarship (POS) (Quinn, Dutton, & Cameron, 2003)? This paper will present a normative, rather than descriptive, conception of positive corporate citizenship, i.e., an aspirational perspective prescriptive of what might be, rather than a description of what actually is. Thus, it represents the opinion of one person, a construction that represents one view of what might be desirable for companies to engage their stakeholders, develop their strategies and practices, and operate in the world.

Leading corporate citizenship, the notion that companies develop and implement strategies and practices that treat all of their stakeholders and the natural environment with respect, dignity, and care (Waddock, 2002) is an aspiration, a goal; it is clearly not the present reality. Like the positive psychology that has been emerging at the individual level through the work of former American Psychological Association president Martin Seligman (2000, 2002), among others (e.g., Csikszentmihalyi, 1991, 1994, 1996, 1997), there is a tremendous need to focus not only on the problems of corporate citizenship, but also on the aspirational, inspirational, and hopeful aspects that have the potential to guide companies and the societies within which they operate in healthy and sustainable directions. Luthans (2002a, b) argues that a concept of positive organizational behavior (POB) at the individual level would emphasize "state-like psychological capacities" such as confidence and self-efficacy, hope, resilience, optimism, subjective well being/happiness, and emotional intelligence.

Translated to the level of corporate citizenship, which represents a company's interactions with "society," we might consider POB to encompass issues related to visioning and positive aspirations to help build a better world through business (hope and optimism), foundational values (creating a sense of subjective organizational well being), adaptiveness, mutuality, and engagement with stakeholders (related to resilience and emotional intelligence). If well implemented, such characteristics might well be expected to add value. This vision, values, value-added framework (Waddock, 2002) with its emphasis on stakeholder engagement suggests that achieving leading corporate citizenship is a long-term process that will never end.

Perhaps an analogy will help set the context. When Executive Head of the UN Global Compact Georg Kell speaks about the Global Compact,[2] a set of ten fundamental principles based on globally-agreed UN documents that companies agree to uphold, he talks about the aspirations inherent to the principles. The GC's fundamental principles focus on human rights, labor rights, and ecological sustainability and establish a high standard for human—and corporate—behavior. They set an expectation that those who are affected by or can affect the firm (the classic definition of stakeholders, Freeman, 1984) will be treated with fairness, dignity, respect, and care, principles founded on fundamental ethical principles (Cavanagh, Moberg, & Velasquez, 1981; Donaldson & Dunfee, 1999).

The media, activists, and public opinion consistently highlight the things companies do that create problems for various stakeholders and nature. Most books on corporate responsibility or corporate citizenship (the words are used interchangeably) focus on the ethical dilemmas created by bad management practices, the consequences of poor decision making for a range of stakeholders or nature.[3] The positive psychology of leading corporate citizenship takes the opposite perspective, in that it is aspirational in the same sense that the Global Compact is, representing what is known about best (or good) practices with respect to stakeholders and the natural environment.

Positive CC is, as Figure 2.1 suggests, built on certain accepted foundational values (Waddock, 2001), and uses *processes* of stakeholder engagement and reciprocity to enact an aspirational responsible vision, and makes both the reasons for and impacts of corporate activities transparent, so that accountability is ensured. Arguably, knowing what to do to be a leading corporate citizen is not rocket science. Making it real, on the other hand, seems to be the difficult task. For that, a shift of perspective or what Senge (1990) calls *metanoia* is needed, possibly for stakeholders them-

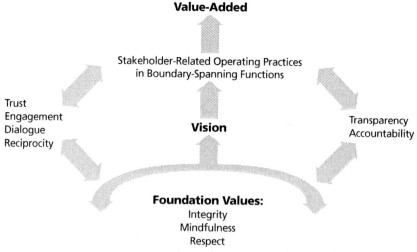

Figure 2.1.   Elements of positive corporate citizenship.

selves—who need to be willing to engage constructively with companies—as well as for corporations.

METANOIA: A SHIFT OF PERSPECTIVE

Developing positive CC calls for nothing less than a shift of mind toward a more aspirational, stakeholder-oriented view of the fundamental purposes of the firm, not to mention the ways in which stakeholder practices are operationalized. This mindset shift is what Peter Senge calls *metanoia*. *Metanoia* literally means a shift of mind, even transcendence toward a higher purpose. The fundamental concept of positive corporate citizenship implies that companies will serve in the role of citizens, contributing to and bettering the societies in which they participate, with a fundamental premise of participation by all (democracy) and an advancement of social (not just company or shareholder) good that differs quite dramatically from the current conception of the firm. Too frequently, in fact, the language of corporate citizenship suggests the separation of business from society, i.e., the term business *and* society implies that business operates alongside of society, which is clearly not the case, since businesses operate *in* society.

Use of the politically-charged word "citizenship" implies that companies are, like individual citizens, granted rights and responsibilities in society by relevant governments. Early conceptions of the corporation had these citizenship responsibilities in mind, with incorporation papers being granted only to firms that served a social purpose—and only granted for as long as that social purpose was served (Derber, 1998). Although the broader role of business in society has largely been subjugated in recent times to the single "objective function" of maximizing shareholder wealth (Jensen, 2002), many stakeholder theorists have argued that both from a managerial perspective and a conceptual perspective, companies do and need to serve the broader interests of society (see, e.g., the essays in Andriof et al., 2002, 2003; Brenner & Cochran, 1991, Wicks & Freeman, 1998). Because companies are not human beings and granting these rights and responsibilities reifies the firm, this usage is sometimes viewed as problematic, in particular because companies control significantly more resources and wield significantly more power than do most individual citizens (Matten, Crane, & Chappel, 2003). But one point is clear, companies as fictitious legal persons (citizens) are subject to laws and regulations of the societies where they operate (e.g., Laufer, 1996; Frederick, 1995).

Votaw (1961) was perhaps the first to use the term corporate citizenship in a business publication, arguing for a holistic conception defining a company's responsibilities as inherent in the fundamental practices that have the biggest impacts on stakeholders and the natural environment. In this early conceptualization, Votaw argued that the corporation's power, accountability, influence, and legitimacy, as well as society's capacity to sanction the firm (1961, p. 111) were critical aspects of establishing corporate citizenship. Since Votaw's argument was published, the question of legitimacy for the corporation on a practical level seems to have settled into the much narrower economic conception of maximizing shareholder wealth, which are what leads stakeholder theorists to argue (without necessarily using the term) for a *metanoia* with respect to corporate purposes that broadens purposes toward serving stakeholder, ecological, and societal interests.

The proposed *metanoia*, shift of mind, inherent in positive corporate citizenship refocuses the purpose of the corporation away from narrow wealth maximization for shareholders toward serving the interests of society, and, indeed, moves the level of analysis away from that of the company (or other institution) toward the health and well-being of society itself as the appropriate unit of analysis. It also focuses attention on the implementation of practices that develop positive relationships between companies and stakeholders, taking multiple interests into account simultaneously. Positive CC moves companies toward a more ecological or systems understanding of their embeddedness, interconnectedness, and interdependence with other institutions in society, the natural environment, and the people in communities, who are their primary and secondary stakeholders (Clarkson, 1995).

Arguably, such a positive vision of corporations as citizens cannot be achieved with the current one-dimensional orientation of corporations toward the maximization of shareholder wealth. Nor can it be achieved with scholarship about corporate citizenship that is predominantly focused on the negative behaviors and impacts of companies. And positive corporate citizenship in practice will require managers and leaders capable of holding multiple perspectives simultaneously, capable of integrating the perspectives of numerous other stakeholders into their own, and working with those stakeholders collaboratively as well as (sometimes) competitively. Here the words of Martin Seligman and Mihaly Csikszentmihhalyi in their framing piece introducing positive psychology to the world are relevant to thinking about what we mean by positive corporate citizenship:

> At the individual level, [positive psychology] is about positive individual traits: the capacity for love and vocation, courage, interpersonal skill, aesthetic sensibility, perseverance, forgiveness, originality, future mindedness, spirituality, high talent, and wisdom. At the group level, it is about the civic virtues and the institutions that move individuals toward better citizenship: responsibility, nurturance, altruism, civility, moderation, tolerance, and work ethic. (Seligman & Csikszentmihhalyi, 2002, p. 6)

At the organizational (company) level, positive corporate citizenship is about other virtues that have come to the public attention in the wake of anti-globalization activism: vision and values resulting in value added, specific processes, such as stakeholder engagement, trust-building, dialogue, reciprocity, transparency, responsibility, accountability. The implication is that company leaders need to act with integrity and mindfulness about impacts on and respect for stakeholders and the natural environment (Waddock, 2001, 2002). Let us explore below some of the core ideas associated with the notion of positive CC, along with some of the shifts in vision, values, and practices that will be necessary to achieve positive or leading corporate citizenship in tomorrow's world.

The Wisdom to Create Vision Linked to Values

Today more than ever leaders need to have the wisdom to ensure that their companies are contributing to society, making things better, not worse. That is the dream of positive corporate citizenship: that companies become actors for the betterment of society, not simply by "doing good" through philanthropy or having employees volunteer (or what corporate community relations professionals call "tee shirts and balloons" or feel good programs), but through refocusing their strategies and operating practices, where their major impacts are felt, and by operating with integrity and mindfulness. What positive CC means is that companies operate with respect for the dignity and worth their stakeholders in society and the natural environment. The *metanoia* embedded in this vision demands wisdom of corporate leaders that is not yet widespread, because traditionally the role of the firm has been viewed solely from the perspective of business, not from that of the good of society as a whole. Business leaders need to learn to think from a more holistic perspective to take the positive CC agenda seriously.

Many people trained in management and business programs today operate by drawing from dominant economic models that lead them to argue that the purpose of business is to maximize shareholder wealth, a solely financial goal benefitting only the shareholders. Positive CC calls for a broader vision that demonstrates not only how the company's products and services better society in some way but also that the practices (processes, policies, and procedures) implemented to deliver those products and services at worst do no harm and may even improve society. Simultaneously, positive CC calls for ensuring that stakeholders are treated well, potentially in accord with the numerous emerging sets of global principles and codes of conduct, like the UN Global Compact, the OECD Guidelines for Multinational Enterprises, the Caux Principles, and the Global Sullivan

Principles, to name only a few. Table 2.1 highlights some of the shifts in vision that are needed to move from current conceptions of corporate vision to leading corporate citizenship.

Table 2.1.   Vision and Positive Corporate Citizenship

Vision shifts from...	to...
Maximizing shareholder wealth without regard for other stakeholders	Doing something important and useful for customers using the full resources of employees in a way that treats all stakeholders with dignity and respect resulting in success and profitability.
General nonspecific core purpose	Building a better world in some way, creating meaning and higher purpose generating passion and commitment to that purpose and vision among stakeholders, especially employees
Corporate vision and strategy are available only to top managers	Corporate vision and strategy are shared by all primary stakeholders, are clearly articulated, and relate to higher purposes
Business is separate from society Responsibility is discretionary	Business is integral to society Responsibility is integral to and implicit in all practices that impact human and natural ecologies, is transparent for accountability
Stakeholder "management" Leaders direct through authority from the top	Stakeholder relationships Leaders generate meaning that guides core purposes and enables others to act in one's own and the enterprise's best interest

Source: Waddock (2002, Ch. 12).

The shifts identified in Table 2.1 move the fundamental concept of the corporation from the top-down, highly bureaucratic enterprises that value profitability above other aspects of organizing and separate business from society toward an integration of the company's activities, vision, values, and operating practices into society itself. The attitude toward stakeholders also changes from that of "managing" them toward the recognition that companies need and can manage *relationships* with their stakeholders but not always the stakeholders themselves. Relationship implies mutuality, interaction, and engagement that result in co-determination, along with a degree of transparency and accountability, not a one-sided, top down authority dictating what is good for stakeholders and the world. The role of leadership in this positive CC perspective also shifts from authority to meaning-maker and guide. But, as the work of Collins and Porras (1997) demonstrates, vision alone is insufficient to create visionary companies and, for sure, positive corporate citizens. If business is to operate successfully in society as a corporate citizen, contributing positively, then values underpinning vision need to be generative with respect to both the business and the societies in which the business operates as the next section will discuss.

Generative Values beyond Economizing

Leaders of corporations tend to focus, as does much of western civilization, on the measurable and quantitative assessments of performance, even in organizational life. Methods of understanding the world generally focus on "objective" indicators that are readily measurable; money becomes the primary measure of success (because it is believed to be objective), and in typical atomistic fashion, the focus is on satisfying the needs and interests of one group of primary stakeholders, the shareholder. This scientific or atomistic perspective, which separates subjective issues of mind, emotion, and spirit from the physical world, typifies western civilization and ends up focusing much attention on material goods as a signifier of wealth (e.g., Cavanagh et al., 2002; De Graaf, Wann, & Naylor, 2001; Schor, 1999) and on financial results as the critical measures of performance without much regard for so-called "softer" or non-quantitative impacts and outcomes.

Frederick (1995) has argued that these emphases of modern business have resulted in two dominant values in business as we know it today (with other supporting values). The dominant value is economizing, which means the prudent and efficient use of resources, i.e., an efficiency motive that results in value added in quantitative (financial) terms. The second value is what Frederick terms power aggrandizing, which means augmenting and preserving the power of managers and the organization itself, which tends to result in a growth orientation (see Table 2.2). Society can be conceived as having three basic spheres of human civilization, business (economic), government (political), and societal (civil society), underpinned by the natural environment (Waddock, 2002). Frederick (1995) argues that in nature, ecologizing, i.e., the tendency of evolutionary and natural processes to "interweave the life activities of groups in ways conducive to the perpetuation of an entire community" (Frederick, 1995, p. 9), is the dominant value, and some (e.g., Moore, 1997; Hawken, 1993; Hawken, Lovens, & Lovens, 1999; McDonough & Braungart, 2002), have argued that businesses also need to take a more ecological perspective. Positive CC adopts this ecological perspective, and moves from organizations structured through hierarchy, authority, growth at all costs, and power dominance toward values of partnership, equality, and democracy, reuse and conservation of resources, and respect for all stakeholders, including the natural environment.

Table 2.2.   Generative Values for Positive Corporate Citizenship

Values shift from...	to...
Economizing and power aggrandizing	... and including civilizing and ecologizing
Imbalance	Balance
No respect or dignity for stakeholders	Respect and dignity for all stakeholders
Hierarchy	Shared power, empowerment with *appropriate* hierarchy
Dominance	Partnership, equality
Authority	Democracy
Competition	Collaboration *and* competition
Control through systems	Control through goals and values
Exclusive	Inclusive, respect and dignity for life
Value the objective, scientific, observable	An integral perspective that values the objective *and* subjective, inter-objective *and* inter-subjective
Disconnected, fragmented, autonomous	Connected, holistic, networked (linked)

Such an orientation toward positive CC requires that companies engage with stakeholders in demanding and interactive relationships around issues that enhance not only corporate results, but also communal and societal aspects of human life with which those stakeholders are involved and about which they are concerned. Arguably, more stakeholder engagement generates sharing of perspectives and can create forces for civilizing humanity and bettering society, rather than generating still more competition, wasted resources, and materialism, factors now dominating much of the industrialized world (e.g., Cavanagh et al., 2002; De Graaf et al., 2001; Schor, 1999). From dog-eat-dog competition as the dominant operating mode, positive CC would move businesses toward the type of understanding that modern biologists and other scientists now have that companies, like nature, thrive on an appropriate mixture of competition *and* cooperation (called symbiosis in biology) (Capra, 1995; Kauffman, 1995; Maturana & Varela, 1998).

An orientation toward positive CC would also bring better balance into societies now dominated by business interests and values of economizing, moving toward allowing for more voice from stakeholders in civil society with values related to something other than monetary success as well as those stakeholders representing the voiceless natural environment. Positive CC values are those of respect, dignity, and appreciation for life in all its diversity that Donaldson and Dunfee (1999) would term hypernorms and Korten (1999) and others (Cavanagh et al., 2002) believe are needed to change the world for the better. Such values might also include relationship, aesthetic appreciation, mind, and spirit, none of which are tangible, and a willingness to make assumptions that stakeholders are people to be valued in their own right as ends, not means, a fundamental ethical premise (see Table 2.2). The rationale for this broadening of values is explained below.

Positive corporate citizenship, with its inherently stakeholder- and eco-logical-orientation, implicitly posits the need for a more integrated set of values that incorporate not only values of economizing and power aggran-dizing, but reach beyond them to encompass sustainability (ecologizing) for the business as well as communities and societies at the more macro level. Positive CC also argues that the civilizing values of relationship embedded in civil society are important to building a world where human-ity can thrive. Achieving the inherent metanoia in this new vision requires that individuals in companies (and society) have the capacity for under-standing different perspectives and even different paradigms. This capabil-ity can be found in individuals who have developed beyond the conventional levels to post-conventional types of cognitive and moral rea-soning (Gilligan, 1982; Kohlberg, 1976; Torbert, 1991; Wilber, 1995) and are therefore able to perspective-take (Waddock, 2001). Philosopher Ken Wilber (1995, 1996, 1998a,b) has offered a useful framework for under-standing why both higher levels of cognitive/moral development are needed and that examines the types of perspectives on any given system that are possible (Figure 2.2). Wilber argues that for every conscious sys-tem (including, arguably, the earth and even the universe) there are four perspectives that need to be taken. In a two-by-two matrix, Wilber's frame-work illustrates four important perspectives that need to be considered so that any system can be fully comprehended: on the vertical axis, consider-ation there are two levels of analysis: individuals and collectives (of varying sizes). On the horizontal axis are subjective (left-hand side) and objective (right-hand side) perspectives.

In every conscious system, Wilber argues, there are components that represent objective or measurable factors, e.g., the individual-objective level of analysis or the "it" perspective, the collective-inter-objective compo-nent or "its." On the subjective side, which is inherently less measurable because of the subjectivity and therefore given short shrift in typical mod-ern corporations and western societies, are subjective elements, expressed as the individual-subjective component or the "I." Individual-subjective ele-ments might cover, e.g., aesthetic appreciation, emotions, and individual awareness. Finally, there is the collective-inter-subjective or "we" compo-nents, which would be expressed in culture, group cohesion, norms, and values as experienced by the group. Since businesses are human or living

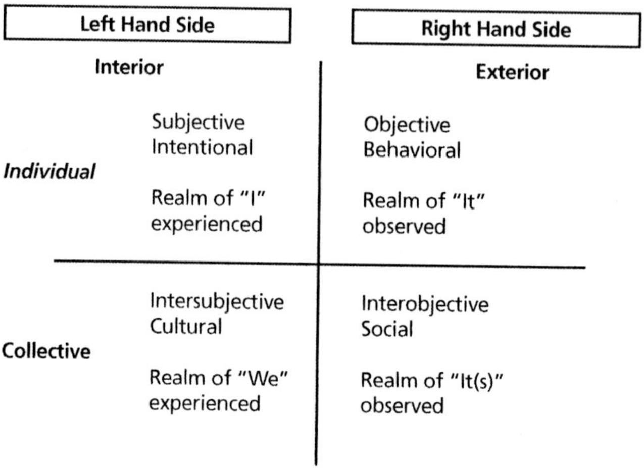

Left Hand Side	Right Hand Side
Interior	**Exterior**

	Interior	**Exterior**
Individual	Subjective Intentional Realm of "I" experienced	Objective Behavioral Realm of "It" observed
Collective	Intersubjective Cultural Realm of "We" experienced	Interobjective Social Realm of "It(s)" observed

Figure 2.2.   Wilber's framework for understanding holons.

systems, a serious understanding of positive CC would incorporate not only traditional quantitative or objectively measurable factors related to objective indicators of performance, but also take into account the subjectively-experienced impacts that companies have on stakeholders and nature at both the individual and collective levels as added performance measures. To a large extent, it is subjectively-important factors that cause many stakeholders to criticize corporate practices, such as human rights abuses, outsourcing practices, ecological abuses, and the like. Positive CC provides a space for the articulation of subjectively-experienced values, emotions, and awareness in addition to traditional quantitative and more objective indicators, thus bringing in and valuing data from all four perspectives.

AN INTEGRAL PERSPECTIVE ON POSITIVE CORPORATE CITIZENSHIP

Gaining the needed new perspective or metanoia that would result in a positive CC involves incorporating into our thinking a new set of "logics" or ways of thinking and new values that accompany those logics. As identified by Austrom and Lad (1989) (see Table 2.3) with additions from Wilber (1995, 1996) and Waddock (2002), these new logics involve moving away from mechanistic thinking that attempts to atomize or fragment the world into smaller pieces toward more ecological or systemic perspectives that rely on organic perspectives based in the emerging sciences of complexity and chaos theories, recognizing a more holistic conception of interrelationships among all aspects of the world, which is a view based on complexity

Table 2.3.   New Logics and New Values

Prevailing Paradigm	Emergent Paradigm
Basic World View	
Mechanistic, simple, linear Cartesian, Newtonian	Organic, complexity, chaotic, ecological, systemic
Atomistic, fragmented	Holistic (holons)
Objective	Objective, subjective, inter-objective, inter-subjective
Disengaged, passive	Engaged, active
"It" orientation	"I," "we," and "it" orientations
Passive and hierarchical	Self-organizing and determining
Implicit Logics: Perspectives	
Focus on distinctions and separations	Focus on interdependence and inter-relatedness, connections
Either/or oppositions	Both/and relationships, linkages
Dualities as opposites and contradictions	Dualities as paradoxes to be lived with
Top down	Top down/bottom up
Leading Values	
Self-contained individualism and agency	Individualism combined with community
Zero-sum game mentality	Positive-sum gain mentality
Win-lose orientation	Win-win orientation
Linear progress toward goals	Ecological/cyclical goal orientation

Sources: This chart is adapted from Austrom and Lad (1989) with additions from Wilber (1998) and Waddock (2002).

theory, concepts of self-organization, and development through multiple states of awareness toward broader, more encompassing perspectives that allow for perspective-taking and understanding of the interrelationship of multiple paradigms. The new views have incorporate both subjective and objective aspects of organizational life as discussed above.

Positive CC emphasizes not only being more holistic and inclusive worldview, but also taking a more integral or integrated perspective as the values on the bottom of Table 2.2 and the new logics of Table 2.3 suggest. The key to successfully developing positive CC is arguably to provide ways for doing what Wilber says must be done to fully comprehend any system: speak simultaneously to and from the perspective of all four quadrants, not just one. For example, company managers employing unskilled workers in developing nations are doing so largely for economic reasons, but may also believe that they are providing jobs to workers who would not otherwise have work. They point to the number of positions created, wages paid, productivity levels, and profitability, all "objective" measures of performance that can be focused on at the individual and collective levels. Managers of large corporations operating from an economizing perspective may see their impacts primarily in terms of financial and productivity gains. Thus, they are largely oriented toward objectively measurable inputs, outputs, and outcomes.

Social activists on human rights and labor conditions, on the other hand, may be discussing issues that, while having some measurable components, largely speak to the quality of human life as experienced by the workers or the cultural impacts of new types of work and jobs on local society. At the more macro level, social activists may be concerned about the impact of corporate activities on local cultures, values, and norms, and the diversity and self-sustainability of local businesses, as well as the quality of life in terms broader than mere material benefits; they are talking about life as it is *experienced* by those affected by corporate actions. When human rights activists ask that people be treated humanely, with respect and dignity, be valued as unique human beings, they are effectively demanding that different cultures and norms be valued for their uniqueness and diversity, rather than being homogenized by the impact of transnational corporations' goods, service, and operating modalities.

Consideration of the differences in language, values, and priorities among the four quadrants in Wilber's framework helps shed light on why issues of positive (or traditional) corporate citizenship may be given short shrift in typical corporate life and why achieving the metanoia has been so difficult. Effectively, social activists and many other stakeholders, speaking about the ways in which they perceive corporate activities affecting them, their communities, their society, or even nature, are speaking from the subjective quadrants. Operating from the perspectives of the subjective experiences of stakeholders, their values, their emotions, thoughts, aesthetic appreciation, and similarly subjective responses to changes in their lives, as well as material benefits that can be measured in more objective terms. Corporate leaders, on the other hand, are speaking from economic, accounting, productivity, and other quantitatively-oriented and measurable "bottom line" results. In many ways, these groups are speaking entirely different languages without understanding that they are doing so.

Under these circumstances, it is hardly surprising that managers and other stakeholders, particularly social activists, take diametrically opposed positions on the role of the corporation in society. And this discussion barely touches on another sensitive issue, that of power, which many stakeholders view the corporation as holding because of the control of money and other resources. Positive CC seeks an integration of understanding of all four different perspectives—both objectively measured performance and subjectively experienced impacts and outcomes—that internal and external stakeholders bring to their interactions with the company. That integration is what the implicit purpose is behind the evolution of stakeholder dialogue and engagement (Calton & Payne, 2003; Payne & Calton, 2002; Svendsen, 1998; Waddell, 2002).

VALUE ADDED OF BEING POSITIVE

A core of positive psychology is that it represents human beings as "self-organizing, self-directed adaptive entities" (Seligman & Csikszentmihhalyi, 2002, p. 10). Translated to the organizational level in a corporate citizenship frame, we can envision companies as self-organizing entities, particularly with respect to boundary relationships, where individual employees at all levels have the awareness and perspective-taking capacity that are needed to understand multiple stakeholders' perspectives and engage productively with them on a variety of different values bases. One thing that the discussion of the four quadrants in Wilber's framework above makes clear is that many of the problems that external stakeholders have in communicating their views successfully to corporate leaders arise from values and perspectives differences when corporate managers and stakeholders fail to appreciate that they are speaking from entirely different quadrants.

Positive corporate citizenship posits that individuals in companies will act with the confidence, capacity, and know-how to engage with the relevant stakeholders affected by and affecting their activities constructively, that they will be able to interpret and communicate in the context of all four perspectives, individual and collective subjective and objective. As an example, the production person or machine operator would understand how the quality of the product affects the customer's experience in using the product and how disseminating that product affects the community, as well its cost, the number sold, and profitability. She would be able to envision how resource use within the firm affects the natural environment. He would be self-directed in his/her job to produce products of high quality that satisfy customer needs, while minimizing waste because of the inherently ecological framing embedded in his and her work. Stakeholder impacts and relationships would naturally be taken into account with every decision made—and decisions themselves would devolve to the lowest level in the enterprise affected by them, engaging stakeholders as needed to ascertain their input and experiences of the company's actions, products, and services.

Companies create value added through their economizing activities, i.e., efficiently creating goods and services. These activities generate wealth, employment, and even structures that create social coherence, progress, and meaning for stakeholders. Businesses also create opportunities for investment, can help to sustain, grow, or destroy local communities, and build important social and physical infrastructure. Clearly, today's businesses are social agents deeply tied to the character of societies and, as with other social agents, there is a social expectation in democracies that they will act to serve the interests of society. To claim that the sole function of business is to maximize wealth for one group of (fairly elite) stakeholders, while simple, clear, and even predictive of financial performance, is to ignore the important social functions and impacts on stakeholders and nature that businesses necessarily have, which the four quadrant framework makes explicit.

Recognition that actions take place within a social context is another important theme of positive psychology (Seligman & Csikszentmihhalyi, 2000). Social context is also a central element of positive corporate citizenship, indeed, perhaps the central element, and is, as subjective experience is, not measurable to the same degree as profitability. Company executives aspiring to leading corporate citizenship *know* that their companies operate *in* society in a relationship that is meant to be mutually beneficial. If we ask the foundational question, "what is business for?" (Handy, 2002) and are somehow able to ignore the dominant economic ideology (i.e., belief system), which suggests that their sole function is to maximize the wealth of shareholders, we might come to answer that involves serving the best interests of *societies*, meeting both quantitatively measurable and material needs and subjectively experienced needs—of customers, employees, investors, allies and partners, governments, and communities. Of course, such an approach might not be profit maximizing in the traditional sense, but from a values-driven basis could be wealth maximizing for societal stakeholders, where wealth is meant to encompass whole sets of values (such as quality of life, health of the natural environment, diversity of species and cultures, as examples) well beyond financial.

Is there, can there be, such a higher purpose to business, something more transcendent that provides vision that inspires, something that is represented by the phrase positive corporate citizenship? Transcendence points toward a conception of businesses *in* society, as part of, integral to, and embedded in societies, not separate from them, and somehow working for the betterment of society. It also points toward an integration of core values, constructive values that build positive relationships with stakeholders and forcefully demonstrate how the company expects to live out its vision. Positive corporate citizenship (CC) is built on such aspirational visions linked to values, vision that includes something of how the company's business strategies and activities build a better world or interact with the company's stakeholders in constructive ways. Perhaps the best known such vision is Johnson & Johnson's famous Credo, which outlines J&J's responsibilities to its patients and health providers, customers, employees, suppliers, and owners.[1]

The new perspective thus asks leaders of and within corporate citizens to think deeply about the meaning and implications of *all* of the decisions they are making and what their impact on the world around us is likely to be. Leading citizens can do this because they explicitly recognize that there will be impacts and consequences of decisions. They know that *all* decisions are embedded with a set of values that either honors the relationships and stakeholders they impact or not. They are *engaged* in ongoing *relationships* with stakeholders and understand their perspectives, even when they are radically different than the company's internal perspective. This *metanoia* asks leading citizens to seek meaning and meaningfulness in decisions so that everyone can bring his or her whole self—mind, heart, body, spirit—to work (as opposed to "checking" their brains or heart at the door).

The changes in organizations and societies today also demand that leadership be distributed throughout the enterprise, rather than held closely in a few top managers' hands. Distributed leadership means taking responsibility for the consequences of one's actions (and thinking through what those consequences are likely to be). It also asks many—most—individuals to assume qualities more like entrepreneurs, self-initiators, and leaders than ever before, to be responsible for their own productive engagement with others and for the results that the decisions they make achieve. Leadership, in this sense, falls to everyone who takes part in bringing to reality the vision embodied in the higher purposes shared by individuals within the enterprise.

Ultimately, this *metanoia* asks leaders in corporate citizens to seek *wisdom* and *mindfulness* in their work as leaders of and within corporate citizens (Ackoff, 1999; Weick, 1999). Mindful and wise leaders think through the consequences of their decisions to all of the stakeholders those decisions impact. Mindful leaders are aware that they do not and cannot know all that they need to know, but take seriously the responsibilities—all of them—attendant upon their leadership. They continue to grow, learn, and develop and embed learning practices within their enterprises as part of the culture. Wisdom among corporate leaders aimed at society would arguably provide the basis for understanding that business, an institution created by society for the benefit of society, ultimately needs to serve *society's* and multiple stakeholders' interests, not merely those of investors, and that the impacts of corporate actions are experienced subjectively as well as objectively recorded. According to Ackoff "*Wisdom is the ability to perceive and evaluate the long-run consequences of behavior.* It is normally associated with a willingness to make short-run sacrifices for the sake of long-run gains"(Ackoff, 1999, p. 16). I would add that the wisdom associated with positive CC argues for companies being both efficient (economizing in the words of Frederick, 1995) *and* effective (in Drucker's sense of doing the right thing) in a logic not of either/or, but of both/and that serves the good of the business, of stakeholders and the natural environment, *and* of societies simultaneously. It is achieving this perspective that is the hope that the waging peace embedded in positive corporate citizenship provides.

NOTES

1. The inspiration for this paper is partially from Chapter 12 of Sandra Waddock, *Leading Corporate Citizens: Vision, Values, Value Added,* New York: McGraw-Hill, 2002.
2. See www.unglobalcompact.org for more information.
3. Recognizing that stakeholders are people, yet needing to also include consequences of corporate actions on the natural environment, I will use the word stakeholder to represent stakeholders and the natural environment, treating the environment "as if" it were a stakeholder (Windsor, 2002).
4. See http://www.jnj.com/our_company/our_credo/index.htm, 9/15/03.

REFERENCES

Ackoff, R.L. (1999). On learning and the systems that facilitate it. *Reflections, 1*(1), 14–24. [Reprinted from The Center for Quality of Management, Cambridge, MA, 1996.]

Andriof, J., & Waddock, S. (2002). Unfolding stakeholder engagement. In J. Andriof, S. Waddock, B. Husted, & S. Rahman (Eds.), *Unfolding stakeholder thinking* (pp. 19–42). Sheffield, UK: Greenleaf.

Andriof, J., Waddock, S., Husted, B., & Rahman, S. (Eds.). (2003). *Unfolding stakeholder thinking 2: Relationships, communication, reporting and performance.* Sheffield, UK: Greenleaf.

Aspinwall, L.G., & Staudinger, U.M. (2003). A psychology of human strengths: Some central issues of an emerging field. In L.G. Aspinwall & U.M. Staudinger (Eds.), *A psychology of human strengths: Fundamental questions and future directions for a positive psychology.* Washington, DC: American Psychological Association.

Austrom, D.R., & Lad, L.J. (1989). Issues management alliances: New responses, new values, and new logics. In J.E. Post (Ed.), *Research in corporate social performance and policy* (Vol. 11, pp. 233–355). Greenwich, CT: JAI Press.

Berle, A., & Means, G. (1932). *The modern corporation and private property.* New York: Macmillan.

Brenner, S., & Cochran, P. (1991, March). A stakeholder theory of the firm. *Proceedings of the International Association of Business and Society,* Sundance, UT.

Burke, E.M. (1999). *Corporate community relations: The principle of the neighbor of choice.* Westwood, CT: Praeger.

Calton, J.M., & Payne, S.L. (2003, March). Coping with paradox: Multistakeholder learning dialogue as a pluralist sensemaking process for addressing messy problems. *Business & Society, 42*(1), 7–42.

Cameron, K.S. (2003). Organizational virtuousness and performance. In K.S. Cameron, J.E. Dutton, & R.E. Quinn (Eds.), *Positive organizational scholarship: Foundations of a new discipline* (pp. 48–65). San Francisco: Berrett-Koehler.

Capra, F. (1995). *The web of life.* New York: Anchor Doubleday.

Cavanagh, G.F., Moberg, D.J., & Velasquez, M. (1981). The ethics of organizational politics. *Academy of Management Review, 6*(3), 363–374.

Cavanagh, J., Mander, J., Anderson, S., Barker, D., Barlow, M., Bellow, W., Broad, R., Clarke, T., Goldsmith, E., Hayes, R., Hines, C., Kimbrell, A., Korten, D., Norberg-Hodge, H., Larrain, S., Retallack, S., Shiva, V., Tauli-Corpuz, V., & Wallch, L. (2002). *Alternatives to economic globalization.* San Francisco: Berrett-Kohler.

Clarkson, M.B.E. (1995). A stakeholder framework for analyzing and evaluating corporate social performance. *Academy of Management Review, 20*(1), 92–117.

Collins, J.C., & Porras, J.I. (1997). *Built to last: Successful habits of visionary companies.* New York: HarperBusiness.

Csikszentmihalyi, M. (1991). *Flow: The psychology of optimal experience.* New York: HarperCollins.

Csikszentmihalyi, M. (1994). *The evolving self: A psychology for the third millennium.* New York: Harperperennial Library.

Csikszentmihalyi, M. (1996). *Creativity: Flow and the psychology of discovery and invention.* New York: HarperCollins.

Csikszentmihalyi, M. (1997). *Finding flow: The psychology of engagement with everyday life.* New York: Basic Books.

D'Aveni, R. (1994). *Hypercompetition: Managing the dynamics of strategic maneuvering.* New York: Free Press.

De Graaf, J., Wann, D., and Naylor, T.H. (2001). *Affluenza: The all-consuming epidemic.* San Francisco: Berrett-Koehler.

Derber, C. (1998). *Corporation nation: How corporations are taking over our lives and what we can do about it.* New York: St. Martin's Press.

Donaldson, T., & Dunfee. T.W. (1999). *Ties that bind: A social contracts approach to business ethics.* Boston: Harvard Business School Press.

Eisler, R. (1988). *The chalice and the blade: Our history, our future.* San Francisco: HarperCollins.

Freeman, R.E. (1984). *Strategic management: A stakeholder approach.* Boston: Pitman.

Gilligan, C. (1982). *In a different voice: Psychological theory and women's development.* Cambridge, MA: Harvard University Press.

Handy, C. (2002, December). What's a business for? *Harvard Business Review,* pp. 49–55.

Hawken, P. (1993). *The ecology of commerce.* New York: HarperBusiness.

Hawken, P., Lovens, A., & Lovens, L.H. (1999). *Natural capitalism: Creating the next industrial revolution.* Boston: Little Brown.

Jensen, M.C. (2000). Value maximization, stakeholder theory, and the corporate objective function. In M. Beer & N. Norhia (Eds.), *Breaking the code of change.* Boston: Harvard Business School Press.

Kauffman, S. (1995). *At home in the universe: The search for the laws of self-organization and complexity.* New York: Oxford University Press.

Kohlberg, L. (1976). Moral stages and moralization: The cognitive-developmental approach. In T. Lickona (Ed.), G. Geis & L. Kohlberg (Consulting Eds.), *Moral development and behavior: Theory, research, and social issues.* New York: Holt, Rinehart and Winston.

Korten, D. (1999) *The post-corporate world.* San Francisco: Berrett-Koehler.

Lutz, W. (1988–89, Winter). Doublespeak. *Public Relations Quarterly, 33*(4), 25–31.

Matten, D., Crane, A., & Chapple, W. (2003, June). Behind the mask: Revealing the true face of corporate citizenship. *Journal of Business Ethics, Part 2, 45,*(1/2), 109–121.

Maturana, H.R., & Varela, F.J. (1998). *The tree of knowledge: The biological roots of human understanding* (rev. ed.). Boston: Shambala Press.

McDonough, W., & Braungart, M. (2002). *Cradle to cradle: Remaking the way we make things.* San Francisco: North Point Press.

Mirvis, P.H. (2000). Transformation at Shell: Commerce *and* citizenship. *Business and Society Review, 105*(1), 63–84.

Mirvis, P.H., Ayas, K., & Roth, G. (2003). *To the desert and back: The story of the most dramatic business transformation on record.* San Francisco: Jossey-Bass.

Moore, J.F. (1997). *The death of competition leadership and strategy in the age of ecosystems.* New York: HarperBusiness.

Payne, S.L., & Calton, J.M. (2002). Towards a managerial practice of stakeholder engagement: Developing multi-stakeholder learning dialogues. In J. Andriof, S. Waddock, B. Husted, & S. Rahman (Eds.), *Unfolding stakeholder thinking* (pp. 121–136). Sheffield, UK: Greenleaf.

Post, J.E. (2003). Meltdown in the Catholic church; or creating a "Voice of the Faithful." *Journal of Corporate Citizenship, 12,* 23–26.

Senge, P.M. (1990). *The fifth discipline.* New York: Currency Doubleday.

Seligman, M. (2002). *Authentic happiness: Using the new positive psychology to realize your potential for lasting fulfillment.* New York: Free Press.

Seligman, M.E.P., & Csikszentmihalyi, M. (2000, January). Positive psychology: An introduction. *American Psychologist, 55*(1), 5–14.

Schor, J. (1999). *The overspent American: Why we want what we don't need.* New York: HarperCollins.

Svendsen, A. (1998). *The stakeholder strategy: Profiting from collaborative business relationships.* San Francisco: Berrett-Koehler.

Torbert, W.R. (1991). *The power of balance: Transforming self, society, and scientific inquiry.* Newbury Park, CA: Sage Publications.

Votaw, D. (1961). The politics of a changing corporate society. *California Management Review, 3*(3), 105–118.

Waddell, S. (2002, Summer). Six societal learning concepts in an era of engagement. *Reflections: The SoL Journal, 3*(4).

Waddock, S. (2001, Spring). Integrity and mindfulness: Foundations of corporate citizenship. *Journal of Corporate Citizenship, 1*(1), 25–37.

Waddock, S. (2002). *Leading corporate citizens: Vision, values, value added.* New York: McGraw-Hill.

Warmoth, A., Resnick, S., & Serlin, I. (2003). Contributions of Humanistic Psychology to Positive Psychology, Divison 32 of the American Psychological Association, posted at http://www.westga.edu/~psydept/os2/papers/serlin2.htm.

Weick, K.E. (1999). *Educating for the unknowable: The infamous real world.* Paper presented at Academy of Management annual meeting, Chicago.

Wicks, A.C., & Freeman, R.E. (1998, March-April). Organization studies and the new pragmatism: Positivism, anti-positivism, and the search for ethics. *Organization Science, 9*(2), 123–140.

Wilber, K. (1995). *Sex, ecology, spirituality: The spirit of evolution.* Boston: Shambala Publications.

Wilber, K. (1996). *A brief history of everything.* Boston: Shambala Publications.

Wilber, K. (1998a). *The eye of spirit: An integral vision for a world gone slightly mad.* Boston: Shambala Publications.

Wilber, K. (1998b). *The marriage of sense and soul: Integrating science and reason.* New York: Random House.

CHAPTER 3

TOWARD A THEORY OF ETHICAL AND SPIRITUAL WELL-BEING, AND CORPORATE SOCIAL RESPONSIBILITY THROUGH SPIRITUAL LEADERSHIP

Louis W. Fry

ABSTRACT

Fry's (2003) causal theory of spiritual leadership was developed within an intrinsic motivation model that incorporates vision, hope/faith, and altruistic love, theories of workplace spirituality, and spiritual survival through calling and membership. The purpose of spiritual leadership is to create vision and value congruence across the strategic, empowered team, and individual levels and, ultimately, to foster higher levels of organizational commitment and productivity. The purpose of this paper is to extend spiritual leadership theory as a predictor of ethical and spiritual well-being as well as corporate social responsibility.

Positive Psychology in Business Ethics and Corporate Responsibility, pages 47–83
Copyright © 2005 by Information Age Publishing
All rights of reproduction in any form reserved.

First, the current malaise in corporate ethics and social responsibility is discussed with roots based on egoism and a perversion of the Protestant Work Ethic. Second, the concept of positive human health and well-being through the four fundamental arenas of human existence—physical, mental, emotional, and spiritual—and their relationship to values, attitudes and behavior is explored. Next, it is argued that recent developments in workplace spirituality, character ethics, positive psychology and spiritual leadership provide a consensus on the content of values, attitudes, and behavior necessary for positive human health and well-being. Then, it is demonstrated that spiritual leadership theory incorporates these values and provides a process that fosters ethical and spiritual well being as well as corporate social responsibility. Finally, how to achieve organizational transformation through spiritual leadership and the learning organizational paradigm to achieve this is discussed.

INTRODUCTION

Enron and WorldCom are two examples of the many scandals that have cast a chilling pall over the way business is conducted in the United States, dealing a major blow to trust and giving many people the perception that corporate America is amoral and corrupt. More and more, business ethics is being jokingly called an oxymoron. At the heart of this issue is a basic mistrust of the dominant capitalist business philosophy, predominantly espoused in Colleges of Business influenced by finance and economics departments, which emphasizes maximizing shareholder value today. Michael Douglas's academy award winning performance in claiming that "Greed is Good" in the movie Wall Street still appears to be the mantra of businesses big and small.

In response to this crisis of trust, universities have been scrambling to design new courses that apply the basics of ethics and leadership to real-life work situations (Treviño & Nelson, 2004). However, such attempts only begin to speak to the seemingly intractable issues that must be addressed to clean up corporate accounting, governance, and ethics to the point that these organizations have a corporate conscience and culture built around an ethical set of moral principles and values (Byrne, 2002; Merritt, 2003; Wee, 2002).

Capitalism is an economic model grounded in a worldview of self-interest. However, the exclusive pursuit of self-interest has been found wanting by most ethicists (Gini, 1995; Price, 2003; Rosenthall & Buchholz, 1995). Underlying capitalism is the core value of modern Western philosophy that affirms individual liberty, inviolability of conscience, self-determination, and choice, with the inherent assumption that the liberty of individuals be maximized subject only to the condition that there be similar liberty for all others (Bass & Steidlmeier, 1999). Thus, there is a need for the individual and community to exist in a delicate tension through social choices to provide for the common good without infringing upon inalienable individual human rights (Bellah, Madsen, Sullivan, Swidler, & Tipton, 1985).

Ethics is primarily concerned with exploring the question of what are the values and principles of morally good behavior, of what is "the good life" in terms of happiness and well-being, and providing justification for the sort of contexts that might help insure morally good decisions (Hill & Smith, 2003). The Dalai Lama (1999) in *Ethics for the New Millennium* notes that at no time in human history has it been more essential that we reach a consensus about what constitutes positive and negative conduct in an increasingly interdependent world to ultimately answer the great question which confronts us all: "How can I be happy?" This fundamental aspiration is inherent in everything we do, not only as individuals but also at the group and organizational levels of society. The desire or inclination to be happy and avoid pain and suffering knows no boundaries.

Spiritual leadership (Fry, 2003) through vision, hope, faith, and altruistic love taps into the fundamental needs of both leaders and followers for spiritual survival through calling and membership so that they become more organizationally committed and productive (see Figure 3.1). Building on Bass and Steidlmeier (1999), a major proposition of this review is that spiritual leadership theory provides the ethical *content* in terms of the values which emphasize the issues of standards and criteria of behavior that lead to positive health and ethical and spiritual well-being. It also provides an ethical *process* that reflects requirements for legitimacy for both leader influence and follower empowerment to facilitate value congruence across the strategic, empowered team, and individual and, ultimately, corporate social responsibility.

First, the current malaise in corporate ethics and social responsibility is discussed with its roots based on a perversion of the Protestant Work Ethic. Second, the concept of positive human health and well-being through the four fundamental arenas of human existence—physical, mental, emotional, and spiritual—and their relationship to values and attitudes, and behavior is explored. Next, it is argued that recent developments in workplace spirituality, character ethics, positive psychology, and spiritual leadership provide a consensus on the values, attitudes, and behavior necessary for positive human health and well-being. Then, it is demonstrated that spiritual leadership theory incorporates these values and provides a process that fosters ethical and spiritual well being as well as corporate social responsibility. Finally, the process of organizational transformation and development through spiritual leadership and the learning organizational paradigm to achieve this is discussed.

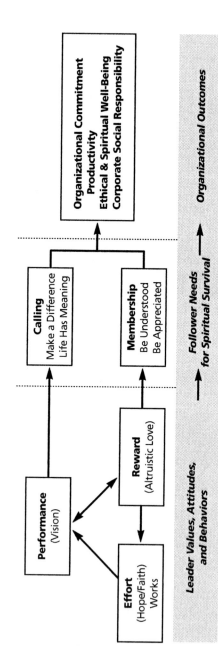

Figure 3.1. Casual model of spiritual leadership.

THE PROTESTANT WORK ETHIC AND CORPORATE GREED

Historically, the roots of modern bureaucratic theory are found in the family, the church, the military, and feudal monarchies. With the advent of the industrial revolution, the Protestant Work Ethic (Weber, 1958) became the general foundation for a work ethic that was, in some sense, an attempt to spiritualize the workplace and provide a moral framework for morally good behavior. Thus "the good life" became defined in terms of the new roles and responsibilities that were developing in newly emerging industrial societies (Buchholz & Rosenthal, 2003). This ethic set forth moral principles that, through the idea of a calling, provided meaning and purpose to work and the workplace. "People had a primary responsibility to do their best at whatever worldly station they found themselves rather than withdrawing from the world to seek perfection" (Buchholz & Rosenthall, 2003, p.152).

However, the values of the Protestant Work Ethic hold certain pessimistic views about mankind (Mobley, 1971)—that man was basically sinful, his punishments and/or rewards were after death, and earthly pleasures and satisfactions were to be denied to oneself in order to avoid hell and reach heaven. In addition, these views were reinforced by the Industrial Revolution which expanded the demand for objective information based on the Newtonian view of a deterministic, machine-like universe that, through the scientific method, removed the free will of man as the focus of observation and interest (Mason, 2003). This classical world-view, coupled with the underpinnings of a structural theology describing a world of "isness," saw the universe, including man, as basically stable and materialistic in nature (Mobley, 1971).

Stability was the prevailing worldview and assumption in both theology and science. The fact that most people held these assumptions led to the development of corresponding ideas about management and corporate ethics. Since, in science, cause effect is unidirectional, the past is supposed to predict the future, social structure needs hierarchy, and a supreme controlling agent must be in power—the President. Therefore, classical management theory is rooted in the Protestant Work Ethic and asserts the need for the exercise of autocratic rule and power including the need to minimize employee conflict and resistance to work. The problem, of course, is that humans are not fixed and do not conform to this kind of universe—we are unpredictable and have free will with characteristics like imagination, hope and faith, ambitions, creativity, growth, and change. "If the universe was good (because God created it) then man must be bad because he doesn't fit into the 'good' machine-like universe" (Mobley, 1971, p. 188).

The Protestant Work Ethic does contain restrictions on consumption in that the wealth one creates should not be lavishly consumed but invested to create more wealth that in turn would lead to greater individual and societal well-being. However, even though the values underlying this ethic may have sought to bring meaning and purpose to the workplace, what it actually did was to make the production of economic wealth an end in itself, which became severed from any higher moral principles related to the ongoing enrichment of human existence. What has ensued is that whatever constraint the Protestant Work Ethic may have provided has disappeared due to an ever increasing demand for the creation of a consumer culture with products and services that could produce pleasure and instant self-gratification. Not only production but also consumption had become an end in itself, divorced from any broader or larger moral purpose beyond the production and consumption of more goods and services themselves to increase economic growth (Buchholz & Rosenthal, 2003).

This relentless pursuit of egoistic gratification has led to the current situation of corporate greed and lack of trust in corporate America noted earlier. Corporate ethics in bureaucracies have tended to be depersonalized with managers and employees expected to place company interests before their own private interests with their ultimate fealty to society. Often, ethical conflicts are legalistically determined with extensive interpretation by laws and court decisions. In nations permitting economic freedom, questions of ethics that do not fall under the scrutiny of law, are subjected to an economic imperative—to create a present value return on capital that is greater than the cost of that capital. People thus have a calling based not on a higher moral purpose of service to enrich human existence but, instead, to egoistically engage the world, work hard, and accumulate as much wealth as possible regardless of the impact on others (Buchholz & Rosenthall, 2003).

In summary, this perversion of the Protestant Work Ethic, which resulted in managers and employees acting out of self-interest and the opportunity to reap great rewards, underlies the current malaise in corporate ethics and social responsibility. The hypothesis that the Protestant Work Ethic underlying the pursuit of egoistic self-interest inherent in Adam Smith's invisible hand theory of capitalism would prevent excessive greed and abuse of other individuals and stakeholders is clearly untenable. This is especially so for today's Internet driven, post September 11, globally competitive business climate which requires organizational effectiveness be achieved through a trust-based, empowered team, and learning organizational paradigm led by vision and the values of altruistic love (Fry, 2003).

POSITIVE HUMAN HEALTH AND WELL-BEING

Webster's dictionary (1976) defines well-being as "the state of being happy, healthy, or prosperous." Throughout human history there have been attempts to develop a normative understanding of well-being or "the good life" in terms of particular human characteristics and qualities that are desirable and worthy of emulation (Christopher, 1999). Moreover, an understanding of well-being may be a transcendental requirement for human existence—what Geertz (1973, p. 363) terms a "pervasive orientational necessity" in that human beings always and of necessity live on the basis of an understanding of what is a better, more desirable, or worthier way of being in the world (Christopher, 1999). Initially philosophy (e.g., ethics) and religion (e.g., spiritual practices) stressed normative understandings that often emphasize the cultivation of certain values or virtues (Coan, 1977; Diener, 1984). Diverse characteristics such as love, wisdom, and nonattachment have been touted as the cardinal elements of a fulfilled existence. Although there are other desirable personal characteristics that result in the presence of pleasure and the absence of pain, well-being actually goes beyond whether a person is happy. In particular, those individuals with abundant joy, peace, and serenity have the key ingredients of a good life (Diener, Lucas, & Oishi, 2001).

In this age of science and technology, these norms of well-being are largely provided by the notions of positive human health and psychological or subjective well-being. Today, well-being plays a crucial role in theories of personality and development in both pure and applied forms (Christopher, 1999), positive psychology (Snyder & Lopez, 2001), physical health (Ryff & Singer, 2001), character ethics (Josephson, 1999, 2002) as well as leadership and organizational behavior (Danna & Griffin, 1999; Fry, 2003). Although the science of positive human health and well-being is in its infancy, recent empirical findings in contemporary social science have begun to discover the components of a science of human betterment. Physical health is viewed as a sub-component of well-being and comprises the combination of such mental/psychological indicators as positive affect, frustration, stress, and anxiety as they impact such physiological indicators as blood pressure, heart condition, and general physical health (Dana & Griffin, 1999; Kaczorowski, 1989; Quick, Nelson, & Hurrell, 1997; Watson, 2001).

This review draws upon the theory-guided dimensions of well-being offered by Ryff and Singer (2001). Together, these dimensions comprise the most complete model of well-being to date and encompass diverse features of what it means to be well, including:

1. *Self-Acceptance*—Possesses a positive attitude toward the self; acknowledges and accepts multiple aspects of self, including good and bad qualities; feels positive about past life.

2. *Positive relations with others*—has warm, satisfying, trusting relationships with others; is concerned about the welfare of others; capable

of strong empathy, affection, and intimacy; understands give-and-take of human relationships.

3. *Autonomy*—is self-determined and independent; is able to resist social pressures to think and act in certain ways; regulates behavior from within; evaluates self by personal standards.

4. *Environmental Mastery*—has a sense of mastery and competence in managing the environment; controls complex array of external activities; makes effective use of surrounding opportunities; is able to choose or create contexts suitable to personal needs and values.

5. *Purpose in Life*—has goals in life and a sense of directedness; feels there is meaning to present and past life; holds beliefs that give life purpose; has aims and objectives for living.

6. *Personal Growth*—has a feeling of continued development; sees self as growing and expanding; is open to new experiences; has sense of realizing his or her potential; sees improvement in self and behavior over time; is changing in ways that reflect more self knowledge and effectiveness.

Empirical findings to date have shown that individuals that score high on these six dimensions experience greater psychological well-being and have fewer problems related to physical health in terms of allostatic load (cardiovascular disease, cognitive impairment, declines in physical functioning, and mortality). Thus, one would experience greater positive human health and well-being to the extent one had a high regard for oneself and one's past life, good-quality relationship with others, a sense that life is purposeful and meaningful, the capacity to effectively manage one's surrounding world, the ability to follow inner convictions, and a sense of continuing growth and self-realization.

Well-being and Ethical Values, Attitudes, and Behavior

People bring to work their values and attitudes that drive their behavior (Olsen & Zanna, 1993). Core values reflect the moral principles that an individual considers to be important. These values are relatively stable over time and have an impact on attitudes and behavior (Ravlin & Meglino, 1987). Values affect one's perception of the situation or problems, how one relates to others, and act as guides for choices and actions. Taken as a set, these core values cause or determine a person's preferences about what they consider to be good or bad and form the foundation for moral principles that then translate into the individual's, team's, or organization's ethical system. For example, honesty is a value that is considered to be good and desirable in all cultures and across all religions (Elm, 2003; Smith, 1992).

Values then help determine attitudes. An attitude is an evaluation that predisposes a person to act in a certain way. Attitudes are relatively lasting cognitions, feelings, and behavioral tendencies toward specific people, groups, ideas, issues, events or objects (Breckler, 1984; Olsen & Zanna, 1993). An attitude consists of three components:

1. A *cognitive component*—the opinions, knowledge, or information the person has about the object of the attitude.

2. An *affective component*—the feelings, sentiments, moods, and emotions about the object of the attitude.

3. A *behavioral component*—the predisposition or intention to act or behave toward the object of the attitude.

The interplay between values and attitudinal components and their effect on behavior and well-being can be extremely complex. In general, however, a leader who highly values honesty, integrity, forgiveness, compassion, and helping others would have different attitudes and behave very differently toward followers than if he or she ultimately valued egoistic need satisfaction and personal ambition (Hughes, Ginnet, & Curphy, 1999; Walsh, 1997).

A major proposition of this review is that there is an emerging theoretical and empirical consensus on the core ethical values that are necessary for positive human health and well-being. Table 3.1 summarizes the universal or consensus values relating to ethical and spiritual well-being from spiritual leadership, religion, workplace spirituality, positive psychology, and character education. Because space limitations preclude exhaustive reviews for each of these areas, only recent representative work is summarized and cited. For workplace spirituality and positive psychology, the entries in Table 3.1 represent the values that were given major chapter focus in two recent seminal paradigm defining works, *Handbook of Workplace Spirituality and Organizational Performance* (Giacalone & Jurkiewicz, 2003) and *Handbook for Positive Psychology* (Snyder & Lopez, 2001).

Workplace Spirituality

A major change is taking place in the personal and professional lives of leaders as many of them more deeply integrate their spirituality with their work. Most would agree that this integration is leading to very positive changes in their relationships and their effectiveness (Neal, 2001). Further, there is evidence that workplace spirituality programs not only lead to ben-

Table 3.1. Comparison of Scholarly Fields Emphasizing Values Relating to Ethical and Spiritual Well-Being

Spirituality & Leadership (Fry, 2003)	Workplace spirituality (Giacalone & Jurkiewicz, 2003)	Religion (Smith, 1992)	Character Ethics & Education (Josephson, 2002)	Positive psychology (Snyder & Lopez, 2001)
Vision	Honesty	Vision	Trustworthiness	Optimism
Hope/Faith	Forgiveness	Honesty	Honesty	Hope
Altruistic Love:	Hope	Veracity	Integrity	Humility
Trust/Loyalty	Gratitude	Charity/Unconditional Love	Reliability	Compassion
Forgiveness/Acceptance/	Humility		(Promise Keeping)	Forgiveness
Gratitude	Compassion		Loyalty	Gratitude
Integrity	Integrity			Love
Honesty			Respect	Altruism
Courage			Civility	Empathy
Kindness			Courtesy	Toughness
Empathy/Compassion			Decency	Meaningfulness
Patience/Meekness/			Dignity	Humor
Endurance/Excellence			Autonomy	
Fun			Tolerance	
			Acceptance	
			Responsibility	
			Accountability	
			Excellence	
			Diligence	
			Perseverance	
			Continuous	
			Improvement	
			Fairness	
			Process	
			Impartiality	
			Equity	
			Caring	
			Citizenship	

eficial personal outcomes such as increased joy, peace, serenity, job satisfaction and commitment but that they also deliver improved productivity and reduced absenteeism and turnover (Giacalone & Jurkiewicz, 2003). Employees who work for organizations they consider being spiritual are less fearful, more ethical, and more committed. And, there is mounting evidence that a more humane workplace is not only more productive, but also more flexible and creative (Eisler & Montouri, 2003).

Although still in the early stages of theory building and testing, the role of workplace spirituality is receiving increasing attention (Conger, 1994; Fairholm, 1998, Giacalone & Jurkiewicz, 2003). In particular, workers who view their work as a called vocation are likely to approach their work very differently than employees who see work primarily as a means to pay bills (Zinnbauer, Pargament, & Scott, 1999). Most important to management and leadership from an organizational effectiveness and performance perspective, is the finding by Mitroff and Denton (1999) that spirituality could be the ultimate competitive advantage.

In their scientific inquiry into workplace spirituality, Giacalone and Jurkiewica (2003, p. 13) define workplace spirituality as:

> A framework of organizational values evidenced in the culture that promotes employees' experience of transcendence through the work process, facilitating their sense of being connected in a way that provides feelings of compassion and joy.

This sense of transcendence—of having a calling through one's work (vocationally)—and the need for membership or social connection are necessary for providing the foundation for a theory of workplace spirituality. Workplace spirituality must therefore be comprehended within a holistic or system context of interwoven cultural and personal values. Also, to be of benefit to leaders and their organizations, workplace spirituality must demonstrate its utility by impacting performance, turnover, and productivity and other relevant effectiveness criteria (Ellis, 2002; Sass, 2000). In fact, recent studies have shown that companies perform higher if they emphasize workplace spirituality through both people-centered values and a high-commitment model of attachment between the company and its employees (Mitroff & Denton, 1999; Giacalone & Jurkiewicz, 2003; Pfeffer, 2003).

Finally, to gain a systemic understanding of how workplace spirituality—through transcendence and value congruence among organizational, team, and individual values—impacts organizational effectiveness, a focus on the interconnectedness and interplay across these levels is required. Giacalone and Jurkiewicz (2003) posit that the greater the value congruence across levels, the more individuals will experience transcendence through their work. To the extent that the organization's culture reflects the general global shift from materialist to altruistic values that tend to be more idealistic and spiritual, the more the individual will have a sense of connection, joy, and completeness.

Religion

Viewing workplace spirituality through the lens of religious traditions and practice can be divisive in that, to the extent that religion views itself as the only path to God and salvation, it excludes those who do not share in the denominational tradition (Cavanaugh, 1999) and often conflicts with the social, legal, and ethical foundations of business and public administration (Nadesan, 1999). Thus, religion can lead to arrogance that a company, faith, or society is "better," morally superior, or worthier than another (Nash, 1994). Translating religion of this nature into workplace spirituality can foster zealotry at the expense of organizational goals, offend constituents and customers, and decrease morale and employee well-being (Giacalone & Jurkiewicz, 2003).

Yet spiritual concerns are separate from the search for God and the sharing of beliefs of any particular religious group (Veach & Chappell, 1991). The renowned Dalai Lama is very clear in making the distinction between spirituality and religion in his search for an ethical system adequate to withstand the moral dilemmas of the new millennium.

> Religion I take to be concerned with faith in the claims of one faith tradition or another, an aspect of which is the acceptance of some form of heaven or nirvana. Connected with this are religious teachings or dogma, ritual prayer, and so on. Spirituality I take to be concerned with those qualities of the human spirit-such as love and compassion, patience, tolerance, forgiveness, contentment, a sense of responsibility, a sense of harmony-which bring happiness to both self and others. (Dalai Lama, 1999, p. 22)

The Dalai Lama notes that while ritual and prayer, along with the questions of heaven and salvation are directly connected to religion, the inner qualities of spirituality, the quest for God, and ultimately joy, peace, and serenity need not be. Also, there is no reason why individuals could not or should not develop these underlying values or inner qualities independent of any religious or metaphysical belief system. "This is why I sometimes say that religion is something we can perhaps do without. What we cannot do without are these basic spiritual qualities" (Dalai Lama, 1999, p. 22).

The common bridge between spirituality and religion is altruistic love— regard or devotion to the interests of others. In this respect, the basic spiritual teachings of the world's great religions are remarkably similar (Bolman & Deal, 1995). In religion this is manifested through the Golden Rule, also called the Rule of Reciprocity—do unto others as you would have them do unto you—which is common to all major religions (Josephson, 1996; *Shared Belief in the Golden Rule*, 2003).

From this perspective, spirituality is necessary for religion but religion is not necessary for spirituality. Consequently, workplace spirituality can be inclusive or exclusive of religious theory and practice. Indeed, Horton (1950) notes that there are many nonexclusive paths to the presence of God through spirituality, including and excluding religion. For example, there are institutionalists or traditionalists who find God through time-honored beliefs and practices of their church, rationalists who find Him through hard study and reflective thought, mystics who find God through silent, intuitive contemplation, and moralists who find Him through active obedience to duty.

While a review of the literature from Christianity, Judaism, and Islam relating to ethical values and well-being is beyond the scope of this review, Huston Smith's influential work, *The World's Religions* (1992), can be used to build upon the fact that every religion has some version of the Golden Rule. Smith (1992) notes that all religions espouse the values of humility, charity, veracity, and vision (see Table 3.1). In other words, ethical and spiritual well-being is found in pursuit of a vision of service to others through: (1) humility which is having the capacity to regard oneself as one, but not more than one, (2) charity, or altruistic love, which considers one's neighbor to be as fully worthy as you are, and (3) veracity which goes beyond basic truth-telling to having the capacity to see things exactly as they are, freed from subjective distortions.

Character Education

Since the very beginning of mankind's quest for knowledge, there has been the realization that, at the core of human existence, there is a set of capital virtues and capital vices and that a major goal of life is to live these virtues and overcome the vices. The Greek philosopher, Aristotle, defined good character as the life of right conduct both in relation to others and in relation to oneself (Lickona, 1991). A major proposition of this review is that the ability to distinguish between morally good and evil acts is critical to the formation of character that enables individuals to adopt the values and attitudes that lead to moral behavior and, ultimately, to well-being and "the good life." However, knowledge of ethical values and moral principles is futile unless the individual makes the effort to habitually incorporate them into his or her attitudes and behavior. Thus, character constitutes an inner-directed and habitual strength of mind and will. At the heart of character formation then are the habits that are acquired through the "practice of virtue"—a process that should also be facilitated by moral mentors who guide both by teaching and example (Kanungo & Mendonca, 1996).

Moral theology has traditionally identified prudence, justice, temperance, and fortitude as the "Cardinal Virtues" because the values underlying them lead to what are universally viewed as morally good attitudes and behaviors or practices. The effort to create, teach, and model this core group of values is at the heart of character education. As the role and influence of family and religious institutions has waned in our society, the education system has assumed a primary role to provide students with the moral and civic values that are an essential part of our social fabric and sense of community (Lickona, 1991). "Character education is a broad term that is used to describe the general curriculum and organizational features of schools that promote the development of fundamental values in children at school" (Peterson & Skiba, 2001, p. 169). Character education of elementary school students is designed to accomplish three goals (Lickona, 1988, p. 420):

1. To promote development away from egocentrism and excessive individualism and toward cooperative relationships and mutual respect;
2. To foster the growth of moral agency—the capacity to think, feel and act morally; and,
3. To develop in the classroom and in the school a moral community based on fairness, caring, and participation.

Specific qualities that are desirable in children are self-respect, social perspective in considering how others think and feel, moral reasoning about right and wrong actions, and moral values that produce supportive attitudes and behavior directed toward the above goals.

Hence character education advocates a common ethical ground even though there are often intense conflicts in our society over moral issues such as abortion, homosexuality, euthanasia, and capital punishment. That, despite this diversity, we can identify basic shared values that enable us to engage in public moral education in a pluralistic society; indeed, democratic pluralism itself is not possible without such agreement:

> There *are* rationally grounded, nonrelative, objectively worthwhile moral values: respect for life, liberty, the inherent value of every individual person, and the consequent responsibility to care for each other and carry out our basic obligations. These objectively worthwhile values demand that we treat as *morally wrong* any action by any individual, group, or state that violates these basic moral values. (Lickona, 1991, p. 230)

In character education there is a developing consensus regarding "Six Pillars of Character" as a set of universal core ethical values that transcend

race, creed, politics, gender, and wealth that honor the dignity and autonomy of each person and cautions against self-righteousness in areas of legitimate controversy (Josephson, 2002; Peterson & Skiba, 2001). These are
(see Table 3.1):

1. *Trustworthiness*—Don't deceive, cheat or steal. Build a good reputation. Be reliable.
2. *Respect*—Be tolerant of differences and considerate of others' feelings.
3. *Responsibility*—Do what you are supposed to do. Be accountable. Persevere.
4. *Fairness*—Take turns. Share. Play by the rules. Don't take advantage
   of others.
5. *Caring*—Forgive others. Help people in need. Express gratitude. Be
   kind.
6. *Citizenship*—Obey the laws. Respect the authority. Stay informed.
   Cooperate.

Incorporating these universal, consensus values with the Cardinal Virtues
defines core values, which, in turn, define one's character and personality.

The core values of the six pillars of character translate into principles
that guide and motivate ethical conduct. For example, honesty, a value of
trustworthiness, gives rise to attitudes, behaviors, and principles in the
form of specific do's and don'ts such as: tell the truth, don't deceive, be
candid, and don't cheat. In situations where one is confronted with conflicting values (e.g., the desire for wealth and prestige versus to be honest
and kind to others), we resort to our core value system, which consists of
the values we consistently rank higher than others. These values then are
the source of the attitudes and, ultimately, the behaviors we choose in
these situations.

Character is the process of putting ethical values into action through
one's attitudes and behavior (Josephson, 2002). One's conscience is the
awareness of the moral and ethical aspects of one's conduct with its urges
to prefer right to wrong. People are not born with good character; it has to
be developed. "Building character," like acquiring a set of any habits, is a
process of instruction, training and mentoring to instill within a person
positive ethical values and principles. From this perspective, well-being is
not to be found in a life focused on pleasure-seeking and material wealth
based on the unrealistic expectation of happiness as a continuous series of
pleasurable emotions and feeling good all the time. Thus, as a theoretical
construct, ethical well-being is defined as the process of living from the
inside-out in creating congruence between universal, consensus values and
one's personal values, attitudes, and behavior. An example of the process

of living from the inside-out is described by Covey (1989, 1991) in his significant works, *The Seven Habits of Highly Effective People* and *Principled-Centered Leadership*. The outcome of ethical well-being is a state of joy, peace, and serenity. It is an emotional resting place of quiet satisfaction with one's life—the art of living a balance between getting what you want and, for today, wanting what you have (Josephson, 2002).

Positive Psychology

The purpose of positive psychology is to scientifically investigate and uncover a vision of "the good life" that is empirically sound while being understandable and attractive. After World War II, the field of psychology became a science almost exclusively devoted to healing and, in doing so, developed a disease model that focused on pathology and neglected the idea of a fulfilled individual and a thriving community (Seligman, 2001). However, psychology is not just the study of pathology, weakness, and damage; it is also the study of strength and virtue. It is not just a branch of medicine concerned with illness or health or fixing what is broken; it is about nurturing what is best in work, education, insight, love, growth, and play (Seligman & Csikszentmihalyi, 2000).

Although there is voluminous literature about how people survive and endure under conditions of adversity (Benjamin, 1992; Smith, 1997), little is known of what makes life worth living or about how normal people prevent life from being barren and meaningless and achieve positive human health and well-being. Positive psychology attempts to refocus psychology from a preoccupation with repairing the worst things in life to building positive qualities (Seligman & Csikszentmihalyi, 2000). The field of positive psychology holistically examines multiple levels of the human experience:

1. The subjective level is about valued subjective experiences—well-being, contentment, and satisfaction (in the past); hope and optimism (in the future); and flow and happiness (in the present).

2. The individual level is about positive human traits—the capacity for love and vocation, courage, interpersonal skill, aesthetic sensibility, perseverance, forgiveness, originality, future mindedness, spirituality, high talent, and wisdom.

3. The group level is about civic virtues and the institutions that move individuals toward better citizenship: responsibility, nurturance, altruism, civility, moderation, tolerance, and work ethic.

The general stance of positive psychology is toward prevention and asserts that certain positive human traits act as buffers against psychopathology.

Positive psychology helps people identify and nurture their strongest qualities, what they own or are best at, and supports them in finding niches in which they best live out these positive qualities. Identifying, amplifying, and concentrating on these strengths in people at risk, aid effective prevention (Seligman, 2001). Positive psychologists recognize that their best work lies in (1) amplifying strengths rather than repairing client weaknesses, and (2) developing contexts and cultures that reinforce and foster these strengths.

Positive Ethics. Handlesman, Knapp, and Gottlieb (2001) call for a shift from negative to positive ethics as central to the development of positive psychology. They argue that currently there is an almost exclusive focus on wrongdoing and disciplinary action. This leads to an erroneous but common belief that ethics consists solely of adherence to laws and codes of conduct with the responsibility for enforcement residing with the courts or the adjudication processes of disciplinary bodies. The result is an emphasis on negative ethical rule adherence or a "Thou shalt not" perspective whereby ethics is considered as a list of prohibitions that must be followed without the need to consider its underlying spirit or philosophy. Such a rule-bound approach to ethics can lead to one experiencing a conflict or disconnect between one's professional roles and one's personal moral philosophies. "A focus on conforming professional behavior to minimum standards may create the impression that professional ethics are separate from our intuitive moral sense" (Handlesman et al., 2001, p. 733).

This negative approach to ethics especially ignores issues of self-care and well-being. To argue that one has no personal stake in the process or outcome of one's work is nonsensical and creates separation between individual and organizational values. Personal well-being then becomes at best irrelevant and at worst in conflict with organizational interests. Positive ethics, therefore, recognizes that it is appropriate to incorporate notions of self-interest into our work in deriving satisfaction from our work behavior. This includes such intrinsically motivating activities as using our skills and creativity, working directly with others for their benefit, and experiencing competence and progress as well as indirectly benefitting society. Cultivating these activities leads to a greater awareness of the boundaries of our work relationships and to a greater ability to actualize our values and ethical well-being at work.

Spiritual Leadership

Spiritual and ethical leadership is an area of research in its early stage of development and, therefore, it lacks a strong body of traditional research findings to substantiate it. Most of the theory that is offered in this area comes from the fields of religious theology and practice (Blackaby & Blackaby, 2001; McNeal, 2000; Sanders, 1986;) and leadership ethics and values (Barrett, 1998, 2003; Covey, 1989, 1991; Fairholm, 1997, 1998, 2001; Greenleaf, 1977, 1978; Kanungo & Mendonca, 1996; Kouzes & Posner, 1987,1993, 1999; Northouse, 2001).

Spiritual leadership theory (Fry, 2003) builds on this work from spiritual, religion, and ethics-based leadership theory. It is based on the definition and generic process of leadership as motivation to change developed by Kouzes and Pozner (1987, p. 30)—"Leadership is the art of mobilizing others to want to struggle for shared aspirations." From this perspective, leadership entails motivating followers by creating a vision of a long-term challenging, desirable, compelling, and different future. When combined with a sense of mission of whom we are and what we do, this vision establishes the foundation for the organization's culture with its fundamental ethical system and core values. The ethical system subsequently establishes a moral imperative for right and wrong behavior which, when combined with organizational goals and strategies, acts as a substitute (Kerr & Jermier, 1977) for the traditional bureaucratic structure (centralization, standardization and formalization). Thus, it is the act of establishing a culture with values that influences others to strongly desire, mobilize, and struggle for a shared vision that defines the essence of motivating through leadership.

Spiritual leadership as vision, hope/faith, and altruistic love taps into the fundamental needs of both leaders and followers for spiritual survival through calling and membership so they become more organizationally committed and productive. Further, this paper proposes that spiritual leadership is a source of ethical and spiritual well-being and corporate social responsibility. Spiritual leadership is defined as the values, attitudes, and behaviors that are necessary to intrinsically motivate oneself and others so that they have a sense of spiritual survival (Fleischman, 1994; Maddock & Fulton, 1998) through calling and membership (see Figure 3.1 and Tables 3.1 and 3.2). This entails:

1. Creating a vision wherein organization members experience a sense of calling in that their life has meaning and makes a difference;
2. Establishing a social/organizational culture based on altruistic love whereby leaders and followers have genuine care, concern, and appreciation for BOTH self and others, have a sense of membership, and feel understood and appreciated.

Mainstream medical research has begun to recognize the power of spirituality in maintaining health during the last 20 years. Recent research tends to support a positive relationship between spirituality and health (Mathews, Larson, & Barry, 1994; Zellars & Perrewe, 2003). The other three arenas—

Table 3.2.   Qualities of Spiritual Leadership

Vision	Altruistic Love	Hope/Faith
Broad Appeal to Key Stakeholders	Trust/Loyalty	Endurance
Defines the Destination and Journey	Forgiveness/Acceptance/ Gratitude	Perseverance
Reflects High Ideals	Integrity	Do What It Takes
Encourages Hope/Faith	Honesty	Stretch Goals
Establishes Standard of Excellence	Courage	Expectation of Reward/ Victory
	Humility	Excellence
	Kindness	
	Compassion	
	Patience/Meekness/ Endurance	

mental/cognitive, emotional, and spiritual—can best be viewed within a conception of positive human health that is fundamentally anchored in psychological and social well-being (Ryff & Singer, 2001). Indeed, the experience of spiritual support may form the nucleus of the spirituality-health connection (Mackenzie, Rajagopal, Meibohm, & Lavizzo-Mourey, 2000).

Spiritual well-being is seen to both feed into and flow from the attainment of goals consistent with one's spiritual values and functioning in society as a whole (Paloutzian, Emmons, & Keortge, 2003). Spiritual well-being is a result of satisfying the spiritual survival needs for: (1) transcendence or calling manifested in the desire to strive for those purposes and values that express whatever a person feels is ultimately meaningful to him or her and (2) membership which is the desire for people, especially at work, to feel understood, and appreciated resulting in a sense of belonging and partnership. Spiritual well-being, however, is not obtained by striving for it directly. Organizational members cannot experience a sense of spiritual well-being by trying to manufacture it. It is not produced when a company focuses on its monetary goals, but instead occurs when leadership first establishes a healthy workplace culture grounded in altruistic values and transcendent goals. When members of an organization have a sense of belonging and a commitment to a common purpose, the organization as a whole is more successful in meeting or exceeding key stakeholder expectations; this is also when sustainable monetary goal achievement is realized.

An essential element of spiritual well-being is the ability to engage in virtuous behavior as one pursues one's calling or purpose. The foundation of such behavior is based in the ethical values and attitudes usually consid-

ered to reflect high moral principles (to show forgiveness, to express gratitude, to be humble, and to display compassion). Thus, ethical well-being is
viewed as a necessary but not sufficient condition for workplace spirituality
and spiritual well-being (Furnham, 2003; Garcia-Zamor, 2003; Paloutzian
et al., 2003).

TOWARD A THEORY OF ETHICAL AND SPIRITUAL WELL-BEING AND CORPORATE SOCIAL RESPONSIBILITY THROUGH SPIRITUAL LEADERSHIP

Table 3.1 demonstrates that vision and the values of hope/faith, and altruistic love in spiritual leadership theory include those emphasized in religion, workplace spirituality, character education, and positive psychology.
Thus, there is an emerging consensus from scholarly areas grounded in
philosophy, religion, and science about the universality of vision and those
values that are the source for attitudes and behavior that lead to positive
health and ethical and spiritual well-being.

For organizations to be effective, leadership to achieve vision and value
congruence is necessary across three distinct levels—strategic, empowered
team, and personal. Figure 3.2 gives a causal model of spiritual leadership
introduced earlier by Fry (2003) that incorporates theories of intrinsic
motivation, vision, hope/faith, altruistic love, and spiritual survival across
these three levels as it positively impacts organizational commitment and
productivity. This review extends the causal impact of spiritual leadership
to ethical and spiritual well-being (manifested through joy, peace, and
serenity) at the personal level, and corporate social responsibility at the
strategic and empowered team levels.

Bass and Steidlmeier (1999) note that any ethical analysis of leadership
must take into account both ethical content and process. Ethical content is
focused on values, which emphasize the issues of standards and criteria of
ethical behavior. Ethical processes reflect requirements for legitimacy for
both leader influence and follower empowerment inherent in relationships between the individual, group, organizational, and societal levels.
The ethics of leadership rests upon three pillars: (1) the leader's moral
character, (2) the ethical legitimacy of the leader's vision and values which
followers either embrace or reject, and (3) the morality of the choices and
actions that leaders engage in and collectively pursue. To be authentic,
leadership must have a moral foundation of legitimate values and congruence between these values and attitudes and behavior. Additionally, leaders
and followers must be willing to have their behavior evaluated against generally applicable moral requirements based in universal, consensus values
that—in today's global Internet world with its requirements for a learning

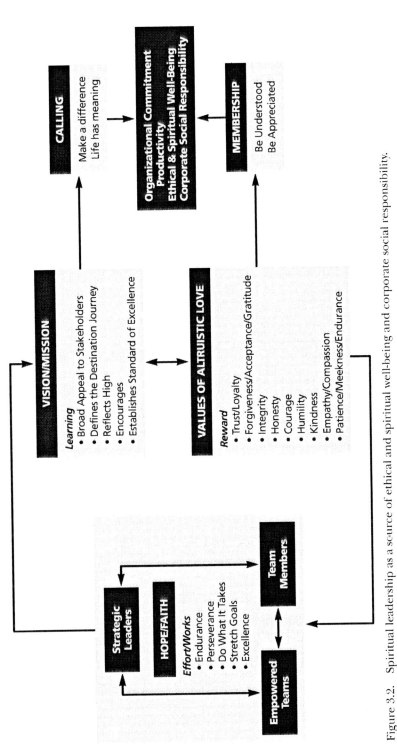

Figure 3.2.   Spiritual leadership as a source of ethical and spiritual well-being and corporate social responsibility.

67

organizational paradigm based on trust and empowerment—finds the attitudes and behavior of all actors together as part of a much larger social and moral framework (Fry, 2003; Price, 2003). Authenticity is especially important and necessary for a theory of ethical and spiritual well-being, since there is a great deal of research on the health benefits of open communication and, in particular, a clear connection between authenticity and increased well-being (Pennebaker, 1990).

Following Bass and Steidlmeier (1999), SLT provides the ethical content that prescribes universal or consensus values distilled from thousands of years of human experience through religion and philosophy as well as the results of emerging scientific research on positive human health and well-being. As an ethical process, SLT prescribes a moral discourse based in stakeholder theory (Freeman, 1984) resting upon the centrality of mutual altruism which incorporates both moral intention and moral consequences in advocating (within the human rights tradition) a balance between egoism and altruism in assessing benefits and costs for both self (e.g., the organization) and others (Bass & Steidlmeier, 1999; Kanungo & Mendonca, 1996).

Earlier, ethical well-being was defined as the outcome of authentically living one's values, attitudes, and behavior from the inside-out in creating a principled-center congruent with the universal, consensus values inherent in spiritual leadership theory (SLT). At the heart, SLT are the values and outcomes of altruistic love—"a sense of wholeness, harmony, and well-being produced through care concern and appreciation for both self and others" (Fry, 2003, p. 712). It is proposed that ethical well-being is necessary but not sufficient for spiritual well-being which, in addition to ethical well-being, incorporates transcendence of self in pursuit of a vision/purpose/mission in service to key stakeholders to satisfy one's need for spiritual survival through calling and membership. SLT then incorporates both ethical and spiritual well-being.

Personal Spiritual Leadership and Ethical and Spiritual Well-being

Leaders as well as followers exercise personal leadership at all levels. Personal leadership is the self-confident ability to crystallize your thinking and establish an exact direction for your life, to commit yourself to moving in that direction and then to take determined action to acquire, accomplish or become whatever you identify as the ultimate goal for your life (Meyer, 1994). Personal leadership is a process of developing a positive self-image that gives you the courage and self-confidence necessary to consciously choose actions that satisfy your needs, to follow that path with perseverance, and accept responsibility for the outcome.

The foundation of personal leadership is a personal mission statement (Covey, 1989). This statement describes a philosophy or creed that focuses on what one wants to be (character) and to do (contributions and achievements), as well as the values and moral principles that drive one's attitudes and behaviors. Much like the United States Constitution, it is a personal constitution that is fundamentally changeless.

> It becomes a personal constitution, the basis for making major, life-directional decisions in the midst of the circumstances and emotions that affect our lives. It empowers individuals with the same timeless strength in the midst of change. (Covey, 1989, p. 108)

At a personal level for both leaders and followers, it is especially important to adhere to and practice five key spiritual practices in a continual quest for strong personal leadership, ethical and spiritual well-being, and professional development and effectiveness (Kurth, 2003):

1. Know oneself.
2. Respect and honor the beliefs of others.
3. Be as trusting as you can be; and
4. Maintain a spiritual practice (e.g., spending time in nature, prayer, mediation, reading inspirational literature, yoga, shamanistic practices, writing in a journal).

These spiritual practices are also necessary for developing the features of well-being (self-acceptance, positive relations with others, autonomy, environmental mastery, purpose in life, and personal growth) offered by Ryff and Singer (2001).

Personal spiritual leadership, by tapping into the fundamental spiritual survival dimensions of calling and membership, creates an intrinsic motivating force that elicits spontaneous, cooperative effort from people, and make it more likely for employees to learn, develop and use their skills and knowledge to benefit both themselves and their organizations.

Through participation in self-directed, empowered teams, both leaders and followers begin to develop, refine, and practice their own personal leadership. Most important, it is necessary for the source of personal leadership to spring from the values underlying altruistic love that reflect a genuine care and concern for both self and others. Through visualization and positive affirmation of the values of hope/faith and altruistic love (see Table 3.4)—which have been shown to be at the heart of effective personal change (Covey, 1989)—leaders and followers at all levels in empowered teams practice personal spiritual leadership by authentically pursuing a personal vision for their own lives through a self-motivated intrinsic process that creates a sense of calling and membership, ethical and spiritual well being, and high levels of organizational commitment and productivity (see Figure 3.2).

Table 3.3. Spiritual Leadership Organizational Transformation Process

Action Plan—Strategic Level

- Conduct strategic level review and analysis.
- Create shared organizational vision.
- Develop stakeholder criteria and goals to meet or exceed expectations.
- Develop strategy to implement goals.
- Review/develop information systems to measure effectiveness.

Action Plan—Empowered Team & Personal Leadership Levels

- Conduct team level review and analysis.
- Define/implement essential elements of empowered teams.
- Create shared organizational/team vision and personal mission statements.
- Develop stakeholder criteria and goals to meet or exceed expectations.
- Develop strategy to implement goals.
- Review/develop information systems to measure effectiveness.

Elements of Empowerment

- Empowerment is power sharing—the delegation of power and authority.
- It creates the cross-level connection between team and individual jobs.
- It provides the basis for strong intrinsic motivation and meets the higher-order needs of individuals.
- Empowered employees are more committed to the organization through trust, hope, and faith.
- Empowered teams receive information about organizational performance.
- Employees receive knowledge and skills to contribute to organizational goals.
- Employees have the power to make substantive decisions.
- Employees understand the meaning and impact of their jobs.
- Employees are rewarded based upon organizational performance.

Exercising personal leadership and reaping the fruits of ethical and spiritual well-being (joy, peace, and serenity) demands conscious assumption of control over one's own destiny through the establishment of a personal mission based on these values with goals that give depth and meaning to every action. Doing what you know is right and productive for you regard-

**Table 3.4.   Values of Hope/Faith and Altruistic Love
as Personal Affirmations**

1. **TRUST/LOYALTY**—In my chosen relationships, I am faithful and have faith in and rely on the character, ability, strength and truth of others.

2. **FORGIVENESS/ACCEPTANCE/GRATITUDE**—I suffer not the burden of failed expectations, gossip, jealousy, hatred, or revenge. Instead, I choose the power of forgiveness through acceptance and gratitude. This frees me from the evils of self-will, judging others, resentment, self-pity, and anger and gives me serenity, joy and peace.

3. **INTEGRITY**—I walk the walk as well as talk the talk. I say what I do and do what I say.

4. **HONESTY**—I seek truth and rejoice in it and base my actions on it.

5. **COURAGE**—I have the firmness of mind and will, as well as the mental and moral strength, to maintain my morale and prevail in the face of extreme difficulty, opposition, threat, danger, hardship, and fear.

6. **HUMILTY**—I am modest, courteous, and without false pride. I am not jealous, rude or arrogant. I do not brag.

7. **KINDNESS**—I am warm-hearted, considerate, humane and sympathetic to the feelings and needs of others.

8. **EMPATHY/COMPASSION**—I read and understand the feelings of others. When others are suffering, I understand and want to do something about it.

9. **PATIENCE/MEEKNESS/ ENDURANCE**—I bear trials and/or pain calmly and without complaint. I persist in or remain constant to any purpose, idea, or task in the face of obstacles or discouragement. I pursue steadily any project or course I begin. I never quit in spite of counter influences, opposition, discouragement, suffering or misfortune.

10. **EXCELLENCE**—I do my best and recognize, rejoice in, and celebrate the noble efforts of my fellows.

11. **FUN**—Enjoyment, playfulness, and activity must exist in order to stimulate minds and bring happiness to one's place of work. I therefore view my daily activities and work as not to be dreaded yet, instead, as reasons for smiling and having a terrific day in serving others.

less of obstacles or the opinions of others is the essence of personal leadership. To exercise strong personal leadership, people must recognize and believe in their own untapped potential, develop a strong self-image, be self-motivated through hope and faith in their personal vision through desire held in expectation with the belief that it will be realized, and define success in terms of the progressive realization of worthwhile predetermined personal goals (Meyer, 1994).

By exercising strong personal leadership and authentically living the values, attitudes, and behavior of altruistic love through the care, concern, and appreciation of themselves, team members, and strategic leaders, participants have the experience of membership and ethical well-being, which is a necessary condition for spiritual well-being. By being committed to a vision grounded in service to key stakeholders and being empowered with the autonomy to act as they see fit, participants have an experience of competence and calling in that, through their work, they are making a difference in other people's lives and therefore their life has meaning. As discussed by Fry (2003), the combined experiences of calling and membership are the essence of spiritual survival and, ultimately, spiritual well-being in the quest for a higher power from which one can draw strength and give their unreserved commitment and devotion.

Outcomes of personal spiritual leadership include ethical and spiritual well-being as manifested through joy, peace, and serenity. These outcomes also are the sources of high organizational commitment, productivity and reduced stress levels that are the goals of most managers and organizations and the most often reported affective outcomes of organizational research. Joy is exultant satisfaction as a source of gladness or delight and is an emotion of keen or lively pleasure arising from present or expected satisfaction. Peace is a state of mind where one is free from mental disturbance, strife or agitation. Serenity encompasses joy and peace and much more.

Put simply, serenity is a deep inner sense that all is well. The experience goes beyond our systems of emotional or rational intelligence. Rather, it is an intuitive or spiritual knowing that produces in us the inner experience of calmness, clarity, and awareness. In serenity, we can live more fully in the now moment, perceiving in acceptance the reality presenting itself without wanting to control things to gratify our selfish desires. There is no need to have or get anything more than what the moment presents; living in serenity itself is sufficient (St. Romain, 1997, p. 2).

Strategic and Empowered Team, Spiritual Leadership and Corporate Social Responsibility

With the dawn of a new century, there is an emerging and exponentially accelerating force for global societal and organizational change. Responding to these forces will require a major organizational transformation to a learning organizational paradigm that is radically different from the traditional centralized, standardized, and formalized bureaucratic organizational form based on fear that has been the dominant organizational paradigm since the beginning of the industrial revolution (Ancona et al., 1999; Fry, 2003; Moxley, 2000).

From a strategic and empowered team spiritual leadership perspective, it is therefore necessary for organizations to adopt a stakeholder approach in viewing social organizations as imbedded in layers or levels (individual, group, organizational, societal) with various internal and external constituencies (employees, customers, suppliers, government agencies, and so

forth), all of whom have a legitimate strategic and moral stake in the organization's performance (Freeman, 1984). Each of these stakeholders may
have different values and interests as well as different stakeholder relationships with other individuals, groups and organizations:

> The core problem is to achieve the common good of the organization, while
> at the same time meeting the needs and safeguarding the rights of the vari-
> ous stakeholders. To achieve such an outcome, people must to some extent
> come together and cooperate on the basis of values interest and social
> choice. (Bass & Steidlmeier, 1999, p. 200)

Because of this, the single-minded focus on measuring organizational
performance through "shareholder value" based primarily on the basis of
stock price must give way to a balanced perspective that elevates the importance of simultaneously satisfying the expectations and interests of employees, customers, and their communities in addition to the bottom line. Even
Milton Friedman (1970), the guru of free markets and profit, in his famous
New York Times article, "The Social Responsibility of Business is to Increase
Profits," proclaimed that the appropriate goal for corporate executive was
to maximize profits as much as possible while conforming to the basic rules
of society—both those imbedded in law and ethical custom. Even for Friedman, legal and ethical norms should act as a guide for establishing and
maintaining stakeholder relationships in distinguishing between responsible and irresponsible notions of profit seeking (Ostas, 2001). In addition,
recent analysis of corporate social responsibility (CSR) utilizing legal and
economic theory suggests that CSR and the profit motive are compatible.
And, when legal and market issues are properly framed, CSR can be gained
or achieved without sacrificing profit (Heinze, Sibary, & Sikula, 1999;
McWilliams & Segal, 2001; Ostas, 2001; Trevinio & Nelson, 2004). "The key
is to throw off ill-fitting habits of thought and to look closely at one's own
values and those of one's trading partners so as to propose new and creative market exchanges" (Ostas, 2001, p. 299). Given the challenges presented by today's rapidly changing and increasingly complex global
business environment, by achieving congruence between customer,
worker, and other key stakeholder values and expectations, leaders will
enhance, rather than detract from corporate profitability.

As outlined in Fry (2003, pp. 718–720) and further detailed in the field
experiment conducted by Malone and Fry (2003), the spiritual leadership
transformation process utilizes a vision and values-driven stakeholder
approach to achieve this congruence and, it is proposed, to ultimately foster CSR. This process is initiated by developing a vision/mission whereby
strategic leaders and/or followers can initiate CSR to serve key stakeholders. This vision must vividly portray a journey which, when undertaken, will

give one a sense of calling, of one's life having meaning and making a difference. The vision then forms the basis for the social construction of the organization's culture as a learning organization and the ethical system and values underlying it. In spiritual leadership, these values are prescribed and form the basis for altruistic love. Strategic leaders then embody and abide in these values through their everyday attitudes and behavior. In doing so, they create empowered teams where participants are challenged to persevere, be tenacious, do what it takes, and pursue excellence by doing their best in achieving challenging goals through hope and faith in the vision, their leaders, and themselves (see Tables 3.3 and 3.4).

Strategic leaders benefit from this personal and team empowerment and self-direction in that they can devote more time to strategic stakeholder issues arising from an ever-changing environment. Empowerment is power sharing in the delegation of power and both authority and all but symbolic responsibility to organizational followers (Conger & Kanungo, 1998; Ford & Fottler, 1995; Hollander & Offerman, 1990; Spreitzer, 1996). Empowered employees commit more of themselves to do the job through trust in the strategic leaders and the hope and faith that ensues from this trust. By providing employees with both the knowledge to contribute to the organization and the power to make consequential decisions and the necessary resources to do their jobs, strategic leaders provide the context for all organizational participants to receive the altruistic love that, in turn, forms the basis for intrinsic motivation through hope/faith in pursuit and implementation of the organization's vision and values in socially responsible service to internal and external stakeholders. It is through participating in these teams that followers, through recognition and celebration, experience a sense of membership and feel understood and appreciated.

Additionally, strategic leaders must provide followers with the knowledge of how their jobs are relevant to the organization's performance and vision/mission. This understanding is necessary to create the cross level connection between team and individual jobs and the organization's vision/mission. Through this experience, followers too can begin to develop, refine, and practice their own personal spiritual leadership that fosters value congruence in social interaction with internal and external stakeholders and, ultimately, ethical and spiritual well-being.

DISCUSSION

Covey (1991, p. 296) gives an example of a universal mission statement, "To increase the economic well-being and quality of life of all stakeholders," which incorporates the essence of both the ethical content and process of implementing corporate social responsibility through spiritual leadership. Following Bass and Steidlmeier (1999), this review has established that, as ethical content, SLT prescribes universal or consensus values distilled from thousands of years of human experience through religion and philosophy as well as the results of emerging scientific research on positive human health and well-being. As an ethical process, SLT prescribes a moral discourse based in stakeholder theory (Freeman, 1984) resting upon the centrality of mutual altruism, which incorporates both moral intention and moral consequences in advocating (within the human rights tradition) a balance between egoism and altruism in assessing benefits and costs for both self and others (Bass & Steidlmeier, 1999; Kanungo & Mendonca, 1996).

Earlier, ethical well-being was defined as authentically living one's values, attitudes, and behavior from the inside-out in creating a principled-center congruent with the universal, consensus values inherent in SLT (Covey, 1991; Fry, 2003). Ethical well-being is then seen as necessary but not sufficient for spiritual well-being which, in addition to ethical well-being, incorporates transcendence of self in pursuit of a vision/ purpose/ mission in service to key stakeholders to satisfy one's need for spiritual survival through calling and membership. Therefore, it is hypothesized that individuals practicing spiritual leadership at the personal level will score high on both life satisfaction in terms of joy, peace, and serenity and the Ryff and Singer (2001) dimensions of well-being discussed earlier. In other words, they will:

1. Experience greater psychological well-being.
2. Have fewer problems related to physical health in terms of allostatic load (cardiovascular disease, cognitive impairment, declines in physical functioning, and mortality).

More specifically, they would have a high regard for oneself and one's past life, good-quality relationship with others, a sense that life is purposeful and meaningful, the capacity to effectively manage one's surrounding world, the ability to follow inner convictions, and a sense of continuing growth and self-realization.

Relative to corporate social responsibility (CSR), a major proposition of this paper is that spiritual leadership—which incorporates ethical and spiritual well-being—is hypothesized to be necessary for CSR. In addition, any balanced theory of CSR must rest upon the underlying assumption inherent in stakeholder theory (Freeman, 1984)—that overall organizational effectiveness (including profits and shareholder value) is a function of meeting or exceeding the expectations of key high power/high importance stakeholders. From this perspective, what is being proposed is a new model of the ideal corporation based on spiritual leadership across the strategic, empowered team, and individual levels that is far more transparent and places greater emphasis on vision and value congruence with key stakeholders (Byrne, 2002; Fry, 2003).

So what is the answer for dealing with the perception that corporate America is amoral and corrupt? At the heart of this issue is a basic mistrust of a business philosophy that emphasizes maximizing shareholder value today. In response to this crisis of trust, universities must do more than just design new courses that apply the basics of ethics and leadership to real-life work situations. They could act more like investigators to ascertain the character of applicants and set strict course criteria with severe penalties for students who exhibit unethical behavior. Alliances could be forged with companies to open their door to faculty that want to study everyday corporate ethics. Company recruiters could also play a vital role by placing as high a value on good ethics as they do on problem-solving skills. Finally, corporations could partner with universities to increase the professionalization of the practice of management and leadership (Filley, House, & Kerr, 1976; Merritt, 2003; Wee, 2002). In doing so, the emphasis should be placed on the positive ethics approach advocated for positive psychology (Handlesman et al., 2001), which recognizes the importance of physical health and well-being.

Since September 11, 2001 with homeland security a top priority, the operating environment for CEO's has fundamentally changed. National governments are increasing financial regulation in order to monitor flows of money that could be used to finance terrorist activity. Corporate scandals such as Enron and WorldCom plus the collapse of faith in financial markets when so many highly touted dotcoms proved worthless have precipitated a crisis in corporate governance. Corporate boards must put a premium on focusing anew on fundamentals and move away from the fad of developing new business models (Garten, 2003). Now the emphasis must be on building great institutions and creating lasting value. Boards must recognize that the single-minded goal of primarily and exclusively enriching its shareholders now is a failed philosophy. In its place the much broader purpose of creating value by also enriching key stakeholders—employees, customers, suppliers, and the communities in which it operates—must become paramount. This calls for a new ethos of corporate governance. At a minimum corporate boards need to redefine the character of leadership and select CEO's who emphasize a constant vision and set of consensus values that everyone knows and can rely on (Byrne, 2002; Garten, 2003). This is especially important in today's business climate of hyper-competitive markets, downsizing and large layoffs, and outsourcing jobs overseas to utilize lower-cost labor. The blot on board and CEO reputations for being rewarded whether the company does well or not must also end. Both strategic leaders and other employees must gear remuneration to long-term performance and putting their compensation at risk when targets are not met, while looking more carefully at ways to protect worker pensions.

As recognition of this call, ISO (International Organization for Standardization)—the developer of ISO 9000, which has become an international reference for quality management requirements in business-to-business dealings—is conducting a survey on the worldwide state of social responsibility codes, guidelines and specifications. The hope is that ISO's network of 148 countries with a Central Secretariat in Geneva, Switzerland, that coordinates the system, will be able to act as a bridging organization in which a consensus can be reached on solutions that meet both the requirements of business and the broader needs of society, such as the needs of stakeholder groups like consumers and users (Quality Digest, 2003).

CONCLUSION

Nearly fifty years ago, Ohmann (1955) argued that people have lost faith in society's basic values and that a spiritual rebirth was needed in industrial leadership. Noting that never in human history had people ever had so much yet enjoyed so little real satisfaction. He proposed that the god of production and profits had feet of clay and that a religion based on materialism, science, and humanism is inadequate. He then argues that man, especially at work, is searching for new "skyhooks"—for an abiding faith around which life's experiences can be integrated and given meaning. Asking the questions, "Production for what?" "Do we use people for production or production for people?" and "How can production be justified if it destroys both personality and human values both in the process of its manufacture and by its end use?" Ohmann (1955, p. 37) makes a persuasive case for the very consensus values offered here. In answering these questions, Ohmann (1955) describes the successful executive as one who provides an invisible, fundamental structure of "skyhooks" into which the experiences of every day are absorbed and given meaning. These include:

1. Providing a vision without which the people perish.
2. Philosophical and character values that help relate the overall goals of the enterprise to eternal values.
3. Setting the climate within which these values become working realities.
4. Integrating the smaller, selfish goals of individuals into larger, more social and spiritual objectives of the group.
5. Resolving conflicts by relating the immediate to long range and more enduring values.

In a very real sense, what is being called for here is what Yogi Berra terms, "Deja vu all over again." "Skyhooks" must be found and issues relating to ethical and spiritual well-being at work resolved if we are ever to effectively deal with the seemingly intractable issues that must be addressed to clean up corporate accounting, governance, and ethics to the point that organizations have a corporate conscience and culture built around an ethical set of moral principles and values and knowing the difference between right and wrong. Fundamentally, strategic leaders must adopt the SLT process to establish congruence of values and interests among stakeholders while avoiding deceit, manipulation, self-aggrandizement, and power abuse. This means establishing and enforcing high standards of conduct as well as recruiting, rewarding, and promoting people of character. "It is better to hire people with good character and train for competence than it is to hire competent but unprincipled people in the hope that their character defects won't hurt the organization" (Josephson, 1999, p. 13).

ACKNOWLEDGMENTS

I give grateful acknowledgment to a number of anonymous reviewers, August Turak, and especially Laura Matherly for their critical, constructive comments, and editorial assistance on earlier versions of this paper.

REFERENCES

Ancona, D., Kochan, T., Scully, M., Van Maanen, J., & Westney, D.E. (1999). *Managing for the future: Organizational behavior and processes.* Boston: Southwestern College Publishing.

Barrett, R. (1998). *Liberating the corporate soul.* Boston: Butterworth-Heinemann.

Barrett, R. (2003). Culture and consciousness: Measuring spirituality in the workplace by mapping values. In R.A. Giacalone & C.L. Jurkiewicz (Eds.), *Handbook of workplace spirituality and organizational performance* (pp. 345–366). Armonk, NY: M. E. Sharp.

Bass, B.M., & Steidlmeier, P. (1999). Ethics, character, and authentic transformational leadership. *The Leadership Quarterly, 10*(2), 181–217.

Bellah, R., Madsen, R., Sullivan, W. M., Swidler, A., & Tipton, S.M. (1985). *Habits of the heart: Individualism and commitment in American life.* Berkeley: University of California Press.

Benjamin, L.T.J. (1992). The history of american psychology [Special issue]. *American Psychologist, 47*(2).

Blackaby, H., & Blackaby, R. (2001). *Spiritual leadership.* Nashville, TN: Broadman & Holman Publishers.

Bolman, L.G., & Deal, T.E. (1995). *Leading with soul.* San Francisco: Jossey-Bass Publishers.

Breckler, S.J. (1984). Empirical validation of affect, behavior and cognition as distinct components of attitudes. *Journal of Personality and Social Psychology,* 1191–1205.

Buchholz, R.A., & Rosenthal, S.B. (2003). Spirituality, consumption, and business: A pragmatic perspective. In R.A. Giacalone & C.L. Jurkiewicz (Eds.), *Handbook of workplace spirituality and organizational performance.* Armonk, NY: M. E. Sharpe.

Cavenaugh, G.F. (1999). Spirituality for managers: Context and critique. *Journal of Organizational Change Management, 12,* 186–199.

Christopher, J.C. (1999). Situational psychological well-being: Exploring the cultural roots of its theory and research. *Journal of Counseling and Development, 77,* 141–152.

Coan, R.W. (1977). *Hero, artist, sage, or saint? A survey of what is variously called mental health, normality, maturity, self-actualization, and human fulfillment.* New York: Columbia University Press.

Conger, J.A., & Kanungo, R.N. (1994). Charismatic leadership in organizations: Perceived behavioral attributes and their measurement. *Journal of Organizational Behavior, 15,* 439–452.

Conger, J.A., & Kanungo, R.N. (1998). *Charismatic leadership in organizations.* Thousand Oaks, CA: Sage.

Covey, S.R. (1989). *The seven habits of highly effective people: Powerful lessons in personal change.* New York: Fireside/Simon & Schuster.

Covey, S.R. (1991). *Principle-centered leadership.* New York: Fireside/Simon & Schuster.

Dali Lama XIV. (1999). *Ethics for the new millennium.* New York: The Putnam Publishing Group.

Danna, K., & Griffin, R.W. (1999). Health and well-being in the workplace: A review and synthesis of the literature. *Journal of Management, 25*(3), 357–384.

Diener. (1984). Subjective well-being. *Psychological Bulletin* (95), 542–575.

Diener, E., Lucas, R.E., & Oishi, S. (2001). Subjective well-being: The science of happiness and life satisfaction. In C.R. Snyder & S.J. Lopez (Eds.), *Handbook of positive psychology.* Oxford/New York: Oxford University Press.

Diener, E., Lucus, R.E., & Oishi, S. (2001). Subjective well-being: The science of happiness and life satisfaction. In C.R. Snyder & S.J. Lopez (Eds.), *Handbook of positive psychology* (pp. 63–73). Oxford/New York: Oxford University Press.

Eisler, R., & Montouri, A. (2003). The human side of spirituality. In R.A. Giacalone & C.L. Jurkiewicz (Eds.), *Handbook of workplace spirituality and organizational performance* (pp. 46–56). Armonk, NY: M. E. Sharp.

Elm, D.R. (2003). Honesty, spirituality, and performance at work. In R.A. Giacalone & C.L. Jurkiewicz (Eds.), *Handbook of workplace spirituality and organizational performance.* Armonk, NY: M. E. Sharpe.

Fairholm, G.W. (1997). *Capturing the heart of leadership: spirituality and community in the new American workplace.* Westport, CT: Preager.

Fairholm, G.W. (1998). *Perspectives on leadership: From the science of management to its spiritual heart.* Westport, CT: Preager.

Fairholm, G.W. (2001). *Matering inner leadership.* Westport, CT: Quorum.

Filley, A.C., House, R.J., & Kerr, S. (1976). *Managerial processes and organizational behavior.* Glenview, IL: Scott, Foresman and Company.

Fleischman, P.R. (1994). *The healing spirit: Explorations in religion & psychotherapy.* Cleveland, OH: Bonne Chance Press.

Ford, R.C., & Fottler, M.D. (1995). Empowerment: a matter of degree. *Academy of Management Executive, 9,* 21–31.

Freeman, R.E. (1984). *Strategic management: A stakeholder approach.* Boston: Pitman Publishing.

Friedman, M. (1970, September 13). The social responsibility of business is to increase profits. *New York Times.*

Fry, L.W. (2003). Toward a theory of spiritual leadership. *The leadership quarterly, 14,* 693–727.

Furnham, A. (2003). Ethics at work: Money, spirituality, and happiness. In R.A. Giacalone & C.L. Jurkiewicz (Eds.), *Handbook of workplace spirituality and organizational performance.* Armonk, NY: M. E. Sharpe.

Garten, J. (2003, January 4). A new year: A new agenda. *The Economist,* 44–56.

Geertz, C. (1973). *The interpretation of cultures.* New York: Basic Books.

Giacalone, R.A., & Jurkiewicz, C.L. (2003). Toward a science of workplace spirituality. In R.A. Giacalone & C.L. Jurkiewicz (Eds.), *Handbook of workplace spirituality and organizational performance* (pp. 3–28). Armonk, NY: M. E. Sharpe.

Gini, A. (1995). Too much to say about something. *Business Ethics Quarterly, 5,* 143–155.

Greenleaf, R.K. (1977). *Servant leadership: A journey into the nature of legitimate power and greatness.* New York: Paulist Press.

Greenleaf, R.K. (1978). *Servant leader and follower.* New York: Paulist Press.

Handlesman, M.M., Knapp, S., & Gottlieb, M. C. (2001). Positive ethics. In C.R. Snyder & S.J. Lopez (Eds.), *Handbook of positive psychology.* Oxford/New York: Oxford University Press.

Heinze, D., Sibary, S., & Sikula, A. J. (2000). Relations among corporate social responsibility, financial soundness, and investment value in 22 manufacturing industry groups. *Ethics & Behavior, 9*(4), 331–347.

Hendricks, K.T., & Hendricks, C.G. (2003). Operational integrity. In R.A. Giacalone & C.L. Jurkiewicz (Eds.), *Handbook of workplace spirituality and organizational performance* (pp. 429–446). Armonk, NY: M. E. Sharpe.

Hill, P.C., & Smith, G.S. (2003). Coming to terms with spirituality and religion in the workplace. In R.A. Giacalone & C.L. Jurkiewicz (Eds.), *Handbook of workplace spirituality and organizational performance.* Armonk, NY: M. E. Sharpe.

Hollander, E.P., & Offerman, L.R. (1990). Power and leadership in organizations. *American Psychology, 45,* 179–189.

Horton, W.R. (1950). *GOD.* New York: Association Press.

Hughes, R.L., Ginnett, R.C., & Curphy, G.J. (1999). *Leadership: Enhancing the lessions of experience.* Boston: Irwin McGraw-Hill.

ISO considers creating social responsibilty standard. (2003). Retrieved December 19, 2003, from the World Wide Web: http://www.qualitydigest.com/april/news.shtml

Josephson, M. (1996). *Making ethical decisions.* Marina del Ray, CA: Josephson Institute of Ethics.

Josephson, M. (1999). Character: Linchpin of leadership. *Executive Excellence*, 13–14.

Josephson, M. (2002). *Making ethical decisions*. Marina del Ray, CA: Josephson Institute of Ethics.

Kaczorowski, J.M. (1989). Spiritual well-being and anxiety in aduldts diagnosed with cancer. *Hospice Journal*, 5(3), 105–115.

Kanungo, R.N., & Mendonca, M. (1996). *Ethical Dimensions of Leadership*. Thousand Oaks, CA: Sage.

Kerr, S., & Jermier, J.M. (1977). Substitutes for leadership: Their meaning and measurement. *Organizational Behavior and Human Performance, 22*, 375–403.

Kouzes, J.M., & Pozner, B.Z. (1987). *The leadership challenge*. San Francisco: Jossey-Bass.

Kouzes, J.M., & Pozner, B.Z. (1993). *Credibility*. San Francisco: Jossey-Bass.

Kouzes, J.M., & Pozner, B.Z. (1999). *Encouraging the heart*. San Francisco: Jossey-Bass.

Kurth, K. (2003). Spiritually renewing ourselves at work. In R.A. Giacalone & C.L. Jurkiewicz (Eds.), *Handbook of workplace spirituality and organizational performance* (pp. 447–460). Armonk, NY: M. E. Sharp.

Lickona, T. (1988). Four strategies for fostering character development in children. *Phi Delta Kappan*, 419–423.

Lickona, T. (1991). *Educating for character*. New York: Bantam Books.

Mackenzie, E.R., Rajagopal, D.E., Meibohm, M., & Lavizzo-Mourey, R. (2000). Spiritual support and psychological well being: Older adult's perceptions of the religion and health connection. *Alternative Therapies, 6*, 37–45.

Maddock, I.I., & Denton, E.A. (1998). *Motivation, emotions, and leadership: The silent side of management*. Westport, CT: Quorum Books.

Maddock, R.C., & Fulton, R.L. (1998). *Motivation, emotions, and leadership: The silent side of management*. Westport, CT: Quorum Books.

Malone, P.F. & L.W. (2003). *Transforming schools through spiritual leadership: A field experiment*. Paper presented at the Academy of Management, Seattle, WA.

Mason, R.O. (2003). Spirituality and information. In R.A. Giacalone & C.L. Jurkiewicz (Eds.), *Handbook of workplace spirituality and organizational performance*. Armonk, NY: M. E. Sharpe.

Matthews, D.A., Larson, D.B., & Barry, C.P. (1994). *The faith factor: An annotated bibliography of clinical research on spiritual subjects*. Rockville, MD: John Templeton Foundation, National Institute for Healthcare Research.

McNeal, R. (2000), *A work of heart: Understanding how God shapes spiritual leaders*. San Francisco: Josey-Bass.

Mcwilliams, A., & Seigel, D. (2001). Corporate social responsibility. *Academy of Management Review, 26*(1), 117–127.

Merritt, J. (2003, January, 17). Ethics is also B-School business. *Business Week*.

Meyer, P.J. (1994). *Effective personal productivity*. Waco, TX: Leadership Management Inc.

Mitroff, I.I., & Denton, E.A. (1999). *A spiritual audit of corporate america: A hard look at spirituality, religion, & values in the workplace*. San Francisco: Jossey-Bass.

Mobley, L.R. (1971). Personal values and Corporate Ethics. In A. Klose & R. Weiler (Eds.), *Men in decision making; Social ethics and the policy of society* (pp. 1887–1199). Freiburg: Herder.

Moxley, R.S. (2000). *Leadership and spirit*. San Francisco: Jossey-Bass.

Nadesan, M.H. (1999). The discourse of corporate spritualism and evangelical capitalism. *Management Communication Quarterly, 13*, 3–42.

Nash, L. (1994). *Believers in business*. Nashville, TN: Nelson.

Neal, J.A. (2001). Leadership and spirituality in the workplace. In R.N. Lussier & C.F. Achua (Eds.), *Leadership theory, application, skill development* (pp. 464–473). South-Western Publishing.

Northouse, P.G. (2001). *Leadership: Theory and practice*. Thousand Oaks, CA: Sage.

Ohmann, O.A. (1955, May-June). "Skyhooks": With special implications. for Monday through Friday. *Harvard Business Review,* 33–41.

Olson, J.M., & Zanna, M.P. (1993). Attitudes and attitude change. In L.W. Porter & M.R. Rosenzweig (Eds.), *Annual review of psychology* (Vol. 44, pp. 117–154). Annual Reviews, Incorporated.

Ostas, D.T. (2001). Deconstructing corporate social responsibility: Insights from legal and economic theory. *American Business Law Journal, 38*, 261–299.

Paloutzian, R.F., Emmons, R.A., & Keortge, S.G. (2003). Spiritual well-being, spiritual intelligenve, and healthy workplace policy. In R.A. Giacalone & C.L. Jurkiewicz (Eds.), *Handbook of workplace spirituality and organizational performance*. Armonk, NY: M. E. Sharpe.

Pennebaker, J.W. (1990). *Opening up: The healing power of confiding in others*. New York: William Morrow.

Peterson, R.L., & Skiba, R. (2001). Creating school climates that prevent school violence. *The Social Studies,* 167–175.

Pfeffer, J. (2003). Business and the spirit. In R.A. Giacalone & C.L. Jurkiewicz (Eds.), *Handbook of workplace spirituality and organizational performance* (pp. 29–45). Armonk, NY: M. E. Sharp.

Quick, J.C., Nelson, D.L., & Hurrell, J.J. (1997). *Preventative stress management in organizations*. Washington, DC: American Psychological Association.

Ravlin, E.C., & Meglino, B.M. (1987). Effects of values on perception and decision making: A study of alternative work value measures. *Journal of Applied Psychology, 72*, 666–673.

Rosenthal, S.B., & Buckholz, R.A. (1995). Leadership: Toward new philosophical foundations. *Business and Professional Ethics Journal, 14*, 25–41.

Ryff, C.D., & Singer, B. (2001). From social structure to biology: Integrative science in pursuit of human health and well-being. In C.R. Snyder & S.J. Lopez (Eds.), *Handbook of positive psychology*. Oxford/New York: Oxford University Press.

Sanders, J.O. (1986). *Spiritual leadership*. Chicago: Moody Press.

Sass, J.S. (2000). Characterizing organizational spirituality: An organizational communication culture approach. *Communication Studies, 51*, 195–207.

Seligman, M.E., & Csikzentmihalyi, M. (2000). Positive psychology: An introduction. *American Psychologist, 55*(1), 5–14.

Seligman, M.E.P. (2001). Positive psychology, positive prevention, and positive therapy. In C.R. Snyder & S.J. Lopez (Eds.), *Handbook of positive psychology*. Oxford/New York: Oxford University Press.

Shared belief in the golden rule. (2003). Religious Tolerance Org. Retrieved, from the World Wide Web: http://www.religioustolerance.org/reciproc.htm

Smith, D.S. (1997). *Caregiving: Hospice proven techniques for healing body and soul*. New York: Macmillan.

Smith, H. (1992). *The world's religions*. New York: Peter Smith.

Spreitzer, G. (1996). Social structural characteristics of psychological empowerment. *Academy of Management Journal, 39*(2), 483–504.

St. Romain, P. (1997). *Reflections on the serenity prayer*. Ligouri, MO: Ligouri Press.

Treviño, L.K., & Nelson, K.A. (2004). *Managing business ethics*. Hoboken, NJ: Wiley.

Veach, T.L., & Chappell, J.N. (1991). Measuring spiritual health: a preliminary study. *Substance Abuse, 13*, 139–149.

Walsh, D.C. (1997). Cultivating inner sources of leadership. In F. Hesslebein, M. Goldsmith, & R. Beckhard (Eds.), *The organization of the future*. San Francisco: Jossey-Bass.

Watson. (2001). Positive affectivity: The disposition to experience pleasurable emotional states. In C.R. Snyder & S.J. Lopez (Eds.), *Handbook of positive psychology*. Oxford/New York: Oxford University Press.

Weber, M. (1958). *The protestant ethic and the spirit of capitalism*. New York: Scribner's.

Webster's New Collegiate Dictionary. (1976). Springfield MA: G & C Merriam Company.

Wee, H. (2002, April, 11). Corporate ethics: Right makes might. *Business Week*.

Zellers, K.L., & Perrewe, P.L. (2003). In R.A. Giacalone & C.L. Jurkiewicz (Eds.), *Handbook of workplace spirituality and organizational performance* (pp. 300–313). Armonk, NY: M. E. Sharp.

Zinnbauer, B.J., Pargament, K.I., & Scott, A.B. (1999). The emerging meanings of religiousness and spirituality: Problems and prospects. *Journal of Personality, 67*, 889–919.

CHAPTER 4

WHISTLE-BLOWING
AND POSITIVE PSYCHOLOGY

Marcia P. Miceli and Janet P. Near

INTRODUCTION

Throughout the world, employees' blowing the whistle on perceived organizational wrongdoing—as in Sherron Watkins' reporting financial wrongdoing at Enron Corporation—frequently makes news (Frey, 2002). For example, during 1989–1995, 30 major newspapers published more than one thousand articles on these topics (Brewer, 1996). Many more articles have been published since that time, particularly recently, regarding the uncovering of scandals involving Enron, WorldCom, Global Crossing, Tyco, the FBI, and other large organizations (e.g., Pressler, 2003).

Many of the news stories have identified substantial negative consequences of organizational wrongdoing for victims, such as employees, customers, and society at large, and two implications have emerged. First, organizational wrongdoing continues to be perceived all too frequently, and societies show considerable interest in reducing its occurrence. Second, in general, actions such as whistle-blowing, that attempt to stop its substantial negative consequences for employees, customers, communities, and societies, are positive behaviors, though certain incidents of whistle-blowing can be antisocial (Miceli & Near, 1997).

Positive Psychology in Business Ethics and Corporate Responsibility, pages 85–102
Copyright © 2005 by Information Age Publishing
All rights of reproduction in any form reserved.

Unfortunately, it is not self-evident that whistle-blowing is a positive behavior, in the minds of corporate leaders who can most directly affect it. Obviously, it can be argued that even if avoiding and stopping wrongdoing benefits society but not the organization, it is still a positive behavior, and managers of that the organization are ethically, and sometimes legally, obliged to put the interests of society first. In other words, we would argue that it is managers' social responsibility to balance their roles as agents of their organization and as citizens of the broader community.

But less obviously, whistle-blowing can help the organization—often the same action that benefits constituents, such as employees and community members, also directly benefits the organization. For example, the very existence of Enron, Arthur Andersen, and Bridgestone/Firestone has been shaken by wrongdoing (*The Economist*, 2002), which might have been avoided had top management responded appropriately to internal whistle-blowers. In addition to anecdotes, there is also preliminary controlled evidence of benefits to organizations of stopping wrongdoing (e.g., Glomb et al., 1997; Miceli, Van Scotter, Near, & Rehg, 2001b). Further, offering the opportunity for employees to voice their concerns creates an alternative to the organization's losing excellent employees who would otherwise choose to leave rather than work for an organization that tolerates wrongdoing and squelches dissent (e.g., Farrell & Rusbult, 1990; Hirschman, 1970). Enlightened managers acting in their organizations' self-interest certainly would prefer to reduce dysfunctional turnover.

Yet, according to a recent article in an influential international publication,

> sadly, few firms are yet persuaded that such procedures (to encourage internal whistle-blowing) are in their own best interests. In America at least, it is almost always thought cheaper to fire whistleblowers than to listen to them, despite years of legislation designed to achieve the opposite. "No matter how many protections whistleblower laws have created over the years," says Kris Kolesnik, director of the National Whistleblower Centre in Washington, DC, "the system always seems to defeat them." (*The Economist*, 2002, p. 56)

This observation suggests that additional work is needed to foster acceptance of the notion that whistle-blowing is a positive behavior; hence, the study of whistle-blowing falls within the realm of positive psychology, the "scientific study of optimal human functioning whose aims are to determine and advance the factors that lead to flourishing individuals, communities, and societies" (Giacalone, Dunn, & Jurkiewicz, 2005). Positive psychology covers a wide range of topics and includes work on positive experience (such as well being and flow), character strengths (such as courage, perseverance and forgiveness) and civic virtues (such as altruism and civility) (Giacalone et al., 2005; Luthans, 2002).

We argue that because whistle-blowing is generally a positive response to negative circumstances, it should be more strongly encouraged by organizations and by society. However, published advice as to how this can be achieved is not always informed by existing scientific literature on the topic.

Accordingly, the purpose of this paper is to utilize existing theoretical and empirical literature to identify ways that managers can more effectively respond to whistle-blowing, and ways to improve public policy toward it in the US. There is substantial evidence that whistle-blowing occurs throughout the world, including Australia (e.g., De Maria & Jan, 1997; *The Economist*, 2002), Hong Kong (e.g., Near & Miceli, 1988), Israel (e.g., Day, 1996; Seagull, 1995), Japan (e.g., Yoshida, 2001), and The Netherlands (e.g., Bates, 1999). Because cultures and laws vary substantially, however, we must limit our focus to the US. We begin by defining whistle-blowing; then we describe how it has been viewed as a positive organizational behavior, and how literature from this perspective suggests actions that can be taken.

DEFINING WHISTLE-BLOWING

Because whistle-blowing is discussed by researchers in a variety of fields, including psychology, sociology, ethics, law, and public policy, it is important to clarify what we mean by whistle-blowing. Whistle-blowing is "the disclosure by organization members (former or current) of illegal, immoral, or illegitimate practices under the control of their employers, to persons or organizations that may be able to effect action" (Near & Miceli, 1985, p. 4).

This definition has been used in studies of persons in a variety of occupations and professions, including nurses (King, 1997), internal auditors (Miceli & Near, 1994; Miceli, Near, & Schwenk, 1991), and managers (e.g., Keenan, 2002b). It has been used in investigations using diverse samples from various industries (e.g., Rothschild & Miethe, 1999), including federal employees (e.g., Miceli, Rehg, Near, & Ryan, 1999), and samples from countries as varying as India and Yugoslavia (e.g., Keenan, 2002a; Tavakoli, Keenan, & Crnjak-Karanovic, 2003). As such, this definition appears to be the most widely used definition in empirical research about whistle-blowing (King, 1997).

Recently, both *Time* magazine and the Academy of Management (in its 2003 national meeting) honored Sherron Watkins as a whistle-blower (Lacayo & Ripley, 2002). Watkins initially wrote a letter to the CEO, and eventually, her letter became known outside the organization (and its advisers) only after investigations of Enron by the federal government were underway. We thus consider her an "internal" whistle-blower, but other observers have argued that whistle-blowing must be defined as involving a complaint recipient outside the organization (e.g., Farrell & Petersen,

1982), and this debate continues today. This question is important ethically, because some ethicists have implied that only the use of internal complaint channels is morally justified (Bowie, 1982; De George, 1986). If only external actions comprise whistle-blowing, then by this reckoning, whistle-blowing is unethical, and hence, could not be considered a positive action. The question is also important legally, because some state and federal statutes protect whistle-blowers from retaliation only when they use internal channels and others only when external channels (e.g., a report to an official body designated to receive complaints such as the police or the Occupational Safety and Health Administration) are used (Near, Dworkin, & Miceli, 1993). An obvious advantage, of course, for organizations that correct wrongdoing in response to valid internal reports, is that they give the whistle-blower no reason to take the process to a party outside the organization, such as a journalist or congressperson. External reports may be more likely to produce adverse consequences such as unwanted publicity, government intervention, negative effects on recruiting or retention (e.g., practitioner surveys show that employees who have not witnessed wrongdoing are more likely to speak well of the organization to recruits [Ridge, 2000]), loss in stock value, or other undesirable consequences.

We believe that the reasons and evidence for considering internal and external whistle-blowing to be two types of one broad class of behavior comprise a more compelling argument than the argument that they are two essentially unrelated behaviors. These reasons have been detailed elsewhere (Miceli & Near, 1992), so rather than repeat them, we will summarize one of the most important of these reasons.

An inclusive definition permits empirical examination of differences among types of whistle-blowers; omitting internal whistle-blowers like Sherron Watkins from study would lead us to ignore information that might be helpful in understanding the process. Does research show that internals and externals are extremely dissimilar, having different characteristics, encountering different situations, and experiencing different reactions from their organizations? Or are externals, for various reasons, simply extending a process that began with an internal report (and hence largely similar to internals)? If so, this would be one factor suggesting that both should be considered whistle-blowers.

The evidence more strongly supports the latter view. Many studies have shown that nearly all whistle-blowers who use external channels do so after first using internal channels; they may go outside because the wrongdoing was not corrected after the internal report, because they experienced retaliation, or because the nature of the wrongdoing required it (e.g., some types of wrongdoing such as fraud or workplace violence must be reported to authorities [Miceli & Near, 1992]). Results of extensive research concerning potential differences between internal and external whistle-blowers have suggested that their characteristics are generally similar (e.g., Dworkin & Baucus, 1998). Research also shows that the two groups of whistle-blowers differ much more from other groups of organizational members, such as persons who believe they have not observed wrongdoing, or those who have, but have chosen not to report it ("inactive observers," Miceli & Near, 1992; Miceli et al., 2001b; Near & Miceli, 1996). Following are three examples. Whistle-blowers tend to be moderately committed to the organization, whereas inactive observers tend to be either uncommitted, or highly committed as in the "organization man" stereotype (Somers & Casal, 1994). Both internals and externals perceive wrongdoing that tends to be more serious than that perceived by inactive observers (e.g., Miceli & Near, 1985). Both internals and externals (along with inactive observers) tend to believe their organizations are less supportive, with less effective channels for whistle-blowing, than do non-observers (e.g., Miceli et al., 2001b).

WHISTLE-BLOWING AS PROSOCIAL ORGANIZATIONAL BEHAVIOR

Consistent with our view of whistle-blowing as typically a positive behavior, for more than 20 years, researchers have viewed whistle-blowing as a prosocial behavior. That is, behavior intended to benefit other persons (Staub, 1978), such as bystander intervention in crime and emergencies, altruism, or other types of helping. Prosocial behavior was first studied by social psychologists; for example, the theory of bystander intervention (e.g., Latané & Darley, 1968, 1970) ultimately formed the basis of social impact theory (e.g., Latané, 1981). To illustrate one element of this theory, Latané, Darley and their colleagues identified a "diffusion of responsibility" effect explaining why none of the more than 40 witnesses who heard a victim screaming while brutally attacked in New York City called the police; each witness knew that others must have heard, and consequently felt less personally responsible for reporting the act than if he or she were the only witness.

Later, organizational researchers extended this theory into organizational contexts, that is, prosocial organizational behavior, including whistle-blowing (Brief & Motowidlo, 1986). Research suggests that many acts of whistle-blowing are prosocial organizational behaviors (Dozier & Miceli, 1985; Miceli et al., 2001a). Prosocial organizational behavior has been defined as behavior that is "(a) performed by a member of an organization; (b) directed toward an individual, group, or organization with whom he or she interacts while carrying out his or her organizational role; and (c) performed with the intention of promoting the welfare of the individ-

ual, group, or organization toward which it is directed" (Brief & Motowidlo, 1986, p. 711).

A model predicting who will blow the whistle, based on this theoretical
tradition, has been developed, and refined based on empirical results
reported over the years (Dozier & Miceli, 1985; Miceli et al., 2001a). The
model proposes that three general phases occur when questionable activity
occurs. In Phase 1, employees assess whether wrongdoing has occurred
(within a specified time period, such as in the past year) by answering such
questions as "do I believe wrongdoing is occurring?" and "is action warranted?" In Phase 2, the model proposes that observing wrongdoing negatively influences how employees view the organization, though this will be
less true for wrongdoing that one believes has been reported or is being
corrected, and that some elements of this negativity will discourage many
employees from taking action. Not surprisingly, this is one hypothesized
reason why so few organization members blow the whistle even when formal complaint channels exist. Many observers may ask, rhetorically, "how
likely is it that any organization that would allow this wrongdoing to occur
in the first place, would maintain effective complaint channels, and that
these channels would spring into action if I were to use them? It's all 'lip
service' and 'CYA'." In Phase 3, observers of wrongdoing who believe some
action is warranted must make further decisions (e.g., "am I responsible
for acting? Is there something that I could do that might stop the wrongdoing? Will the benefits of a considered action outweigh the costs?"). Thus,
any variables that theory would suggest might influence any of these considerations, could be expected to influence how employees perceive and
react to questionable activity.

The prosocial model has been generally supported, but the correspondence with the bystander literature is imperfect, not surprisingly. For
example, conflicting results have emerged regarding whether the number
of other observers of organizational wrongdoing (perceived or actual)
affect whistle-blowing, perhaps because of situational interactions (Miceli
et al., 1991). Whistle-blowers usually have much more time to think before
acting than do witnesses to an emergency, and interrelationships with
other members of their employing organization, and other variables,
would differ from those of strangers who might encounter street crime
(Dozier & Miceli, 1985).

Behavior does not have to be altruistic to be considered prosocial
(Dozier & Miceli, 1985); whistle-blowers can have mixed motives at the
time of deciding to act (and it is often difficult empirically to ascertain
motives). After the fact, they can experience some personal gain while
behaving prosocially. For instance, whistle-blowers who complain about
unsafe working conditions benefit personally—along with coworkers—if
those unsafe conditions are remedied. Likewise, whistle-blowers who

receive cash awards are still whistle-blowers; they are acting to stop wrong-doing and often take on huge career risks as do other whistle-blowers. For example, Douglas Durand, a pharmaceutical sales representative, certainly benefitted handsomely from blowing the whistle on physicians' over-charges of government medical programs for the prostate cancer drug Lupron; he received 14% of the $875 million fine imposed on manufactur-ers, because he saved the federal government far more (Haddad & Barrett, 2002). Yet perhaps because he knew changing practices that yielded such a tidy profit to wrongdoers would be highly threatening (perhaps like the internal whistle-blowing at Enron), he said "the idea of suing as a whistle-blower intimidated me. Nobody likes a whistle-blower. I thought it could end my career" (Haddad & Barrett, 2002, p. 130). And obviously, at the time he reported the problems, he had no guarantee of a payoff, and knew the process would likely be long and arduous. Although the number of such cases has grown quickly since the inception of legal processes for pro-viding cash awards to whistle-blowers, the effects of cash awards are just beginning to receive empirical attention (e.g., Callahan & Dworkin, 1992).

Therefore, although research suggests that whistle-blowers feel more morally compelled to act than do inactive observers (Miceli et al., 1991), researchers generally agree that requiring that whistle-blowing be purely altruistic in order to be morally acceptable imposes an unrealistically high standard (Dozier & Miceli, 1985; Perry, 1991). If altruism involves no bene-fit to the actor, there could be virtually no whistle-blowing. Whistle-blowers would almost always benefit from the cessation of wrongdoing, at least psy-chologically, if not more tangibly as in the case of cash rewards. For exam-ple, research shows that employees are less satisfied when sexual harassment occurs in the workplace, regardless of whether they personally are directly targeted by the harasser (Glomb et al., 1997); therefore, even a male whistle-blower who took on the risks and costs of fighting harassment directed at a female co-worker would not be purely altruistic.

The model of whistle-blowing as prosocial organizational behavior has suggested many variables that may affect the decision to blow the whistle, and while nearly two decades of research has produced some useful results (Near & Miceli, 1996), many hypotheses remain untested. One area that has generally received little attention is that of personality or dispositional determinants of whistle-blowing; however, two personality variables—nega-tive affectivity and proactive personality—have been examined recently.

Recent research (Miceli et al., 2001b) has suggested that employees high in negative affectivity are more likely to perceive wrongdoing. Theory on negative affectivity clearly suggests a basis for individual differences that could lead different individuals to judge the same event to be more or less wrongful (in Phase 1 of the prosocial model). Negative affectivity is an enduring disposition to experience subjective distress (Watson & Walker,

1996). Persons high in negative affectivity are more critical of themselves and others, and they experience more stress, anxiety, nervousness, anger, fear, and guilt (Watson & Clark, 1984). This trait influences the way employees perceive and react to objects and events in the work environment (e.g., Watson & Clark, 1984), in that they interpret neutral or ambiguous situations more negatively and experience more work-related stress than do other people (Parkes, 1990). Hence negative affectivity may influence perceptions that wrongdoing is occurring and that action is warranted. Preliminary empirical evidence suggests support for the model, in that observers of perceived wrongdoing had higher levels of negative affectivity than did nonobservers (Miceli et al., 2001b).

Similarly, research on positive psychology implies that disposition would affect whistle-blowing or would interact with events to do so. Specifically, research on subjective well-being or happiness (Diener, 2000) suggests that both events and how people interpret them (i.e., because of their dispositions or demographic characteristics) affect happiness. One such disposition is optimism (Seligman & Csikszentmihalyi, 2000); people high in optimism tend to have better moods and to be more persevering and successful (Peterson, 2000). This suggests that, although some optimists may not correctly perceive wrongdoing, those optimists who believe they have seen wrongdoing will be more likely to take action to get it corrected and push back if they encounter resistance.

Such reasoning is consistent with findings in the whistle-blowing literature concerning another personality variable, proactive personality, which is expected to influence the decisions in Phase 3 of the model. Proactivity is likely related to positive organizational behavior (Luthans, 2002). In their early theoretical and empirical work on proactive personality, Bateman and Crant (1993) proposed specifically that whistle-blowers would be more proactive than other persons who have observed wrongdoing, for reasons detailed below. Proactive personality stems from people's need to control their surroundings, and it is reflected in the extent to which individuals take action to influence their environments (Bateman & Crant, 1993; Langer, 1983). Research shows that proactive personality is a narrowly focused personality trait that is consistently associated with two of the "Big Five" factors, Conscientiousness and Extraversion, yet it explains variance in organizational phenomena beyond that explained by the Big Five (Crant, 1995; Crant & Bateman, 2000; Seibert, Kraimer, & Crant, 2001). The "prototypic proactive personality" is "relatively unconstrained by situational forces, and . . . effects environmental change"; thus, when high proactives observe wrongdoing, they will be more likely than other organizational members to blow the whistle (Bateman & Crant, 1993, p. 105). Consistent with these predictions (and hence supportive of the model), empirical research has shown that whistle-blowers (internal and external) have more proactive personalities than do inactive observers (Miceli et al., 2001b).

Other dispositions examined in the positive psychology literature are hope, gratitude, and generativity (concern for future generations [Giacalone et al., this volume]). We can speculate about these dispositions, though no existing research on whistle-blowing has included them. Specifically, we would propose that higher levels of hope and generativity might increase whistle-blowing among observers of wrongdoing. However, the role of gratitude might be more complex. For example, as described in the literature on prosocial behavior (e.g., Brief & Motowidlo, 1986), gratitude toward the organization the organization may disincline an observer of questionable activity to view it as wrongdoing and to act on it. However, if a grateful observer believes that the organization is a victim of wrongdoing committed by some of its members, such as in the case of Watkins (at Enron), she may be more likely to want to help the organization by calling attention to the problem. Or, if the grateful observer believes that the organization really does want the information so that it can self-correct, the employee may feel compelled by the norm of reciprocity (e.g., Gouldner, 1960) to return the good treatment that she or he is grateful to have received from the munificent employer.

Obviously, much remains to be done to determine all the factors that affect whether whistle-blowing will occur in a given situation. Despite the incompleteness of the literature, we believe it is worthwhile to suggest applications of what is known, to managerial practice and public policy.

IMPLICATIONS FOR THEORY AND PRACTICE

Throughout this paper, we have described theory and empirical research done to date. One implication of existing theory and research is clearly that there are many untested ideas that may prove fruitful in helping to understand "who blows the whistle, and why do they do so? The positive psychology literature, particularly that on dispositions such as hope, optimism, and generativity, should be integrated into empirical tests. For example, is there an inverted U relationship between optimism and whistle-blowing, as the literature discussed earlier seems to suggest? As another example, while employees with children may have higher levels of generativity, as they have a very salient reason to be concerned for the effects of their actions (or inactions) on future generations, will high generativity translate into greater whistle-blowing (because the costs of inaction and the sense of responsibility for stopping harm to others are great)? Or, will this make the risks of dissenting so high (e.g., the fear that one will lose one's job over reporting wrongdoing, and will not be able to support his or her family) that the employee cannot justify, in his or her own mind, taking those risks? Clearly, research is needed to address these questions.

As for practice, despite the impression that may be left by the nearly daily reports of corporate wrongdoing, which almost always include a claim that someone on the inside tried but failed to get the wrongdoing stopped, whistle-blowing is a relatively rare event. Unfortunately, this is not because organizational wrongdoing is also unusual, thus rendering whistle-blowing unnecessary. Instead, research indicates that most employees who perceive that wrongdoing is occurring do not act on it, primarily because they believe nothing will be done to correct the problems (Miceli & Near, 1992).

Sadly, evidence suggests that this belief is well founded. While obviously some whistle-blowers are mistaken, or may find objectionable certain types of behavior that are not widely defined as wrongdoing, there have been many documented cases where valid concerns were ignored. As noted earlier, employers do not respond well to whistle-blowers, and legal protections in the United States are inadequate (Dworkin & Near, 1997; *The Economist*, 2002).

Further, reports indicate that many employers perceive that only a tiny minority of internal complaints are valid (Miceli & Near, 1992). External complaint recipients may agree; for example, according to the *Wall Street Journal*, the EEOC "dismisses" 90% of discrimination cases (Karr, 1998). However, other data suggest that in reality many more have substance, at least under certain circumstances. A study of directors of internal auditing who reported wrongdoing suggested that well over half of the time they are able to get changes made and frequently they were rewarded for their efforts, which would be highly unlikely had their reports been invalid (Miceli et al., 1991). But because these whistle-blowers may be more powerful or more capable of sorting out valid cases before going forward than others, these results may not seem inconsistent with the perception that complaints are nearly always frivolous.

However, other findings, where auditors are serving as complaint *recipients*, may be more compelling. Tavakoli et al. (2003, p. 62) reported, "a survey (Figg, 2000) of more than 125 chief internal auditors concluded that 76% of employee whistleblowing complaints were found to be true." We are unaware of any other published studies documenting validity. But these preliminary findings certainly raise a critical point: Obviously, employers who perceive that complaints are frivolous are unlikely to take corrective action, and if they refuse to act on a large proportion that are valid, then even employees with valid concerns will quickly conclude that nothing will happen if they complain.

Legal and Public Policy Implications

As these observations suggest, the irony is that—as positive as whistle-blowing can be for society and other parties (often including the organization in which the wrongdoing is occurring)—it is remarkable that anyone ever chooses to report on organizational wrongdoing. Why? Because most employees in the US are essentially employed at the will of their employers, and legal exceptions to the "at will" doctrine are not comprehensive (Werhane & Radin, 1997). Further, the law has generally focused on protecting whistle-blowers from retaliation. This is true even for the newest federal law—Sarbanes-Oxley—which extends statutory protections for the first time to many private sector whistle-blowers (under certain conditions); for example, "an executive who retaliates against a corporate whistleblower can be held criminally liable and imprisoned for up to 10 years. That's the same maximum sentence a mafia don gets for threatening a witness" (Dwyer, Carney, Borrus, Woellert, & Palmeri, 2002). The emphasis on retaliation protection was partially in reaction to the revelation that Sherron Watkins' bosses at Enron considering firing her even though she kept her expression of concerns entirely in-house (Zellner, 2002).

Yet research described earlier strongly suggests that legal changes focused on encouraging organizations to change the wrongdoing, and punishing organizations who ignore whistle-blowers, would have greater impact. Sarbanes-Oxley does require some additional actions focused on effectiveness in correcting wrongdoing rather than preventing retaliation, e.g., requiring that corporate lawyers report misconduct to top management and, if there is no response, to the board (Dwyer et al., 2002). It remains to be seen whether this is sufficient incentive to organizations to take responsive action.

The National Whistleblower Center provides an updated listing of proposed federal legislation (The National Whistleblower Center, 2004). At the time this chapter was prepared, some examples of legislation under consideration included the Federal Employee Protection of Disclosures Act, the Women and Children in Conflict Protection Act, and the Registered Nurse Safe Staffing Act. The summaries of these and other laws on their website emphasize protection from retaliation. Unfortunately, while many people understand the need for public sector whistle-blowing to be protected and encouraged, there may not yet be equal acceptance of the notion in a "free market" economy, of the critical need to support private sector whistle-blowers. Yet the Enron case and other private sector scandals have shown that legal protections for whistle-blowers are very limited, and that many people—employees, stockholders, the public in general—are harmed when whistle-blowers are unable to speak out.

The literature on sexual harassment law can serve as an example for how whistle-blowing law and corporate practice (e.g., training) could be improved (e.g., Dwyer et al., 2002). Over the past 20–25 years, U.S. Supreme Court decisions have provided more incentives and penalties for employers, and surveys indicated that there is much greater awareness and disapproval of sexual harassment in varying forms than previously (e.g., Erdreich, Slavet, & Amador, 1995). Thus, one effect of oversight of employers seems to be that employees show greater awareness of wrongdoing and their legal rights in the workplace. In fact, a new law applies to federal agencies and requires them to pay for settlements and judgments against them in discrimination and whistle-blower cases, out of their agency budgets, and thus "will hit agencies in their pocketbooks" (Barr, 2002, p. B2). Further, agencies are required to file reports with Congress and the attorney general on data such as the number of complaints filed against them by employees, the disposition of these cases, the total monetary awards charged against the agency and the number of agency employees disciplined for wrongdoing involving discrimination or harassment (Barr, 2002).

Managerial Actions

Recent research (e.g., Glomb et al., 1997; Miceli et al., 2001b) suggests that organizations reap significant benefits by preventing wrongdoing, besides fulfilling their ethical obligations to employees, customers, and society. Thus, managers who wisely and ethically do not wish to wait for the law to further intervene in their activities can take a number of steps to improve conditions for whistle-blowers. These steps may encourage whistle-blowers to limit their reports to internal channels, thus reducing the risks and costs associated with external disclosure, such as bad publicity.

Select positive employees. To the extent that dispositions are important determinants of employee behavior, the research on positive dispositions suggests that the selection process is important. One implication of research on positive psychology, if confirmed in research on whistle-blowing, would be that if dispositions such as optimism contribute to whistle-blowing, then human resources managers could take steps to ensure that optimistic applicants are included in those selected. Similar arguments could be made for employees who are hopeful and generative, particularly given that these employees could bring other positive behavior to the workplace. Of course, there is another side to this argument. As suggested in the research on negative affectivity and speculation on the effects of extreme optimism, highly positive people may distort reality, e.g., by not seeing wrongdoing when it is occurring (Peterson, 2000). Perhaps a middle ground, or a commitment to diversity of personalities, will be shown to be ideal.

*Research on
preventing
wrongdoing.*

restigations. Clearly, validity is important. Organi-
ved by ignoring real discrimination or serious
ns. But they are also not well served by rewarding
v performer seeking to distract attention, nor by
is complaints. "Although the authenticity of a whis-
nay be irrelevant for the organization that chooses
te against the whistle-blower, it is clearly relevant to
ishes to respond appropriately. Responsive organi-
vestigating the complaint to identify whether it is
" (Perry, 1991, p. 12).

Protect the whistle-blower who acts in good faith. Prevailing legal arguments,
both in US law (Miceli & Near, 1992) and British law (Vinten, 1994), suggest that "whistle-blowing is warranted if the whistle-blower believes, in
good faith, that the wrongdoing has implications for public policy; that is,
some portion of society is endangered by the organization's actions" (Near
& Miceli, 1996, p. 508). Further, ethicists have indicated that whistle-blowers should "perceive serious danger that can result from the violation"
(Bowie, 1982, p. 143), or else the act of reporting is not moral. Clearly such
prescriptions depend on the accuracy of the potential whistle-blower's
observation of the facts surrounding the wrongdoing (Near & Miceli,
1996), and they imply that the nature of the wrongdoing is critical. They
may also depend on the process used by the whistle-blower (e.g., taking
steps to embarrass a perceived wrongdoer or interfere with legitimate work
processes, rather than focusing on solving the problem).

*Correct wrongdoing quickly and, to the extent appropriate, communicate that this
has occurred.* Once wrongdoing has occurred, it is not too late to realize
benefits; research (Miceli et al., 2001b) suggests that encouraging reporting and immediate correction may also have equally desirable effects as
preventing wrongdoing in the first place. These benefits go *beyond* reducing tangible costs to the organization associated with wrongdoing itself
(e.g., adverse publicity, damaged reputation, lawsuits); managers who prevent or correct wrongdoing may engender positive feelings and favorable
consequences among employees. Communications obviously must be
informed by privacy considerations.

*Recognize the role of personality or dispositions in employee reactions to
wrongdoing.* It's not clear whether employees with high negative affectivity, or low hope or optimism, more *correctly* recognize wrongdoing than do
people with low negative affectivity scores. If they correctly identify wrongdoing, they would be valuable employees, but if they tend to be overly critical, perhaps training would help to clarify organizational definitions of
wrongdoing. Similarly, gratitude may be a two-edged sword when it comes
to wrongdoing and whistle-blowing. Employees who feel very grateful
toward their employers may be reluctant to see and report wrongdoing,

but on the other hand, employers who genuinely encourage self-correction may find that grateful employees will be the most likely to step up to the plate, because they wish to reciprocate the good treatment they feel they have received.

There seems to be little downside risk regarding proactivity. Managers need to recognize that proactive personality is associated not only with whistle-blowing within the organization, but also with other positive outcomes such as sales success (e.g., Crant, 1995). These findings (Miceli et al., 2001b) provide even more reason for those critical of whistle-blowing to rethink their views. Proactive people can provide a very positive resource to the organization—in sales, in prosocial organizational behavior, in problem-solving—though some managers may feel threatened by them.

CONCLUSION

As long as society, organizations, and organizational members continue to view whistle-blowing as negative—something about which to feel shame or guilt—we will continue to experience unethical corporate behavior. Valid whistle-blowing, executed appropriately, can be a positive experience for most parties involved, and provide the opportunity to stem what appears to be a veritable tidal wave of recent corporate wrongdoing. Changing the law to reflect a more positive interpretation of whistle-blowing may not be enough: managers, employees and members of society need to undergo a cultural transformation such that whistle-blowing is viewed as potentially positive for those involved. Only with this changed view of whistle-blowing will it prove more effective as a mechanism for corporate and societal change.

ACKNOWLEDGMENT

This work was supported by the Ronald W. and Arleigh L. Tysoe Faculty Research Fellowship provided to the first author by the McDonough School of Business, Georgetown University. We thank the editors and reviewers for their helpful comments on an earlier draft of this chapter.

REFERENCES

Barr, S. (2002, May 16). Making agencies pay the price of discrimination, retaliation. *Washington Post*, p. B2.
Bateman, T.S., & Crant, J.M. (1993). The proactive component of organizational behavior: A measure and correlates. *Journal of Organizational Behavior, 14*, 103–118.

Bates, S. (1999, January 11). Europe is out to get me. *The Guardian*, T8.

Bowie, N. (1982). *Business ethics*. Englewood Cliffs, NJ: Prentice-Hall.

Brewer, G.A. (1996). *Incidence of whistleblowing in the public and private sectors* (Working Paper). Athens: Department of Political Science, The University of Georgia.

Brief, A.P., & Motowidlo, S. (1986). Prosocial organizational behaviors. *Academy of Management Review, 4*, 710–725.

Callahan, E.S., & Dworkin, T.M. (1992). Do good and get rich: Financial incentives for whistle-blowing and the False Claims Act. *Villanova Law Review, 37*, 273–336.

Crant, J.M. (1995). The Proactive Personality Scale and objective job performance among real estate agents. *Journal of Applied Psychology, 80*(4), 532–537.

Crant, J.M., & Bateman, T.S. (2000). Charismatic leadership viewed from above: The impact of proactive personality. *Journal of Organizational Behavior, 21*(1), 63–75.

Day, S.H., Jr. (1996). Rotblat Nobel gives hope to "Free Vanunu" campaign. *Bulletin of the Atomic Scientists, 52*(1), 5–6.

De George, R.T. (1986). *Business ethics* (2nd ed.). New York: Macmillan.

De Maria, W., & Jan, C. (1997). Eating its own: The whistleblower's organization in vendetta mode. *Australian Journal of Social Issues, 32*(1), 37–59.

Diener, E. (2000). Subjective well-being: The science of happiness and a proposal for a national index. *American Psychologist, 55*, 34–43.

Dozier, J.B., & Miceli, M.P. (1985). Potential predictors of whistle-blowing: A prosocial behavior perspective. *Academy of Management Review, 10*, 823–836.

Dworkin, T.M., & Baucus, M.S. (1998). Internal vs. external whistle-blowers: A comparison of whistle-blowing processes. *Journal of Business Ethics.*

Dworkin, T.M., & Near, J.P. (1997). A better statutory approach to whistle-blowing. *Business Ethics Quarterly, 7*(1), 1–16.

Dwyer, P., Carney, D., Borrus, A., Woellert, L., & Palmeri, C. (2002, December 16). Year of the whistleblower: The personal costs are high, but a new law protects truth-tellers as never before. *Business Week*, 106.

The Economist. (2002, January 12). Whistleblowing: Peep and weep. *The Economist*, 55–56.

Erdreich, B.L., Slavet, B.S., & Amador, A.C. (1995). *Sexual harassment in the federal workplace: Trends, progress, continuing challenges.* (Report of the Merit Systems Protection Board). Washington, DC: U.S. Government Printing Office.

Farrell, D., & Petersen, J.C. (1982). Patterns of political behavior in organizations. *Academy of Management Review, 7*, 403–412.

Farrell, D., & Rusbult, C. (1990). *Impact of job satisfaction, investment size, and quality of alternatives on exit, voice, loyalty, and neglect responses to job dissatisfaction: A cross-lagged panel study.* Best Paper Proceedings of the national Academy of Management meeting, San Francisco.

Figg, J. (2000). Whistleblowing. *The Internal Auditor, 57*, 30–37.

Frey, J. (2002, January 25). The woman who saw red: Enron whistle-blower Sherron Watkins warned of the trouble to come. *Washington Post*, pp. C1, C8.

Giacalone, R., Dunn, C., & Jurkiewicz, C. L. (2005). Foreword. In R. Giacalone, C. Dunn, & C.L. Jurkiewicz (Eds.), *Positive psychology in business ethics and corporate social responsibility* (Vol. 1). Greenwich, CT: Information Age Publishing.

Glomb, T.M., Richman, W.L., Hulin, C.L., Drasgow, F., Schneider, K.T., & Fitzgerald, L.F. (1997). Ambient sexual harassment: An integrated model of antecedents and consequences. *Organizational Behavior and Human Decision Processes, 71*(3), 309–328.

Gouldner, A.W. (1960). The norm of reciprocity. *American Sociological Review, 25,* 161–178.

Haddad, C., & Barrett, A. (2002, June 24, 2002). A whistle-blower rocks an industry. *Business Week,* 126–130.

Hirschman, A.O. (1970). *Exit, voice, and loyalty.* Cambridge, MA: Harvard University Press.

Karr, A.R. (1998, December 15). New EEOC chairwoman Ida Castro's first meeting. *Wall Street Journal,* p. 1.

Keenan, J.P. (2002a). Comparing Indian and American managers on whistleblowing. *Employee Responsibilities and Rights Journal, 14*(2/3), 79–89.

Keenan, J.P. (2002b). Whistleblowing: A study of managerial differences. *Employee Responsibilities and Rights Journal, 14*(1), 17–32.

King, G., III. (1997). The effects of interpersonal closeness and issue seriousness on blowing the whistle. *Journal of Business Communication, 34*(4), 419–436.

Lacayo, R., & Ripley, A. (2002, December 22). Persons of the Year 2002: Cynthia Cooper, Coleen Rowley and Sherron Watkins. *Time Magazine,* (online).

Langer, E. (1983). *The psychology of control.* Beverly Hills, CA: Sage.

Latané, B. (1981). The psychology of social impact. *American Psychologist, 36,* 343–356.

Latané, B., & Darley, J.M. (1968). Group inhibition of bystander intervention. *Journal of Personality and Social Psychology, 10,* 215–221.

Latané, B., & Darley, J.M. (1970). *The unresponsive bystander: Why doesn't he help?* New York: Appleton-Century-Crofts.

Luthans, F. (2002). Positive organizational behavior: Developing and managing psychological strengths. *Academy of Management Executive, 16*(1), 57–72.

Miceli, M.P., & Near, J.P. (1985). Characteristics of organizational climate and perceived wrongdoing associated with whistle-blowing decisions. *Personnel Psychology, 38,* 525–544.

Miceli, M.P., & Near, J.P. (1992). *Blowing the whistle: The organizational and legal implications for companies and employees.* New York: Lexington.

Miceli, M.P., & Near, J.P. (1994). Relationships among value congruence, perceived victimization, and retaliation against whistle-blowers: The case of internal auditors. *Journal of Management, 20,* 773–794.

Miceli, M.P., & Near, J.P. (1997). Whistle-blowing as antisocial behavior. In R. Giacalone & J. Greenberg (Eds.), *Antisocial behavior in organizations* (pp. 130–149). Thousand Oaks, CA: Sage.

Miceli, M.P., Near, J.P., & Schwenk, C.P. (1991). Who blows the whistle and why? *Industrial and Labor Relations Review, 45,* 113–130.

Miceli, M.P., Rehg, M., Near, J.P., & Ryan, K. (1999). Can laws protect whistle-blowers? Results of a naturally occurring field experiment. *Work and Occupations, 26*(1), 129–151.

Miceli, M.P., Van Scotter, J., Near, J.P., & Rehg, M. (2001a). Responses to perceived organizational wrongdoing: Do perceiver characteristics matter? In J.M. Darley, D.M. Messick, & T.R. Tyler (Eds.), *Social influences on ethical behavior* (pp. 119–135). Mahwah, NJ: Lawrence Erlbaum Associates, Inc.

Miceli, M.P., Van Scotter, J.R., Near, J.P., & Rehg, M.T. (2001b). *Individual differences and whistle-blowing.* Paper presented at the 61st Annual Meeting of the Academy of Management, Best Paper Proceedings, Washington, DC.

National Whistleblower Center. (2004). *Whistleblower laws introduced in the 108th Congress.* Retrieved February 11, 2004, from http://www.whistleblowers.org/html/whistleblower_legislation.html.

Near, J.P., Dworkin, T.M., & Miceli, M.P. (1993). Explaining the whistle-blowing process: Suggestions from power theory and justice theory. *Organization Science, 4*(393–411).

Near, J.P., & Miceli, M.P. (1985). Organizational dissidence: The case of whistle-blowing. *Journal of Business Ethics, 4,* 1–16.

Near, J.P., & Miceli, M.P. (1988). *The internal auditor's ultimate responsibility: The reporting of sensitive issues.* Altamonte Springs, FL: The Institute of Internal Auditors Research Foundation.

Near, J.P., & Miceli, M.P. (1996). Whistle-blowing: Myth and reality. *Journal of Management, 22*(3), 507–526.

Parkes, K.R. (1990). Coping, negative affectivity, and the work environment: Additive and interactive predictors of mental health. *Journal of Applied Psychology, 75,* 399–409.

Perry, J.L. (1991). *The organizational consequences of whistleblowing* (Working paper). Bloomington: Indiana University.

Peterson, C. (2000). The future of optimism. *American Psychologist, 55,* 44–55.

Pressler, M.W. (2003, July 12). Coke says accounting is under U.S. probe. *Washington Post,* p. 1.

Ridge, P.S. (2000, May 11). Ethics programs aren't stemming employee misconduct, a study indicates. *Wall Street Journal,* p. A1 (column 5).

Rothschild, J., & Miethe, T.D. (1999). Whistle-blower disclosures and management retaliation: The battle to control information about organizational corruption. *Work and Occupations, 26*(1), 107–128.

Seagull, L.M. (1995). Whistleblowing and corruption control—the GE case. *Crime, Law, and Social Change, 22*(4), 381–390.

Seibert, S., Kraimer, M.L., & Crant, J. M. (2001). What do proactive people do? A longitudinal model linking proactive personality and career success. *Personnel Psychology, 54*(4), 845–874.

Seligman, M.E.P., & Csikszentmihalyi, M. (2000). Positive psychology: An introduction. *American Psychologist, 55,* 5–14.

Somers, M.J., & Casal, J.C. (1994). Organizational commitment and whistle-blowing: A test of the reformer and the organization man hypothesis. *Group and Organization Management, 19*(3), 270–284.

Staub, E. (1978). *Positive social behavior and morality: Social and personal influences* (Vol. 1). New York: Academic Press.

Tavakoli, A.A., Keenan, J.P., & Crnjak-Karanovic, B. (2003). Culture and whistle-blowing: An empirical study of Croatian and United States managers utilizing Hofstede's cultural dimensions. *Journal of Business Ethics, 43,* 49–64.

Vinten, G. (1994). Whistleblowing—fact and fiction: An introductory discussion. In G. Vinten (Ed.), *Whistleblowing: Subversion or corporate citizenship* (pp. 1–20). New York: St. Martin's Press.

Watson, D., & Clark, L.A. (1984). Negative affectivity: The disposition to experience aversive emotional states. *Psychological Bulletin, 96*, 465–490.

Watson, D., & Walker, L.M. (1996). The long-term stability and predictive validity of trait measures of affect. *Journal of Personality and Social Psychology, 70*(3), 567–577.

Werhane, P.H., & Radin, T.J. (1997). Employment at will and due process. In T.L. Beauchamp & N.E. Bowie (Eds.), *Ethical theory and business* (pp. 275–283). Upper Saddle River, NJ: Prentice-Hall.

Yoshida, S. (2001). *Business ethics.* Tokyo: Jichousha.

Zellner, W. (2002, December 16). Was Sherron Watkins really so selfless? *Business Week*, p.110.

CHAPTER 5

EXECUTIVE INFLUENCE ON ETHICAL CULTURE

Self Transcendence, Differentiation, and Integration

Jeanne M. Logsdon and John E. Young

INTRODUCTION

Ethical leadership of responsible organizations is the socially desired and expected model for business as well as for government and nonprofit entities. Yet many contemporary organizational crises and business failures are blamed on the ethical lapses of top executives, involving misappropriation of funds, lying about business performance and product characteristics, exploitation of employees, political manipulation, and many other illegal and unethical practices. Accusations of excessive pride, personal greed, expediency, and other human failings are common criticisms of executives. In other cases, organizations seem to operate amorally by not considering the impacts of their activities on everyone who is affected.

Top executives can have enormous influence on how well their organizations meet ethical expectations through both formal and informal

Positive Psychology in Business Ethics and Corporate Responsibility, pages 103–122
Copyright © 2005 by Information Age Publishing
All rights of reproduction in any form reserved.

means. The challenge is how to select, develop, and support executives who will make ethical decisions and nurture strong ethical cultures. Executives themselves often seek counsel about ethical leadership and find many helpful sources of advice. Business ethicists provide normative concepts based upon fundamental ethical principles, such as rights and duties, justice, utilitarianism, and social contract theory (e.g., Cavanagh, Moberg, & Velasquez, 1981; Donaldson & Dunfee, 1999). Scholars in the social sciences focus on descriptive models and empirical studies of individual ethical decision making (e.g., Ford & Richardson, 1994; Loe, Ferrell, & Mansfield, 2000; May & Pauli, 2002), organizational ethical culture and climate (e.g., Treviño, Butterfield, & McCabe, 1998; Vidaver-Cohen, 1998), and business responsibility to stakeholders (e.g., Agle, Mitchell, & Sonnenfeld, 1999; Carroll, 1979; Wood, 1991). Executives themselves also contribute to the popular literature about how to operate ethically and successfully (e.g., Chappell, 1993; Rosenbluth & Peters, 1998).

What is missing from this rich menu of sources is the contribution from positive psychology on individual perceptions and group processes to improve the ethical functioning of organizations. This chapter examines a potentially significant contribution from the emerging field of positive psychology on the influence of executives on the ethical culture of organizations. In particular, we expand the analysis beyond existing literature in business ethics to include the executive's capacity for self transcendence and the impacts from engaging in processes of differentiation and integration. These executive traits and activities are proposed as having significant impacts on organizational ethical culture.

ETHICAL CULTURE OF ORGANIZATIONS

In this chapter, we focus initially on models that integrate normative and descriptive approaches to the study of the nature of an organization's ethical culture and the impacts of executives on ethical decisions. We emphasize the influence of individual personality characteristics and values of top-level executives in this brief review although it is clear that external and situational factors also impact ethical culture (e.g., Logsdon & Corzine, 1999; Sethi & Sama, 1998). It is also recognized that ethical culture is only one component of the organization's culture (Treviño, 1990; Waters & Bird, 1987), and that immoral and amoral ethical (sub)cultures can also exist within an organization even when top executives are personally ethical.

Two factors deserve particular attention when addressing the concept of organizational ethical culture. One involves the nature of formal and informal social control factors, and the other relates to the distinction between "positive" and "negative" ethical cultures.

Formal and Informal Social Control Mechanisms

The ethical culture of an organization consists of the formal and informal social control factors that shape perceptions of "right" and "wrong" behavior of the organization's employees (Treviño, 1990). These factors should ideally work consistently and even synergistically to produce ethical outcomes, but they do not necessarily work together, and this can cause problems for employees and those affected by organizational decisions.

The formal element that most significantly relates to ethical culture is the nature of the organization's formal policies, such as its code of ethics and content of the policy manual. Codes of ethics have become common in large U.S. corporations (Weaver, Treviño, & Cochran, 1999). Growth in the number of firms with ethics codes during the 1990s was stimulated in part by incentives to strengthen organizational compliance programs that were provided in the U.S. Sentencing Guidelines in 1991. Other elements relating to ethical culture include the importance given to ethics in company training programs, the frequency and tone of communications about ethics, the organization's treatment of whistle-blowers, the presence of ethical consideration in official reward systems, and enforcement mechanisms for violators of ethical standards. Assignment of an ethics officer to oversee the organization's ethics effort is useful in coordinating the diverse elements that reflect the organization's commitment to a sound ethical culture (Morf, Schumacher, & Vitell, 1999).

Informal elements of social control in organizational ethical cultures consist of role models, development of organizational norms, and other aspects of the socialization process (Treviño, 1990). Role models have been found to be the most important influence on employee ethical attitudes and behavior in a number of studies, particularly the example set by superiors (e.g., Brenner & Molander, 1977; Posner & Schmidt, 1984). Organizational norms determine the types of responsibilities the organization identifies as legitimate (such as obeying the requirements for accurate financial reporting vs. searching for loopholes in the requirements in order to record more revenue) and those it is willing to tolerate (such as minor overcharging on expense reports by sales personnel vs. strict accountability for reporting expenses).

Positive and Negative Ethical Cultures

Ethical cultures can also be distinguished as "positive" or "negative" (Logsdon & Corzine, 1999). Positive ethical cultures support taking into account the legitimate concerns and expectations of stakeholders affected by a company's decisions. In these cultures, honest and equitable processes represent the norm or the ideal to which the company aspires. Within negative cultures the opposite holds true. In these cultures, executive problem-solving takes only a few of the organization's stakeholders into consideration—for example, those with power (Mitchell, Agle, & Wood, 1997). Within these cultures, organizational processes are not perceived as fair, and stakeholders are less likely to trust what executives say.

The formal and informal social control mechanisms will operate differently in positive and negative ethical cultures (Logsdon & Corzine, 1999). It has been argued that, even though virtually every large firm has an ethics code today, at least in the United States, these codes are not equivalent in their content and impact. For example, the ethics code in a positive ethical culture is broadly conceived to include the interests of the full range of organizational stakeholders. It is distributed with clearly expressed and personalized top management support for the ethical application of its values and guidelines. All employees are requested to read the document carefully and bring any confusing or unclear statements to the appropriate party's attention. By contrast, a negative ethical culture is likely to have an ethics code that focuses narrowly on the organization's short-term interests or on protection of top management from responsibility. In negative cultures, the code is distributed in a legalistic fashion. For example, it is sent via email from the head of the legal department with instructions to sign and return a hard copy that will be kept on file. Employees often perceive such a request as an attempt to protect top managers from blame and personal liability, rather than as a sincere effort to foster ethical awareness and responsibility throughout the organization.

In terms of ethics training and communication, the positive ethical culture is more likely to have frequent, meaningful, and proactively developed training programs. In these cultures, two-way communication is encouraged, and ways of obtaining ethical assistance are well publicized. For example, ethics "hotlines" or "helplines" are available for anonymous reporting of ethical concerns and for seeking information about ethically questionable situations. By contrast, the negative ethical culture would institute such programs only if they are mandated to do so by an external force. For example, federal government procurement guidelines may require ethics training as a condition for winning or maintaining contracts to supply equipment or services, as the Department of Defense does for defense contractors. No formal methods for employees to communicate ethical concerns or report unethical incidents are created in organizations with negative ethical cultures, or the informal norms may discourage inquiries on the ethics "hotline" about questionable practices.

The other elements of organizational ethical culture also vary by type of culture. In positive ethical cultures, whistle-blowers are encouraged to provide information internally, managers are evaluated according to ethical as well as business performance, and violators are penalized, while the opposite takes place within negative ethical cultures (Logsdon & Corzine, 1999).

INDIVIDUAL EXECUTIVE CHARACTERISTICS INFLUENCING ETHICAL CULTURES AND DECISIONS

Several models have been proposed to identify factors that influence ethical decision making and ethical culture in organizations. As noted earlier, these models typically include individual characteristics of organizational leaders and decision makers as well as organizational and external characteristics. In keeping with the topic of this chapter, we focus here on individual psychological characteristics and values that may influence organizational ethics.

A brief review of the components of personality is helpful here because a comprehensive understanding of these components is not always evident in research in the business ethics and business and society fields. This review will also be useful in integrating elements of positive psychology into research in these fields. According to James and Mazerolle (2002), a complete theory of human personality needs to join and synthesize concepts about individual traits and social cognition. The *trait perspective* focuses on individual dispositions to behave consistently over time and in diverse situations. Traits reflect differences in behaviors that are caused by one's needs and motives. For example, the need for achievement is a widely studied individual trait manifested in those who have a preference for selecting demanding tasks and pursuing them with tenacity and intensity (James & Mazerolle, 2002). The *social cognitive perspective* focuses on how motives cause the behaviors that reflect various traits and has two components, cognitive processes and cognitive structures. Cognitive processes are the "actual mental operations of perceiving, thinking, and feeling" that result in behavioral adjustments (James & Mazerolle, 2002, p. 34). For example, the process of "framing" or "sense making" for an individual with a high need for achievement involves interpreting information according to such criteria as likelihood of succeeding at the task, the amount of control one will have over the task, etc.

Cognitive structures include the cognitive schema that provides the bases for framing information. Cognitive schema are the mental models (Gentner & Stevens, 1983) or mental maps (Eden, 1992; Scheper & Faber, 1994) that individuals create to aid in understanding relationships that comprise their situational contexts. Cognitive structures also include values, beliefs, knowledge, self-concepts, emotional repertoires, etc., that shape one's interpretation of the environment and thus make meaning of goals, events, and facts. For example, individuals with a high need for

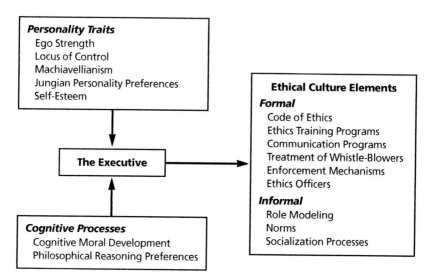

Figure 5.1.   Traditional theoretical model of individual psychological factors influencing organizational ethics. *Source:* Adapted from Treviño (1986) and Logsdon & Corzine (1999)

achievement are likely to ascribe behavior to personal or internal characteristics, such as initiative or persistence, because they believe that success can be achieved through their own efforts, i.e., they can control outcomes through their own efforts.

Theoretical developments and empirical research on individual factors influencing ethical culture and decisions have included both the trait perspective and the social cognitive perspective of human personality. Figure 5.1 synthesizes some of the theoretical work that has been done in the business ethics and business and society fields about the executive's individual traits, cognitive processes, and values that influence organizational ethical culture and decisions.

Treviño's model was one of the first in the management literature to hypothesize about the factors that influence an organization's ethical decisions. She identified several individual personality factors that were expected to have a significant impact on organizational ethics, specifically the traits of ego strength, locus of control, field dependence, and the cognitive process of level of moral development. Logsdon and Corzine's (1999) theoretical model examined the psychological characteristics of chief executive officers that are likely to influence the ethical culture of their organizations. Their model focused on personality traits and cognitive processes that were measurable and thus more easily amenable to empirical testing. The four personality traits were locus of control, Machiavellianism, Jungian personality references, and self-esteem. The two cognitive processes were cognitive moral development and philosophical reasoning preference.

Another stream of research relevant to the impact of individual factors on ethical culture and decisions has focused on values, which are a component of cognitive structure. Rokeach described a value as a prescriptive belief that can be either terminal (relating to an ultimate goal) or instrumental (relating to the means to attain an ultimate goal) and found 20 specific values in each category (Rokeach, 1973).

Empirical research has found a number of significant relationships between traditional psychological characteristics and ethical attitudes, intentions, or decisions. Table 5.1 lists the supported relationships in a sampling of the empirical literature.

Table 5.1. Significant Findings in Empirical Studies of Personality Characteristics Influencing Ethical Intentions, Behaviors, or Outcomes

Locus of Control	Hegarty and Sims (1978)
	Zahra (1989)
	Treviño and Youngblood (1990)
	Baehr, Jones, and Nerad (1993)
	Cherry and Fraedrich (2000)
	Beu, Buckley, and Harvey (2003)
Machiavellianism	Hegarty and Sims (1978, 1979)
	Singhapakdi and Vitell (1990)
	Bass, Barnett, and Brown (1999)
	Beu, Buckley, and Harvey (2003)
Cognitive Moral Development	Treviño and Youngblood (1990)
	Weber (1990)
	Cherry and Fraedrich (2000)
	Beu, Buckley, and Harvey (2003)

For example, having the trait of an internal locus of control has been associated with more ethical analysis or decisions in studies by Hegarty and Sims (1978), Zahra (1989), Treviño and Youngblood (1990), Baehr, Jones, and Nerad (1993), Cherry and Fraedrich (2000), and Beu, Buckley, and Harvey (2003). The Machiavellian trait is negatively related to ethical attitudes or intentions in studies by Hegarty and Sims (1978, 1979), Singhapakdi and Vitell (1990), Bass, Barnett, and Brown (1999), and Beu et al. (2003).

The social cognitive perspective is represented by extensive use of Kohlberg's model of moral development to identify reasoning processes that are linked with various types of ethical decisions or intentions. For example, studies by Weber (1990), Treviño and Youngblood (1990), Cherry and Fraedrich (2000), and Beu et al. (2003), among others, confirm the relationship between Kohlberg's levels and stages of moral development and ethical reasoning and intentions.

In terms of Rokeach's work on values, surveys of managers have found consistent support for three top terminal and three top instrumental values (cited in Fritzsche, 1997). The terminal values are self-respect, family security, and freedom; the instrumental values are responsible, honest, and capable. Despite the extensive research on values (Agle & Caldwell, 1999), little research has found linkages between executive ethical values and ethical culture. Most values research involving managers has focused on the values that managers have, but not on how their values impact organizational characteristics and processes (e.g., Frederick & Weber, 1987).

Past theories and empirical research have typically identified traditional personality traits, cognitive processes, and executive values as stable attributes that are measured at a single point and correlated with various ethical behaviors or decisions. Positive psychology offers the opportunity for the *dynamic* development of one's cognitive structure, which is likely to significantly influence one's cognitive processing of information, and subsequent behavioral manifestations (traits). This dynamic evolution in turn should inspire the affected executive to improve the ethical culture of his or her organization.

WHAT POSITIVE PSYCHOLOGY CAN CONTRIBUTE

The field of positive psychology focuses on the study of individual and collective strengths that lead to optimal human functioning. Many psychologists believe that nurturing these strengths can be the most effective strategy in the treatment of various dysfunctional human traits (Seligman & Csikszentmihalyi, 2000; Seligman, 2002), but more importantly for business organizations, these strengths can lead to extraordinary organizational performance. At the individual level, positive psychology is concerned with characteristics that enhance personal functioning, including the capacity for love and vocation, courage, spirituality, optimism, and wisdom (Seligman & Csikszentmihalyi, 2000; Seligman, 2002). At the more macro level, it is concerned with civic virtues and the institutions that move individuals toward enhanced citizenship, responsibility, nurturance, altruism, civility, moderation, tolerance, and work ethic (Seligman & Csikszentmihalyi, 2000; Seligman, 2002). Within organizations, positive organizational scholarship, which is developing in part from the emergence of positive psychology, gives attention to theories of excellence, positive deviance, extraordinary performance, transcendence, and other individual and group characteristics that improve organizational functioning and that increase human satisfaction in organizations (Cameron, Dutton, & Quinn, 2003).

Cognitive structures are particularly important in distinguishing how individuals make ethical decisions. Cognitive structures are "the enduring mental components... on which individuals rely in giving meaning to their environments and in thinking and feeling" (James & Mazerolle, 2002, p. 34). Such structures include beliefs, values, goals, emotional repertoires, self-concepts, and cognitive schemata, defined as "internal prisms through which external stimuli pass, and in passing they are translated into interpretative adjectives that indicate personal meaning" (James & Mazerolle, 2002, p. 35). Cognitive structures shape the implicit assumptions we make about how to interpret information and events and then how to analyze and make decisions "rationally." That is, they help us to give meaning to or make sense (Weick, 1995) of what is happening in our environment.

A significant concept in positive psychology that has implications for organizational functioning is the capacity for self transcendence, which emerges from one's level of consciousness, a construct that reflects one's view of the self. The "self" is defined as "the sum of the contents of consciousness and the structure of its goals" (Csikszentmihalyi, 1990, p. 34). A behavioral manifestation or trait that is positively linked to self transcendence is the capacity for empathy. We argue that the executive who expands his or her capacity for empathy will create positive ethical cultures. These relationships are shown in Figure 5.2.

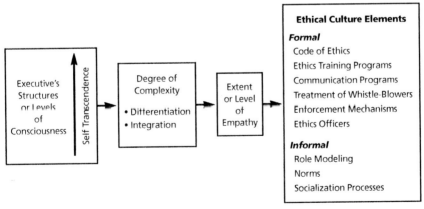

Figure 5.2.   Additional individual factors from positive psychology influencing organizational ethical culture.

The Capacity for Self Transcendence

Self transcendence can be defined as the inclination of individuals to take worldviews or perspectives larger than themselves. In other words, as one moves toward greater degrees of self transcendence, one moves psychologically from greater to lesser degrees of egocentrism. Self transcendence is motivated by the human drive toward greater complexity. The concept of increasing psychological complexity is clearly addressed in positive psychology. Csikszentmihalyi (1993) coined the term "transcender," or "T-person," for one who successfully transcends to higher levels of psychological complexity and consciousness. Transcenders have the capacity to see the world from a wider perspective, and therefore they are able to see, appreciate, and empathize with the views of others. They invest their psychic energies in concerns and goals that are larger than their own individual self-interests. By contrast, individuals whose life motives and goals are generally self-centered are not as transcendent as those concerned with family, who are in turn less transcendent than those concerned with the community, the nation, the world, and the cosmos or universe at large.

One's capacity for self transcendence is related to one's state or level of consciousness. Beck and Cowan (1996) developed a hierarchical framework of consciousness, or levels of existence, based upon the earlier work of psychologist Clare Graves (1959/2001, 1961/2001). Eight levels are distinguished: the lower levels relate to instinct, magic, and impulse; the middle levels relate to conformity with societal rules, understanding of science and natural laws, and connections of individuals freely with others; the highest levels relate to an understanding of integrative natural hierarchies and holistic systems. Their theory asserts that, as individuals move to higher levels of consciousness, their worldviews become more inclusive and their moral reasoning becomes more comprehensive and complex.

A similar perspective is offered by philosopher Ken Wilber (1999), drawing upon conceptualizations of human evolution from many fields. In his original work, *The Spectrum of Consciousness*, Wilber identified six major levels of consciousness, ranging from the Shadow level to the Level of Mind (Wilber, 1999). The hierarchical levels take into account that human development involves decreasing narcissism and an increasing transcendence or the ability to take other people, places, and things into account, thereby increasingly extending one's care, concern, or empathy toward others (Wilber, 2000). Thus, self transcendence involves the gradual elimination of egocentrism, nepotism, ethnocentrism, and anthropocentrism as individuals become capable of greater complexity at higher levels of consciousness. When individuals engage in self transcendence, their identification with the "self," as defined earlier, becomes more expansive. Young (2002) explained that organizational leaders who experience progressively higher levels of self transcendence are more effective at problem solving because they can be more objective and comprehensive in their analysis. Similarly, he suggested that they are likely to make more ethical decisions at higher levels of transcendence.

Individuals can facilitate their own self transcendence by increasing their psychological complexity and consciousness. Complexity is increased by enhancing individual uniqueness (differentiation) and integration (Csikszentmihalyi, 1993).

Differentiation

Differentiation occurs as individuals select personal challenges for growth and development and is analogous to Maslow's (1968) concept of self-actualization. In order to move effectively toward self-actualization, one must be open to new ideas and approaches, engage in creative ways of viewing selected avenues for growth, and be willing to enhance one's skills and level of knowledge with regard to the selected activities for development. Furthermore, one must approach his or her developmental activities with a perspective of not only learning, but perhaps more important, continuous unlearning, which should be employed as one modifies or replaces old cognitive schema—mental models (Gentner & Stevens, 1983) or mental maps (Eden, 1992; Scheper & Faber, 1994)—with new ones as one's skill level improves.

The challenge for individuals seeking greater growth through differentiation is to discover which paths, methods, or vehicles for development are most appropriate as they traverse the course of their life spans. Wilber (2002) described this process as "discovering one's judo." Csikszentmihalyi (1975, 1990, 1997) suggested that individuals generally select activities for growth and development that allow them to experience positive or rewarding states of consciousness. He refers to these optimal experiences as the experience of *flow.* A characteristic of the flow experience is intrinsic motivation, which is enjoyment of the activity for itself rather than for external rewards (Deci & Ryan, 1985). Other characteristics cited by Csikszentmihalyi that characterize the flow experience are clear goals, balance between opportunity and capacity, deep concentration, and immersion into the present. A characteristic of the flow experience that may have direct relevance to executive self transcendence and consequent positive influence on ethical culture is the loss of ego-centeredness or transcendence of ego boundaries, a sense of growth and of being a part of some greater entity (Csikszentmihalyi, 1993).

The more one is able to participate in flow activities, which require increasing skills matched with more challenging opportunities, the more one will move toward self-actualization and differentiation. However, the experience of flow alone will not in itself lead toward greater individual complexity. For instance, as differentiation has been described above, terrorists, world-class jewel thieves, juvenile delinquents, and corporate embezzlers can all experience flow by becoming very involved in the pursuit of these activities. In order for one to achieve complexity, the second criterion, greater integration, must also be achieved.

Integration

Integration, the second attribute of complexity, occurs when the T-person "balances a healthy pride in one's uniqueness with a deep interest and concern for others" (Csikszentmihalyi, 1993, p. 238). Integration is said to occur when one entity within a system communicates with and enhances the goals of other entities within the system. The greater one's level of self transcendence, the more likely one is able to utilize his or her uniqueness for the greater good. Therefore, self transcendence is a requisite for true integration, which requires one to see and empathize with the goals, feelings, and rights of others.

Integration takes place in a hierarchical manner and is a function of one's level of self transcendence. For instance, one can progressively integrate one's "self" with the family, community, nation, or the universe at large. Integration reflects one's worldview of the self and as such it reflects an ontological state of being. Ultimately, the extent or depth of one's ethical behavior is impacted by the degree of his or her integration within a hierarchical system. To the extent that individuals integrate themselves at higher situational levels of cultural contexts, both individual and social ethics will be enhanced. The greater the extent of self transcendence one is able to achieve over longer periods of time, the more he or she will reflect ethical behavior that takes into account an empathetic concern for the goals and well-being of others.

IMPLICATIONS FOR EXECUTIVES AND ETHICAL CULTURE

Executives who want to strengthen their moral character and moral leadership capabilities should examine self transcendence as the means of enhancing their moral growth, which can be a self-chosen ongoing process. Executives desiring to improve their effectiveness, on-the-job satisfaction, and moral leadership should strive to enhance their individual complexity by focusing on its two cognitive processes, differentiation and integration (Csikszentmihalyi, 2003). These activities will contribute to the creation and maintenance of more positive ethical cultures.

Differentiation

Regarding the realm of differentiation, as executives learn to take on various roles entailing greater responsibility (Hill, 1992), they must not only modify existing mental models, but they must also develop new mental models through continual learning and unlearning. This development and modification of cognitive schema (i.e., mental models or maps) occur when executives continually enhance their skills and capabilities as their businesses grow, decline, and enter new environments. Successful executives will be those who are flexible in modifying their mental maps and who react appropriately in response to and in preparation for the environments they face.

Integration

The realm of integration also has significant and perhaps even more profound implications for executives. Integration takes place as a result of the T-executive's successful efforts in transcending one's definition of the "self." As one identifies with broader definitions of the "self," his or her conceptualization of "right" and "wrong" begins to shift in a similar sequence to Kohlberg's theory of moral development (Kohlberg, 1969). For instance, if one's consciousness is more egocentric or "preconventional" in Kohlberg's terms, "right" could include motives such as "doing whatever is necessary," as long as it's legal, in order to promote one's career and rise in the organization or generate greater corporate profits. More ego-centered executives would also tend to focus on short-term performance goals as opposed to longer-term performance criteria. However, as one's sense of self begins to broaden, and one identifies with the community or the nation, then engaging in behaviors that could harm members of the community or the nation at large would not be acceptable. This is the level of conventional moral development, according to Kohlberg (1969). Similarly, as one identifies with nature, the environment, and with humankind in general, then performing actions or developing company policies harmful to the environment or humankind, in any location, would be unacceptable, Kohlberg's post-conventional level.

Implications for Personality Traits

Positive psychology's emphasis on self transcendence suggests that one's sense of empathy becomes progressively more profound as one moves to higher levels of self transcendence or consciousness. In other words, one's degree of empathy increases as one's view of the "self" (Csikszentmihalyi, 1990, 1993) transcends the family, community, nation, world, and beyond. How might this affect an executive's personality traits?

More advanced T-executives would begin to experience effects on various personality characteristics. In addition to exhibiting higher levels of cognitive moral development as their decision making begins to reflect post-conventional characteristics as indicated above, they would exhibit more ego strength and less Machiavellian tendencies. The impact on locus of control, which is the degree to which individuals believe that they control their destinies, is likely to reinforce a strong internal locus of control because the individual is more able and willing to take action and accept personal responsibility for what happens to him or her. Self-esteem would be enhanced as executives experience greater control over negative emotions, less attribution of setbacks to others, and an enhanced sense of well-being as their egocentrism lessens and their self transcendence deepens. No impact is expected on the executive's Jungian personality preferences.

Implications for Ethical Cultures

Because more complex and self transcendent executives will be happier and more caring individuals (Csikszentmihalyi, 2003), they will tend to promote and facilitate the development of positive ethical cultures, in which their peers and subordinates can also be empowered to develop complexity and achieve greater degrees of happiness. Self transcended or T-executives would tend to be more empathetic to the needs of a greater number of external and internal stakeholders. Empathy or concern for others will be expressed in personal interactions as well as in decision making criteria so that role modeling is perceived as authentic and consistent with the executive's verbal and written statements.

Formal rules and policies for ethical behavior developed by T-executives who have achieved high levels of self transcendence would differ from those developed by more ego-centered executives. Because they are more likely to perceive interdependencies between parts of the relevant systems, as well as the interdependence between systems themselves (Kegan, 1994), codes of ethics in their companies are more likely to be broad in scope and explicit in identifying the ethical principles and values that undergird the codes, rather than sets of rules to assure legal compliance. Ethics training is likely to be integrated into all regular company training programs. Communications about ethical standards and issues will be unambiguous with respect to potential conflicts with other corporate goals, such as growth and profitability. Information received from any source about possible ethical violations will be carefully examined, and if unethical behavior is confirmed, appropriate remedies will be enforced. In a positive ethical culture, there may be more inquiries on the ethics "helpline" but likely will be less external whistle-blowing because employees' ethical concerns are heard and addressed internally.

Self transcended executives would tend to see the underlying causes and subtle influences of situational contexts, thereby making better use of existing informal norms and role behaviors that support ethical behaviors throughout the organization. They would be continuously aware of the power of their words and actions as role models for ethical analysis and decision making. In particular, such executives would think carefully about possible mixed messages that could be interpreted from their behavior about what is really important in this organization.

PARADOXES OF T-EXECUTIVES

As executives move up the consciousness hierarchy, they would be able to see beyond dichotomous categorization of viewing all behaviors as either right or wrong, black or white. Executives at higher levels of consciousness are better equipped to see the comprehensive nature of situational analyses and problem solving. They are better able to perceive interdependencies that executives occupying lower levels of consciousness are unable to detect. Beck and Cowan (1996) refer to this ability to see the comprehensive nature of situational contexts as "second tier" thinking. Rooke and Torbert (1998) discuss how executives at higher levels of consciousness experience a greater disintegration of ego-identity, have the capacity to blend opposites during problem solving, and experience the interplay between intuition, thought, and action. Kegan (1994) discusses how individuals at higher levels of consciousness, the reconstructive postmodern stage of development, not only see the interdependencies between multiple systems perspectives, but also they are more comfortable with paradox.

Therefore, "right" and "wrong" at higher levels of integration are viewed from a broader perspective, and what's "right" behavior from the perspective of an executive utilizing a "universal" worldview may not necessarily be "right" from the perspective of one utilizing an egocentric perspective. This paradox can occur despite the fact that both executives consider their problem solving processes and decision outcomes perfectly rational.

The dilemma of executives utilizing higher perspectives therefore becomes obvious. As Kohlberg (1969), Beck and Cowan (1996), Graves (1959/2001, 1961/2001), Kegan (1994), and others all attest, the rationales utilized by individuals problem solving at higher levels will not be understood by associates and subordinates problem solving at lower level of consciousness. This makes leadership of groups and organizations comprised of mixed structures a challenge. Virtually all organizations include employees of mixed consciousness structures and have external stakeholders with mixed structures (Cowan & Tordorovic, 2000). However, while individuals at lower levels may not be able to appreciate rationales of those problem solving using higher-level worldviews, individuals utilizing higher-level perspectives should be able to understand and appreciate lower-level perspectives.

Executives desiring to increase their managerial effectiveness by enhancing their own complexity should engage in regular self-reflection and improve requisite managerial skills and capabilities. They should seek to facilitate their own transformation and conscious development by engaging in various transformational practices (e.g., Leonard & Murphy, 1995). Finally, they should also make opportunities available for complexity development of other organizational associates and subordinates (Csikszentmihalyi, 2003).

RESEARCH IMPLICATIONS AND CONCLUSIONS

This chapter has reviewed the literature on the characteristics of executives that may influence an organization's ethical culture and then identified a potentially significant contribution from the emerging field of positive psychology that may contribute to positive ethical cultures. We argue that expanding one's capacities for self transcendence and developing greater psychological complexity through differentiation and integration can be invaluable in enhancing an executive's capacity for empathy and interest in creating a positive ethical culture. We suggest that executives embarking upon such self-development can be referred to as T-executives.

Regarding future research on the development of T-executives and the organizations they manage, the first challenge is to develop effective measures of self transcendence. Several methods and measures of self transcendence have already been created (Braud & Anderson, 1998). For example, Rooke and Torbert (1998) measured levels of development of executive consciousness as they occurred in organizational settings. They used Loevinger's Washington University Sentence Completion Test to empirically assess the ego development of executives in their research (e.g., Hy & Loevinger, 1996; Loevinger, 1998). Also, more sophisticated measures of the nature of an organization's ethical culture must be developed. It is not sufficient to simply check whether an ethics code is in place.

It is also likely that other positive psychology characteristics, such as wisdom, self-efficacy, optimism, and authentic behavior, will be enhanced as T-executives develop. In turn, these characteristics will have a positive impact on organizational ethical culture. Measures of these characteristics that fit organizational roles and contexts will strengthen empirical research to determine how positive psychology variables relate to one another and to organizational impacts.

As the field of positive psychology and its numerous subfields continue to develop, the empirical testing of concepts such as self transcendence, or ego development, will continue to experience greater sophistication. In the interim, we believe that the notions of self transcendence and complexity offer invaluable insights to the field of ethical behavior and cultures in organizations. The implications for executive moral development and consequent ethical cultures in organizations are profound.

REFERENCES

Agle, B.R., & Caldwell, C.B. (1999). Understanding research on values in business: A level of analysis framework. *Business & Society, 38*, 326–387.

Agle, B.R., Mitchell, R.K., & Sonnenfeld, J.A. (1999). Who matters to CEOs? An investigation of stakeholder attributes and salience, corporate performance, and CEO values. *Academy of Management Journal, 42*, 507–525.

Bass, K., Barnett, T., & Brown, G. (1999). Individual difference variables, ethical judgments, and ethical behavior intentions. *Business Ethics Quarterly, 9*, 183–205.

Beck, D.E., & Cowan, C.C. (1996). *Spiral dynamics: Mastering values, leadership, and change.* Malden, MA: Blackwell Publishers.

Beu, D.S., Buckley, M.R., & Harvey, M.G. (2003). Ethical decision-making: A multidimensional construct. *Business Ethics: A European Review, 12*, 88–107.

Braud, W., & Anderson, R. (1998). *Transpersonal research methods for the social sciences: Honoring human experience.* Thousand Oaks, CA: Sage.

Brenner, S., & Molander, E. (1977). Is the ethics of business changing? *Harvard Business Review, 55*, 57–71.

Cameron, K.S., Dutton, J.E., & Quinn, R.E. (Eds.) (2003). *Positive organizational scholarship: Foundations of a new discipline.* San Francisco: Berrett-Koehler Publishers.

Carroll, A.B. (1979). A three-dimensional conceptual model of corporate social performance. *Academy of Management Review, 4*, 497–505.

Cavanagh, G.F., Moberg, D.J, & Velasquez, M.G. (1981). The ethics of organizational politics. *Academy of Management Review, 6*, 363–374.

Chappell, T. (1993). *The soul of a business: Managing for profit and the common good.* New York: Bantam.

Cherry, J., & Fraedrich, J. (2000). An empirical investigation of locus of control and the structure of moral reasoning: Examining the ethical decision-making processes of sales managers. *Journal of Personal Selling & Sales Management, 20,* 173–188.

Cowan, C.C., & Todorovic, N. (2000). Spiral dynamics: The layers of human values in strategy. *Strategy and Leadership, 28,* 4–11.

Csikszentmihalyi, M. (1975). *Beyond boredom and anxiety.* San Francisco: Jossey-Bass.

Csikszentmihalyi, M. (1990). *Flow: The psychology of the optimal experience.* New York: Harper Collins.

Csikszentmihalyi, M. (1993). *The evolving self: A psychology for the third millennium.* New York: Harper Perennial.

Csikszentmihalyi, M. (1997). *Finding flow: The psychology of engagement with everyday life.* New York: Basic Books.

Csikszentmihalyi, M. (2003). *Good business: Leadership, flow, and the making of meaning.* New York: Viking.

Deci, E.L., & Ryan, R.M. (1985). *Intrinsic motivation and self-determination in human behavior.* New York: Putnam Press.

Donaldson, T., & Dunfee, T.W. (1999). *Ties that bind: A social contracts approach to business ethics.* Boston: Harvard Business School Press.

Eden, C. (1992). On the nature of cognitive maps. *Journal of Management Studies, 29,* 261–265.

Ford, R.C., & Richardson, W.D. (1994). Ethical decision making: A review of the empirical literature. *Journal of Business Ethics, 13,* 205–221.

Frederick, W.C., & Weber, J. (1987). The values of corporate managers and their critics: An empirical description and normative implications. In W.C. Frederick (Ed.), *Research in corporate social performance and policy* (Vol. 9, pp. 131–152). Greenwich, CT: JAI Press.

Fritzsche, D.J. (1997). *Business ethics: A global and managerial perspective.* New York: McGraw-Hill.

Gentner, D., & Stevens, A.L. (Eds.). (1983). *Mental models.* Hillsdale, NJ: Lawrence Erlbaum.

Graves, C.W. (1959/2001). *An emergent theory of ethical behavior.* Presentation at The Unitarian Society, available at www.clarewgraves.com.

Graves, C.W. (1961/2001). *On the theory of ethical behavior.* Presentation at The Unitarian Society, available at www.clarewgraves.com.

Hegarty, W.J., & Sims, Jr., H.P. (1978). Some determinants of unethical decision behavior: An experiment. *Journal of Applied Psychology, 63,* 451–457.

Hegarty, W.J., & Sims, Jr., H.P. (1979). Organizational philosophy, policies, and objectives related to unethical decision behavior: A laboratory experiment. *Journal of Applied Psychology, 64,* 331–338.

Hy, L.X., & Loevinger, J. (1996). *Measuring ego development* (2nd ed.). Mahwah, NJ: Lawrence Erlbaum.

James, L.R., & Mazerolle, M.D. (2002). *Personality in work organizations.* Thousand Oaks, CA: Sage.

Kegan, R. (1994). *In over our heads: The mental demands of modern life.* Cambridge, MA: Harvard University Press.

Kohlberg, L. (1969). Stage and sequence: The cognitive-developmental approach to socialization. In D.A. Goslin (Ed.), *Handbook of socialization theory and research* (pp. 347–480). Chicago: Rand McNally.

Leonard, G., & Murphy, M. (1995). *The life we are given: A long-term program for realizing the potential of body, mind, heart, and soul.* New York: Jeremy P. Tarcher/Putnam.

Loe, T.W., Ferrell, L., & Mansfield, P. (2000). A review of empirical studies assessing ethical decision making in business. *Journal of Business Ethics, 25,* 185–204.

Loevinger, J. (Ed.). (1998). *Technical foundations for measuring ego development: The Washington University Sentence Completion Test.* Mahwah, NJ: Lawrence Erlbaum.

Logsdon, J.M., & Corzine, J.B. (1999). The CEO's psychological characteristics and ethical culture. In M.A. Rahim, R.T. Golembiewski, & K.D. Mackenzie (Eds.), *Current topics in management* (pp. 63–79). Stamford, CT: JAI Press.

Maslow, A. (1968). *Toward a psychology of being* (2nd ed.). Princeton, NJ: Van Nostrand.

Massimini, F., & Fave, A. D. (2000). Individual development in a bio-cultural perspective. *American Psychologist, 55,* 24–33.

May, D.R., & Pauli, K.P. (2002). The role of moral intensity in ethical decision making: A review and investigation of moral recognition, evaluation, and intention. *Business & Society, 41,* 84–117.

Mitchell, R.K., Agle, B.R., & Wood, D.J. (1997). Toward a theory of stakeholder identification and salience: Defining the principle of who and what really counts. *Academy of Management Review, 22,* 853–886.

Morf, D.A., Schumacher, M.G., & Vitell, S.J. (1999). A survey of ethics officers in large organizations. *Journal of Business Ethics, 20,* 265–271.

Posner, B.Z., & Schmidt, W.H. (1984). Values and the American manager: An update. *California Management Review, 26*(3), 202–216.

Provenzano, J.P. (1993). *The philosophy of conscious energy: Answers to the ultimate questions.* Nashville, TN: Winston-Derek Publishers, Inc.

Rokeach, M. (1973). *The nature of human values.* New York: Free Press.

Rooke, D., & Torbert, W.R. (1998). Organizational transformation as a function of CEO's developmental stage. *Organizational Development Journal, 16,* 11–28.

Rosenbluth, H.F., & Peters, D.M. (1998). *Good company: Caring as fiercely as you compete.* Reading, MA: Addison Wesley.

Scheper, W.J., & Faber, J. (1994). Do cognitive maps make sense? In C. Stubbart, J.R. Meindl, & J.F. Porac (Eds.), *Advances in managerial cognition and organizational information processing* (pp. 165–185). New York: John Wiley and Sons.

Seligman, M.E.P. (2002). Positive psychology, positive prevention, and positive therapy. In C.R. Snyder & S.J. Lopez (Eds.), *Handbook of positive psychology* (pp. 3–9). New York: Oxford University Press.

Seligman, M.E.P., & Csikszentmihalyi, M. (2000). Positive psychology: An introduction. *American Psychologist, 55,* 5–14.

Sethi, S.P., & Sama, L. M. (1998). Ethical behavior as a strategic choice by large corporations: The interactive effect of marketplace competition, industry structure and firm resources. *Journal of Business Ethics, 8,* 85–104.

Singhapakdi, A., & Vitell, S.J. (1990). Marketing ethics: Factors influencing perceptions of ethical problems and alternatives. *Journal of Macromarketing, 10,* 4–18.

Treviño, L.K. (1986). Ethical decision-making in organizations: A person-interactionist model. *Academy of Management Review, 11*, 601–617.

Treviño, L.K. (1990). A cultural perspective on changing and developing organizational ethics. In *Research in organizational change and development* (pp. 195–230). Greenwich, CT: JAI Press.

Treviño, L.K., Butterfield, K.D., & McCabe, D.L. (1998). The ethical context in organizations: Influences on employee attitudes and behaviors. *Business Ethics Quarterly, 8*, 447–476.

Treviño, L.K., & Youngblood, S.A. (1990). Bad apples in bad barrels: A causal analysis of ethical decision-making behavior. *Journal of Applied Psychology, 75*, 378–385.

Vidaver-Cohen, D. (1998). Moral climate in business firms: A conceptual framework for analysis and change. *Journal of Business Ethics, 17*, 1211–1226.

Waters, J.A., & Bird, F. (1987). The moral dimension of organizational culture. *Journal of Business Ethics, 6*, 15–22.

Weaver, G.R., Treviño, L.K., & Cochran, P.L. (1999). Corporate ethics practices in the mid-1990s: An empirical study of the *Fortune* 1000. *Journal of Business Ethics, 18*, 283–294.

Weber, J. (1990). Managers' moral reasoning: Assessing their responses to three moral dilemmas. *Human Relations, 43*, 687–702.

Wilber, K. (1999). The spectrum of consciousness. In *The Collected Works of Ken Wilber* (Vol. 1, pp. 33–414). Boston: Shambhala.

Wilber, K. (2000). *A theory of everything: An integral vision for business, politics, science, and spirituality.* Boston: Shambhala.

Wilber, K. (2002, August 10). Personal interview with Ken Wilber by representatives of the Management, Spirituality, and Religion Interest Group of the Academy of Management, Denver, CO.

Wood, D.J. (1991). Corporate social performance revisited. *Academy of Management Review, 16*, 691–718.

Young, J.E. (2002). A spectrum of consciousness for CEOs: A business application of Ken Wilber's "Spectrum of Consciousness." *International Journal of Organizational Analysis, 10*, 30–54.

Zahra, S.A. (1989). Executive values and the ethics of company politics: Some preliminary findings. *Journal of Business Ethics, 8*, 15–29.

CHAPTER 6

LEADING THROUGH POSITIVE DEVIANCE

A Developmental Action Learning Perspective on Institutional Change

Pacey C. Foster and William R. Torbert

INTRODUCTION

In recent years, scholars have begun to recognize that more is known about individual, group and organizational dysfunction than about individual, group and organizational health and flourishing. As it did for psychologists, after Martin Seligman's (1998) introduction of the subfield of positive psychology, this insight has given rise to a new subfield in organizational research called positive organizational scholarship (POS) (Cameron, Dutton, & Quinn, 2003). Like research in positive psychology, this new research program seeks to replace a long-standing negative bias in organizational research with a more balanced approach that investigates positive deviance in organizational contexts.

Positive deviance refers to "intentional behaviors that depart from the norms of a referent group in honorable ways" (Spreitzer & Sonenshein,

Positive Psychology in Business Ethics and Corporate Responsibility, pages 123–142
Copyright © 2005 by Information Age Publishing
All rights of reproduction in any form reserved.

2003, 2004) and is a central construct in positive organizational scholarship. However, because of this sanguine view about the potential for positive deviance in organizations, this new sub field runs against a well-established tradition in organizational theory that sees social structures as replicated regardless of their objective value (DiMaggio & Powell, 1991). In particular, positive organizational scholarship, "advocates the position that the desire to improve the human condition is universal and that the capacity to do so is latent in most systems" (Cameron et al., 2003). Existing macro organizational theory argues that there is an "inexorable push toward homogenization" in well established fields (DiMaggio & Powell, 1991). Because positive organizational scholars may encounter resistance from some quarters in academia (Peterson & Seligman, 2003), it is critical that this new approach explain what it contributes to understanding organizational phenomena over and above explanations offered by existing theories.

Toward this end, this chapter compares and contrasts how two apparently contradictory theories, action learning and institutional theory, address the critical issue of transformational change. On the one hand, the positive psychological theories of action learning (Argyris & Schön, 1974, 1978; Nielsen, 1996; Senge, 1990; Torbert, 1976, 1987, 1991) emphasize the ability of agentic actors to facilitate transformational group, organizational and institutional change (Fisher, Rooke, & Torbert, 2001). On the other hand, institutional theory emphasizes the constraints on individual agency represented by existing institutional logics and views the reproduction of existing social orders as the norm (Barley & Tolbert, 1997; DiMaggio, 1988). We argue that these two theories, although apparently contradictory, have numerous areas of overlap.

Specifically, developmental action learning theory provides a framework that accounts for both the unconscious reproduction of social orders described by institutional theorists and the increasing possibility of agentic action and transformational change described by positive organizational scholars (Cooperrider & Sekerka, 2003; Spreitzer & Sonenshein, 2003, 2004). At the center of this framework is the notion that individuals, organizations, and broader institutions can be characterized as evolving through a series of developmental stages or action-logics. Moreover, earlier work has established a parallelism between different ethical theories, different types of power, and different developmental action-logics (Lichtenstein, Smith, & Torbert, 1995; Torbert, 1991). This work shows that leaders and organizations operating at earlier action-logics treat either a utilitarian, a communitarian, or a principled ethical approach as primary, whereas later action-logics become capable of optimizing multiple ethical perspectives and multiple bottom-lines.

Toward the end of the chapter, we offer the case of the rise of Socially Responsible Investing between 1982 and 2001 as an illustration of how, in spite of strong initial change-inhibiting institutional pressures, a leader who operates at a relatively late developmental action-logic through transforming action learning has created a company and a series of widening networks that support widespread institutional transformation and growing legitimacy for a socially responsible triple bottom-line approach that balances financial, social equity, and environmental sustainability concerns.

Our aim is to develop a realistic and balanced theory of agency and institutional change that simultaneously explains: (1) the prevalence of resistance to change in institutions of all kinds; (2) the numerous examples of initiatives that transform whole institutional fields (Austin, 1997; Kraatz & Zajac, 1996); and (3) the developmental process through which persons and organizations become capable of transforming action learning and institutional entrepreneurship. In addition, we will show how current efforts in institutional theory to explain change can be augmented by incorporating insights from action learning theory. At the broadest level, we join ongoing efforts among macro organizational scholars to balance the "undersocialized" rational choice theory of agency in economics (Aldrich & Pfeffer, 1976; Hannan & Freeman, 1977; Williamson, 1981) with the "oversocialized" institutional theory of constraint on choice in sociology (DiMaggio & Powell, 1991; Emirbayer & Mische, 1998; Granovetter, 2002; Kraatz & Zajac, 1996). Our unique contribution is to introduce a theory of developmental stages that include both individual rational choice and institutional constraint on choice as two of eight possible action-logics that may characterize particular individuals, organizations, or institutional fields. Because these action-logics apply to multiple levels of analysis, they help to bridge the apparent disconnects between the typical micro orientation of psychological theories (such as positive psychology and action learning theory) and the macro orientation of institutional theory. By using a theory that crosses levels of analysis, we connect individual cognitions, with micro-organizational processes like leadership, meso-level organizational development, and field-level institutional changes. By using developmental theory in particular, with its progression from empirically more prevalent action-logics that reinforce the status quo to empirically rarer action-logics that support first incremental and then transformational change, we believe we can improve on recent ambitious and helpful efforts to describe and explain how institutional change occurs (Collins, 2001; Huff, Huff, & Barr, 2001; Kraatz, 2002). We argue that the later developmental action-logics provide the basis for institutional entrepreneurship (Fligstein, 1997, 2001).

We also view this effort as contributing to the development of positive organizational scholarship. First, by identifying how positive views of leadership culled from action learning theory add to existing institutional explanations of change, we help to specify how a positive view of organizational phenomena dovetails with and extends existing organizational scholarship. Second, by specifying developmental factors that make large-scale organizational change possible, we contribute to the ongoing effort among positive organizational scholars to define central constructs like positive deviance (Spreitzer & Sonenshein, 2003, 2004). Because our goal is to illustrate broad connections among disparate theoretical views of change, we are unable to fully represent the spectrum of existing research on either institutional change or action learning. However, we hope that the value obtained by integrating these research areas will make up for any omissions caused by the broad view required for such an effort.

JUXTAPOSING INSTITUTIONAL THEORY AND DEVELOPMENTAL ACTION LEARNING THEORY

There are at least three ways in which the institutional and action learning literatures already share common language and concerns. First, like institutionalists, some action learning scholars acknowledge that social structures tend to be reproduced and that the action-logics of most people, organizations, and institutional fields reinforce such reproduction (Argyris & Schön, 1974, 1978; Fisher et al., 2001). Second, both literatures are informed by the cognitive revolution in psychology, with its concern for different logics of action, whether institutional or personal. And third, recent work in both the institutional and action learning literatures increasingly seeks to determine how change can and does occur (Collins, 2001; Huff et al., 2001; Kraatz, 2002).

Let us review first how the two theories converge in explaining broad-based resistance to personal, organizational, and institutional transformation. Next, we will examine how developmental action learning theory diverges from institutional theory by highlighting action-logics that support transformational change. We conclude by using a case of major institutional change—the development of the socially responsible investing sub-industry between 1982 and 2002—to illustrate institutional entrepreneurs intentionally engaging in transformational institutional change.

The similarities in how both theories explain resistance to change

Institutional theory holds that institutional forces of coercion, mimesis, and professionalism tend to focus and limit change toward reproduction of legitimate institutional practices (DiMaggio, 1988; DiMaggio & Powell, 1991). Early action learning theory (Argyris & Schön, 1974) also focused on how dominant logics of action inhibited change, but they focused on how micro, interpersonal logics of action inhibit change at the group level (rather than how macro institutional logics limit change at the institutional level). They called this most common interpersonal action-logic "Model I." In describing the Model I action logic, Argyris and Schön (1974, p. 67) describe forces that seem to track the coercive, mimetic and normative isomorphic forces identified by institutional theory. According to Argyris and Schön (1974, p. 64), due to this Model I logic, people in groups "use whatever means will assure success" (e.g., use coercion), "never... diminish status of parties by upsetting them" (e.g., attend to the status differences that drive mimetic isomorphism) and strive to "be objective, intellectual... demonstrate... command of the facts" (e.g., demonstrate conformance to normative beliefs about rational action). Just as institutional theory predicts that isomorphic pressures tend to reinforce existing social structures at the macro level, the Argyris and Schön theory predicts that the Model I action-logic reinforce the status quo at the group level.

Developmental action learning theory (Alexander & Langer, 1990; Cook-Greuter, 1999; Fisher et al., 2001; Kegan, 1994; Rooke & Torbert, 1998; Sherman & Torbert, 2000; Torbert, 1987, 1991; Wilber, 1995, 2000) is a more recent action learning theory that is also broadly cognitive in nature and broadly congruent with both institutional theory and Argyrisian action learning theory. It holds that three early developmental action-logics each respond primarily to one of the three forces in institutional theory (see Action-logics II–IV in Table 6.1) in reinforcing the status quo.

Action-logic II in developmental theory (the Opportunist action-logic typical of six to ten-year-olds and of new organizations seeking resources before they have marketable products or services) focuses on concrete choices bounded by coercive limits within a short time horizon. This action-logic implicitly corresponds both with rational-choice theory (utilitarianism) and with the institutional force of coercion. This is the action-logic that neoclassical economics and Hobbesian political theory explicate and treat as the basic action-logic guiding all human affairs. (This and the following extremely abbreviated outlines of each action-logic are fleshed out in whole chapters on each individual and organizational action-logic in Torbert, 1987.)

Action-logic III (the Diplomat action-logic typical of early teenagers) is based on playing an appealing role in a larger group culture, through past-oriented, other-focused behavioral mimesis of existing social norms. This is the action-logic that Rousseauvian political theory, sociological theory in general, and institutional theory in particular, with its emphasis on mimesis, explicate and take to be the basic action-logic guiding human affairs.

Action-logic IV (the Expert action-logic toward which late teens going to college often evolve) entails a future-oriented commitment to high quality work, based on predefined, internally consistent craft, professional, scien-

Table 6.1.   Analogies among Personal, Organizational, and Social Scientific Developmental Action-Logics

Personal Development Action-Logics	Organizational Development	Social Scientific Development
I. Birth-Impulsive	**I.** Conception	**I.** Anarchism (Feyerabend, 1975)
(multiple, distinctive impulses gradually resolve into characteristic approach [e.g. many fantasies into a particular dream for a new organization])		
II. Opportunist	**II.** Investments	**II.** Behaviorism
(dominant task: gain power [e.g. bike riding skill] to have desired effects on outside world)		
III. Diplomat	**III.** Incorporation	**III.** Gestalt Sociologism
(looking-glass self: understanding others'/markets' expectations and molding own actions to succeed in those terms)		
IV. Expert	**IV.** Experiments	**IV.** Empirical Positivism
(intellectual mastery of outside-self systems such that actions = experiments that confirm or disconfirm hypotheses and lead toward valid certainty)		
V. Achiever	**V.** Systematic Productivity	**V.** Multi-Method Eclecticism
(pragmatic triangulation among plan/theory, operation/implementation, and outcome/assessment in incompletely pre-defined environment; regularly acts on single-loop feedback to achieve incremental change)		
VI. Strategist	**VI.** Collaborative Inquiry	**VI.** Postmodern Interpretivism
(self-conscious mission/philosophy, sense of timing/historicity, invitation to conversation among multiple voices and to mutual reframing of boundaries—hence, double-loop, transformational feedback occasionally acted upon)		
VII. Alchemist	**VII.** Foundational Community	**VII.** Ecological Cooperative Inquiry
(life/science = a mind/matter, love/death/tranformation praxis among others, cultivating interplay and reattunement among inquiry, friendship, work, and material goods—continual triple-loop feedback sought among intent, strategy, action, and effects)		
VIII. Ironist	**VIII.** Liberating Disciplines	**VIII.** Developmental Action Inquiry
(full acceptance of multi-paradigmatic nature of human consciousness/reality, including distances/alienations among paradigms, such that few recognize paradigm differences as cause of wars, few seek action-logic disconfirmation and transformation, and few face dilemma/paradox of 'empowering leadership': that it must work indirectly through ironic words, gestures, and event-structures that invite participants gradually to attune themselves to listen for and play with single-, double-, and triple-loop feedback)		
IX. Elder (undefined, unresearched)	**IX.** ?	**IX.** ?

tific, and/or ethical standards that aspire to universalizability. This is the action-logic that Kantian philosophy explicates and that corresponds to the force of professionalism in institutional theory. It is based on subordinating both short-term, physical outcomes and middle-term, emotional inclusion in a group's performance to a longer-term, internally consistent intellectual plan/system for accomplishing a new project.

Two different empirical measures of adults' action-logics find that, along with virtually everyone below the age of 21, 58% of persons over 21 in managerial/professional positions are found to be operating at the Opportunist, Diplomat, or Expert action-logics (Kegan, 1994, $n = 342$; Torbert, 1991, $n = 497$). The fact that a significant majority of the population operates under these action-logics that tend to reproduce existing structures through processes of coercion, mimesis, and adherence to predefined professional norms, both confirms institutional theories and illustrates the relative difficulty of facilitating large scale organizational or institutional change.

Having demonstrated the similarities between institutional theory and two action learning theories (Argyrisian and developmental), let us now describe how they diverge. In particular, we will show how action learning theories move beyond existing institutional theories of change.

How action learning theory explains change

Traditionally, institutional theory has presumed that change is primarily frictional, quasi-accidental, and in the direction of reinforcing current norms (recent exceptions that begin to account for strategic change will be discussed in the next section). By contrast, both Argyrisian and developmental action learning theories describe action-logics that facilitate different orders of change (Argyris, Putnam, & Smith 1985; Fisher et al., 2001; Raelin, 1999). First-order change is incremental, tactical, behavioral, in the service of the original goal (e.g., when I see I'm not convincing you, I change from "advocating" my point of view to "asking" what *your* goals are; then I use something you say to help persuade you). In contrast, second-order change is transformational, strategic, structural, changing the goal itself (e.g., when I see I'm not convincing you, I retire temporarily, reconsider and reprioritize my strategy, and set a different goal). Third-order change is continual, visionary, spiritual (e.g., when I see I am not persuading you, I suddenly feel a much larger pattern of unilateralness throughout my life and social history and feel called to listen deeply and seek mutuality in every encounter) (Bartunek & Moch, 1987, 1994; Nielsen, 1996; Torbert & Fisher, 1992; Torbert & Associates, 2004).

Argyris and Schön claim that their second (rarely exercised) interpersonal action logic ("Model II") generates effective second-order change ("double-loop learning" in their terminology). But they also acknowledge that it is difficult to teach many people (even successful, mid-life professionals who return to graduate school) this interpersonal action-logic. Moreover, although they document interventions that generate instances of second-order organizational change (Argyris, 1994), they present no clear cases of, or ways of measuring, sustained organizational or field transformation. Nielsen (1996) has argued that changing traditional institutional frameworks requires third-order change (or triple-loop learning), and gives occasional historical examples of when such triple-loop, attention-and-institution-changing learning has occurred (e.g., when John Woolman engaged in an inquiry with other Pennsylvania Quakers that resulted in the nonviolent abolition of slavery in Pennsylvania before 1800 [110–112]).

The developmental action learning perspective both explains why first-, second-, and third-order learning are so difficult to generate and provides a clearer roadmap for planning, implementing, and measuring change efforts. As already discussed, it shows that most managers, organizations, and institutional fields are found operating at Action-logic IV (Expert) or earlier. Yet, according to developmental theory, the capacity for intentional and reliable first-order change only develops at Action-logic V (Achiever), the capacity for intentional second-order change only develops in the transition to Action-logic VI (Strategist), and the capacity for third-order change only develops in the transition to Action-logic VII (Alchemist) (see Table 6.2) (Torbert & Associates 2004).

Table 6.2.   How Different Developmental Action-Logics Relate to Institutional Constraints on, and Opportunities for, Change

Developmental Action-logics	% of Actors Operating from	Predominant Influence Process	Effects on Continuity & Change
I–IV	58%	Coercion Mimesis Professional norms	Replicate with frictional change (Reinforce isomorphism)
V	35%	Coordination thru single-loop learning	Participates in first-order change initiatives
VI	6%	Mutual transformation thru double-loop learning	Leads first- and second-order change initiatives
VII–VIII	1%	Liberating disciplines with timely use of all types of power	Enacts first-, second-, and third-order integrity/transformation

The multiple different samples aggregated in the two studies cited earlier (Kegan, 1994; Torbert, 1991) find 35–36% of adults operating at Action-logic V, the Achiever action logic where single-loop learning becomes a regular, systemic practice. Market-oriented modern businesses particularly cultivate this institutional logic of action because they tend to die if they cannot regularly make first order adjustments in performance (how frequently they die anyway testifies to their relative failure in cultivating Action-logic V and the still later action-logics). Action-logic V attempts to generate norms of organized cooperation across the first five action-logics, in order to achieve success according to a criterion outside the performing system (e.g., winning votes or selling goods).

According to developmental action learning theory, a still more creative level of institutional change and transformation is possible for the few organizations/members/leaders who, today, evolve to Action-logic VI, the Strategist/Collaborative Inquiry action logic and later. (The cited studies find about 6% at Action-logic VI and 1% at the following action logic.) Action-logic VI includes a concern for the unique—unique market niches, uniquely timely action at a particular historical moment, uniquely configured organizational structures—along with the capacity for double loop, transformational learning as well as single loop, incremental learning. Strategist leaders can personally model the vulnerability of transformational learning, and this is a necessary skill if they are to inspire others and whole organizations or institutional fields to transform, because intentional transformational learning occurs voluntarily and mutually (conformity can be coerced unilaterally, but not transformation [Collins, 2001; Torbert, 1991; Torbert & Associates, 2004]).

These theoretical claims about the capacity of leaders operating at Action-Logic VI to generate organizational transformation have been quantitatively tested at both the individual and organizational levels. The individual action-logic measure (the Leadership Development Profile) is among the most well-validated and predictively robust measures in the social sciences (Cook-Greuter, 1999, cites and critiques the entire methodological literature on the measure). The organizational measure is "younger," having been used for a quarter century in intervention case studies (Fisher et al., 2001; Torbert, 1987) and having shown high inter-rater reliability (above .90) in the study we are summarizing here. This study (Rooke & Torbert, 1998) examines ten cases of attempted organizational transformation (of attempted second-order change across action-logics). In each case, the top management team received long-term consulting support from consultants measured at Action-logic VI or later. The study shows that all five CEOs at Action-logic VI or beyond were successful in generating organizational transformation, with four of the five participating in two or more transformations. By contrast, three of the five CEOs prior to Action-logic VI were unsuccessful in generating transformational change in their organizations. Looking still more closely, we find the one case of organizational regression in the study associated with the CEO at the earliest action-logic in this sample (Action-logic III/Diplomat). Despite the relatively small size of the sample, the results achieve significance at the .05 level (using the Spearman rank order test) and account for an unusually robust 42% of the variance. A later re-analysis of the data, adding together the consultant and CEO action-logic scores (hypothesizing that they are the two primary change agents) and correlating the resulting ranks with the number of organizational trans-formations in each case, accounts for 59% of the variance and achieve a .01 level of significance on the same test.

How the developmental action learning approach relates to recent work on change in institutional theory.

Now, let us examine how these tentatively empirically confirmed insights from the developmental action learning approach relate to recent work on change in institutional theory. This recent work is represented both by detailed case studies of change (Creed, Scully, & Austin, 1999; Els-bach & Sutton 1992; Foldy & Creed, 1999; Kraatz & Zajac, 1996; Scully & Meyerson, 1996) and by theoretical work (Fligstein, 1997, 2001; Green-wood & Hinings, 1996).

Looking at the case studies through the developmental action learning lens, we find examples where agentic groups engage in first-order tactics to accomplish what is arguably a second-order strategic change. For example, Creed et al. (1999) found that proponents of domestic partner benefits were able to mobilize support for their causes by framing changes in terms of existing "legitimate accounts" (in this case, civil rights and cost/benefit arguments). In this view, the institutional landscape is littered with multi-ple "ready to wear" accounts and frames that can be used by strategic agents to support or oppose change. The agents capable of such a change strategy must be capable of seeing beyond "a single right answer" (Action-logic IV/Expert), but are not yet fashioning uniquely timely arguments and actions (Action-logic VI/Strategist). Developmental action learning lens predicts that such agents are likely to be operating from Action-logic V/Achiever and will be limited in their effectiveness if second-order change on their own part is required.

A slightly different view of institutional agency comes from work by Els-bach and Sutton (1992) in a paper that links institutional and impression management theories. They describe a series of steps through which activist organizations facilitated radical social changes by sequencing different kinds of legitimate justifications for "illegitimate" actions. In stage one, members perform an illegitimate action (e.g., civil disobedience) that attracts atten-tion to the organization. In step two, the activist organization displays its legitimacy through the use of culturally acceptable structures like profes-sional spokespersons and press releases. At the same time, the organization decouples these legitimate structures from the illegitimate actions of "rogue members." In steps three and four, the organization uses justifications and defenses to reduce negative public perceptions of the event while highlighting the positive outcomes that resulted. In step four, the organization receives endorsement and support for the positive outcomes of the event without incurring reputational damage due to the illegitimate means of achieving them. Here, we see evidence, not just of Action-logic V/Achiever capacities, but also of a sense of strategic timing characteristic of Action-logic VI/Strategist. However, there is no evidence of the activist group engaging in second-order transformation of its own operating strategy, so its action-logic may be in transition from Action-logic V to Action-logic VI.

When we look carefully at Fligstein's (1997, 2001) theoretical notions of the social skills required for institutional change, we find resonances with particular developmental action-logics. The very choice of the word "skills" suggests an Action-logic V/Achiever sense, and this is reinforced by Fliegstein's (1997, pp. 399–401) unsystematic (but interesting and useful) list of fifteen "tactics" that support change. These tactics can be roughly ordered as follows, using the developmental lens (see Table 6.3). Although this list of titles omits the descriptive paragraphs, we believe they are roughly intuitively interpretable, and we provide additional commentary and quotes below.

Table 6.3. Developmental Action-Logics Implied by Fligstein's List of Social Skills for Institutional Change

Fligstein's Social Skills	Developmental Action-Logics
Direct authority	Opportunist
Convincing people one has more cards than one does	
Maintaining "goallessness" and selflessness	Diplomat
Making others think they are in control	
Not disturbing dominant groups	
Wheeling and dealing (in relation to subordinate parties)	Expert
Agenda setting	Achiever
Taking what the system gives	
Brokering	
Asking for more, settling for less	
Aggregating interests	
Trying five things to get one	
Networking to outliers who have no coalitions or isolating particularly difficult outliers	
Framing action	Strategist
Maintaining ambiguity	

The most obvious aspect of Table 6.3 is that roughly half the tactics reflect Action-logic V/Achiever. In addition, six of the remaining eight tactics reflect earlier action-logics. According to developmental theory, persons or organizations at later action-logics maintain access to the tactics and understandings of the earlier action-logics through which they have evolved, and can intersperse such tactics strategically, rather than by necessity. Thus, a true Diplomatic action-logic actually experiences others and existing norms as in control (and conforming to norms and high status others as good), whereas the tactic of *Making others think they are in control* actually implies either the earlier Opportunist action-logic, or a later action-logic using a Diplomatic pattern to mask a deeper strategy. Similarly, when we examine what Fligstein actually says about them, the two Strategist-sounding tactics do not actually reflect the Action-logic VI spirit of mutual transformation toward actualization of some higher principle. For example, of *Framing action* he says, "Strategic actors have to convince others who do not necessarily share interests that what will occur is in their interests. This can be done by selling pie in the sky (i.e., overriding values that all accept) or convincing them that what will happen will serve their own narrow interests" (Fligstein, 1997, p. 399). Were Fligstein approaching institutional change from a Strategist or later action-logic, he would *not*: (1) treat the notion of constructing a principled, mutual frame cynically ("pie in the sky"); or (2) take for granted that "skilled actors of dominant groups generally defend the status quo even in a crisis" (Fligstein, 2001, p. 118).

Thus, from a developmental point of view, Fligstein (2001) is constructing an institutional change strategy based predominantly in the Achiever action-logic, the next action-logic beyond the three developmental action-logics already implied in institutional theory. This makes all the sense in the world, developmentally, for two reasons: (1) because the Achiever is the first skillful practitioner of cooperation and incremental change among the otherwise clashing early action-logics; and (2) because the Achiever action-logic is far more prevalent than any other later-stage action-logic.

However, the developmental action learning approach highlights the still higher potential for mutual, nonviolent, transformational institutional change that practitioners and organizations operating at still later action-logics bring. We have offered one study that tentatively confirms the unusual organization transformation skills with which the Strategist action-logic endows leaders. But the question remains whether such leaders can and do successfully generate transformation in wider institutional fields. We now offer an extended case that illustrates the quality of such transformational change in a wider institutional field—the development of socially responsible investing between 1982–2002.

THE CASE OF SOCIALLY RESPONSIBLE INVESTING

Our case concerns the development, over the past twenty years, of the Socially Responsible Investing sub-industry within investment advising. This case illustrates institutional entrepreneurship, not from an established seat of institutional power, but by acts of true economic entrepreneurship, followed by acts of social entrepreneurship, and culminating in field-wide institutional entrepreneurship.

In 1982, Joan Bavaria founded Trillium Asset Management (then called Franklin Research & Development Corporation), responding to client requests to somehow screen their investments not only for optimal short-term financial gains, but also for companies' longer-term, not-directly-financial impacts on social equity and environmental sustainability. (Today, attempting to jointly optimize economic profitability, social equity, and environmental sustainability is known as managing the triple bottom line [Waddock, 2001].) Trillium became the first company solely dedicated to defining and practicing socially responsible investment advising, research, and advocacy, and it remains the largest such company to this day.

The company has been consistently profitable and has grown modestly but steadily over 19 years, expanding to four sites, with nearly $1 billion under investment in 2001. Thus, it has steadily proven itself in first-order change terms, finding and growing a market. But, for its first fifteen years, this approach to investing was treated as a laughable proposition by the big, traditional investment advising corporations, mutual funds, and mainstream economists and finance professors, because narrowing one's investment portfolio on criteria other than shareholder wealth maximization cannot help but reduce one's financial return, according to short-term rational choice criteria. (The work of 1998 Nobel Laureate in Economics, Amartya Sen [1982, 1987; Klamer, 1989], is rare in recognizing that this isn't necessarily so.) Thus, institutional forces (not only in the financial industry, but in academia) acted strongly to maintain isomorphism within the industry during this period, as institutional theory would predict. But then, during the late 1990s, two-thirds of the socially screened equity funds outperformed the average equity mutual fund over a three-year period, and major investment houses were suddenly advertising "social" funds as quickly as they could mount any facsimile of one (Becker, 1999; Torbert, 1999). Moreover, between 1999 and the end of 2001, socially screened investment portfolios under professional management grew 1.5 times as fast all investment assets, topping $2 trillion and accounting for more than 10% of all invested funds (Social Investment Forum, 2001) for the first time. What had happened?

First and most obvious, socially screened equity funds had proved they could match or exceed the financial returns of traditional funds. Moreover, in addition to their financial return, one gained the benefits of supporting companies that addressed social equity and ecological sustainability concerns in relatively positive ways. Thus, in Action-logic V, first-order change terms, people were learning that they could do better with socially screened funds.

But how did this sub-industry arise in the first place and develop to the point of generating this data? First, Joan Bavaria was measured by the Leadership Development Profile (Cook-Greuter, 1999) as an Action-logic VI/Strategist leader, in the 1980s. Second, she created an Action-logic VI/Collaborative Inquiry organization from the outset, not only creating a unique market niche, but also incorporating as a worker-owned cooperative, with women and minorities constituting a majority of the employee/owners. Bavaria also initiated and participated in companywide learning throughout the next twenty years, seeking out a variety of consultants. Retention and longevity are far better than the industry norm, and the few employees who have gradually "moved on" through processes of performance reviews, personal choice, and company discipline have largely been those who have not been able to support the trans-conventional integration of competition and collaboration and of economics and politics in the company's strategies and daily activities. Third, over the first decade of developing Trillium Asset Management, Bavaria gradually attracted a Board of Directors with similar ideals and action-logics and, with their support, overcame a potentially crippling law suit from a disgruntled Board member operating at an earlier action logic. (All these and the following facts and inferences about Trillium derive from Brown [1987], a doctoral dissertation on the earliest years of the company, and from the fifteen-year association of one of the authors with the company as a board member.)

In the middle 1980s, Bavaria became one of the leading cofounders of the Social Investing Forum, serving as its chairperson for a time, thus creating an inter-organizational network that could create and maintain the integrity of the new subfield. In 1989, Bavaria coauthored the Valdez Environmental Principles (soon renamed the CERES Environmental Principles) and played a key role in attracting signatories such as General Motors. By 1999, CERES, which she now chaired, organized 19 institutional investment groups, representing $195 billion, for a year-long drive to dialogue with leading companies about endorsing the code of conduct on corporate accountability. During this same period, through CERES, Bavaria and colleagues launched the Global Reporting Initiative, a set of global sustainability guidelines supported by both corporate and NGO partners, with a $3 million grant from the United Nations Foundation. "We're moving beyond the concept stage and into the implementation stage," she said. "Our goal is simply to make environmental reporting standard procedure for public companies around the world" (Bavaria, 2000).

By initiating CERES and GRI, Bavaria participated in creating entirely new standards of legitimacy, not just within the field of investing itself, but among business corporations nationally and globally.

Finally, for the purposes of this brief reprise, Bavaria was chosen as a *Time* magazine "Hero of the Planet" in 1999 as well. (Bavaria herself has reviewed this description for accuracy and, as might be predicted of an Action-logic VI practitioner of collaboration, mutuality, and distributed leadership rather than "heroic" leadership, she doesn't much like being singled out like this. And, indeed, a notable feature of her leadership has been the assemblage of a very strong senior team that works together smoothly and creatively, and any of whom represent the company well.)

In this case, we see an entrepreneur with an at-least-second-order-change vision focus from the start on first-order economic success in the market. At the same time, she begins to create a succession of ever-wider new institutions that support a second order transformation in financial advising, in corporate reporting, and in economic theorizing, including first the members and Board of her own company, then the widening networks of the Social Investing Forum, CERES, and the Global Reporting Initiative.

She started from the at-that-time-not-yet-fully-explicated theory that companies that disciplined themselves, not only to generate good short-term financial results (a single bottom line), but also good longer-term, social equity results (a double bottom line), and inter-generationally sustainable ecological results (the triple bottom line symbolized by the three-petal trillium) would be better, long-term financial bets than companies fixated by a single time horizon and a single bottom line.

This Action-logic VII vision will probably take generations to embody fully. Indeed, the recent popularity of social investing, based on its single-loop financial returns, threatens to erode its triple-loop principles and practices, as more large investment houses mount superficial social screens for the purposes of short-term sales alone (Torbert, 1999). Furthermore, because SRI funds tend to eschew big oil companies, they also tend toward high tech companies. As a result, since 2001, the combination of war and recession has reduced SRI financial returns. Moreover, the entire SRI movement is still in its infancy, including all its methods of assessment (even "straight" financial accountants have been having a good deal of trouble cranking out the true numbers in the late 1990s and early 2000s!). Therefore, there is appropriate continuing controversy about all the claims made in these paragraphs on behalf of Socially Responsible Investing, and the reader is invited to inquire further (e.g., Entine, 2003; Waddock 2003).

CONCLUSION

This chapter has juxtaposed institutional and action learning theories, showing where they overlap and parallel one another. Then it has shown how the positive psychology of developmental action learning theory in particular describes action logics (that are today empirically relatively rare) that go beyond reinforcing the status quo or allowing incremental change, to nurturing personal, organizational, and institutional transformations. It has illustrated these theoretical claims with a long-term case of transformational change in an institutional field, the case of introducing socially responsible investing in the finance industry.

The foregoing suggests that action learning and institutional theories not only share common theoretical interests, but that these interests complement each other in important ways. If institutional theory has lacked a coherent model of institutional entrepreneurship and transformation, developmental action learning theory offers such a model. At the same time, early action learning approaches tended to overlook just how the normative features of institutional fields enable and constrain change agents. Until now, institutional theory has explained stability better than change, while action learning has explained change better than stability. But now, we can begin to see how institutional theory and developmental action inquiry theory together point toward just which types of agentic, organizational, and institutional action-logics (Action-logics I–IV) constrain anything but frictional change, which support incremental change (Action-logics V and later), and which support transformational change (Action-logics VI and later). Thus, the chapter develops a contextually sensitive theory of institutional agency that explains both stability and positive change.

The major questions that are likely to arise for interested readers are: (1) how can persons and institutions (including the social sciences) help themselves to evolve to later developmental action-logics? and (2) how can leaders, consultants, teachers, and the systemic processes of later action-logic organizations help to catalyze development to later action-logics? These are profound psychological, social, and political, mysteries that few scholars or practitioners have as yet directly addressed (Argyris, 1994; Burns, 1978; Erikson, 1969; Reason & Torbert, 2001; Senge, Scharmer, Jaworski, & Flowers, 2004; Sherman & Torbert, 2000; Torbert, 1991; Torbert & Associates, 2004). These questions stand as a challenge for future research and practice in the realm of positive organizational scholarship.

REFERENCES

Aldrich, H.E., & Pfeffer, J. (1976). Environments of organizations. *Annual Review of Sociology, 2,* 79–105.

Alexander, C., & Langer, E. (Eds.). (1990). *Higher stages of human development.* New York: Oxford University Press.

Argyris, C. (1994). *Knowledge for action.* San Francisco: Jossey-Bass.

Argyris, C., Putnam, R., & Smith, D.M. (1985). *Action science: Concepts, methods and skills for research and intervention.* San Francisco: Jossey-Bass.

Argyris, C., & Schön, D.A. (1974). *Theory in practice: Increasing professional effectiveness.* London: Jossey-Bass.

Argyris, C., & Schön, D.A. (1978). *Organizational Learning.* Reading MA: Addison-Wesley.

Austin, J. (1997). A method for facilitating controversial change in organizations. *Journal of Applied Behavioral Science, 33*(1), 101–118.

Barley, S.R., & Tolbert, P.S. (1997). Institutionalization and structuration: Studying the links between action and institution. *Organization Studies, 18*(1), 93–117.

Bartunek, J.M., & Moch, M.K. (1987). First order, second order, and third order change and organization development interventions: A cognitive approach. *Journal of Applied Behavioral Science, 23*(4), 483–500.

Bartunek, J.M., & Moch, M.K. (1994). Third-order organizational change and the western mystical tradition. *Journal of Organizational Change, 7*(1), 24–41.

Bavaria, J. (2000). The Global Reporting Initiative. *Investing in a Better World, 15*(2), 1.

Becker, E. (1999). Social funds track record lengthens, strengthens. *Investing in a Better World, 14*(8), 1–6.

Brown, I. (1987). *Responsive enterprise: Creating and developing entrepreneurial vision.* Chestnut Hill MA: Boston College doctoral dissertation.

Burns, J. (1978). *Leadership.* New York: Harper & Row.

Cameron, K.S., Dutton, J.E., & Quinn, R.E. (Eds.). (2003). *Positive organizational scholarship: Foundations of a new discipline.* San Fransisco: Barrett-Koehler.

Collins, J. (2001). *Good to great.* New York: Harper Business.

Cook-Greuter, S. (1999). *Postautonomous ego development: A study of its nature and measurement.* Unpublished doctoral dissertation, Harvard Graduate School of Education, Cambridge, MA.

Cooperrider, D.L., & Sekerka, L.E. (2003). Toward a theory of positive organizational change. In K.S. Cameron, J.E. Dutton, & R.E. Quinn (Eds.), *Positive organizational scholarship: Foundations of a new discipline* (pp. 225–240). San Fransisco: Barrett-Koehler.

Creed, D.W.E., Scully, M., & Austin, J.R. (1999). *Ready to wear: The tailoring of legitimating accounts.* Paper presented at the annual meetings of the Academy of Management, Chicago.

DiMaggio, P. (1988). Interest and agency in insitutional theory. In L.G. Zucker (Ed.), *Institutional patterns and organizations: Culture and environment* (pp. 3–21). Cambridge, MA: Ballinger Publishing Co.

DiMaggio, P.J., & Powell, W.W. (1991). The iron cage revisited: Insitutional isomorphism and collective rationality in organizational fields. In W.W. Powell & P.J.

DiMaggio (Eds.), *The new institutionalism in organizational analysis* (pp. 63–82). Chicago: University of Chicago Press.

Elsbach, K.D., & Sutton, R.I. (1992). Acquiring organizational legitimacy through illegitimate actions: A marriage of institutional and impression management theories. *Academy of Management Journal, 35*(4), 699–738.

Emirbayer, M., & Mische, A. (1998). What is agency? *American Journal of Sociology, 103*(4), 962–1023.

Entine, J. (2003). The myth of social investing: A critique of its practice and consequences for corporate social performance research. *Organization and Environment, 16*(3), 349–368.

Erikson, E. (1969). *Gandhi's truth.* New York: Norton.

Fisher, D., Rooke, D., & Torbert, W. (2001). *Personal and organizational transformations: Through action inquiry.* Boston: Edge\Work Press.

Fligstein, N. (1997). Social skill and institutional theory. *American Behavioral Scientist, 40*(4), 397–405.

Fligstein, N. (2001). Social skill and the theory of fields. *Sociological Theory, 19*(2), 105–125.

Foldy, E.G., & Creed, W.E.D. (1999). Action learning, fragmentation and the interaction of single, double, and triple loop change. *Journal of Applied Behavioral Science, 35*(2), 207–227.

Granoveter, M. (2002). Oral communication. Harvard Kennedy School of Government Seminar 4/22.

Greenwood, R., & Hinings, C.R. (1996). Understanding radical organizational change: Bringing together the old and the new institutionalism. *Academy of Management Review, 21*(4), 1022–1054.

Hannan, M.T., & Freeman, J. (1977). The population ecology of organizations. *American Journal of Sociology, 82*(5), 929–964.

Huff, A., Huff, J., & Barr, P. (2001). *When firms change direction.* New York: Oxford University Press.

Kegan, R. (1994). *In over our heads: The mental demands of modern life.* Cambridge MA: Harvard University Press.

Klamer, A. (1989). A conversation with Amartya Sen. *Journal of Economic Perspectives, 3*(1), 135–150.

Kraatz, M., & Zajac, E. (1996). Exploring the limits of the new institutionalism: The causes and consequences of illegitimate organizational change. *American Sociological Review, 61*, 812–836.

Kraatz, M. (2002). Review of Huff, Huff & Barr, When Firms Change Direction. *Academy of Management Review. 27*(3), 464–467.

Lichtenstein, B., Smith, B., & Torbert, W. (1995). Leadership and ethical development: Balancing light and shadow. *Business Ethics Quarterly, 5*(1), 97–116.

Nielsen, R. P. (1996). *The politics of ethics: methods for acting and learning, and sometimes fighting with others in addressing ethics problems in organizational life.* Oxford: Oxford University Press.

Peterson, C.M., & Seligman, M.E.P. (2003). Positive organizational studies: Lessons from positive psychology. In K.S. Cameron, J.E. Dutton, & R.E. Quinn (Eds.), *Positive organizational scholarship: Foundations of a new discipline* (pp. 14–27). San Fransisco: Barrett-Koehler.

Raelin, J. (1999). Special issue: The action dimension in management: Diverse approaches to research, teaching, and development. *Management Learning, 30*(2), 115–248.

Reason, P., &, Torbert, W. (2001). The action turn toward a transformational social science: A further look at the scientific merits of action research. *Concepts and Transformation, 6*(1), 1–37.

Rooke, D., &, Torbert, W. (1998). Organizational transformation as a function of CEO's developmental stage. *Organization Development Journal, 16*(1), 11–28.

Scully, M., &, Meyerson, D. (1996). Before isomorphism: The dynamics of legitimation in the early days of corporate ethics programs. *MIT/Sloan Working Paper.*

Seligman, M.E.P. (1998). The President's address. *American Psychologist, 54,* 559–562.

Sen, A. (1982). *Choice, welfare and measurement.* Cambridge, MA: MIT Press.

Sen, A. (1987). *On ethics and economics.* London: Blackwell.

Senge, P. (1990). *The fifth discipline.* New York: Currency Doubleday.

Senge, P., Scharmer, C., Jaworski, J., & Flowers, B. (2004). *Presence: Human purpose and the field of the future.* Cambridge MA: The Society for Organizational Learning.

Sherman, F., & Torbert, W. (2000). *Transforming social inquiry, transforming social action: New paradigms for crossing the theory/practice divide in universities and communities.* Boston MA: Kluwer.

Social Investment Forum. (2001). *2001 Report on Responsible Investing Trends in the United States.* www.socialinvest.org

Spreitzer, G., & Sonenshein, S. (2003). Positive deviance and extraordinary organizing. In K.S. Cameron, J.E. Dutton, & R. E. Quinn (Eds.), *Positive organizational scholarship: Foundations of a new discipline* (pp. 207–224). San Fransisco: Barrett-Koehler.

Spreitzer, G.M., & Sonenshein, S. (2004). Toward the construct definition of positive deviance. *American Behavioral Scientist, 47*(6), 828–847.

Torbert, W. (1976). *Creating a community of inquiry.* London: Wiley.

Torbert, W. (1987). *Managing the corporate dream: Restructuring for long-term success.* Homewood, IL: Dow Jones-Irwin.

Torbert, W. (1991). *The power of balance: Transforming self, society, and scientific inquiry.* Newbury Park, CA: Sage.

Torbert, W. (1999). The meaning of social investing. *Investing in a Better World, 14*(10), 2.

Torbert, W., &, Fisher, D. (1992). Autobiographical awareness as a catalyst for managerial and organisational development. *Management Education and Development, 23*(3), 184–198.

Torbert, W., & Associates (2004). *Action inquiry: The secret of timely and transforming leadership.* San Francisco: Berrett-Koehler.

Waddock, S. (2001). *Leading corporate citizens: Vision, values, value added.* New York: McGraw-Hill.

Waddock, S. (2003). Myths and realities of social investing. *Organization and Environment, 16*(3), 369–380.

Wilber, K. (1995). *Sex, ecology, spirituality.* Boston: Shambala.

Wilber, K. (2000). *A theory of everything: An integral vision for business, politics, science, and spirituality.* Boston: Shambhala.

Williamson, O.E. (1981). The economics of organization: The transaction cost approach. *American Journal of Sociology, 87*(3), 548–577.

CHAPTER 7

PHOENIX RISING

Positive Consequences Arising from Organizational Crisis

Judith A. Clair and Ronald L. Dufresne

ABSTRACT

Is it possible that organizations can flourish *as a result of having experienced* a crisis? In this chapter we draw from and integrate multidisciplinary research to consider the ways that traumatic organizational events can have highly positive consequences for an organization. We also discuss some of the reasons why organizations may or may not accrue these positive consequences. Finally, we consider research directions for those interested in further developing knowledge in this new line of inquiry.

... but as when the bird of wonder dies, the maiden phoenix, her ashes new create another heir, as great in admiration as herself; so shall she leave her blessedness to one, when heaven shall call her from this cloud of darkness, who from the sacred ashes of her honour shall star-like rise, as great in fame as she was, and so stand fix'd: peace, plenty, love, truth, terror.... (Shakespeare, *King Henry VIII*)

Positive Psychology in Business Ethics and Corporate Responsibility, pages 143–164
Copyright © 2005 by Information Age Publishing
All rights of reproduction in any form reserved.

As is evident from some of the most notorious disasters such as Chernobyl, 3 Mile Island, Challenger (and now Columbia), and most recently, 9/11/ 2001, Enron, and recent deaths of children in the ICU at Children's Hospital in Massachusetts (Barnard, 2003a, 2003b) organizational crises threaten human life, environmental and community sustainability, and organizational profitability. Scholarly research reveals human, technical, and organizational errors and dysfunctions that lead to these tragic outcomes (i.e., Perrow, 1984; Shrivastava, 1987; Turner, 1976). This research exposes the most negative, least desirable aspects of and consequences from human and organizational behavior.

Positive outcomes of organizational crises are usually not the focus of scholarly research, though 15 years ago Mitroff and Pauchant (1990) acknowledged that one of the greatest myths about organizational crises is that they are purely destructive. Research on the impacts of trauma at the individual level of analysis shows that some people grow and even thrive as a result of traumatic experiences, and reach even higher level functioning than they experienced before the trauma (Linley & Joseph, 2003). Is it possible that, like individuals who grow as a result of having experienced trauma, organizations can also flourish in the face of and *even as a result of having experienced* a crisis? While the main focus of crisis research is on negative outcomes, there is some research that considers how organizational change and learning are triggered from crisis. In this article we draw from and integrate this research with research at the individual level on learning and development triggered from trauma experiences to consider the ways that organizational crises can create highly positive consequences.

Our interest in the positive consequences of organizational crises is motivated by Seligman's work on positive psychology (Seligman, 2000; Seligman & Csikszentmihalyi, 2000) and by the urging of organizational scholars who seek to build a body of positive organizational scholarship (POS) (i.e., Cameron, Dutton & Quinn, 2003). A POS perspective encourages organizational scholars to build knowledge on individual, organizational, community, and societal flourishing rather than on dysfunctional or acceptable organizational behaviors (Cameron et al., 2003). Our work is especially encouraged by Aspinwall and Staudinger's (2003, p. 16) assertion that a psychology of human strengths must not only examine highly positive states but also needs to include close examination of "...the positive aspects of negative states and the negative aspects of positive states...."

This chapter is organized as follows. First, we provide a general overview of scholarly research that suggests that positive outcomes can arise from crises and trauma. Second, we explore some of the types of positive consequences that may follow an organizational crisis. Third, we discuss some of the conditions that explain why more organizations don't realize highly positive consequences in the wake of a crisis. Finally, we end the paper with a brief discussion of research directions.

Before moving forward, we want to note that we do not mean to underplay the tragic outcomes arising from organizational crises through our focus on positive consequences. The horrors of events such as September 11, 2001 cannot be ignored, nor should they. Our hope is that, through a highlighting of positive consequences arising from organizational crises, we motivate research and practice that also provide hope and inspiration even in tragedy.

In addition, we want to share our expectation that highly positive consequences are unlikely to materialize regularly for an organization without particular facilitating conditions. For example, of all organizations over the last twenty years having experienced a major organizational crisis, Johnson and Johnson (with regard to its response to the Tylenol poisonings) is the most salient example of an organization that experienced highly positive consequences. We hope that our highlighting of these consequences will encourage scholars to explore and practitioners to create organizational conditions that make these positive outcomes more likely in the event of an unavoidable crisis.

POSITIVE PERSPECTIVES ON CRISES AND TRAUMA

Organizational crises are low-probability, high-impact events that threaten an organization's viability and are characterized by ambiguity of cause, effect, and means of resolution, as well as by a belief that decisions must be made swiftly (Pearson & Clair, 1998).

Organizational crises are distinct from natural disasters such as earthquakes or hurricanes in that they are human-caused rather than acts of nature (Shrivastava, Mitroff, Miller, & Miglani, 1988). While the scholarly work on organizational crises is notable for its cross-disciplinary nature and poor integration (Pearson & Clair, 1998), it is possible to identify general trends in the direction of research. Recently, Rudolph and Repenning (2002) characterized scholarly work related to organizational crises as including in-depth case studies of disasters, such as the chemical leak at Union Carbide in Bhopal, India (Shrivastava, 1987); studies of learning from accidents and errors (e.g., Cook & Woods, 1994); theories of high-hazard or accident-prone organizations (e.g., Perrow, 1994); theories of high-reliability organizations (e.g., Weick & Roberts, 1993); and theories of how to manage accident and error (e.g., Reason, 1997). Scholars who study crisis cases and crisis-prone organizations seek to highlight the variables that have led, or can lead, to tragedies and explicitly or implicitly seek to identify ways that future crises can be avoided or losses can be minimized (e.g., Pearson & Clair, 1998). In contrast, high-reliability scholars study organizations that are highly successful at avoiding crisis (e.g., Weick & Roberts, 1993). Similarly, research on how to manage accident and error and research on learning from crisis demonstrates ways that losses can be minimized and new ways of organizational functioning adapted to avoid future crisis (e.g., Carroll, Rudolph, & Hatakenaka, 2002). As this brief overview of the crisis literature illustrates, an important focus of prior research is on why crises occur and how organizations can avoid them or minimize their negative impacts if unavoidable.

In contrast to this traditional approach to crisis research, a positive psy-chology or POS perspective urges organizational scholars to consider ques-tions and outcomes that populate the exemplary, positive, glorious aspects of the individual and organizational experience such as hope (Luthans, 2002), virtue (Park & Peterson, 2003), positive organizing (Lee, Caza, Edmondson, & Thomke, 2003; Weick, 2003), transcendent behavior (Bate-man & Porath, 2003), and resilience (Coutu, 2002; Sutcliffe & Vogus, 2003; Vickers & Kouzmin, 2001). While a positive psychology perspective can already be found in theory on organizational crises to some extent (Weick, 2003), this perspective motivates scholars to ask a different set of questions regarding organizational crises. How can one imagine such exemplary, positive, glorious outcomes to arise from tragic events? Is there an ethical imperative for organizations to seek and reap the positive outcomes of cri-ses? Stated somewhat differently, the positive psychology perspective leads us to ask whether and how highly positive outcomes arise from organiza-tional events characterized by trauma and loss. Some research on individu-als' experiences of trauma, organizational change, and learning from organizational crisis can inform our thinking about positive outcomes from traumatic experience and crisis.

At the individual level of analysis, as we mentioned previously, a growing body of research explores the ways that traumatic experience—such as the death of a loved one—not only has negative consequences for the individ-ual but also can have highly positive consequences. This research demon-strates that trauma can trigger highly positive consequences such as personal and social transformation, growth in relationships, and existential and spiritual growth (Calhoun & Tedeschi, 2001; Davis, 2001; Linley & Joseph, 2003). This research demonstrates that some growth may only be possible because of losses (Baltes, Lindenberger, & Staudinger, 1998). Thus, while organizations may be able to accrue some of the positive bene-fits that we discuss in this paper without ever experiencing a crisis, the research on trauma and loss at the individual level of analysis suggests that crisis experiences can be an essential trigger for organizational change and transformation.

Similarly, at the organizational level of analysis, some organizational scholars discuss how organizational crises can trigger positive consequences. For example, Bartunek's (1984, 1993) work on "first-order" and "second-order" change and Turner's (1976) work on disasters demonstrate that reassessments of shared organizational assumptions and goals are often initiated by a crisis situation. Similarly, Greiner's (1972) well-known theory of organizational life cycles asserts that most organizations undergo an invariable growth and development process where stages of evolution are punctuated by revolutionary crises. In this model, crisis is the inevitable outcome of an organization's development, and it is only by successfully navigating through these crises that the organization can continue growth.

Some organizational scholars also explore learning outcomes that arise from organizational crisis, noting how the Chinese ideogram for crisis (*wei ji*) contains the sense of both danger and opportunity (e.g., Nathan, 2000; Turner & Pidgeon, 1997). While it is common for models of the stages of organization crises to culminate with the learning stage (Shrivastava et al., 1988; Stead & Smallman, 1999; Turner, 1976), relatively few empirical studies have explored how learning is motivated by organizational crises. For example, in their study of the environmental crisis that emerges from uncontrollable tire fires, Simon and Pauchant (2000) explain how such a crisis can reveal paradigmatic and systemic relationships not previously seen. In another example, Kim (1998) showed how Hyundai Motors created organizational crises to learn how to transform itself from a vehicle assembler to a true vehicle developer and producer.

In the following sections, our chapter integrates and builds beyond this prior research to provide opportunities for further research exploring positive consequences of organizational crises.

POSITIVE CONSEQUENCES ARISING FROM ORGANIZATIONAL CRISES

Building on the observation that in certain circumstances crises can indeed have some non-detrimental—or even highly positive—outcomes (Mitroff & Pauchant, 1990), in this section we ask explicitly what positive consequences might flow from an organizational crisis. We explore just five of these positive consequences in this section: (1) heightened attention to stakeholder relationships; (2) transformed organizational identity and deeper member identification; (3) heightened insight into organizational vulnerabilities; (4) issue leadership; and (5) enhanced sense of the emotional, spiritual, and existential aspects of organizational life. Rather than attempt to discuss all possible positive outcomes, our purpose in this section is to motivate scholars to further explore the implications of the positive psychology perspective for organizational crises. Further, we expect that the consequences we discuss in this section will interact with one another. For example, insights into particular organizational vulnerabilities are likely to transform the organizational self-concept, in other words, its organizational identity. For clarity purposes, we discuss each consequence separately.

Heightened Attention to Stakeholder Relationships

As Shrivastava et al. (1988) assert, crises often entail multiple stakeholders, either as victims, instigators, or mitigators of a crisis event and its effects. Whereas most crises involve parties previously known as stakeholders of the organization-in-crises, sometimes crises uncover stakeholder relationships that were previously unknown. For example, the improper use of DDT in fertilizers might have been foreseen as harmful to people living near farms and drinking from the local groundwater. Through the crisis of declining bald eagle populations, though, came the revelation that rare wildlife was also a stakeholder to the farmers' operations.

As highlighted by stakeholder theory (Freeman, 1984; Mitchell & Agle, 1997), organizations exist in a web of relationships of various types. These relationships can be with people and organizations including employees, suppliers, customers, shareholders, neighbors, competitors, regulators, media, and wildlife (among others). While a crisis can have obvious deleterious effects on some—or all—of these stakeholders, more positively, the crisis can also signal to members of the focal organization the true nature and magnitude of the interdependencies. In the midst of the crisis, this knowledge could help the organization to minimize the negative impact of the events on the organization's stakeholders.

Mitchell and Agle (1997) assert that three specific combinations of factors influence the degree to which stakeholders become salient to an organization's managers and leaders: power, legitimacy, and urgency. Rather than existing in steady-state, these factors in flux combine together to influence the salience of stakeholders:

> Urgency by itself is not sufficient to guarantee high salience in the stakeholder-manager relationship. However, when it is combined with at least one of the other attributes, urgency will change the relationship and cause it to increase in salience to the firm's managers. Specifically, in combination with legitimacy, urgency promotes access to decision-making channels, and in combination with power, it encourages one-sided stakeholder action. In combination with both, urgency triggers reciprocal acknowledgment and action between stakeholders and managers. (Mitchell & Agle, 1997, p. 870)

It is our sense that an organizational crisis can shift the balance of these three factors in such a way that particular organizational stakeholders become more salient to managers and leaders and thus generate organizational attention to previously unrecognized stakeholder groups. Organizational crises that impact particular stakeholders can provide a legitimate basis for stakeholder action, urgency on the part of stakeholders to take action to protect their interests or identities (i.e., Rowley & Moldoveanu, 2003), and/or stakeholder power to the extent that stakeholders who have been visibly impacted by a crisis may be able to force an organization (which previously did not recognize the stakeholder) to attend to its interests.

While in the short term an organization may experience this shift of stakeholder salience as threatening, there might also be the delayed positive effect of an improved and more ethical internal process when making decisions. For example, within the contractualist theory of ethics, an act is moral if the principle motivating that act is reasonably defensible to others in the community (Scanlon, 1998). To the extent that an organization better understands who exactly composes its "community," its decisions could be more reasonably defensible—and thereby more ethical.

A case that illustrates this argument is the Shell Oil crisis in Nigeria and its immediate fallout (Lawrence, 2002; Mirvis, 2000). Prior to 1995, Shell, like most other multinational oil corporations, focused its attention on the more proximate stakeholders: shareholders, customers, employees, and—when mandated—the environment. In 1995, activist Ken Saro-Wiwa protested the pollution by Shell's drilling operations in Nigeria and was subsequently tried and executed by the Nigerian government. A reputational crisis ensued when the international media learned of the execution and Shell's silence about the issue, and several non-governmental organizations (NGOs) joined in protest of Shell's complicity. In responding to this crisis, Shell recognized numerous stakeholders they had previously not sufficiently considered, including NGOs, local governments, and indigenous people. By integrating these stakeholders into its "community" of affected others, the managers were better equipped to incorporate their perspective when making decisions, resulting in more ethical processes and outcomes.

Clarified Organizational Identity and Deepened Member Identification

Organizational crisis can also lead to a clearer understanding of the organization's identity and stronger identification of the organization's members. Organizational identity is a set of characteristics that are core, distinctive, and enduring in an organization (Albert & Whetten, 1985).

When a crisis occurs, organizations are afforded the opportunity to see what image they have projected. Their image is how others—particularly the media and other salient stakeholders—see the organization and perceive its identity (Berg, 1985), and in the comparison of the image and self-perceived identity an organization can discover an opportunity to revisit what it would desire its identity and image to be. This renewed attractive identity may lead organization members to increase their identification with the organization (Dutton, Duckerich, & Harquail, 1994).

It is not uncommon for organizations operating in the status quo to ignore asking identity questions such as "who are we" or "what do we stand for." In the midst of crisis, however, as fundamental assumptions are tested or violated, these questions take on greater salience. This is especially the case when the media, customers, and shareholders express to members of the organization who these stakeholders think the organization is (Gioia, Schultz, & Corley, 2000). As Hatch and Schultz (2002) argue, an organization's identity is an expression of its culture, and its image is the impression an organization's identity leaves on others. When discrepancies exist between the identity and the image, one potential remedy to the gap is to change the identity to generate a more desirable image. Crises, then, can provide leverage for an organization to see and possibly change its essential character.

In a related manner, a clarified organizational identity that follows from crisis may result in an enhanced identification of members with the organization. Identification entails the degree to which members feel that their sense of self is wrapped up with the organization and the organization's identity (Ashforth, 1998). So when someone primarily introduces herself to another as an employee of the XYZ Corporation, her identification with XYZ is strong. It is possible that strong identification, in turn, may create a variety of organization benefits such as reduced turnover, greater commitment, and a higher probability of organizational citizenship behaviors. Crisis can act to reaffirm one's identification with an organization, just as a critical event may strengthen one's love for one's partner (Ashforth, 1998). Lastly, it is also possible that a redefinition of the organizational identity may lead to an identity that feels more authentic to the members, thereby also strengthening identification.

Some of these identity processes can be seen in the case of Cantor Fitzgerald in the aftermath of the September 11, 2001 tragedies. A leading financial services firm through the 1990s, Cantor Fitzgerald was headquartered between the 101st and 105th floors of One World Trade Center in New York City. On September 11, almost seven hundred employees were killed and the company's headquarters were destroyed. Soon thereafter, even as the firm was uncertain how it would resume operations, the firm's CEO and other partners announced they would expedite payment of end-of-year bonuses to the families of the lost employees. The partners also committed to allocating 25% of all profits to an employee victim fund to pay for families' health care costs and to provide some residual income for those families (Henriques, 2002; Zuckerman, 2002).

Although anecdotal, we can see indications here that the crisis had effects on the organization's identity. Before 9/11, Cantor Fitzgerald's identity appeared to be defined by its technological savvy and its ability to return solid profits to the firm's partners. In the fallout of the tragedy, as CEO Howard Lutnick responded to television interviews, the identity seemed to be shifting to that of a company that existed to help the families of those killed in the terrorist attacks and to provide opportunities for meaningful and challenging work. After negotiating between the firm's previous identity, espoused future identity, and perceived external image, the company instituted the 25% policy and embedded that artifact in its current identity. Televised interviews with surviving employees lead us to speculate that, following the crisis, members' identification with Cantor Fitzgerald was strengthened. The fact that the survivors of the attack were able to resume the company's operations within two days might also be a manifestation of the heightened identification.

Increased Mindfulness of Organizational Vulnerability

Just as the individual who survives trauma can emerge with a greater recognition and appreciation of his or her vulnerability (Tedeschi & Calhoun, 1995), experience of an organizational crisis may lead to greater insight into and appreciation of the organization's vulnerability to harm. This idea is implicit within Turner's (1976) well-known theory of the evolution of organizational crises, which highlights how standard organizational practices assumed to be normal and safe may be out of line with the real circumstances. When a crisis occurs, organizational members can gain insights into new realities as shared assumptions about safety are shattered and reformed so that they are more in line with these real circumstances (Turner, 1976). Thus, a crisis can heighten the awareness and attention of organizational members (Nathan, 2000; Stern, 1997) to an organization's vulnerabilities. While much of organizational life is routinized and enables mindlessness (Ashforth & Fried, 1988; Langer, 1989), crises can shake organizations and their members to attend to what is occurring and why. This increased awareness can facilitate learning from crisis. Such learning can also benefit society if knowledge is subsequently applied to other organizations (Shepherd, 2003).

Failure to appreciate the significance of information is not exclusively the result of organizational members' inability to "correctly" gather, perceive, and interpret information. In addition, organizational members engage in collectively held illusions of invulnerability such as "we are all-powerful" (Mitroff & Pauchant, 1990) that lead to "encased learning" (Nystrom & Starbuck, 1984) where knowledge and responsibility are negated or disowned (Brown & Starkey, 2000). These processes produce organizational blindness and rigidity and can make an organization more prone to experiencing a crisis (Mitroff & Pauchant, 1990; Nystrom & Starbuck, 1984). For example, with regard to the Challenger disaster, Vaughan (1996, p. 394) describes how shared beliefs at NASA produced "... a way of seeing that was simultaneously a way of not seeing." Illusions of invulnerability can arise as collective defenses against anxiety-provoking challenges to organizational identity (Brown & Starkey, 2000) and lead to dangerous and unhealthy behaviors such as ignoring safety regulations. While the traumas associated with an organizational crisis are an undesirable outcome of illusions of vulnerability, a crisis—which is difficult to deny or disclaim—can also be a positive influence because it challenges illusions of invulnerability (Tedeschi & Calhoun, 1995) and, under certain conditions, may lead to more realistic assumptions and healthy behaviors.

Issue Leadership

When a crisis prompts an organization to sense its vulnerability and learn ways to overcome that vulnerability, another positive outcome is for the organization to become a leader in the institutional field concerning ways others might avoid such a crisis. The possibility of other organizations—not just the one encountering the crisis—learning vicariously is enhanced by the focal organization's transparency and honesty. Airing the organization's "dirty laundry" and becoming the leader around an issue may be limited by the risk of facing litigation, but the benefits to other organizations—and their stakeholders—may be great.

We call this positive outcome "issue leadership," and it is closely related to the concept in the literature known as issues management (Gonzales-Herrero & Pratt, 1996; Jaques, 2002). Issues management concerns a strategy managers can employ to improve a reputation that may have been negatively affected by a crisis event. Issues management tactics include when an organization takes measures to offset negative media coverage (Gonzales-Herrero & Pratt, 1996), promotes a favorable policy agenda (Crable & Vibbert, 1985), and seeks to benefit its own as well as society's interests (Bucholz, Evans, & Wagley, 1989). The difference, we feel, hinges on intentions: whereas issues management is intended to help an organization "get through" a crisis, issue leadership is intended to help others learn from one's own failings. As such, issue leadership has at its root altruism—a concern for the well-being of others (Batson et al., 2002).

An example of issue leadership following an organizational crisis can be found in the story of the Dana-Farber Cancer Institute in Boston. In 1994, one patient died and another patient was badly injured when they received an overdose of a chemotherapy drug. Following the incident, the hospital undertook a review of their procedures and pursued several steps to ensure such medication errors could be avoided in the future, including new order entry computers and support for reporting potential mishaps. Dana-Farber also aggressively publicized their problems and their solutions, participating nationwide in more than forty seminars on medication errors in the three years following the tragedy. The hospital's staff also produced an educational video chronicling its crisis and its response; this video is now used by many hospitals to fulfill their continuing education requirements (Stratos Institute, 2000). These public acts of issue leadership resulted in a majority of the major cancer centers following suit and revising their internal systems as well (Romano, 1999).

Enhanced Emotional, Spiritual, and/or Existential Aspects of Organizational Life

Organizational crises, which involve major losses, can enhance emotional, spiritual, and existential aspects of organizational life. Especially when an organizational crisis leads to loss of human life, organizational members are likely to experience an array of negative emotional reactions—including guilt, anger, fear and depression (Tedeschi & Calhoun, 1995). In the wake of these losses, organizational members may also experience grief for their own and the organization's losses. While individuals express a wide array of reactions to a crisis, a perceived loss and attendant negative emotional and grief reactions is likely to trigger a process of meaning re-creation as individuals attempt to make sense of (and assign meaning to) the event within the context of their lives.

There are several positive consequences of organizational grieving. First, an organization may be better prepared to work through emotional reactions to future organizational loss experiences. In other words, an organization increases its emotional capability, which Huy (1999) defines as an organization's ability to acknowledge, recognize, monitor, discriminate, and attend to its members' emotions. In addition, an organization may be better prepared to integrate the spiritual and existential aspects of human existence into everyday work. For example, employees may react to losses by seeking more meaningful work and meaningfulness at work (Pratt & Ashforth, 2003). Organizations may be more aware of and responsive to such needs as a result of having to work through loss of meaning attendant to a crisis event.

These are just five potential highly positive consequences that can result from an organizational crisis. While they do not represent all possible positive outcomes, as foretold by Mitroff and Pauchant (1990, p. 95), they do highlight that "...one of the most persistent myths about crises is that they are solely negative in their impacts both on individuals and organizations...."

WHY DON'T MORE ORGANIZATIONS REALIZE HIGHLY POSITIVE CONSEQUENCES FROM THEIR CRISIS EXPERIENCE?

Certainly not all—or even a majority—of organizations realize these positive outcomes. Why is this so? In this section, we briefly highlight three reasons: (a) defensive and protective reactions; (b) inability to unlearn; and (c) a rush to put the crisis behind the organization and return to standard operating procedures.

First, since crises threaten the viability of organizations, it is natural for an organization to react defensively. However, in order to accrue some of the benefits we described earlier, leaders of organizations in crisis need to open themselves to unknown, risky opportunities. When the Dana-Farber Cancer Institute illuminated the dark realm of their own medication errors, its transparency allowed others to benefit from its crisis. As Le Menestrel (2002) writes, transparency and openness afford stakeholders the opportunity to determine the ethicality of an organization's behavior. Indeed the fact that an organization is attempting to be transparent is in itself an indicator of ethicality (Pearson, 2000). However, organizations' defensive reactions may be fueled by the view that a crisis is solely negative, and contains no potentially positive consequences. Research on issue framing by Dutton and Jackson (1987; Jackson & Dutton, 1988) shows that managers tend to have a threat bias, whereby managers tend to see not only threats, but also ambiguous and neutral information, as potentially threatening. Moreover, once an issue is perceived as a threat, others in the organization attend to threat-congruent data and ignore opportunity-congruent data (Dutton & Jackson, 1987). Since, as we and others (Jackson & Dutton, 1988; Mitroff & Pauchant 1990; Turner & Pidgeon, 1997) have argued, crises have threat *and* opportunity aspects, leaders need to overcome the threat bias and focus others in the organization on the latent opportunities to realize positive outcomes. Specifically, we want to suggest that organizational leaders are less likely to be highly defensive, and more likely to be transparent and open about a crisis experience, when the crisis is framed as having both possible negative and positive consequences. Also, positive consequences are seen as more possible when the organization invites stakeholders to engage with its crisis experience rather than shutting the organizational doors to stakeholders. In so doing, as described in the case of Millstone by Carroll and Hatakenaka (2001), an organization signals that things have changed for the better through its honesty and transparency. In other words, honesty and openness signals that the organization is ready to take positive action in response to the crisis.

Second, as Hedberg (1981) has argued, one of the key steps to learning is unlearning. Unlearning, he wrote, "... is a process in which learners discard knowledge. Unlearning makes way for new responses and mental maps" (Hedberg, 1981, p. 18). Even in the face of crisis, organizations are still unable to discard unreliable mental maps and see the need for new ways of thinking and operating. To realize the positive outcomes of organizational crises, managers need to be able to see mental models that may have led to the crisis in the first place and hold them lightly. For example, Mitroff and Pauchant (1990) found that a series of assumptions about properties of the organization, environment, crises themselves, and how crises should be handled made organizations more crisis prone. These assumptions included: "our size will protect us," "each crisis is unique and it is not possible to prepare for them," and "we are a team that will function well during a crisis." It is possible that one positive consequence of the crisis is that it reveals new insights about dangerous implicit assumptions and beliefs, as we discussed above. Further, as Tushman and Romanelli (1985) point out, sometimes the leaders of the previous "status quo" fall victim to the turmoil of the crisis and are replaced by people previously external to the organization. The outsiders may lack the burdensome assumptions and beliefs that could limit the ability of leaders within the organization to develop and communicate a transformational vision for the future.

Third, scholars have long lamented that organizational leaders usually rush to sweep crisis events "under the carpet" and to resume standard operating procedures as soon as possible rather than attempting to learn from their experiences (i.e., Pearson, Clair, Kovoor Misra, & Mitroff, 1997). However, in order to accrue positive consequences from an organizational crisis, leaders need to recognize that a crisis creates positive opportunities for organizational change and learning. For some organizations, crises can provide powerful motivation to engage in personal and organizational learning (Borodzicz & van Haperen, 2002); when confronted with the gap between desired and actual outcomes, organizational members are motivated to learn how to close that gap. Whether the crisis occurred in an individual's own organization or in a closely related one (i.e., in the same industry or in the same location), the motivation to learn can be strong as a result (Stern, 1997). Furthermore, since there isn't likely to be a single quick-fix solution, it is important that the motivation be able to sustain the commitment to learning from and through the crisis situation. This motivation can increase the chances of discovering the deep lessons that can lead to systemic learning (Carroll et al., 2002). Carroll and Hatakenaka (2001) describe how one organization institutionalized its learning from crisis with the goal of creating a safety-conscious work environment, for example, by building supportive organizational structures (i.e., accountability at senior levels and participation throughout the organizational structure) and creating measurement tools that allowed the organization to measure its progress and detect problems.

DISCUSSION

Is it possible that organizations can flourish in the face of and even *as a result of having experienced* a crisis? In this chapter, we drew from and integrated multidisciplinary research on positive psychology and crisis learning and change at the individual and organizational levels to consider this question. We explored five specific ways that a traumatic organizational crisis can have highly positive consequences for an organization. We also discussed how three factors (organizational defensiveness, failure to unlearn, and an urge to put the crisis behind the organization and get back to standard operating procedures) make it less likely that organizations will accrue these positive consequences.

The crisis literature provides a prime example of an area where a positive perspective can yield a new universe of understanding. Most research energy has been devoted to the project of uncovering and seeking to avoid the dangerous aspects of crisis. Where there has been work in the opportunity aspects, it's been individual forays rather than a concerted campaign. By asking questions from within a positive perspective, we hope to encourage a new research agenda focused on "upward spirals" (Cameron et al., 2003) triggered from the experience of an organizational crisis.

There are many opportunities for those interested in pursuing this new research agenda. Most obviously, scholars need to explore the conditions under which the positive consequences highlighted in this chapter are more likely to take place. For example, Mitroff and Pauchant (1990) discuss a range of organizational behaviors and beliefs which make an organization more crisis prone. A number of the variables discussed in this work may also influence the extent to which an organization experiences highly positive consequences from a crisis experience. In this section we briefly consider additional prime opportunities for scholarly research that builds on and moves beyond our ideas presented in this chapter.

Crisis' Ethical Mandate

We have presented several positive potential outcomes of organizational crisis, some of which had expressly ethical implications. Increased awareness of stakeholders can improve ethical decision making, issue leadership is based on an altruistic motivation of concern for others, and enhancing the spiritual aspects of organizational life can have reverberations that will affect ethicality of intra- and inter-organizational behaviors. What we have not yet mentioned, however, is that there may indeed be an ethical mandate to realize these and other positive outcomes of crises. Wildavsky (1988) argues that seeking to avoid crises altogether may increase danger and accepting the risk of crises can increase safety in the long run. What is needed to make this logic work is the realization of the positive outcomes of crises, especially personal and vicarious learning. Since it is impossible to avoid all crises, the response that fulfills the ethical requirement of defensibility (Scanlon, 1998) is to attempt to gain some positive outcome. What fails the defensibility test is to count an organization's losses and hope the crisis doesn't strike again. Organizational ethicists may better be able to determine the scope and boundaries of this ethical mandate to realize positive consequences of organizational crises.

Organizational Identity and Identification

Scholars have recently expressed much interest in issues of organizational identity and identification (i.e., Dukerich, Golden, & Shortell, 2002; Dutton et al., 1994; Whetten & Godfrey, 1998). One area of research that has not been explored much is the link between the experience of organizational crises and organizational identity and identification. Several scholars have investigated organizational identity conflicts or breakdowns in meaning as a source or as an illustration of an organizational crisis (i.e., Glynn, 2000; Stjernberg & Tillberg, 1998). In contrast, as suggested earlier in our paper, the POS perspective opens new avenues for research which investigates how organizational crises offer opportunities to transform organizational identity, external images, and deepen member identification. Using longitudinal research designs, scholars could explore how such changes occur over time in response to a crisis experience. Additionally, scholars should investigate the conditions under which a positive identity and external images and deepened member identification can be fostered following a crisis (in contrast to organizational crises where an organization's identity and external image are marred by the crisis itself and the organization's response, as illustrated by Exxon's notorious Valdez disaster [Dutton et al., 1994]).

Stakeholder Relationships

As we suggested earlier in the paper, organizational crises can open organizations' awareness to the array of stakeholders that are impacted by and impact an organization in the face of an organizational crisis. Scholarly research looking at the intersection between stakeholder relationships, organizational crises, and positive perspectives on organizational behavior could also investigate the conditions under which stakeholder relationships are deepened and made more positive in the wake of a crisis. Positive psychology scholars have started to look at the power of high-quality connections (i.e., Dutton & Heaphy, 2003) and energizing relationships (Baker, Cross, & Wooten, 2003) within organizations. This focus could be broadened to investigate how stakeholder connections with an organization are energized and deepened when a crisis occurs and the conditions under which stakeholders work effectively together to contain the crisis and return to normalcy. This research focus would move beyond current approaches by illustrating how stakeholder groups work together courageously to respond to the crisis-in-the-moment.

Transcendent Behavior

Relatedly, research should also use organizational crises as a context to deepen our understanding of transcendent behavior in organizations (Bateman & Porath, 2003)—where individuals perform above and beyond the call of duty—in the context of organizational crises. Rarely do scholars account for the type of courageous behavior that take place during a crisis as people are rescued and losses are minimized through the selfless acts of others. Certainly, the events of September 11, 2001 offer many anecdotal stories of transcendent behaviors of emergency workers as well as victims who sought to save others and in some instances sacrificed their own lives in doing so. These examples of transcendent behavior under extreme organizational conditions may offer greater insight into the positive behaviors and performances that are generated during a crisis that may not be visible in day-to-day organizational routines under normal non-crisis conditions.

Meaning and Meaningfulness at Work

Furthermore, scholars interested in the creation of meaningfulness at work may look at how and under what conditions the experience of an organizational crisis triggers individuals to form a new sense of meaning and meaningfulness at work. Work on individuals' experience of a trauma demonstrates how traumatic experiences force individuals to search for a sense of meaning in the event and triggers some people to seek out greater meaning in their lives (Tedeschi & Calhoun, 1995). Rather than illustrating how organizational crises either represent or trigger losses of existential meaning, as is more typical of research on organizational crises, scholars could explore how organizational trauma can be a tool for transformation in how individuals understand their work. Some questions that come to mind for us include: To what extent do individuals reformulate their organizational roles or even careers after having gone through an organizational crisis? In what ways does a crisis trigger an organization to offer greater opportunities for meaningful work to its employees? Or, in what ways does it trigger, if at all, individuals to reformulate their work in a way that contains greater meaning and meaningfulness, akin to Wrzesniewski and Dutton's (2001) concept of job crafting?

Initial Conditions

Finally, there is ample opportunity for researchers to uncover the factors and mechanisms that can act as initial conditions for future positive outcomes of organizational crisis. Positive initial conditions may act as the launching pad for the upward spiraling positive outcomes, and these initial conditions might best be developed in times of relative stability. How can leaders grow to balance their threat bias (Dutton & Jackson, 1987) with a tendency to see opportunities in ambiguous situations as well? How do organizations build structure both to learn and to unlearn (Hedberg, 1981) in their daily operations? These questions concerning initial conditions are not only of great concern to organizational scholars, but also to managers who wish to be able to realize the potential benefits when they are beset with crisis. Given the propensity toward the threat-rigidity effect (Staw, Sandelands, & Dutton, 1981), it is unlikely that managers in crises will stumble upon a positive mechanism or outcome; it would be a wiser investment if they were to lay the foundation before the storm.

In closing, we return to the venerable Bard:

Sweet are the uses of adversity, Which, like the toad, ugly and venomous, Wears yet a precious jewel in his head; And this our life, exempt from public haunt, Finds tongues in trees, books in the running brooks, Sermons in stones, and good in everything. (Shakespeare—*As You Like It*)

AUTHOR NOTE

The authors contributed equally to the development of ideas in this chapter.

REFERENCES

Albert, S., & Whetten, D. (1985). Organizational identity. In L.L. Cummings & B.M. Staw (Eds.), *Research in organizational behavior* (Vol. 7, pp. 263–295). Greenwich, CT: JAI Press.

Ashforth, B.E. (1998). Becoming: How does the process of identification unfold? In D.A. Whetten & P.C. Godfrey (Eds.), *Identity in organizations: Building theory through conversations* (pp. 213–222). Thousand Oaks, CA: Sage.

Ashforth, B.E., & Fried, Y. (1988). The mindlessness of organizational behaviors. *Human Relations, 41,* 305–329.

Aspinwall, L.G., & Staudinger, U.M. (2003). A psychology of human strengths: Some central issues of an emerging field. In L.G. Aspinwall & U.M. Staudinger (Eds.), *A psychology of human strengths: Fundamental questions and future directions for a positive psychology* (pp. 9–22). Washington, DC: American Psychological Association.

Baker, W., Cross, R., & Wooten, M. (2003). Positive organizational network analysis and energizing relationships. In K.S. Cameron, J.E. Dutton, & R.E. Quinn (Eds.), *Positive organizational scholarship: Foundations of a new discipline* (pp. 328–342). San Francisco: Berrett-Koehler.

Baltes, P.B., Lindenberger, U., & Staudinger, U.M. (1998). Life-span theory in developmental psychology. In W. Damon & R.M. Learner (Eds.), *Handbook of child psychology, Vol. 1: Theoretical models of human development* (5th ed. , pp. 1029–1143). New York: Wiley.

Bartunek, J.M. (1984). Changing interpretive schemes and organizational restructuring: The example of a religious order. *Administrative Science Quarterly, 29,* 355–372.

Bartunek, J.M. (1993). The multiple cognitions and conflicts associated with second order organizational change. In J.K. Murnighan (Ed.), *Social psychology in organizations: Advances in theory and research* (pp. 322–349). Englewood Cliffs: Prentice-Hall.

Bateman, T.S., & Porath, C. (2003). Transcendent behavior. In K.S. Cameron, J.E. Dutton, & R.E. Quinn (Eds.), *Positive organizational scholarship: Foundations of a new discipline* (pp. 122–137). San Francisco: Berrett-Koehler.

Batson, C.D., Ahmad, N., Lishner, D., Tsang, J. (2002). Empathy and altruism. In C.R. Snyder, & S.J. Lopez (Eds.), *Handbook of Positive Psychology* (pp. 485–498). New York: Oxford University Press.

Berg, P.O. (1985). Organization change as a symbolic transformation process. In P. Frost, L. Moore, M.R. Louis, C. Lundberg, & J. Martin (Eds.), *Reframing organizational culture* (pp. 281–300). Beverly Hills, CA: Sage.

Borodzicz, E.P., & van Haperen, K. (2002). Individual and group learning in crisis simulations. *Journal of Contingencies and Crisis Management, 10,* 139–147.

Brown, A.D., & Starkey, K. (2000). Organizational identity and learning: A psycho-dynamic perspective. *Academy of Management Review, 25*, 102–120.

Bucholz, R.A., Evans, W.D., & Wagley, R.A. (1989). *Management response to public issues.* Englewood Cliffs, NJ: Prentice-Hall.

Calhoun, L.G., & Tedeschi, R.G. (2001). Postraumatic growth: The positive lessons of loss. In R.A. Neimeyer (Ed.), *Meaning reconstruction and the experience of loss* (pp. 157–172). Washington, DC: American Medical Association.

Cameron, K.S., Dutton, J.E., & Quinn, R.E. (Eds.). (2003). *Positive organizational scholarship: Foundations of a new discipline.* San Francisco: Berrett-Koehler.

Carroll, J.S., & Hatakenaka, S. (2001). Driving organizational change in the midst of crisis. *Sloan Management Review, 42(3),* 70–79.

Carroll, J.S., Rudolph, J.W., & Hatakenaka S. (2002). Learning from experience in high-hazard industries. In L.L. Cummings & B.M. Staw (Eds.), *Research in organizational behavior* (Vol. 24, pp. 87–137). Greenwich, CT: JAI Press.

Cook, R.I., & Woods, D.D. (1994). Operating at the sharp end: The complexity of human error. In B.S. Bogner (Ed.), *Human error in medicine* (pp. 255–310). Hillsdale, NJ: Lawrence Erlbaum.

Coutu, P.L. (2002, May). How resilience works. *Harvard Business Review,* 46–55.

Crable, R.E., & Vibbert, S.L. (1985). Managing issues and influencing public policy. *Public Relations Review, 7,* 3–16.

Davis, C.G. (2001). The tormented and the transformed: Understanding responses to loss and trauma. In R.A. Neimeyer (Ed.), *Meaning reconstruction and the experience of loss* (pp. 137–155). Washington, DC: American Medical Association.

Dukerich, J.M., Golden, B.R., & Shortell, S.M. (2002). Is beauty in the eyes of the beholder? Predicting organizational identification and its consequences using identity and image. *Administrative Science Quarterly, 47,* 507–533.

Dutton, J.E., Dukerich, J.M., & Harquail, C.V. (1994). Organizational images and member identification. *Administrative Science Quarterly, 39,* 239–263.

Dutton, J.E., & Heaphy, E.D. (2003). In K.S. Cameron, J.E. Dutton, & R.E. Quinn (Eds.), *Positive organizational scholarship: Foundations of a new discipline* (pp. 263–278). San Francisco: Berrett-Koehler.

Dutton, J.E., & Jackson, S.E. (1987). Categorizing strategic issues: Links to organizational actions. *Academy of Management Review, 12,* 76–90.

Freeman, R.E. (1984). *Strategic management: A stakeholder approach.* Boston, MA: Pitman.

Gioia, D.A., Schultz, M., & Corley, K.G. (2000). Organizational identity, image, and adaptive instability. *Academy of Management Review, 25,* 63–81.

Glynn, M.A. (2000). When cymbals become symbols: Conflict over organizational identity within a symphony orchestra, *Organization Science, 11,* 285–298.

Gonzalez-Herrero, A., & Pratt, C.B. (1996). An integrated symmetrical model for crisis-communications management. *Journal of Public Relations Research, 8,* 79–105.

Greiner, L.E. (1972, July/August). Evolution and revolution as organizations grow. *Harvard Business Review,* 37–46.

Hatch, M.J., & Schultz, M. (2002). The dynamics of organizational identity. *Human Relations, 55,* 989–1018.

Hedberg, B. (1981). How organizations learn and unlearn. In P. Nystrom & W. Starbuck (Eds.), *Handbook of organizational design* (pp. 1–27). New York: Oxford University Press.

Henriques, D.B. (2002, January 3). Horrible year ends on up note at Cantor. *The New York Times.*

Huy, Q.N. (1999). Emotional capability, emotional intelligence and radical change. *Academy of Management Review, 24,* 325–345.

Jackson, S.E., & Dutton, J.E. (1988). Discerning threats and opportunities. *Administrative Science Quarterly, 33,* 370–387.

Jaques, T. (2002). Towards a new terminology: Optimising the value of issue management. *Journal of Communication Management, 7,* 140–147.

Kim, L. (1998). Crisis construction and organizational learning: Capability building in catching-up at Hyundai Motor. *Organization Science, 9,* 506–521.

Langer, E.J. (1989). *Mindfulness.* Reading, MA: Merloyd Lawrence Book.

Lawrence, A.T. (2002). The drivers of stakeholder engagement: Reflections on the case of Royal Dutch/Shell. In J. Andriof, S. Waddock, B. Husted, & S.S. Rahman (Eds.), *Unfolding stakeholder thinking: Theory, responsibility and engagement* (pp. 185–199). Sheffield, UK: Greenleaf Publishing.

Lee, F., Caza, A., Edmondson, A., & Thomke, S. (2003). New knowledge creation: A study in positive organizing. In K.S. Cameron, J.E. Dutton, & R.E. Quinn (Eds.), *Positive organizational scholarship: Foundations of a new discipline* (pp. 194–206). San Francisco: Berrett-Koehler.

Le Menestrel, M. (2002). Economic rationality and ethical behavior: Ethical business between venality and sacrifice. *Business Ethics: A European Review, 11,* 157–166.

Linley, P.A., & Joseph, S. (2003). Trauma and personal growth. *The Psychologist, 16,* 135.

Luthans, F. (2002). The need for and meaning of positive organizational behavior. *Journal of Organizational Behavior, 23,* 695–706.

Mirvis, P.H. (2000). Transformation at Shell: Commerce *and* citizenship. *Business and Society Review, 105*(1), 63–84.

Mitchell, R.K., & Agle, B.R. (1997). Toward a theory of stakeholder identification and salience. *Academy of Management Review, 22,* 853–886.

Mitroff, I.I., & Pauchant, T.C. (1990). *We're so big and powerful nothing can happen to us.* New York: Carol Publishing.

Nathan, M. (2000). The paradoxical nature of crisis. *Review of Business, 21*(3), 12–16.

Nystrom, P.C., & Starbuck, W.H. (1984). To avoid organizational crisis, unlearn. *Organizational Dynamics, 12,* 53–65.

Park, N., & Peterson, C.M. (2003). Virtues and organizations. In K.S. Cameron, J.E. Dutton, & R.E. Quinn (Eds.), *Positive organizational scholarship: Foundations of a new discipline* (pp. 33–47). San Francisco: Berrett-Koehler.

Pearson, C.M., & Clair, J.A. (1998). Reframing crisis management. *Academy of Management Review, 23,* 59–76.

Pearson, C.M., Clair, J.A., Kovoor Misra, S. & Mitroff, I.I. (1997). Managing the unthinkable. *Organizational Dynamics, 26,* 51–64.

Pearson, G. (2000). Making profits and sweet music. *Business Ethics: A European Review, 9,* 191–199.

Perrow, C. (1984). *Normal accidents: Living with high-risk technologies.* New York: Basic Books.

Pratt, M.G., & Ashforth, B.E. (2003). Fostering meaningfulness in working and work. In K.S. Cameron, J.E. Dutton, & R.E. Quinn (Eds.), *Positive organizational scholarship: Foundations of a new discipline* (pp. 309–327). San Francisco: Berrett-Koehler.

Reason, J. (1997). *Managing the risks of organizational accidents.* Aldershot UK: Ashgate.

Romano, R. (1999, March 15). Fatal error becomes catalyst for reform. *The Boston Globe,* p. A11.

Rowley, T.I., & Moldoveanu, M. (2003). When will stakeholder groups act? An interest- and identity-based model of stakeholder group mobilization. *Academy of Management Review, 28,* 204–219.

Rudolph, J.W., & Repenning, N.P. (2002). Disaster dynamics: Understanding the role of quantity in organizational collapse. *Administrative Science Quarterly, 47,* 1–30.

Scanlon, T.M. (1998). *What we owe to each other.* Cambridge, MA: Belknap Press.

Seligman, M.E.P. (2000). Positive psychology. In J.E. Gillham (Ed.), *The science of optimism and hope* (pp. 415–429). Radnor, PA: Templeton Foundation Press.

Seligman, M.E.P., & Csikszentmihalyi, M. (2000). Positive psychology: An introduction. *American Psychologist, 55,* 5–14.

Shepherd, D.A. (2003). Learning from business failure: Propositions of grief recovery for the self-employed. *Academy of Management Review, 28,* 318–328.

Shrivastava, P. (1987). *Bhopal: Anatomy of a crisis.* Cambridge, MA: Ballinger.

Shrivastava, P., Mitroff, I.I., Miller, D., & Miglani, A. (1988). Understanding industrial crises. *Journal of Management Studies, 25,* 285–304.

Simon, L., & Pauchant, T.C. (2000). Developing three levels of learning in crisis management. *Review of Business, 21*(3), 6–11.

Staw, B.M., Sandelands, L.E., & Dutton, J.E. (1981). Threat rigidity effects in organizational behavior: A multilevel analysis. *Administrative Science Quarterly, 26,* 501–524.

Stead, E., & Smallman, C. (1999). Understanding business failure: Learning and un-learning from industrial crises. *Journal of Contingencies and Crisis Management, 7,* 1–18.

Stern, E. (1997). Crisis and learning: A conceptual balance sheet. *Journal of Contingencies and Crisis Management, 5,* 69–86.

Stjernberg, T., & Tillberg, U. (1998). When structure and meaning break down: Taking responsibility in downsizing. *European Journal of Work and Organizational Psychology, 7,* 355–371.

Stratos Institute. (2000). *Preventing medication errors for the oncology nurse.* Video produced by the Oncology Nursing Society. Laguna Niguel, CA: Stratos Institute.

Sutcliffe, K.M., & Vogus, T.J. (2003). Organizing for resilience. In K.S. Cameron, J.E. Dutton, & R.E. Quinn (Eds.), *Positive organizational scholarship: Foundations of a new discipline* (pp. 94–110). San Francisco: Berrett-Koehler.

Tedeschi, R.G., & Calhoun, L.G. (1995). *Trauma & transformation: Growth in the aftermath of suffering.* Thousand Oaks, CA: Sage.

Turner, B.A. (1976). The organizational and interorganizational development of disasters. *Administrative Science Quarterly, 21,* 378–397.

Turner, B.A., & Pidgeon, N.F. (1997). *Man-made disasters* (2nd ed.). Oxford: Butterworth-Heinemann.

Tushman, M.L., & Romanelli, E. (1985). Organizational evolution: A metamorphosis model of convergence and reorientation. In L.L. Cummings & B.M. Staw (Eds.), *Research in organizational behavior* (Vol. 7, pp. 171–222). Greenwich, CT: JAI Press.

Vaughan, D. (1996). *The Challenger launch decision: Risky technology, culture and deviance at NASA.* Chicago: University of Chicago Press.

Vickers, M.H., & Kouzmin, A. (2001). 'Resilience' in organizational actors and rearticulating 'voice.' *Public Management Review, 3,* 95–119.

Weick, K.E. (2003). Positive organizing and organizational tragedy. In K.S. Cameron, J.E. Dutton, & R.E. Quinn (Eds.), *Positive organizational scholarship: Foundations of a new discipline* (pp. 66–80). San Francisco: Berrett-Koehler.

Weick, K.E., & Roberts, K.H. (1993). Collective mind in organizations: Heedful interrelating on flight decks. *Administrative Science Quarterly, 38,* 357–381.

Whetten, D.A., & Godfrey, P. (1998). *Identity in organizations: Building theory through conversations.* Thousand Oaks, CA: Sage.

Wildavsky, A. (1988). *Searching for safety.* New Brunswick, NJ: Transaction Books.

Wrzesniewski, A. & Dutton, J.E. (2001). Crafting a job: Revisioning employees as active crafters of their work. *Academy of Management Review, 26,* 179–201.

Zuckerman, G. (2002, March 8). Rebuilding Wall Street: Six months after. *The Wall Street Journal,* p. C1.

CHAPTER 8

POSITIVE AGENCY

Barry M. Mitnick

INTRODUCTION

The study of agency has acquired an academic reputation at least as dismal as the economic science to which the theory of agency is often attributed. As an approach said to assume relentlessly self-interested decision making, it would seem to be a poor candidate to examine for its "positive" attributes. But, in fact, the institutional study of agency reveals many circumstances that display positive behaviors and outcomes; theory about agency has not always reflected an opportunistic view of the world. This paper will examine several of these "positive" features. It turns out that there are many key contexts in which agency produces important social advantages.

AGENCY

In social and organizational life, agency relationships are pervasive. Agency relationships arise when the principal lacks the capability (e.g., in expertise) to act for him or herself, when the principal finds for technical or structural reasons that it is inefficient to act for him or herself, or when agency is needed to resolve questions of collective action. In any of these

Positive Psychology in Business Ethics and Corporate Responsibility, pages 165–189
Copyright © 2005 by Information Age Publishing

cases, agency may be elected for either substantive or symbolic reasons, i.e., in order to appeal to the perceptions of third party observers (Mitnick, 1993, ch. 4). These are extraordinarily common circumstances, and so the functions of agency in society are myriad. Indeed, it would be strange if the behaviors of ubiquitous agents, unlike those of other social actors, never displayed positive attributes.

The explicit, systematic study of agency relationships in social science dates to 1973 (Mitnick, 1973, 1975a,b; Ross, 1973), and is thus just 30 years old, though the use of agency concepts in social science, and, of course, in legal studies, is far older. Though the approach is often relevant to the study of social and organizational relationships, and has found applications almost throughout the social sciences, it is most commonly associated with the application of economic modeling to these relationships. In fact, it is far broader-based, and has an institutional stream that extends its theory logics considerably beyond economics.

The theory of agency that has developed to describe these relationships has acquired the reputation of being a formal theory based on the assumption that agents are self-interested and opportunistic. As a result, principals find it costly to instruct and control their agents. Indeed, principals choose to forgo some of those costs whenever the gains to be made by exerting perfect control are simply not worth it. Thus, the classic failures of control in economic agency stem importantly from opportunistic agents that principals choose, rationally, not to control perfectly.

The very terms used in the economic literature to identify the characteristic problems of agency display this dismal view of the nature of agent-principal relations. Under "moral hazard," principals find it costly to observe agent behavior, making it possible for those opportunistic agents to take advantage of their relationship with the principal; the agent's action may be "hidden" from the principal. Thus, agents who purchase insurance take less care with their valuables because they will be reimbursed should those valuables suffer loss; their careless behavior is hidden from the principal. Under "adverse selection," information about the agent's qualities is hidden from the principal (i.e., costly to reveal to the principal), though known to the agent. This permits opportunistic agents to take advantage of their knowledge. Thus, agents misrepresent their real abilities in order gain employment, and employees deliberately underperform or shirk because they know that the principal lacks the expertise to know that higher levels of performance are possible. Arrow terms these two problems of agency, hidden action (moral hazard) and hidden information (adverse selection), respectively (see Arrow, 1985). As developed below, it turns out that reliance on these two problems misrepresents important aspects of agency, some of which produce far more positive outcomes than the classic model would suggest.

The literature on economic agency worries about the ways in which the principal can compensate the agent in order to generate incentives to ameliorate or eliminate these problems. It also observes that external processes, such as competition among agents, can cause them to behave closer to desired standards, squeezing out the residual surplus generated by the imperfections of agency control (see Fama, 1980; on producing congruence between agent and principal, see, e.g., Oviatt, 1988).

I shall take a much broader view of the functions of and performance of agency relationships. Agency is not merely an essential building block of social systems that brings with it unavoidable imperfections in performance. Agency is often used in social relationships as a means of permitting positive outcomes that would be inhibited by self-performance by principals. In this paper, I shall suggest some of the contexts in which "positive" behavior emerges from agency relationships and can be studied by methods consistent with the institutional theory of agency. As noted below, the broader field of positive studies is itself not cohesive, and this short paper will provide only a speculative tour of some of agency's less dismal aspects.

By way of introduction, consider the following "positive" application of agency.

SANTA CLAUS AS AGENT

In a delightful, and at the same time profound piece, Warren Hagstrom (1966) explores the sociological theories that might explain the use of the myth of Santa Claus. He reviews and discounts applications of a series of classic theoretical approaches in the behavioral sciences, such as positivism, naturism, historicism, psychoanalytic theory, Marxism, and the sociology of Emile Durkheim. Applying the insights of Marcel Mauss (1967) on gift-giving in exchange, Hagstrom concludes that Santa Claus is an invention made necessary by the norm of reciprocity and the desire that giving associated with the religious as well as social holiday of Christmas be untainted. Gifts normally create the expectation of reciprocity by placing a burden on the recipient to express thanks to the giver and to prepare to return the favor. By inserting a mythical Santa as the gift-giver, no obligation is created to another person. We note, however, that there remains an obligation to Santa on the contingent basis of continued morally upright behavior; gifts may not be received in the next round if children do not behave themselves. But, as Hagstrom observes, no tangible obligations are left toward the actual donors, e.g., parents. Indeed, completely consistent with the themes of positive psychology, he comments that "whenever we place a high value on the possession of certain positive sentiments we are likely to value the anonymous gift" (Hagstrom, 1966, p. 252).

This may be recognized as a common agency role. That is, agents like Santa Claus are often created in order to bear social burdens that otherwise may pollute social relationships, whether as the result of the norm of reciprocity or because certain processes of attribution are at work that must be dodged, displaced, or refined. Principals displace their problems onto their agents, who, in a way, stand in front and receive the attribution in place of the principal. In other words, agents take the heat for their principals.

Furthermore, Santa, as an invented agent, is always perfect in motivation. Thus, the agent cannot only be a substitute (and, sometimes, protective) recipient, but also take on qualities not available to the principal acting as him or her actual self. Though gift recipients may find that their most desired gifts are not delivered, it is never Santa's fault—indeed, Santa is a means of ensuring that it is no one's fault. Santa's role as agent both protects the hidden donors against creating obligations of reciprocity and insulates the donors against blame for the limitations of gift identification and acquisition. Thus, going beyond Hagstrom's insights, we observe that the agent of Santa Claus is also a means of guaranteeing that the disappointments resulting from the imperfect agency of the gift selector are disarmed or cloaked: No one gets mad at Santa Claus for picking the wrong or inappropriate present. By definition, Santa knows all and is a perfect agent, a perfect gift giver. In Santa's presence, the sour grapes of bad choices become holiday punch.

This highlights an important positive function of agency: agency can be *critically transformational.* Just as anthropologists study liminality in the processes of social ritual (e.g., rites of passage; Moore & Meyerhoff, 1977), so that identities become transformed via the ritual, so do the far more common relationships of agency convert action by the principal to action by the agent: Principal is transformed and appears in the person or actor of the agent. The agent acquires powers that the principal may be denied and/or steps into the principal's place. Third parties see agents rather than principals and act or interpret accordingly. And all this occurs without benefit of phone booth or magic elixir. And, like the world of comic book superheroes, agents can use their powers for good or ill, for "positive" social functions or to create harm. As we shall see below, the study of "positive" behaviors in society has also displayed transformational properties, if only in identifying some of the relatively poorly-understood "positive" attributes and behaviors that sometimes accompany other, less "positive" dimensions of social ties, structures, or institutions.

POSITIVE PSYCHOLOGY AND THEORY FLIPPING

The developing field of positive psychology focuses on such positive aspects of social behavior. The field's founder, Martin Seligman, writing with another major contributor, Mihaly Csikszentmihalyi, observes that the field contributes insights at three levels: At the "subjective level," it seeks to understand "valued subjective experiences," including the sense of well-being, hope, optimism, "flow," and happiness. At the "individual level," it is focused on traits like "capacity for love," forgiveness, originality, spirituality, and wisdom. Finally, at the "group level," it deals with "civic virtues," altruism, tolerance, and "work ethic" (Seligman & Csikszentmihalyi, 2000, p. 5). Cameron, Dutton, and Quinn (2003, p. 7) characterize these as focuses on "positive experiences," "positive individual traits," and "positive institutions." Luthans (2002, p. 698) offers an application to organizational behavior contexts, defining "positive organizational behavior" in terms of "the study and application of positively oriented human resource strengths and psychological capacities that can be measured, developed, and effectively managed for performance improvement in today's workplace." This gives positive psychology an enormous canvas—perhaps impossibly so, were the goal to build anything like a cohesive field with integrated and consistent foci of study and theory logics.

Indeed, however compelling the case for focusing work on areas such as these, a less "positive" observer might complain about an absence of clear field definition and boundaries. Positive psychology cannot extend to all good things that happen in society or that happen to individuals or as part of individual life experiences. If it did, we might come perilously close to coming full circle in an explanation of its relevance to the theory of agency: If agency behavior done relentlessly in self-interest, policed only by competition and the structured institutions of principal instruction to and policing of the agent, leads to greater efficiency, would that be a "positive" result? If dismal methods produce happy outcomes, are they "positive?" Is positive psychology all about process and the quest, about particular positive outcomes, or both—but with what limits?

Social science fields rarely have rigid, easily identifiable boundaries; one has only, for example, to look at the literature's discussion over whether political science is about the "authoritative allocation of values for a society" (Easton, 1953) or something else to see the range of disagreement about a field definition. At the same time, however, fields cannot be so overly inclusive that their subjects of study have little in common, and do not permit the generation of conceptual approaches, including theories, useful across those subjects. The identification of the domains of a field—the characteristic problems, variables, investigative techniques, etc.—presented by a field helps to advance research by focusing it. It economizes by telling researchers what tools should be used so that their work will "fit" with and, perhaps, advance the similarly-based work of others and be more successful in generating meaningful insights about phenomena. If fields are almost randomly scattershot in focus, the development of cumulative understanding via work in the field will be inhibited. Of course, this can be exclusionary by denying legitimacy to innovative work perceived as outside the field's focus. Still, there clearly exist grounds for concern if fields appear too inclusive.

The study of the positive sides of social relationships may also be seen as part of a larger process of backfilling our understandings in social science. This process has moved across the social sciences; it is not just a product of the insights of the important movement advanced by Martin Seligman and others in psychology. Indeed, some of the "discoveries" of the importance of "positive" features of individual, group, and societal behaviors seem to be new only to the psychologists who declared them so. In psychology, the focus of the new positive studies has been on individual-level mechanisms, though some require a relational setting, secondary or target actor, or collective setting for understanding. The study of what are essentially problematic or even pathological aspects of human cognition and emotion have been *flipped* to examine their positive counterparts. Examples in psychology (see, e.g., Snyder & Lopez, 2002) include resilience, creativity, optimism, hope, authenticity, humility, compassion, forgiveness, gratitude, love, empathy, altruism, morality, toughness, humor, and spirituality. But studies of altruism, of gift-giving, and of helping behavior, for example, are considerably older than the positive psychology movement (for older references, see, e.g., Berkowitz, 1972; Bar-Tal, 1976; Leeds, 1963; Macaulay & Berkowitz, 1970; Schwartz, 1967; cf. the famous controversy about Titmuss 1971; there are many other older references on positive psychology topics that appeared before Seligman's call for study of this area). Studies of emotion in organizations (e.g., Fineman, 1993) were already in the literature when Seligman launched the movement.

In sociology, the focus on such concepts as social stratification, prestige systems, authority, power, deviant behavior, and so on, that relate to distinction-producing mechanisms in social systems has long ago been amended with attention to relational factors in exchange that reflect factors of mutual benefits, attractors, dependencies, and so on (e.g., the classic social psychological work of Thibaut and Kelley (1959) and the stream of scholars who developed sociological exchange theory, such as Homans, Blau, Emerson, Anderson, Cook, and others). There is a large literature on social norms that is very relevant to the positive psychology argument. Sociological exchange theory has made it possible to improve our understanding of things like trust, altruism, justice, equity, varieties of social norms, and so on. And several of the classical theorists in sociology worried about the nature of community and/or paid important attention to positive topics, such as understanding of the "other" (e.g., Mead). In anthropology, the study of exchange and of symbolic processes has long identified both positive and negative characters (e.g., Mauss, 1966 and the classic work of Claude Levi-Strauss).

In management theory, we have seen the traditional rationales behind corporate governance flipped with the theory of stewardship. In traditional models of firm governance, the managers are seen as controlled by the shareholders via their representatives on the board of directors. The trick is to prevent the managers from indulging in the opportunistic behavior to which all rational, self-interested actors would be prey. Such managers will use their discretion to steer firm benefits to themselves when that action cannot be observed or corrected by the board. A stewardship theory flips the logic—it assumes that managers will value action for the shareholders first (they will act as stewards), and take benefits to themselves only as a secondary process (Davis, Schoorman, & Donaldson, 1997).

The point is not that positive theory is the proverbial old wine in new bottles—indeed, many features of positive behavior are receiving new and/or greatly expanded attention. But social science has not been as deaf to these issues as the literature implies. In addition, however, it has long been clear that at least some of the areas now thrust forward for their positive characters can exhibit a dark side. In any situation in which social actors seek guidance by external or externalized fixed norms or ideologies, the possibilities span both the positive character of reference to fundamental values, and rigidity of analysis and response. For example, spirituality may bring deep insights and comfort as well as produce rigid, maladaptive responses to environmental challenges. Reference to values can freeze action as well as inform and guide it (on processes of normative referencing, see, e.g., Mitnick, 1995).

I refer to these processes of theory development as *theory flipping* or *turning*. Flipping might be criticized as traditional academic game-playing—developing analysis by taking perverse views contrary to received wisdom. If A is interesting, now claim its opposite, not-A, and develop reasons why not-A could be equally or even more valid than A. Thus the notion that the Interstate Commerce Act of 1887 was the result of pressure from farmers, i.e., the Grange, was countered with the argument that it was merchants, not farmers, was countered with arguments that the firms being regulated wanted it from the start, and was countered by showing how the new agency took balancing or country development interests as central, and so on (for a discussion, see, e.g., Mitnick, 1980). Stake a position; stake the contrary; claim complementary or supplementary arguments; claim unappreciated complexities; and so on—these are the standard elements of field development, and reflect the normal processes of academic evolution.

Besides the dangers of relatively simplistic theory flipping, positive research tends to overemphasize the individual level, including individual cognition and emotion. Many of the qualities studied can only be held or expressed by individual human actors. For example, can organizations be said, meaningfully, to be optimistic? To have humor? To express compassion? To feel empathy? To be spiritual? This raises, implicitly, the conceptual and/or theoretical question of what constitutes "positive" behavior at other levels. In the definitions noted above it is apparent that understanding of what is "positive" at these higher levels is often merely an extension or aggregation of the individual-level qualities. Thus, Luthans (2002) speaks of the "human resource strengths and psychological capacities" in the management setting—but these are, of course, individual in character. Seligman and Csikszentmihalyi (2000) lump such things as "civic virtues," altruism, tolerance, and "work ethic" together—but, except for the somewhat vague reference to "civic virtues," the others are largely individual qualities that are applied or realized in a public or collective setting. Hence there is a real issue of what is "positive" at other levels in the same conceptual or theoretical sense as "positive" qualities at the individual level. Is this really a coherent approach, or merely the shaky extrapolation of a varied class of individual qualities?

Finally, positive research tends to undervalue the role of both cooperative behavior in complex systems and the functional nature of authority and control systems. It is easy to understand the dysfunctions of blind obedience to authority (e.g., Milgram 1974) as a negative character of some agency relationships. But there is an enormous literature, going back to the roots of our understanding of bureaucratic organizations (e.g., Weber), and, indeed, to classic political philosophy (e.g., no less than Hobbes), that has argued for the functionality of systems of central controls. Centralized controls, up to the level of coercion, can, after all, at least in a mythical costless world, freeze out the natural chaos of human systems. Does that make coercion "positive?" Where, then, should the boundaries of "positive" behavior be found? If by some magic an "objective" outside observer could judge that the outcome of the collective institution would be a net benefit, would that be "positive" behavior? Are all behaviors with net positive outcomes, "positive?" So is the study of "positive" behaviors merely the study of all the things that lead to benefits to individuals, organizations, and/or society? Surely that is not much of a boundary at all.

Perhaps one answer may be found in identifying the qualities of social life that either build a positive affect toward others in society or toward society in general, or those qualities that contribute directly to the construction of social ties. "Positive" attributes are *qualities of individual, organizational, or societal behaviors that construct and/or reinforce social ties.* In essence, social structure is seen not only as a kind of placement mechanism that locates social actors and their behaviors, hence distinguishing and differentiating them, but as a system of ties that builds greater wholes because of what holds the pieces in place. And the study of the "positive" aspects of this system focuses on this cement that binds actors to one another and to the system (cf. Elster, 1989). It may be just another way of looking at features of another vague term with much currency in recent research, social capital.

The sources and nature of the "cement" may be subtle, distributed, and embedded in social systems; they need not be simply limited to extensions of the social scientific pantheon of well described and coherent concepts or constructs, so that we merely shelve things like "sense of well-being" or "sense of flow" next to other familiar concepts, such as status, power, or authority. When we speak of trust as "resilient," for example (cf. Ring, 1996), we have identified a subtle yet essential feature of the performance of trust in a system. While trust itself might be labeled, intrinsically, as "positive," there are degrees and qualities of trust. "Resilient trust" is more "positive" than "fragile trust": Resilient trust is based in simple, noncalculative faith in the "goodwill of others" (Ring, 1996, pp. 155–156); fragile trust is based on calculations that assess risk and make predictions about future behavior, concluding that it is rational to trust the other. Institutional features can develop that remove the perceived need for calculation. They inspire faith—generating automatic belief in the benign intentions of physicians that are strangers to us, for example, so that initial fragility can be transformed into resilience. It is not commonplace to make calculations regarding the survivability of a visit to the doctor, and patients accept all manner of personal intervention—blood drawing, tubes and pokes and whatnot, with nary a calculation as to their efficacy or danger to the self. Physicians receive a measure of resilient trust that few would provide to their auto mechanics. The "cement" of trust is subtle and of varied character; because resilient trust is more "positive" than fragile trust, it has different functions and effects in social systems. Thus, movement among dimensions of degree of "positive" character—*positivity?*—as the result of subtle processes in social systems can have critical consequences for the ultimate performance of such systems.

A special interest of the literature on "positive" psychology is what might be termed the *reflective humanism of social ties*. Rather than work from variables that describe dimensions and dynamics of social ties, this literature prefers to focus on the individual and social *experience* of participating in social ties. In essence, it is social ties as seen, every day, from the inside. Thus concepts like "flow," gratitude, empathy, forgiveness, compassion, humility, optimism and hope, humor, and so on, become important topics for research. Some of these are not well-studied, and the positive psychology literature makes an important contribution just by drawing scholarly attention to them.

One potential approach to the problem of field definition for positive psychology is to focus not on the domains of study with the aim of developing and testing descriptive theory—i.e., not on what is or is not included as variables, topics, phenomena for investigation, and so on, but on the *functions* of study in the area and how they can serve social purposes. Robert Giacalone (personal communication, March 8, 2004) argues that "one of the critical components is 'what makes life worth living,'" and that the aim of work in the area should be at least in part also normative—"to find out . . . how we can help make people's lives more worth living." Positive psychology was originally offered for study by its founders (see Seligman's work, cited above) partially as a counter to what were said to be postwar trends in psychology to analyze abnormal and/or undesirable individual and social behaviors and find ways to ameliorate them. In that respect, by focusing on "positive" rather than abnormal or problematic behaviors, positive psychology would also serve the wider social purpose of seeking ways to attain more fulfilling lives.

The concerns about what is "positive" in positive approaches that were expressed above raises the critical issue of what about agency *relationships* will qualify as "positive." Agency is a relationship—it is not some psychological preference, quality, affective condition, or whatever, like many of the targets of current work in positive psychology. It involves a social construction among multiple actors. How can we say that the things that occur in or as a consequence of the operation of this relationship are somehow "positive," and that this "positive" is the same kind of "positive" that research at the individual level describes? If aspects of those relationships, by themselves or emergent in social systems of agency, are embedded and produce the "positive" outcomes by subtle processes, how can we extract and understand them?

Ironically, because it is at base a relationship, not a condition of a solitary actor, agency's economic literature has focused on the impacts on such actors of the distribution of incentives—but not on the relationship implicitly constructed between senders and receivers of incentives (on the incentive *relation*, see Mitnick & Backoff 1984). Thus, those aspects of the theory of agency that are needed to deal with "positive" agency are likely to focus not on reward or incentive-driven behavior, as an economics-derived approach might do, but on institutional structuring of behavior in the relationship. Agency is as much a structural or institutional theory as an incentives theory.

In order to explore the positive features of institutional agency, I shall touch on three topics: Transformational agency; abandonment (orphaned) agency; and one of the characteristic norms of agency, the fiduciary norm.

There are many more such topics that may warrant study in a "positive" analysis of agency.

TRANSFORMATIONAL AGENCY

Implicit understanding of the positive functions of transformational agency is deeply embedded in cultural and organizational life. I began this exercise with a discussion of the social role of Santa Claus, who steps in the way of attributions of obligational reciprocity toward gift originators, and absolves such givers of blame for their poor choices of gifts. Another such example is the biblical agency role of the sacrificial scapegoat, said to take sins into the wilderness. Rather than lay the sources of sins on selves, or on the provocation of others, it allows them to be projected onto a socially-constructed and transformed third party, the goat. This inhibits the destructive effects of focusing on the ill consequences of harmful behavioral decisions—one can move on, as it were—and prevents recriminations and loops of reciprocal blame for the poor behavior. In essence, the goat becomes the agent of both efficiency and stability, preventing the diversion of effort to nonproductive blaming processes and ensuring that social ties remain robust.

But besides the peculiar, specialized institutions like Santa and scapegoats, we see a far more fundamental and pervasive process occurring at the boundaries of every organization. We have seen how agency problems have been sorted by economists into moral hazard (hidden action) and adverse selection (hidden information). Consider the organizational manifestations of adverse selection.

All organizations must import new members. This involves a creation of agency: The external actor is in the position of a supplicant to the organization; he or she desires to become an organizational member or employee (on supplicants and mendicants, see Galaskiewicz, 1985). Organizations establish gatekeepers and processes for entrants' evaluation. Once inside the organization, the new member becomes part of the internal agency system of action. Economists observe that because the new agent has better information on his or her capabilities than that held by his or her organizational principals, the agent can behave opportunistically, diverting value to self-consumption that might have gone to more aggressive service to the principal.

The problem with this model in the context of organizational behavior is that the condition of entry is qualitatively different from the condition of internal agency. The applicant provides claims about past and future performances to the organization, providing such things as letters of reference, resumes, transcripts, and oral claims via interview. Knowing his or her own performance better than the evaluator, the applicant can offer materials selectively and even misrepresent performance quality. Once inside the organization, however, the measures taken of agent performance change dramatically. The agent is no longer judged by the claims of unobservable actions, but potentially by actual, if possibly still limited, observations—after all, the agent is inside. Organizational supervisors might still find difficulty in evaluating the true potential level of agent performance, as well as the actual performances provided. But this situation is now transformed from what existed at entry.

Moreover, it is costly for boundary evaluators to ensure that the agent they obtain for the organization is prepared precisely to perform the tasks needed inside—it is prohibitively expensive to identify and hire perfect agents. Indeed, due to uncertainty and change in task demands, it may be counterproductive to pierce the veil of agent opportunism and hire agents who are perfect for present tasks. Rather, it makes far more sense to economize by hiring agents who are more generalist, who have broader preparations and claimed capabilities, and who can then be specialized over time, once inside, to meet the organization's needs. Thus organizations *do not in general seek to hire perfect agents.* Organizations hire agents whose performance range is at least partially unknown, and then socialize them to the organization's needs (for a development of this argument, see Mitnick, 1994). Organizations deliberately hire imperfect agents because it is more efficient to do the training inside the organization. Hence, were all agents perfect coming in (to specifications in effect when the hire is made), they would soon fail due to performance rigidity as conditions and the organization itself change. The problem of adverse selection then divides into what I have labeled *adverse claims,* the entry problem, and *adverse performance,* the internal agency problem.

Note that by splitting adverse selection into adverse claims and adverse performance, we have a mechanism to "forgive" the unavoidably excessive claims made under job competition and an inexpert principal doing the hiring. That is, all new hires enter with honeymoons, having gone through the ritual transformation of liminality as they cross the organization border. Consider the alternative—organizations would find it difficult to assign and sustain negative labels to each entrant based on perceived inadequacies, a kind of albatross of entry. This is not to say that organizations do not initially recognize the limitations of new hires based on the evidence they presented before entry and the evaluation done in hiring. But there is a bias toward forgiveness and a willingness to be surprised that is extremely functional. Once inside, the applicant has been transformed into a member or employee, and enjoys the membership rights that others enjoy. While the candidate is still new and his or her capabilities at least partially unknown, opportunities are provided to display those capabilities according to internal measures, not according to the previous external claims. In essence, the member can redefine him or herself in terms of the organization's internal expectations and evaluation procedures. When a task is performed, it is unlikely that supervisors will consult the member's resume to assess the quality of task performance. Furthermore, by admitting agents with a range of capabilities that may differ from and/or exceed the needs of present task performance, the organization permits the possibility of *adapting to the agent*, as the new agent injects new and unanticipated insights and unforeseen but needed capabilities into the organizational setting. That is, the transformational process can go both ways.

Thus, the nature of agency relationships and the institutional structure of organizations combine to provide "positive opportunities" both for the transformed agent and the adapting organization.

ORPHANED GOODS AND PARENTED GOODS

Some years ago, I owned a Jeep Grand Wagoneer. It spent most of its time at the dealer's, in repair. Chrysler had just acquired American Motors, the Jeep's manufacturer, and refused to accept the burdens of repairing American's defective products. We had owned it over a year (our mistake), and so it was past the black letter warranty period. I counted more than 50 trips for repairs before we finally traded it in. Usually, the list of items needing repair was long. The dealer was perfectly willing to repair the car (at our cost, after the warranty expiration, of course). Sometimes the dealer's mechanics were incompetent, and sometimes the car's problems were subtle and unusually resistent to intervention even by competent mechanics. We always brought the car in with the expectation that it would be repaired. When we picked the car up, some of the problems would be fixed and some would not be fixed, either because the mechanic failed or the mechanic forgot. If the uncompleted repairs did not relate to a safety issue, we would usually just take the car home, though sometimes I did ask for the minor repairs to be completed as well. I can even remember neglecting to call more minor oversights to the attention of the service manager, and omitting some of the more minor items from the list for the next visit. In general, items would eventually be repaired if we insisted, and persisted.

Getting that car fixed took an awful lot of time and effort. With other issues competing for our time, it was rational to just leave some of the more minor repairs "on the table"—just forgetting about them. That is, there were factors both inside and outside the agency relationship that I had with the repair shop that affected my choices of whether to accept the results of agent action. When dealing with mechanics I thought usually competent, I was reluctant to insist that minor repairs be redone, or completed if they had been overlooked. Besides the costs to me of insisting and persisting, I judged it likely that the mechanic would become less sympathetic to the problems of my "lemon" and, hence, less careful to repair those issues that were safety related. It was in my self-interest to preserve the agency relationship because of the likelihood of repeat performance, and to try to ensure that, when preserved, the agency relationship would be capable of acceptable performance.

In addition, I did not want to appear petty and unreasonable. Despite the fact that the problems were indeed in the car, I felt that insistence on perfect performance would transfer some of the car's problems to me, at least in the eyes of the service manager. Nobody brings in a car for repair 50 times (though the service manager should have had ample experience with other owners of the same model vehicle).

Early in the repair cycles, it seemed to me that the competent mechanics were nice people bearing up under an unreasonable car, and in order to be sensitive to this I did not want to place excessive burdens on someone trying to do a good job. Later, this motivation to be sensitive disappeared. As time went by, I also worried less about appearing unreasonable. In addition, I tended to focus more on the major, safety-related problems, and all but abandoned asking repeatedly about relatively minor repairs.

I could have insisted that the car be repaired in every instance, but chose not to. In other words, I left some of the repairs "on the table." We could understand this simply in terms of the costs of policing the mechanic, and of specifying repeat repairs, exceeding the benefits. That is, we could understand this as a classic agency problem.

But what do we really understand by noting that we left it on the table because the costs exceeded the benefits? That we acted rationally? Perhaps better understanding would be generated if we specified carefully, first, the conditions that led us to abandon some of the expected gain or value that had been established within the terms of the nominal agency task or mission as well as within the expectations or contract set up to govern it, and, second, those conditions that were essentially external to the task that caused us to modify our action with regard to the task. We list these two groups of factors for this example in Table 8.1.

Over time, factors related to effects of the complaints on the other party, and reaction of the other party to the complaints, faded.

Moreover, as noted above, these lists of reasons changed over time. As the repair attempts mounted, I became less concerned about minor repairs and more insistent that the major ones related to safety issues and the reliable operation of the vehicle be completed. I also lost my interest in appearing unreasonable, and lost my interest in being considerate of mechanics. Over time, what I left on the table, and my reasons for what I left, changed.

Table 8.1.   A Catalog of Costs: Leaving It on the Table in Auto Repair

Factors Internal to the Agency Relation

1. *Direct process costs such as time and other resources:* Time and complexity in explaining performance failures, i.e., specification costs in telling the service manager to fix it again. Time in taking the car back again.

2. *Process reactance costs:* Aggravation in repeat specification of the repairs needed and in taking the car back again.

3. *Process projection costs:* Concern about effects on future repair quality from irritating the mechanic.

Factors External to the Agency Relation

4. *Process appearance costs:* Concern about appearing petty and unreasonable.

5. *External impacts of the process; external harm creation:* Concern for the mechanic's feelings.

6. *Opportunity costs* generated by being unable to complete other necessary, unrelated tasks because of the time taken in bringing the car back for repair again.

One of the key logics of agency concerns the production of surplused value between the agent and principal: Because it does not pay the principal to expend resources on ensuring agent behavior that is exactly as desired by the principal, a kind of waste is generated. This may be captured by the agent, as when the agent successfully engages in shirking behavior that exists alongside compliance behavior in service of the principal. Or it may, in effect, just be left on the table, captured by no one or by third parties outside the agency relationship. The approach of economic agency views this as a residual to the agency relationship (cf. Jensen & Meckling, 1976). One of the tasks of the design of economic agency relationships is to reduce the residual as much as possible; the residual is seen as either wasteful and hence properly reducible in the interests of efficiency, or as property that should as much as possible be assigned to and under the direction of the principal. In either case, the residual, uncaptured, unassigned agency cost is treated as exactly that—a cost that the principal might covet as lost, or the agent covet as stolen, or the environment absorb as waste.

What this perspective ignores is that some of what the principal appears to lose in the agency relationship may be deliberately lost, or serve positive social functions outside the realm of principal- or even agent-valued property. I term the value that is, as it were, left on the table, an *orphaned good*. Orphaned goods can be generated *even where the benefits of recovery of the goods exceed the costs*. Such goods should be distinguished from orphan goods in microeconomics, i.e., goods that no one wishes to produce, such as orphan drugs, often because it does not pay them to produce the goods. Orphaned goods, on the other hand, are produced—they are generated and seemingly abandoned by their producer, but that abandonment has a rational basis. A concept somewhat parallel to that of orphaned goods is that of *parented goods*, goods that are deliberately recovered and possessed by the principal *even when the costs of recovery exceed the nominal or objective benefits* (on these goods, see Mitnick, 2004; the arguments in this section are drawn largely from this work).

Obviously, the determination of whether goods are orphaned or parented depends heavily on the metric used to determine rational action in the agency relationship. One can always redefine the boundaries to include the goals of orphaning or parenting, so that they accompany other goals related to the bases of the agency relationship. That is, orphaning and parenting are simply external mechanisms that could always be internalized, restoring the narrow logic of agency. Doing so, however, obscures key understandings behind the rationale, dynamics, and contents of actions by the agent and principal. Indeed, with respect to the nominal grounds establishing the agency relationship, orphaning and parenting appear as irrational acts that are difficult for observers to understand. In addition, orphaning and parenting often appear *in the path* of agent action; they are not always anticipated in the nominal agency relationship. Decisions to "leave it on the table" are often made in process, not by antecedent contract; they reflect in part the uncertainties and casual cost impositions of agency. By recognizing orphaning and parenting processes, we can expand our understanding of the range of behaviors that accompany agent actions for principals.

Orphaned goods that are left on the table because of costs appearing within the agency relationship may be termed *endogenous orphaned goods*. Those that are tabled, yet would appear to provide net abandonment benefits within the relationship—that is, whose orphaning appears irrational within but not necessarily outside the relationship—may be termed *exogenous orphaned goods*. We can similarly identify *endogenous* vs. *exogenous parented goods*, depending on whether there are net recovery benefits identified within or outside the relationship.

Consider now the "positive" features of orphaning and parenting. Orphaning and parenting involve choices about compliance with, or, alternatively, divergence from, the strict logics of agent service and control. They typically involve factors that are *experienced* by the agent or principal as outside the relationship, though a global analysis could simply redefine them as endogenous. And they are often choices that evolve through the process of agency, as agent and/or principal encounter unanticipated factors. Within the logic of agency, they can reflect unexpected costs that cause abandonment ("cutting it adrift") or unexpected benefits that lead to recovery ("pulling it back" or "reeling it in").

We may thus understand orphaning and parenting as among the circumstances defining such "positive" phenomena as the leaving of thoughtful and/or generous gifts, the capturing of external benefits such as "peace of mind," or the termination or avoidance of aggravation, on the one hand, and the assertion of responsibility or accountability or the assertion of unique or nonsubstitutable value, on the other. These phenomena are characteristically "positive" in the sense it is treated most commonly in the recent literature in this area. They represent humanistic expressions of value within the experience of the social tie, depicting such conditions as psychological states of mind; emotional conditions; sensitivity to the other; norms, ethical statements, or values; and so on.

Returning to the Jeep Grand Wagoneer example, note how the mix of items left "on" or "off" the table changed, and for what reasons. My initial inclination was to not appear unreasonable and to have concern for the mechanic's feelings, factors that may be viewed as exogenous (they were not directly related to the agency task requested, repair of the car). These factors, which had influenced what I left on the table, were now excluded. My concerns narrowed to safety issues, the core concern of an auto repair, as well as to basic items that were needed to keep the car running. I continued to *not* insist that all the requested repairs be completed—so items were still being left on the table—because of the direct costs to me of insisting on perfect repair. But the list of items requested was itself narrowing to the core items important to safe and reliable operation of the vehicle. The niceties of declining to request perfection over small issues were no longer left on the table, and I resolved the dilemma involved by simply not requesting the small repairs. In essence, the exogenous factors that caused me to leave items on the table were ignored, and only endogenous factors influenced the agency relationship.

To put it simply, the supply of orphaned goods depends on the hassle both of leaving and of retrieving them. What we leave on the table is usually not a significant component of the core agency task. We leave pennies in the cup by the cash register for the convenience of the next purchaser. We round up when dividing the check among a group of diners. We leave gas in the car and oil in the furnace when we leave. We don't ask the mechanic a second or third time to fix the trim problem on the auto dash when he or she has forgotten to do it while engaged for hours in replacing virtually the entire electronic system of a year-old car. Orphaned goods relate typically to our senses of grace, of consideration, of pettiness. They make the donor of such goods feel generous and connected to the social fabric of interpersonal exchange; they are a way of doing uncompensated, unexpected favors. Much like the case of transformational agency, orphaned goods are quietly but knowingly left on the table by both parties and become a way to give gifts without triggering the obligation of reciprocity. Orphaned goods that are highlighted by the donor will elicit reciprocity, and will tend to become endogenous to the relationship; true orphaned goods are "quiet" goods. But if exchange partners act in clear violation of the core agency tasks, the rationale for providing gifts at the margins fades.

Orphaned goods can also be seen as a way of declining to insist on perfection. Insisting on perfect performance has costs that go beyond the strict ones of instructing and monitoring agents in and for the performance. Perfection generates conflict at the margins, and, unless involved in performance in high reliability technologies, such as nuclear reactor maintenance or aircraft carrier operations (see, e.g., Roberts, 1993, 1998), it is often not necessary for task completion. Declining to push for perfection smooths transitions and encourages repeated relationships. It reduces conflict and creates reputations of being "easy to work with" and "being reasonable" in work settings. Thus the "positive" aspects of use of orphaned goods in agency include both the efficient maintenance of social ties and the "quiet" utility that individuals receive from participating in agency relationships.

THE FIDUCIARY NORM: A NORM OF AGENCY

Several social norms appear characteristically in agency relationships. They are responsible for a number of the "positive" features that can be observed in agency.

Where both the agent and the principal consent to the agency, but not as part of a mutual agreement or contract regarding their subsequent relationship, we may see norms of giving, helping, and reciprocity. Where there is a mutual agreement or contract, we may see the promise-keeping/"valid agreements should be kept" norm (Macaulay, 1963) as well as the fiduciary norm (for a more complete analysis, see Mitnick, 1973, 1974, 1975a). In what follows, I shall focus on the fiduciary norm.

The fiduciary norm was first identified as a genuine social norm (as against a "principle") by Mitnick (1973, 1974, 1975a, b) and by Stinchcombe (1986; original paper, 1975). More recent work in the law and economics literature on agency and the fiduciary principle has included Clark (1985), Easterbrook and Fischel (1991), and Cooter (1991). In sociology, Shapiro (1987) discusses the social functions of fiduciary-like relationships. There is of course a huge literature in the law on the fiduciary principle and its role in the laws of trust, contract, and agency.

As a social norm, the fiduciary norm instructs the agent under contract to act diligently, with the skills at his or her disposal, solely in the interest of the principal, without reference to any agent self-interests that may appear in the course of performing the agency. The norm is triggered in social relationships of "acting for" when the agent, having agreed to act for the principal, must take discretionary agency for a dependent principal. Agents have *discretion* with respect to their principals to the extent that they can make choices of actions that make a difference to the principals. In other words, discretion means not just the existence of choice, but that the choice available make a substantive difference to the party the choice affects, the principal. The greater the discretion of the agent, and, consequently, the more dependent the principal on the agent's actions, the more strongly the norm is prescribed.

In its role as a social norm, the fiduciary norm is a recognition that society as well as legal practice recognize that when one party is dependent on the action of another, the agent must not be allowed to take self-interested advantage of that dependence. The fiduciary norm is a true norm, and not just a standard, rule-of-thumb, or legal principle. In social circumstances of discretion/dependency, societal actors will sanction the agent for nonperformance to the strictures of the norm, whether or not the context is a formal legal relationship such as trustee-beneficiary. If a young person agrees to mow the lawn of an elderly neighbor, but forgets and goes to play ball with his friends instead, all the neighbors will be upset. They will deliver sanctions to the young person in forms ranging from icy social relations to outright scolding. When we vote for a President who promises to save Social Security, and nothing of the sort occurs, we perceive a violation of the trust in the agency created by the election. And we vote him or her out of office at the next opportunity (or so theory would predict!).

The fiduciary norm carries with it several subnorms, each an elaboration of the agent's need to act with full devotion to the principal, causing no harm to the principal: Confidentiality between the agent and principal so that nothing adversely affecting the principal might become known by others; full disclosure to the principal of all relevant information, including potential conflicts of interest; and good conduct by the agent, because the agent's poor behavior might harm the principal, given the externally-held knowledge that the agent is engaged in action for the principal.

The sensitivity of the fiduciary's duty of care is traditionally illustrated by Chief Justice Cardozo's expressive, if florid language in the case of *Meinhard* vs. *Salmon*, 249 N.Y. 458 (1928), at p. 464:

Many forms of conduct permissible in a workaday world for those acting at arm's length, are forbidden to those bound by fiduciary ties. A trustee is held to something stricter than the morals of the market place. Not honesty alone, but the punctilio of an honor the most sensitive, is then the standard of behavior. (See, e.g., Scott, 1949, p. 555.)

Thus agency, by creating the conditions in which the fiduciary norm might be active, can generate an important range of "positive" social behaviors. The agent as fiduciary is a mechanism well designed to guard institutions that must protect the vulnerable. Such beneficiaries of fiduciary agency often cannot express their wishes, or their detailed wishes, directly; they may be ill, incompetent, or deceased. Perhaps the best understood case is trusteeship, in which the trustees must operate under strict fiduciary guidelines.

Indeed, trust itself is a relationship based in part on there being a vulnerable party who elects to place reliance on an agent (e.g., Mayer, Davis, & Schoorman 1995), generating trust in the agent. Thus the operation of the fiduciary norm is coextensive with the creation of trust—by the principal and/or beneficiary (in the three-party case, the agent can be serving a principal by acting as trustee for a beneficiary) and in those who observe or otherwise interact with the agency relationship (Shapiro, 1987). Hence we see immediately the relevance to "positive" concerns: By triggering trust, agency is an important mechanism by which dependent relationships in society receive care.

Because agents can generate trust, agents in relationships in which the fiduciary norm is operative can perform effectively as certification and legitimizing agents. Agents can provide *assurance* of the credibility and legitimacy of both public and private sector activities. Thus, CPAs certify tax returns for clients who are dependent on their esoteric and expert knowledge of the tax code. Boards of directors legitimize the corporation for dependent shareholders, holding a fiduciary relationship to those shareholders both in descriptive and normative roles, at least in the narrowly classic concept of corporate governance.

Operation of the fiduciary norm significantly lowers the costs of agency: Principal costs in specifying to the agent what is to be done, monitoring what is actually done, and policing the agent's possibly deviant efforts so that they produce outcomes closer to principal preferences, are all reduced by having agents dedicated to serving the principal. In the best of worlds, the principal who lacks expertise to act on his or her own would engage a perfectly expert agent who would discern what the principal wants and devise solutions in agency. Indeed, by specialization—hiring an agent who is both loyal and expert, freeing the principal to focus on tasks for which he or she is already capable—agency relationships capture one of the key reputed Weberian advantages of bureaucratic systems. Bureaucracies are hierarchies of agency relationships. Like markets, hierarchies of perfect agencies can thus capture benefits that are only available in systems of social exchange (cf. Miller, 1992). Hence the concept of "loyalty" as a *normative* component of the fiduciary *principle* (e.g., Michalos, 1995) has its counterpart in the *descriptive* phenomena of the obligations placed on social actors subject to the fiduciary *norm*.

Agents who provide good service are efficient and reliable in doing their agency tasks; in roles requiring repeated activities, they are predictable. Hence, third parties enjoy interactions with agents who are subject to the fiduciary norm—having reliable, predictable exchange partners reduces the costs of the third parties who interact with them as well. Thus, there is external support for the practice of fiduciary agency. This tends to provide support for the creation of institutions of agency: In essence, there is both an internal and an external market for such reliable agents. Professional roles that involve such agency, such as CPAs, lawyers, physicians, pharmacists, and so on, develop institutions that formalize and police the fiduciary role. The professional role has a formalized statement of the fiduciary norm in its code of ethics, and it requires specialized training to ensure the perfection with which the professional is able to assess what the client wants and provide the services to satisfy those wants.

Because agents are often employed due to a disability of the principal—the principal is unavailable to do the task, or lacks competence to do the task—the principal is inherently unable to evaluate whether the agent is actually providing the quality of service for which he or she was engaged as agent. This produces some of the central problems of agency noted earlier: the inability to observe, and the inability to evaluate, the agent's work. Ensuring that the agent acts with the fiduciary norm is a way of compensating for these characteristic problems; one simply lets the agent correct the problems by him or herself. But real world agents are not likely to be so solicitous of their principals, nor are they likely to be perfect agents, even when such agency is prescribed by the norm. There is, of course, a very large and often critical literature on the performance of professionals.

What can be of even more concern, however, is what can occur when agents, acting under high levels of uncertainty, pursue their tasks as agents all too well. Incompetent or unaware principals cannot tell their agents that they have done enough, stop. It is reasonable for careful agents instructed by the norm to give their principals at least as much as they think they want; in most economic relationships, the assumption is that the other party is greedy, i.e., that more is always better. But in social relationships, as against the market, more is not always better, and principal preferences may not be shaped in the simple way assumed by agents hired for narrowly-defined tasks. It is also possible that agents are engaged precisely because the principal wants distasteful tasks performed in an extreme way; the principal him or herself would not be capable of the maximizing behavior that the fiduciary agent would display.

Furthermore, as noted earlier in this paper, agency is transformational—the fiduciary agent is able to perform distasteful, even extreme actions, because it is not the person of the agent that is perceived *by the agent* to be doing the task. It is, rather, the principal acting via the conduit of the agent. Thus, ironically, the fiduciary norm both permits soldiers to kill who would not kill in ordinary social life, and physicians to take extraordinary efforts to save the lives of mutely ill patients.

Thus, far from being "positive," the logic of agency brings us full circle to among the darkest behaviors recorded—those done "under orders." What the logic of agency tells us is that the problem is not merely that of obedience to authority, as in Milgram's classic work (1974), and in that of other social psychologists who have studied the alteration of behaviors once the individual has been placed in a role (e.g., Zimbardo's prison experiment). It is not just the role that takes over, or the response to authoritative instruction. It is the norm of fiduciary service that converts "positive" help for the dependent into mindless and extreme agency. It is not just that the agent does things that the principal wants; it is also that what is done is done with such ruthless efficiency.

CONCLUSION: AGENCY AND POSITIVE BEHAVIOR

In conclusion, agency provides many contexts and opportunities for the expression of positive behaviors: Agency is a means of jettisoning social burdens via the creation of symbolic agents, as in scapegoats and Santa Clauses, and for transforming the character of the principal and/or agent so that the agent appears as the principal or in another guise. This can facilitate a variety of organizational and social functions. Even the residuals of agency—the nominal costs or unrecovered byproducts of agency—can be employed in "positive" ways, as when orphaned goods smooth transactions and remove potential social frictions. The fiduciary norm acts as a double-edged sword, permitting increased trust, efficiency, and reliability in agency, as well as providing a mechnanism by which principals acquire both relentless agents and escape the direct consequences of those agents' work.

This paper has focused on the intrinsic or characteristic features of agency relationships that would be of interest to a positive psychologist. What is left unsaid here, however, is what consequences would follow from agents and principals who as individuals in the social fabric adopted behavior patterns consistent with the normative aims of the positive psychologists. That is, what would things be like if all agents and principals were hopeful, optimistic, both trusting and trustworthy, were capable of loving one another and of offering forgiveness, could act as altruists, were tolerant, were sensitive to duties to the common weal, and so on? Surely the repair of Grand Wagoneers would be different (Utopia at the repair shop at last?)! Left for study are what changes/improvements in the status of any of these individual experiences/traits/social attitudes would mean for the performance of the social institutions that so often have depended on the development of efficient means to control the dismal features of agency.

These observations do not exhaust the areas in which agency has relevance for "positive" analysis. Agency is a fundamental part of social and organizational behavior, and if "positive" approaches are to generate new insights into such behavior, we expect that at least some of those insights will be found in the pervasive behaviors of agents.

ACKNOWLEDGMENTS

I would like to thank the three editors for inviting my participation in this volume, and Robert Giacalone for supplying some extremely helpful comments and references.

REFERENCES

Arrow, K.J. (1985). The economics of agency. In J.W. Pratt & R.J. Zeckhauser (Eds.), *Principals and agents: The structure of business* (pp. 37–51). Boston: Harvard Business School Press.

Berkowitz, L. (1972). Social norms, feelings, and other factors affecting helping and altruism. In L. Berkowitz (Ed.), *Advances in experimental social psychology* (Vol. 6, pp. 63–108). New York: Academic Press.

Cameron, K.S., Dutton, J.E., & Quinn, R.E. (Eds). (2003). *Positive organizational scholarship: Foundations of a new discipline.* San Francisco: Berrett-Koehler.

Clark, R.C. (1985). Agency costs versus fiduciary duties. In J.W. Pratt & R. Zeckhauser (Eds.), *Principals and agents: The structure of business* (pp. 55–79). Boston: Harvard Business School Press.

Cooter, R., & Freedman, B.J. (1991). The fiduciary relationship: Its economic character and legal consequences. *New York University Law Review, 66,* 1045–1075.

Davis, J.H., Schoorman, F.D., & Donaldson, L. (1997). Toward a stewardship theory of management. *Academy of Management Review, 22,* 20–47.

Easterbrook, F.H., & Fischel, D.R. (1991). *The economic structure of corporate law.* Cambridge: Harvard University Press.

Easton, D. (1953). *The political system: An inquiry into the state of political science.* New York: Alfred A. Knopf.

Elster, J. (1989). *The cement of society: A study of social order.* Cambridge: Cambridge University Press.

Fama, E.F. (1980). Agency problems and the theory of the firm. *Journal of Political Economy, 88,* 288–307.

Fineman, S. (Ed.). (1993). *Emotion in organizations.* Newbury Park, CA: Sage Publications.

Galaskiewicz, J. (1985). *Social organization of an urban grants economy: A study of business philanthropy and nonprofit organizations.* Orlando, FL: Academic Press.

Gouldner, A.W. (1960). The norm of reciprocity: A preliminary statement. *American Sociological Review, 25*(2), 161–178.

Granovetter, M.S. (1973). The strength of weak ties. *American Journal of Sociology, 78*(6), 1360–1380.

Granovetter, M. (1985). Economic action and social structure: The problem of embeddedness. *American Journal of Sociology, 91*(3), 481–510.

Hagstrom, W.O. (1966). What is the meaning of Santa Claus? *The American Sociologist, 1*(5), 248–252.

Jensen, M.C., & Meckling, W.H. (1976). Theory of the firm: Managerial behavior, agency costs and ownership structure. *Journal of Financial Economics, 3,* 305–360.

Leeds, R. (1963). Altruism and the norm of giving. *Merrill-Palmer Quarterly, 9,* 229–240.

Luthans, F. (2002). The need for and meaning of positive organizational behavior. *Journal of Organizational Behavior, 23,* 695–706.

Macaulay, S. (1963). Non-contractual relations in business: A preliminary study. *American Sociological Review, 28,* 55–67.

Macaulay, J., & Berkowitz, L. (Eds.). (1970). *Altruism and helping behavior.* New York: Academic Press.

Mauss, M. (1966). *The gift.* New York, W.W. Norton.

Mayer, R.C., Davis, J.H., & Schoorman, F.D. (1995). An integrative model of organizational trust. *Academy of Management Review, 20*(3), 709–734.

Michalos, A.C. (1995). *A pragmatic approach to business ethics.* Thousand Oaks, CA: Sage Publications.

Milgram, S. (1974). *Obedience to authority.* New York: Harper and Row.

Miller, G.J. (1992). *Managerial dilemmas: The political economy of hierarchy.* Cambridge: Cambridge University Press.

Mitnick, B.M. (1973). *Fiduciary rationality and public policy: The theory of agency and some consequences.* Paper presented at the 1973 Annual Meeting of the American Political Science Association, New Orleans, LA. *Proceedings of the APSA, 1973* (University Microfilms).

Mitnick, B.M. (1974). *The theory of agency: The concept of fiduciary rationality and some consequences.* Unpublished Ph.D. dissertation, Department of Political Science, University of Pennsylvania.

Mitnick, B.M. (1975a). *The theory of agency: The fiduciary norm.* Paper presented at the 1975 Annual Meeting of the American Sociological Association, San Francisco, CA.

Mitnick, B.M. (1975b). The theory of agency: The policing "paradox" and regulatory behavior. *Public Choice, 24,* 27–42.

Mitnick, B.M. (1980). *The political economy of regulation: Creating, designing, and removing regulatory forms.* New York: Columbia University Press.

Mitnick, B.M. (1985). *Agents of legitimacy: Pantheonic directorates and the management of organization environments.* Paper presented at the Fifth Annual Sunbelt Social Networks Conference, Palm Beach Hilton Hotel, Palm Beach, FL, February 14–17.

Mitnick, B.M. (Ed.). (1993). *Corporate political agency: The construction of competition in public affairs.* Newbury Park, CA: Sage Publications.

Mitnick, B.M. (1994). *Delegation of specification: An agency theory of organizations.* Paper presented at the 1994 Annual Meeting of the Academy of Management, Loews Anatole Hotel, Dallas, TX, August 14–17.

Mitnick, B.M. (1995). Systematics and CSR: The concept of normative referencing. *Business & Society 34*(1), 5–33.

Mitnick, B.M. (2004). *Leaving it on the table: A theory of orphaned and parented goods.* Unpublished paper.

Mitnick, B.M., & Backoff, R.W. (1984). The incentive relation in implementation. In G. C. Edwards, III (Ed.), *Public policy implementation* (Vol. 3, pp. 59–122) of S. Nagel (Ed.), *Public policy studies: A multi-volume treatise.* Greenwich, CT: JAI Press.

Moore, S.F., & Myerhoff, B.F. (1977). *Secular ritual.* Assen/Amsterdam: Van Gorum; Humanities Press.

Oviatt, B.M. (1988). Agency and transaction cost perspectives on the manager-shareholder relationship: Incentives for congruent interests. *Academy of Management Review, 13*(2), 214–225.

Pratt, J.W., & Zeckhauser, R. (Ed.). (1985). *Principals and agents: The structure of business.* Boston: Harvard Business School Press.

Ring, P.S. (1996). Fragile and resilient trust and their roles in economic exchange. *Business & Society 35*(2), 148–175.

Roberts, K.H. (1990). Managing high reliability organizations. *California Management Review, 32*(4),101–113.

Roberts, K.H. (Ed.). (1993). *New challenges to understanding organizations.* New York: Macmillan.

Ross, S.A. (1973). The economic theory of agency: The principal's problem. *American Economic Review, 62*(2), 134–139.

Schwartz, B. (1967). The social psychology of the gift. *American Journal of Sociology, 73*(1), 1–11.

Scott, A. (1949). The fiduciary principle. *California Law Review, 37,* 539–555.

Seligman, M.E.P., & Csikszentmihalyi, M. (2000). Positive psychology: An introduction. *American Psychologist, 55*(1), 5–14.

Shapiro, S.P. (1987). The social control of impersonal trust. *American Journal of Sociology, 93*(3), 623–658.

Snyder, C.R., & Lopez, S.J. (Eds.). (2002). *Handbook of positive psychology.* Oxford: Oxford University Press.

Stinchcombe, A.L. (1986). *Stratification and organization: Selected papers.* Cambridge: Cambridge University Press. (Includes original paper on the fiduciary norm presented at 1975 Public Choice Society meeting.)

Thibaut, J.W., & Kelley, H.H. (1959). *The social psychology of groups.* New York: Wiley.

Titmuss, R.M. (1971). *The gift relationship.* New York: Vintage.

CHAPTER 9

"THAT AT WHICH ALL THINGS AIM"

Happiness, Wellness, and the Ethics of Organizational Life

James O. Pawelski and Isaac Prilleltensky

INTRODUCTION

Recent scandals in the business world have underscored the need for a more effective application of ethics in organizational life. Business executives, governmental regulators, and educators at all levels have been asking tough questions about how moral reasoning and ethical behavior can be most effectively cultivated. These scandals, we believe, also point out a need for a more adequate theoretical understanding of ethics. In order to create more responsible organizational structures, more enlightened public policy, and more relevant curricula, we need to have a more articulate understanding of the good we are trying to achieve.

Aristotle (1934) understood the importance of a careful study of the Good as a beginning point for ethics. The entire first book of his *Nicomachean Ethics* is dedicated to a detailed analysis of the Good, which he defines

Positive Psychology in Business Ethics and Corporate Responsibility, pages 191–208
Copyright © 2005 by Information Age Publishing

as "That at which all things aim" (I. i. 2). In the realm of ethics, he concludes, the End at which all actions aim is happiness (*eudaimonia*) (I. vii. 8).

More recently, positive psychologists have initiated a program for research that intends to help "articulate a vision of the good life that is empirically sound . . ." (Seligman & Csikszentmihalyi, 2000, p. 5). Still in its infancy, positive psychology (PP) is already making important empirical contributions to our understanding of the good life and how it can be cultivated. The vision of the good life articulated by PP, however, must not only be empirically sound; it must also be theoretically sound. As with any empirical inquiry, PP is in need of continual care to ensure that the data being collected is interpreted properly and is properly integrated into the developing vision. This theoretical work is especially important now, when PP is still in its formative stages.

We believe careful attention to a theoretical understanding of the Good is crucial for PP. Since different teams of researchers are investigating different positive aims, it is easy to become confused by the various terms used in PP and by the different ways in which the same terms are sometimes used.

By paying careful attention to conceptual clarification, positive psychologists can avoid the unfortunate and dangerous confusions to which the vague and ambiguous use of terms typically leads. As PP moves more and more into the realm of practice, the need for avoiding these confusions becomes especially acute. Adequate clarity will help protect practitioners of PP from the dangers of overreach—of claiming more for their interventions than is empirically warranted.

We believe a comparison of the aims of PP with those of wellness can help make valuable contributions to the conceptual clarifications of which PP is in need. Accordingly, we discuss the relation between the Good at which PP aims and the Good at which wellness aims. This comparison makes possible some suggestions for the application of PP to organizational life in a way that minimizes the risk of overreach.

POSITIVE PSYCHOLOGY AND WELLNESS

The Good at which PP aims is clearly happiness. Martin Seligman, the acknowledged leader of the field, chose "*Authentic Happiness*" as the title of his book on positive psychology. Elsewhere, Seligman (2003) writes, "Positive psychology is about 'happiness. . . .'" Acknowledging that "happiness" is a "promiscuously overused word," he explains more clearly what he means by it: "I use 'happiness' and 'well-being' as soft, overarching terms to describe the goals of the whole positive psychology enterprise" (p. 127). Happiness can be achieved, he explains, in a variety of ways. Most basically, it can be achieved through the pleasant life (through cultivating positive emotions), through the good life (through cultivating strengths and virtues), and through the meaningful life (through cultivating the application of one's strengths and virtues to something much larger than oneself).

The Good at which wellness aims is broader than the happiness of PP. Wellness is a positive state of affairs brought about by the simultaneous and balanced satisfaction of personal, relational, and collective needs; needs that are met by cogent values and adequate material and psychological resources (Nelson & Prilleltensky, in press; Prilleltensky, Nelson, & Peirson, 2001). This definition is readily applicable to organizations, whereby the wellness of individual workers is contingent upon the fulfillment of personal needs, collaborative relationships, and supportive and effective environments. It is hard to imagine how workers may be fully satisfied if they attain wellness in only one of these three domains. For personal satisfaction, however high, cannot neutralize the negative effects of conflictive relationships and corrosive environments. Organizations cannot thrive in the absence of any one of the three domains of wellness. Harmonious corporate cultures and friendly relationships, however desirable, cannot compensate for unhealthy occupational conditions afflicting individual workers. Personal wellness and organizational wellness are highly interdependent (Barrett, 2003; Burke, 2002; Chowdhury, 2003; Paloutizian, Emmons, & Keortgee, 2003; Putnam & Feldstein, 2003).

Our conception of wellness, as illustrated in Figure 9.1, entails four domains created by two intersecting continua. The individual—collective continuum tells us that wellness is a function of attributes present in both people and communities. The deficits—strengths continuum, in turn, indicates that wellness increases by reducing negative factors and enhancing positive qualities in people, communities, and environments. Thus, while wellness is experienced at the individual level in terms of happiness, joy, meaning, longevity and health, many of its enabling factors extend well beyond the individual. Similarly, while wellness promotion strives to increase the joy, meaning, health and longevity of individuals, its strategies go well beyond the individual and include organizational, environmental, social and collective interventions (Stokols, 2000, 2003). The basic assumption behind this conceptualization, well-supported by extensive research, is that the wellness of the individual is influenced not only by internal factors, but also by transactions between the person and the organizational, social and physical environment (Eckersley, Dixon, & Douglas, 2001; Jamner & Stokols, 2000; Keating & Hertzman, 1999; Marmot & Wilkinson, 1999; Shinn & Toohey, 2003).

Our definition of wellness entails the balanced satisfaction of needs at three points along the individual—collective continuum: (a) personal needs such as physical and psychological well-being, (b) relational needs

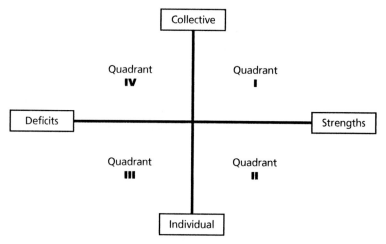

Figure 9.1.   Domains of wellness.

such as social support, affection, caring and compassion, and (c) collective needs such as social justice, fairness, equality, and public resources (Nelson & Prilleltensky, in press; Prilleltensky & Nelson, 2002; Prilleltensky et al., 2001). Organizations can be sites of wellness or sites of suffering, sites of justice or sites of exploitation. By striving to fulfill personal, relational, and collective needs of employees, managers, and the community at large, organizations can become powerful vehicles of wellness. By ignoring any one of these domains, for any one of these populations, they can cause considerable harm. Workplace spirituality is one force pushing organizations and businesses to engage in the former and avoid the latter (Cavanagh & Bandsuch, 2002; Giacalone & Jurkiewicz, 2003). An inspirational example comes from Aaron Feuerstein, CEO of Malden Mills, who in 1995 witnessed how fire destroyed his textile mill. Without hesitation, he announced that he would keep all the 3200 workers on his payroll until the plant was rebuilt (Cavanagh & Bandsuch, 2002). Counter examples, where corporations abandon communities in terrible shape, also abound (Bakan, 2004; Korten, 1995).

Within the context of the wellness framework, one would expect PP to be located mostly within Quadrant II. Among the social sciences, psychology is the one that has historically focused most on the individual, and the very name of PP is intended to distinguish it from the deficits approach of Quadrant III. Indeed, this expectation is born out in the current development of PP. Although it acknowledges the value and importance of deficit approaches in mainstream psychology, PP is focused on the development of a strengths approach to human flourishing. And although it defines itself as a "science of positive subjective experience, positive individual traits, and positive institutions" that seeks to "understand and build the factors that allow individuals, communities, and societies to flourish" (Seligman & Csikszentmihalyi, 2000, p. 5), PP has so far made the most progress at the subjective and individual levels of development. Research on subjective well-being, positive affect, and life satisfaction, the development of the Values in Action Classification of Strengths, and the study of how those strengths can be applied by individuals in their social interactions are all very important components of Quadrant II. But these important components are circumscribed areas of research residing within this quadrant. Physical health, educational attainment, and economic security, as measured by fairly objective tools, are other key components of wellness located within Quadrant II.

While PP represents a significant advance in wellness in the domains in which it is active, the position it occupies in the total landscape of wellness presents potential ethical dilemmas related to its scope. As with all approaches to human and organizational health and development, proponents should make sure to define what aspects of wellness are covered by their research and what kinds of persons and organizations they are uniquely qualified to help.

ETHICS OF SCOPE

As we have noted, the Good at which PP aims is happiness. Yet it is as true today as it was in Aristotle's that "What constitutes happiness is a matter of dispute" (1934, I. iv. 2). Ken Sheldon, Sonja Lyubomirsky, and David Schkade (2003) understand happiness to be a technical term within PP, a term roughly synonymous with "subjective well-being." They write, ". . . we will define happiness as it is most often defined in the literature—that is, in terms of frequent positive affect, high life satisfaction, and infrequent negative affect. These three constructs are the three primary components of subjective well-being, according to Diener and colleagues. . . . [W]e will use the terms 'happiness' or 'subjective well-being,' although we will also discuss mood and life satisfaction at times, based on the specific ideas and data being presented" (p. 11). These writers continue:

> It is also important to note that we use a subjectivist definition of happiness, which commonly relies on people's self-reports. We believe this is appropriate and even necessary given our view that happiness must be defined from the perspective of the person. In other words, happiness is primarily a subjective phenomenon, for which the final judge should be "whoever lives inside a person's skin". . . . Our primary focus in this article is on a person's characteristic level of happiness during a particular period in his or her life which we term the *chronic happiness level*. We define happiness this way because we wish

to identify a quantity that is more enduring than momentary or daily happiness, but that is also somewhat malleable over time, and thus amenable to meaningful pursuit. By this definition, while it is possible to alter one's chronic happiness level, it is much more difficult to do so than to alter one's happiness level at a particular moment or on a particular day. Operationally, one might define a person's chronic happiness level in terms of his or her retrospective summary judgments regarding his/her mood and satisfaction during some recent period (such as the last 2, 6, or 12 months), or as the average of momentary judgments of mood and satisfaction made at several times during the selected period. (Sheldon et al., 2003, pp. 12–13)

Mihaly Csikszentmihalyi takes a very different approach to happiness. Although much of his work on happiness antedates the official beginning of positive psychology, it has been grandfathered into the current movement. For Csikszentmihalyi, happiness can best be understood in terms of optimal experience, which is "based on the concept of *flow*—the state in which people are so involved in an activity that nothing else seems to matter; the experience itself is so enjoyable that people will do it even at great cost, for the sheer sake of doing it" (Csikszentmihalyi, 1990, p. 4). On this view, happiness is an ordered state of consciousness that comes from learning how to control one's experience. Csikszentmihalyi is quick to point out, however, that this state of consciousness may not be particularly pleasurable at the time it occurs.

For Martin Seligman, as we have seen, happiness serves as the ultimate goal of PP, but it is not a technical term in the movement. Seligman tries to integrate the various approaches of PP researchers not so much by focusing on the attempt to find a rigorous definition for the term as by working to describe various paths to its attainment. For Seligman (2002), there are three general means of access to happiness: the pleasant life (which includes the subjective well-being of Diener and of Sheldon et al.), the good life (which includes the flow experience of Csikszentmihalyi), and the meaningful life. The pleasant life is about maximizing one's good feelings about the past (through gratitude and forgiveness), about the present (through savoring and mindfulness), and about the future (through optimism and hope); the good life is about finding flow by cultivating the strengths and virtues; and the meaningful life is about applying these strengths and virtues in the service of something larger than oneself. The full life—a life that integrates the pleasant, good, and meaningful lives— would then seem to be, for Seligman, the ultimate desideratum of PP. This ultimate desideratum is similar in important ways to what others have called the spiritual life (Ingersoll, 2003).

How satisfied would Aristotle be with any of these definitions of happiness? For Aristotle, it is impossible to separate one's happiness from external goods. Aristotle argues that there are certain external factors, such as good birth, satisfactory children, and personal beauty that are essential for a happy life. He also points out that friends, wealth, or political power are often prerequisites for noble action. He concludes that happiness seems to require external prosperity (1934, I. viii. 15–17). While we might take issue with the specific items (such as good birth) that Aristotle finds essential for happiness, his approach underscores the important relation between happiness and objective factors in our environment. This seems to point beyond the scope of PP proper to the entire domain of wellness.

We believe the particular challenges of conceptual clarification PP must meet are not due simply to differences of opinion or usage among positive psychologists. Rather, they are due in part to the origins and dialectical trajectory of the PP movement itself. Its origins lie in a reaction against the tendency of mainstream psychology to focus predominantly on the amelioration of deficits. PP, by contrast, emphasizes the importance of the cultivation of human strengths in the quest for human flourishing. This opposition between the thesis of mainstream psychology and the antithesis of PP is an unstable one, however, since it is clear that deficits and strengths cannot be held absolutely separate. Both the reduction of deficits and the cultivation of strengths are essential for human flourishing. The irony in mainstream psychology is that it has failed to acknowledge adequately the deficit inherent in the deficit approach itself. While removing negatives yields overall progress, this process by itself can never take us into positive territory. Paying off one's debts increases one's net worth but not one's income. The irony in PP is that the human flourishing we seek is more positive than that which PP alone can yield, and that this higher level of flourishing comes precisely through the acknowledgment of the importance of the deficits approach. Increasing one's income may not increase one's net worth if one's debts are large enough.

The instability of this polarity points to the need for a synthesis between mainstream psychology and PP—for, say, an "optimal psychology." An optimal psychology would study when it is best to use a deficits approach and when it is best to use a strengths approach to human flourishing. But an optimal psychology is also unstable, since human flourishing is not dependent solely on psychology. Also at issue here are questions of economics and sociology, of politics and law, of business and the physical environment. In short, the dialectic that begins with PP must end with wellness. That is, a dissatisfaction with the limited approach to human flourishing provided by mainstream psychology will not be overcome until we have a science that covers the full scope of human flourishing. Similarly, the current discontent with limited organizational development approaches will not be alleviated until we have a theory of organizational wellness that encompasses personal, relational, and collective domains, that emphasizes both the enhancement of strengths and the reduction of deficits, and that recognizes the importance of both subjective and objective measures of well-being (Burke, 2002).

This inexorable drive is something of which many positive psychologists are at least implicitly aware. Positive psychologists are quick to point out that their work is intended as a complement to, and not a replacement for, mainstream psychology—thus allowing room for an optimal psychology that integrates both. Positive psychologists are also interested in fostering the development of a positive social science and a positive humanities, thus acknowledging the importance of integrating psychology with other disciplines. The scope of the science and profession that Seligman and Csikszentmihalyi envision for the coming century must then be broader than that of PP proper. It must cover the entire scope of wellness.

Clearly, much more needs to be done to work out the details of this dialectical complexity. Provisionally, we suggest that the current PP movement is both about the science of PP and about something much larger and more comprehensive. PP proper involves the application of the methods of empirical psychology in the development of a strengths-based approach to psychology. The larger science of which PP itself will be only a part has yet to be named. But we predict that its scope will be roughly coterminous with that of wellness.

What then is the Good at which PP aims? Understood as a discrete science, PP aims at happiness—at understanding the nature and causes of subjective well-being, but also at understanding the cultivation of strengths and the finding of meaning in life. Understood developmentally, however, PP is aiming toward something larger than itself. In this sense, the Good at which PP aims seem quite similar to the Good at which wellness aims.

This dynamic state of affairs in PP is quite understandable in a nascent area of study. But it also has important and profound implications for the application of PP in individual, relational, organizational, and communal contexts. One of the greatest dangers presented by this state of affairs is that of overreach. By confusing the domain of PP proper with that of the larger science of human flourishing, practitioners could unwittingly become blind to important factors crucial for wellness in a variety of contexts. Let us consider more carefully how this might happen.

Imagine a positive psychology practitioner (PPP) just beginning her career. She reads in the PP literature that happy people have greater longevity, better health, and increased productivity over unhappy people. She notes Seligman's statement that research leads to an "unambiguous picture of happiness as a prolonger of life and improver of health" (2002, p. 40). She wants these important benefits for her clients, and she wonders what sorts of interventions will work best. She is told by PP researchers that circumstances typically do not matter very much for people's happiness. With respect to socioeconomic level, they state that above a certain threshold wealth adds little to reported happiness. With respect to physical conditions, they claim that "objective good health is barely related to happiness" (Seligman, 2002, p. 58). Finally, with respect to education, climate, race and gender, they observe that "surprisingly, none of them much matters for happiness" (Seligman, 2002, p. 58).

If the PPP understands her job to be that of helping her clients become happier, she may discourage them from focusing too much attention on the circumstances of their lives in favor of interventions focused on savoring, gratitude, mindfulness, the cultivation of signature strengths, and the like. While there is nothing wrong with these interventions, the danger comes in forgetting that happiness might include anything outside of them. If Aristotle is right that happiness is the End at which all actions aim, then it would be a mistake simply to identify happiness with subjective well-being. Overreach would occur if the PPP were to take subjective well-being to cover the entire domain of happiness, not making room for the important elements of happiness that lie outside of subjective well-being.

If subjective well-being were taken to be the End at which all actions aim, then there would be little incentive for working on the objective factors that underlie so much of wellness. One of these factors, for example, is social justice. If the PPP's clients belong to a relatively high socioeconomic class (which is likely to be the case, since they can afford to work with her), working for social justice may have only very marginal effects on their subjective well-being. Or it may have significant negative effects if it presents obstacles to their life satisfaction. So if the PPP takes subjective well-being to be the End at which all actions aim, it seems unlikely that she would encourage her clients to fight for social justice. All the more since one could argue that being the victim of social injustice does not necessarily result in a sustained decrease in one's subjective well-being. So if the victims of injustice are happy, why should a client risk making himself unhappy in order to change their social conditions, which will not likely have much of an effect on their happiness, anyway? Seen in this way, the practice of PP could become an unwitting argument for and a dangerous ally of injustice. In redefining injustice in the workplace as mere maladjustment of disaffected workers, organizational consultants face a similar risk. Ever since Baritz published *Servants of Power* in 1974, organizational consultants have been warned not to distort oppression into private dysfunction (Prilleltensky, 1994; Prilleltensky & Nelson, 2002).

Clearly, the full life and wellness must help fill out our conception of happiness. Subjective well-being by itself is insufficient to cover the entire domain of human flourishing. Indeed, at times it seems difficult to reconcile self-reports of subjective well-being with more objective perspectives that take into account more of the wellness domain. As Eckersley has noted, "there is a range of evidence that suggests a positive bias in the results of happiness and life satisfaction surveys" (2001, p. 63). In a careful review of measures used in assessing levels of happiness and life satisfaction, Eckersley (2000) found great inconsistencies between people's report of happiness and a number of objective measures of well-being. He found that levels of happiness reported by people, usually quite high across a number of countries and contexts, are incommensurate with rather pronounced levels of stress, mental health, sleeping problems, depression, low self-esteem, lack of energy, worries about weight, lack of satisfaction with their economic situation, and other measures. The inconsistency between elevated reports of subjective happiness and depressed measures of physical, psychological, and collective wellness was found in studies across different countries and contexts. In summary, Eckersley writes, "there are several aspects of measures of subjective well-being (SWB) or happiness that present a problem. . . . These are the relative stability of SWB despite dramatic social, cultural and economic changes in recent decades; the complex, nonlinear relationship between objective conditions and subjective states; and the positive biases in measures of SWB" (2000, p. 274).

This situation could lead to the overreach of PP and to the undermining of objective factors in well-being, a conclusion reinforced by PP's claim that happiness is determined largely by genetics (50%) and volitional factors (40%) and only moderately by circumstances (10%) (Seligman, 2002; Sheldon et al., 2003). Although positive psychologists claim that circumstantial factors account for only about 10% of happiness and volitional factors for about 40%, we should keep in mind—as indeed Sheldon et al. (2003) point out—that the psychological and behavioral variables said to account for the 40% cannot be easily disentangled from the circumstances of people's lives (McGue & Bouchard, 1998; Turkheimer, 1998). In our view, some positive psychologists risk engaging in what Shinn and Toohey have recently called the "context minimization error," according to which there is a "tendency to ignore the impact of enduring neighborhood and community contexts on human behavior. The error has adverse consequences for understanding psychological processes and efforts at social change" (2003, p. 428). Shinn and Toohey argue that:

> Psychologists should pay more attention to the community contexts of human behavior. Conditions in neighborhoods and community settings are associated with residents' mental and physical health, opportunities, satisfactions, and commitments. They are associated with children's academic achievement and developmental outcomes, from behavior problems to teenage childbearing. Contexts also moderate other individual or family processes, suggesting that many psychological theories may not hold across the range of environments in which ordinary Americans live their lives. For example, optimal types of parenting may depend on levels of neighborhood

risk. Further...contextual effects may masquerade as effects of individual characteristics, leading to flawed inferences. (2003, p. 428)

Like psychologists, organizational consultants and leaders have a proclivity to explain systemic phenomena, such as corporate inefficiency or corruption, not in systemic terms, but rather in person-centered terms. Corrupt leaders and inept workers account for negative developments, while superb captains and well-trained sailors account for achievement. While paying lip service to organizational culture and external forces, this trend is noticeable in recent organizational development and leadership volumes (e.g., Chowdhury, 2003; Goleman, 1998; Goleman, Boyatzis, & McKee, 2002; Senge, Ross, Smith, Roberts, & Kleiner, 1994). Unemployment, under-employment, outsourcing, injustice, discrimination, and lack of health benefits are dynamics that affect the wellness of workers at least as much as personal attributes such as emotional intelligence or spiritual conviction, however vital for organizational wellness these might be. It is a question of scope. If the phenomena relate to systemic barriers, systemic barriers ought to be removed. But if in such situations the phenomena are narrowly defined in terms of micro segments, the attempt will likely be made to restore the health of the whole by simply removing a few malfunctioning parts. Such attempts are almost certain to fail. It is not easy to find in the organizational development literature conceptualizations of wellness that attend to the various subjective, objective, personal, relational, and collective domains at once.

ETHICS IN ORGANIZATIONAL LIFE

Positive psychologists wish to promote values that enhance personal and institutional development. While most attention has hitherto been devoted to the former, the latter remains an unrealized but important goal (Henry, 2003; Seligman, 2002; Snyder & Lopez, 2002). The cultivation of strengths and virtues and of positive institutions is paramount in the pursuit of authentic happiness (Seligman, 2002, 2003; Seligman & Royzman, 2003) and workforce spirituality (Barrett, 2003; Cavanagh & Bandsuch, 2002; Paloutizian et al., 2003). This is where PP and wellness promotion converge, for both treat the individual as an agent of change, and both consider the role of institutions, even if PP has not yet fully developed this consideration.[1] Agents of change can develop virtues related to the improvement of personal, relational, and collective wellness through the enhancement of organizations, communities and social institutions. Herein lies the potential contribution of PP for the three levels of wellness, namely, the use of proven techniques that enhance satisfaction in life, caring and compassion in relationships, and justice in society. It is definitely within the scope of PP to connect the private pursuit of the good life with the public concern for fairness, equity and justice (Baltes & Kunzman, 2003).

The main challenge in organizational life is to identify the persons and contexts most likely to benefit from PP. The goal is the application of PP to the right people, in the right way, at the right time, in the right place (Pawelski, 2003a,b).

To achieve these goals we need to be clear with respect to *whose* pleasant, good, and meaningful life we are talking about. In any organizational context, we can identify at least three main constituencies or stakeholder groups: (a) employers, (b) employees, and (c) the community at large that is affected by the operations, products, and services of the organization. These three groups are potential recipients and agents of the four types of happiness reviewed at the outset of this chapter: (a) subjective well-being, (b) flow, (c) the full life (composed of the pleasant life, the good life, and the meaningful life), and (d) wellness (pursued in all four quadrants of Figure 9.1).

In an ideal situation, the three groups would work together to maximize the four kinds of happiness. In actual fact, however, the three groups are often in conflict. Different interests and levels of power often interfere with the pursuit of wellness for the common good. As a microcosm of society, organizations reflect conflicts and dynamics affecting the well-being of communities around the world. The challenge to harmonize values and interests among groups is, to say the least, humbling. To face that challenge, we identify four tasks for organizational leaders and positive psychologists alike (Prilleltensky, 2000).

1. Clarify the position of the organization with respect to the pleasant life, the good life, and the meaningful life, and articulate means of achieving these three outcomes for employers, employees, and the community at large.

The needs of the individual have to be in harmony with the needs of the collective. To achieve a balance between individual and collective needs we require processes that can mediate between conflicting interests (Barrett, 2003). The role of the leader is to help the organization clarify its values and suggest means for balancing the personal wellness of workers with the well-being of the organization and the community as a whole. Such processes usually encourage participation and collective ownership of the mission (Maton & Salem, 1995; Racino, 1991; Senge, 1990). Although leaders may be sincere in their desire to formulate a mission statement that balances competing interests and values, their good intentions are threatened by a number of risks. The first risk is to remain at a level of abstraction that makes for an internally coherent set of values that are theoretically beautiful but practically useless. A second risk is the confusion between personal preferences and ethical principles (Becker, 1998). Some management books outline processes that rely on what workers prefer, but not necessarily on what is morally right (e.g., Senge et al., 1994).

2. Promote a state of affairs in which personal power and self-interests do not undermine the wellness or interests of others, but rather contribute to the highest levels of happiness for all.

This calls for an awareness of how personal power and vested interests suffuse leadership (Boonstra, Bennebroek Gravenhorst, 1998; Bradshaw, 1998). Workers and leaders need to reflect on how their personal lives and subjective experiences influence what they deem ethical for the organization and for the public they serve. Awareness, however, is only the first step. The satisfaction of personal needs is another important requisite. Workers are more likely to abide by collective values and norms when they feel that their personal needs are adequately met by the organization (Bolman & Deal, 1997; Lee, Sirgy, Efraty, & Siegel, 2003).

The process of balancing interests with values can be subverted. One way to subvert it is by developing a discourse that overemphasizes self-interests. For example, the notion of a "self-made person," so prevalent in North America, can lead to a justification of privilege and discrimination (Prilleltensky, 1994). Self-determination, skills and perseverance are, in principle, desirable values, but not when they justify dominance and exploitation.

3. Enhance zones of congruence among communities, employees and employers.

Leaders need to create partnerships among these groups in order to foster concordance of values and practices. The primary task in the creation of partnerships is the establishment of trust (Block, 1993; Nelson, Prilleltensky, & MacGillivary, 2001). This is achieved by meaningful and collaborative participation in decision-making processes. Democratic and participatory processes among multiple stakeholders require the prolonged engagement of leaders and the avoidance of tokenism. Token consultative processes subvert the intent of true partnerships.

4. Confront people and groups subverting values, abusing power, or allowing self-interests to undermine the well-being of others in the organization or in the community at large.

A culture of openness and self-reflection facilitates the resolution of conflict. In a climate of healthy and respectful debate, opposing parties may reach an agreement in line with organizational values. There are situations, however, in which a healthy climate may not prevent disagreements. If the conflict is about ideas and interpretations, chances are that a resolution can be reached. But if the conflict is about personal interests or power, differences may be irreconcilable, in which case confrontation takes place. Confrontation may be used for the good of the organization and the good of the public. But it may also be used to suppress legitimate discontent. Leaders can impose their power to silence opposing views.

CONCLUDING CAVEATS

PP is very much concerned with the promotion of strengths and virtues. The context for the promotion of these qualities is crucial. In organizations, there are two contextual forces that threaten and enable the implementation of values at the same time: interests and power. Leaders and positive psychologists invested in the enhancement of institutional life must confront these issues and find ways of enhancing the zones of congruence among power and interests of all concerned. Otherwise, insidious power dynamics and conflicting interests impede the implementation of values and virtues.

We espouse neither Romantic nor Machiavellian views of organizational life. Positive institutions must embrace cogent values, but they must also understand power dynamics (Chambliss, 1996; Dokecki, 1996). We strongly endorse the values of wellness and the virtues of PP. But we also appreciate the context where values are supposed to work. Just like Romantic notions of virtue must consider power dynamics, Machiavellian impulses must be tempered by virtues and values. The promotion of happiness at all levels must take both into account.

New disciplines, movements, and theories usually seek to compensate for the shortcomings of their predecessors. PP strives to rectify the inattention to strengths and virtues of many previous schools. Its historical role, however, need not be one of the promotion of positive qualities at the expense of the elimination of negative forces; nor should it be the promotion of person-based solutions at the expense of collective actions. Rather, its aim should be to reach a balance among multiple approaches. Happiness at any of the levels we have discussed here is unlikely to emerge from unidimensional approaches that exalt, however innocently, fragmented solutions. Persons flourish in environments. Their very qualities of hope, optimism, wisdom and gratitude develop in interactions with others, in favorable proximal conditions, which are, in turn, affected by enabling distal conditions. Leaders and positive psychologists can work together to make sure that the institutions that affect our lives become distal as well as proximal sites to the promotion of subjective well-being, flow, the full life, and wellness for employers, employees, and the communities they serve. This is an End at which the ethics of organizational life must aim.

NOTE

1. Positive Organizational Scholarship is an important and growing related area in organizational behavior research that focuses specifically on the positive in group contexts. (See Roberts, Spreitzer, Dutton, Quinn, Heaphy, & Barker, 2005).

AUTHOR NOTE

Correspondence may be addressed to James O. Pawelski at the Positive Psychology Center, University of Pennsylvania, 3701 Market Street, Suite 200, Philadelphia, PA 19104; or to Isaac Prilleltensky at the Department of Human and Organizational Development, Peabody College, Box 90, Vanderbilt University, Nashville, TN 37203. Emails: pawelski@psych.upenn.edu or isaac.prilleltensky@vanderbilt.edu

REFERENCES

Aristotle. (1934). *Nicomachean ethics* (rev. ed., H. Rackham, trans.). Cambridge, MA: Harvard University Press.

Baltes, P., & Kuntzman, U. (2003). Wisdom. *The Psychologist, 16*, 131–133.

Bakan, J. (2004). *The corporation: The pathological pursuit of power and profit.* New York: Free Press.

Baritz, L. (1974). *The servants of power: A history of the use of social science in American industry.* Westport, CT: Greenwood.

Barrett, R. (2003). Culture and consciousness: Measuring spirituality in the workplace by mapping values. In R. Giacalone & C.L. Jurkiewicz (Eds.), *Handbook of workplace spirituality and organizational performance* (pp. 245–266). Armonk, NY: M.E. Sharpe.

Becker, T.E. (1998). Integrity in organizations: Beyond honesty and conscientiousness. *Academy of Management Review, 23*, 154–161.

Block, P. (1993). *Stewardship: Choosing service over self-interest.* San Francisco: Berrett-Koehler.

Bolman, L., & Deal, T. (1997). *Reframing organizations: Artistry, choice, and leadership.* San Francisco: Jossey-Bass.

Boonstra, J.J., & Bennebroek Gravenhorst, K.M. (1998). Power dynamics and organizational change: A comparison of perspectives. *European Journal of Work and Organizational Psychology, 7*(2), 97–120.

Bradshaw, P. (1998). Power as dynamic tension and its implications for radical organizational change. *European Journal of Work and Organizational Psychology, 7*(2), 121–143.

Burke, W. (2002). *Organization change.* London: Sage.

Cavanagh, G., & Bandsuch, M. (2002). Virtue as a benchmark for spirituality in business. *Journal of Business Ethics, 38,* 109–117.

Chambliss, D. (1996). *Beyond caring.* Chicago: University of Chicago Press.

Chowdhury, S. (Ed.). (2003). *Organization 21C.* New York: Financial Times/Prentice Hall.

Csikszentmihalyi, M. (1990). *Flow: The psychology of optimal experience.* New York: HarperCollins.

Dokecki, P. (1996). *The tragi-comic professional: Basic considerations for ethical reflective-generative practice.* Pittsburgh, PA: Duquesne University Press.

Eckersley, R., (2000). The mixed blessing of material progress: Diminishing returns in the pursuit of progress. *Journal of Happiness Studies, 1,* 267–292.

Eckersley, R. (2001). Culture, health and well-being. In R. Eckersley, J. Dixon, & B. Douglas (Eds.), *The social origins of health and well-being* (pp. 51–70). New York: Cambridge University Press.

Eckersley, R., Dixon, J., & Douglas, B. (Eds.). (2001). *The social origins of health and well-being.* New York: Cambridge University Press.

Giacalone, R., & Jurkiewicz, C. (Eds.). (2003). *Handbook of workplace spirituality and organizational performance.* Armonk, NY: M.E. Sharpe.

Goleman, D. (1998). *Working with emotional intelligence.* New York: Bantam.

Goleman, D., Boyatzis, R., & McKee, A. (2002). *Primal leadership: Realizing the power of emotional intelligence.* Boston: Harvand Business School Press.

Henry, J. (2003). Positive organisations. *The Psychologist, 16,* 138–139.

Ingersoll, R. E. (2003). Spiritual wellness in the workplace. In R. Giacalone & C. L. Jurkiewicz (Eds.), *Handbook of workplace spirituality and organizational performance* (pp. 289–299). Armonk, NY: M.E. Sharpe.

Jamner, M.S., & Stokols, D. (Eds.). (2000). *Promoting human wellness.* Los Angeles: University of California Press.

Keating, D.P., & Hertzman, C. (Eds.). (1999). *Developmental health and the wealth of nations: Social, biological, and educational dynamics.* New York: The Guilford Press.

Korten, D.C. (1995). *When corporations rule the world.* San Francisco: Berret-Koehler.

Lee, D.J., Sirgy, J., Efraty, D., & Siegel, P. (2003). A study of quality of work life, spiritual well-being, and life satisfaction. In R. Giacalone & C. L. Jurkiewicz (Eds.), *Handbook of workplace spirituality and organizational performance* (pp. 193–208). Armonk, NY: M.E. Sharpe.

Marmot, M., & R. Wilkinson (Eds.). (1999). *Social determinants of health.* New York: Oxford University Press.

Maton, K.I., & Salem, D.A. (1995). Organizational characteristics of empowering community settings: A multiple case study approach. *American Journal of Community Psychology, 23,* 631–656.

McGue, M., Bouchard, T.J. (1998). Genetic and environmental influences on human behavioural differences. *Annual Review of Neuroscience, 21,* 1–24.

Nelson, G., & Prilleltensky, I. (in press). *Community psychology: In pursuit of liberation and well-being*. New York: Palgrave/MacMillan.

Nelson, G., Prilleltensky, I., & MacGillivary, H. (2001). Building value-based partnerships: Toward solidarity with oppressed groups. *American Journal of Community Psychology, 29,* 649–677.

Paloutzian, R., Emmons, R., & Keortge, S. (2003). Spiritual well-being, spiritual intelligence, and healthy workplace policy. In R. Giacalone & C.L. Jurkiewicz (Eds.), *Handbook of workplace spirituality and organizational performance* (pp. 123–136). Armonk, NY: M.E. Sharpe.

Pawelski, J. O. (2003a). William James, positive psychology, and healthy-mindedness. *Journal of Speculative Philosophy, New Series, 17,* 53–67.

Pawelski, J. O. (2003b, Fall). Is healthy-mindedness healthy? *Cross Currents,* 404–412.

Prilleltensky, I. (1994). *The morals and politics of psychology: Psychological discourse and the status quo.* Albany: State University of New York Press.

Prilleltensky, I. (2000). Value-based leadership in organizations: Balancing values, interests, and power among citizens, workers, and leaders. *Ethics and Behavior, 10,* 139–158.

Prilleltensky, I., & Nelson, G. (2002). *Doing psychology critically: Making a difference in diverse settings.* London: Macmillan/Palgrave.

Prilleltensky, I. Nelson, G., & Peirson, L. (Eds.). (2001). *Promoting family wellness and preventing child maltreatment: Fundamentals for thinking and action.* Toronto: University of Toronto Press.

Putnam, R., & Feldstein, L. (2003). *Better together.* New York: Simon and Schuster.

Racino, J.A. (1991). Organizations in community living: Supporting people with disabilities. *The Journal of Mental Health Administration, 18,* 51–59.

Roberts, L. M., Spreitzer, G., Dutton, J., Quinn, R., Heaphy, E., & Barker, B. (2005). How to play to your strengths. *Harvard Business Review, 83,* 74–80.

Seligman, M.E.P. (2002). *Authentic happiness.* New York: The Free Press.

Seligman, M.E.P. (2003). Positive psychology: Fundamental assumptions. *The Psychologist, 16,* 126–127.

Seligman, M.E.P., & Csikszentmihalyi, M. (2000). Positive psychology: An introduction. *American Psychologist, 55,* 5–14.

Seligman, M.E.P., & Royzman, E. (2003). *Happiness: The three traditional theories.* Electronic Authentic Happiness Newsletter. http://www.authentichappiness.org

Senge, P. (1990). *The fifth discipline: The art and the practice of the learning organization.* New York: Doubleday.

Senge, P., Ross, R., Smith, B., Roberts, C., & Kleiner, A. (1994). The fifth discipline fieldbook. New York: Doubleday.

Shinn, M., & Toohey, S. (2003). Community contexts of human welfare. *Annual Review of Psychology, 54,* 427–459.

Sheldon, K., Lyubomirsky, S., & Schkade, D. (2003). *Pursuing happiness: The architecture of sustainable change.* Submitted for publication.

Snyder, C.R., & Lopez, S.J. (Eds.). (2002). *Handbook of positive psychology.* New York: Oxford University Press.

Stokols, D. (2000). The social ecological paradigm of wellness promotion. In M. S. Jamner & D. Stokols, (Eds.), *Promoting human wellness* (pp. 21–37). Los Angeles: University of California Press.

Stokols, D. (2003). The ecology of human strengths. In L. Aspinwall & U. Staudinger (Eds.), *A psychology of human strengths: Fundamental questions and future directions for a positive psychology* (pp. 331–343). Washington, DC: American Psychological Association.

Turkheimer, E. (1998). Heritability and biological explanation. *Psychological Review, 105,* 782–791.

CHAPTER 10

THE ROLE OF EMOTIONAL INTELLIGENCE IN ETHICAL DECISION MAKING AT WORK

Robert S. Rubin and Ronald E. Riggio

*As soon as questions of will or decision or reason or choice
of action arise human science is at a loss.*

—Noam Chomsky

INTRODUCTION

Chomsky's keen observation unfolds daily as organizational scientists and practitioners grapple with why good people (and organizations) often do bad things. Numerous formerly respected executives of companies such as Tyco, WorldCom, and Enron made unethical decisions that derailed their own careers, as well as their organizations (see Kramer, 2003). For example, former United Way of America President, William Aramony, was, for many years, considered to be a model leader in the nonprofit sector before his poor decisions tarnished the reputation of one of the world's most respected charities (Ciulla, 2004; Riggio, Bass, & Orr, 2004). America's domestic icon, Martha Stewart, has been convicted of insider trading. If one listens to some of the recent exposés about the corporate ethics crisis

Positive Psychology in Business Ethics and Corporate Responsibility, pages 209–229
Copyright © 2005 by Information Age Publishing
209

in the United States, it may get worse before it gets better (e.g., Sloan, 2003). No doubt, ethics researchers will continue to struggle with this conundrum for years to come.

Central to this struggle is the conflict between a person and his/her environment. Clearly, the study of ethical decision making is complex and involves an interaction between individual, situational and issue-contingent forces (Jones, 1991). However, our perspective is in line with Flannery and May (2000), that ultimately, ethical decision making in organizations is an individual-level phenomenon whereby organizational participants make choices about what is right and wrong. That is not to say that social contexts (e.g., organizational culture) do not matter; rather, that at the end of the day, the decision regarding ethics must be made within individuals, before it can be made between individuals. Further, it is individual differences that allow workers to more adeptly interpret social pressures and environments that often bias the decision making process. Thus, in this chapter, we focus primarily on the influence of individual differences on ethical decision making and more specifically about the potential contribution of emotions.

It has long been acknowledged that an individual's personal characteristics are integral to explaining human behavior in organizations. As Murphy (1996) noted, "Individual differences in abilities, personality attributes, values, outlook, affective state, and so on profoundly affect our behavior" (p. xvi). Given the important role individual differences play in organizational behavior, it is certainly not surprising that much of the literature on ethical decision-making includes individual differences. However, new research developments in this domain could augment this literature nicely.

One such recent development is that of *emotional intelligence*. Vastly popular and often misunderstood, research on emotional intelligence has the potential to substantially contribute to our understanding of the ethical decision making process. Before delving into emotional intelligence however, we first briefly discuss some of the ways in which individual differences have been examined in prior ethical decision making research. This is by no means an exhaustive review, but serves to set the stage for how emotional intelligence fits within the larger framework of individual differences and ethics. Second, we provide an overview of emotional intelligence, to help in understanding this new and often misunderstood construct. Third, we will explore new ground by offering multiple ways in which emotional intelligence could be used to inform ethical decision making.

INDIVIDUAL DIFFERENCES
AND ETHICAL DECISION MAKING

Treviño (1986) conceptualized ethical decision making through an inter-actionist model whereby both individual and situational factors moderate the relationship between individual cognitions and ethical (or unethical) behavior. With respect to individual differences, Treviño draws heavily on Kohlberg's (1969) work on cognitive moral development. Kohlberg described six stages of moral development through which people are able to progress. These six stages can be collapsed to form three stages of ethical concern. In level one (Preconventional—stages 1 and 2), individuals are concerned with strict obedience as well as compliance with rules in order to benefit one's own needs or concerns. The second level, also known as the conventional level (stages 3 and 4), describes individuals' development as concerned with significant others and their expectations for individuals. The conventional level extends to following through on obligations and contributing to society. Finally, the principled level (stages 5 and 6) involves a developed sense of value awareness that transcends laws and authority. Individuals who have reached this highest level often follow self-selected ethical guidelines which are considered to be nonnegotiable. Treviño asserts that particular stages of moral development may lead different views of a given ethical dilemma.

Treviño contends that the vast majority of managers grapple with ethical dilemmas at the conventional level. Further, managers who have reached the principled level of moral reasoning are more likely to "...exhibit consistency between moral judgment and moral action than those at lower stages" (p. 608). Thus, differences in moral reasoning could lead to large gaps in how practicing managers view ethical dilemmas and the resulting action that are taken. Some empirical work supports this perspective (Treviño & Youngblood, 1990).

Treviño also discusses multiple individual difference (i.e., personality) variables that may influence ethical decision making including ego strength, field dependence and locus of control. Ego strength refers to an individual's level of personal conviction such that individuals with a great deal of ego strength can resist impulses and outside pressures, staying true to their personal conviction. Similarly, field independent individuals rely less on others to inform their understanding of ambiguous situations or dilemmas.

Finally, individuals with an internal locus of control (or perception that one controls one's own fate) are more likely to take personal responsibility for their decisions and rely on their own guidelines of ethical behavior. Treviño purports that these three individual differences moderate the relationship between moral development and ethical (or unethical behavior).

Put simply, individual differences among decision makers are likely to influence managers' ability to exhibit consistency between how they think about a decision and how they act.

In addition to moral reasoning and locus of control, Bommer, Gratto, Gravander, and Tuttle (1987) added personal demographics, as well as self-concept, life experiences and other personality dimensions, including one linked to emotions. For example, Bommer et al. argue that older, more educated and emotionally mature individuals are more likely to engage in higher moral behavior. Their model suggests that these individual differences also influence individuals' cognitive processes of decision making.

Similarly, Ferrell and Gresham (1985) suggest that an individual's knowledge, values attitudes and intentions all factor into forming his/her personal philosophical perspective on ethical behavior such as (e.g., utilitarianism). For instance, in their model, beliefs affect attitude formation and intentions of the decision maker. Recent work by Flannery and May (2000) confirms Ferrell and Gresham's thinking demonstrating individual attitudes do indeed have an effect on behavioral intention to make ethical decisions. Research in the area of whistle blowing makes similar assertions, noting that attribution style (i.e., attributing the cause of events to primarily internal or external factors) plays a role in determining whether to hold others responsible for unethical acts or wrongdoings (Gundlach, Douglas, & Martinko, 2003).

The brief review above demonstrates the broad treatment given to individual differences in ethical decision making theory. Most conceptual models include the notion that moral reasoning (or judgment) and other individual factors (e.g., personality, attitudes) are important in making ethical decisions; we certainly do not disagree. As Treviño (1986) duly notes however, moral judgments are limited to cognitive processes and thus largely exclude explorations into other potential influences. Yet, any casual observer of organizational life is sure to note that emotions play a major role in everyday work-life events. Historically, that role has often been viewed as negative, such that expressed emotions interfere with a rational-cognitive "well-oiled machine" approach to work.

More recently however, researchers and practitioners alike have synthesized decades of work on emotions and have shown that emotion in organizations is critical to individual and organizational success. As Lord and Kanfer (2002) suggest, emotions in the work place have multiple direct and indirect pathways of influencing organizational behavior. For instance, they maintain that strong evidence exists for clear emotion-to-behavior linkages such that certain types of emotions will consistently lead to specific behavior and that emotions are important mechanisms for informing cognitive processing. Such processing is at the heart of decision making and problem solving necessary for individual, group and organizational performance.

Indeed, the last decade has witnessed an explosion of empirical research examining how emotions and emotional abilities positively influence many aspects of individual and organizational success including leadership (e.g., George, 2000), work achievement (e.g., Staw, Sutton, & Pelled, 1994), motivation (Ashforth & Humphrey, 1995), turnover intention (e.g., Wong & Law, 2002), turnover (Shaw, 1999), work attitudes (e.g., Ashkanasy & Daus, 2001), and service quality (e.g., Pugh, 2001).

Although much of the recent research has attempted to show how emotions positively influence organizations, negative influences do exist. For example, some research has suggested that suppression of emotion (i.e., not displaying emotion) has harmful effects on the health, as well as, the psychological well-being of employees (Berry & Pennebaker, 1998; Brotheridge & Grandey, 2001). Others have shown that employees who must fake emotions or "put on a smile" to perform their jobs are likely to express intent to leave the organization (Grandey, 1999). Thus, for better or for worse, employee emotions are strongly linked to employee behavior and performance (Brief & Weiss, 2002).

Research on decision making has generally focused on cognitive elements, ignoring the input of emotions. Given the importance of emotions to organizational behavior, we believe that ethical decision making theory and practice could benefit from a systematic examination of emotions. Though emotions broadly speaking are garnering great attention, perhaps the most attention has been given to the promise of emotional intelligence. Below we discuss how emotions and in particular, emotional intelligence, can complement and augment what is known about individual differences in ethical decision making.

EMOTIONAL INTELLIGENCE: A PRIMER

Since the release of Goleman's (1995) best-selling book, considerable attention has been given to emotional intelligence from academics, practitioners, and laypersons alike (e.g., Cooper & Sawaff, 1997; George, 2000; Goleman, 1998; Jordan, Ashkanasy, & Hartel, 2002). Goleman's (1995) provocative title which included the phrase, "why it [emotional intelligence] can matter more than IQ" seemed to strike a chord with the American public, confirming what many claimed to already know; that there is more to life success than intelligence. In practice however, research on emotional intelligence has been slower to empirically demonstrate its purported contributions. One reason for this is that there is considerable disagreement on the exact nature of the construct (Daus & Ashkanasy, 2003).

Specifically, two perspectives have emerged. One approach to the study of emotional intelligence has occurred through a mixed-model of emotional intelligence which includes abilities, motives and other personality factors within the construct (e.g.,Bar-On, 1997; Goleman, 1995). Another approach follows a more strict ability framework (Mayer, Salovey, & Caruso, 2000) and excludes non-ability type indicators. Regardless of the approach however, these researchers agree that individuals differ greatly in their ability to create and/or respond to emotional stimuli both within themselves and from others. That is, some people are simply more adept than others at managing their emotions in a way that is socially adaptive and leads to increased success in a number of life domains.

Emotional intelligence emerges from a tradition of research that examined alternatives and/or complementary concepts to traditional (analytic) intelligence (i.e., cognitive ability). For example, Cantor and Kihlstrom (1987) describe the notion of social intelligence and its adaptive functioning. An individual who is socially intelligent might be described as having the ability to perceive and understand his/her own internal state, which in turn focuses behavior that is geared toward productively solving problems. Although emotional intelligence has been highly touted, its critics have argued that it by no means qualifies as "intelligence" and some have suggested that its potential benefits have been heavily exaggerated (Davies, Stankov, & Roberts, 1998).

In response, some researchers argue that for the construct to be labeled "intelligence" it must truly reflect criteria set forth for intelligence. Mayer and Salovey (2000) described three criteria for determining the appropriateness of labeling a construct as intelligence. First, the construct should conceptually reflect mental performance, not behavior, the self, or nonintellectual achievements. Second, a set of descriptive abilities (properties) should be closely related to but distinct from other known forms of intelligence. Third, a developmental component exists such that the intelligence increases as a function of age and experience. Mayer and Salovey (1997) showed evidence that emotional intelligence indeed meets these three criteria and should be classified within the array of intelligences, specifically as a property of social intelligence. In addition, they proposed a four-dimension model of emotional intelligence that includes the ability to: (1) perceive, appraise and express emotion, (2) facilitate thinking using emotional information, (3) understand and analyze emotion and (4) reflectively regulate emotion (Mayer & Salovey, 1997). Emotional intelligence then is multidimensional and based on a variety of emotional abilities. We elaborate briefly on these core abilities below.

Appraisal and expression of emotion.   People who are considered emotionally intelligent have a strong ability to recognize and interpret their own emotions, often well before others are able to view that emotion (Wong &

Law, 2002). This heightened sensitivity to one's own emotions allows an individual unique insight permitting them to quickly label their own internal experiences. Emotionally intelligent individuals are also adept at accurately identifying various emotions communicated through facial expressions (Ekman, Friesen, & Ancoli, 1980), postures, and voice intonation (Nowicki & Duke, 1994), as well as appraisal of emotional content in art or music than non-emotionally intelligent individuals. In addition, emotionally intelligent individuals have the ability to accurately express and/or display their emotions through nonverbal expressions or through verbal communication. In some extreme cases, individuals who suffer from *alexithymia* (an inability to appraise and verbally express one's own emotions) demonstrate how debilitating the lack of emotional appraisal and expressive abilities can be in appropriate social functioning. Damasio (1994) showed how alexithymic individuals make poor decisions simply because they lack the input of emotion in the decision making process. For example, they are unable to consider the emotional consequences of certain courses of action on themselves and on others (i.e., they lack empathy), and they presumably do not experience anticipatory fear, guilt, or anxiety that are associated with the negative outcomes of a potentially wrong decision.

Empathy, or "the ability to comprehend another's feelings and to re-experience them oneself" (Salovey & Mayer, 1990, p. 194) is another ability related to the appraisal and expression of emotion. The importance of empathy to successful behavior should be underscored (e.g., Davis & Oathout, 1987). In particular, the ability to be empathic leads to genuineness and social appropriateness, whereas a lack of empathy leads to apparently ill-mannered behaviors.

In an ethical dilemma, participants often mention the difficulty they have in dealing with their own, often mixed emotions. For example, FBI whistleblower, Colleen Rowley, who revealed the FBI's mishandling of a terrorist investigation that might have prevented the 9/11 tragedy, has discussed the internal struggle to control her conflicting feelings of anger over the FBI's actions, her positive feelings for the organization that she dedicated many years to (and still works for) and some fear for her own career, in bringing critical information to the attention of FBI Director Robert Mueller.

Empathy for victims of unethical behavior can also play a part in helping individuals make ethical decisions, and in motivating them to action. This was definitely the case for famed legal assistant-turned-victims'-advocate, Erin Brockovich. Brockovich asserts that it was her empathy for the suffering victims of pollution caused by Pacific Gas and Electric's irresponsible actions that helped fuel her decision to continue to pursue legal action against the powerful corporation, and it is what helps her continue her efforts to help victims of corporate-caused environmental dangers.

Regulating emotion.   Research has suggested that individuals are generally motivated to maintain or prolong pleasant moods and curtail unpleasant moods. This behavior is often referred to as "mood maintenance" (Isen, 1985). Mood maintenance has adaptive advantages in that it allows individuals control over otherwise negatively related stimuli. Regulation of emotion in others involves the manipulation of others' emotional reactions through specific emotionally based behavior. For example, most people have had the experience of "being moved" by a particularly powerful speaker. Technically, the speaker has regulated the emotions of the audience.

Emotion regulation allows individuals to keep a close watch on their emotional states, monitoring them for fluctuations that might indicate a need to react behaviorally. For example, when a customer service agent is encountered by an irate customer, the employee may have immediate feelings of anger. The ability to regulate this behavior allows the employee to make a choice about whether or not that emotion is appropriate or conducive to the situation (Gross, 1999). How well this employee regulates his/her emotion has important consequences for his/her success on the job (Rubin, Tardino, Munz, & Daus, 2005). On the other hand, the ability to regulate emotions in others could have similar positive effects. For example, a particularly adept customer service agent could respond to the irate customer by inducing a feeling of compassion for the company or special circumstances of the customer service agent. In all, regulating emotion has important consequences for judgment and behavior.

The importance of emotional regulation emphasizes that for emotional intelligence, unlike perhaps verbal intelligence (i.e., IQ), more of it is not necessarily better. Research on emotional and social skills—constructs that are closely related to emotional intelligence—suggests that emotional abilities need to be "in balance" (Riggio, 1986; Riggio & Carney, 2003). In other words, too much expression of emotion, or being too emotionally sensitive (e.g., to the extent of sympathetically feeling another's pain or grief), may be inconsistent with true possession of emotional intelligence. The construct of emotional intelligence may be more "qualitative" than "quantitative."

Facilitate thinking and understanding emotions.   Emotions and reactions to emotions alert human beings to problems and events that need immediate attention. Therefore, emotions have the power to inform and focus thinking (Pizarro & Salovey, 2002). However, understanding these emotions and how to best utilize them is complex. The complexity comes from the range and combination of emotions people experience at any one time. For example, an employee giving a sales presentation with a colleague notices that his colleague is struggling to respond appropriately to a question. This simple event may trigger multiple emotions. He may on one hand, feel compassion for his colleague and at the same time feel anger at the fact that their meeting is not going well. Both emotions will undoubtedly facilitate a cognitive reaction perhaps leading to a "face saving" behavior to save his colleague from embarrassment while simultaneously aimed at improving the outcome of the meeting. Further, because of their ability to understand emotion and its byproducts, emotionally intelligent individuals are able to anticipate future emotion and understand its potential impact. For instance, people may be less likely to engage in unethical behavior when they are able to fully understand the emotional consequences of such action (Pizarro & Salovey, 2002). In other words, knowing in advance that a particularly unethical decision will bring with it a sense of remorse or regret may significantly deter such a decision in the first place.

In many ways, U.S. President Bill Clinton's decision to lie to the American public about his affair with intern Monica Lewinsky reveals a potential deficit in Clinton's ability to realize the emotional fallout of his dishonesty. It could be the case that an individual's success in lying over time may lead to a disassociation between the unethical act and the emotional consequences, so that the liar begins to ignore the emotional warning signs accompanying the deception.

HOW EMOTIONAL INTELLIGENCE INFORMS ETHICAL DECISION MAKING

We follow Jones's (1991) definition of an ethical (i.e., one that is both legal *and* morally acceptable to the larger community) and unethical (i.e., one that is either illegal *or* morally unacceptable to the larger community) decision. This conceptualization is largely utilitarian and does exclude other ethical decision making perspectives and criteria. However, it is important to note that although emotional intelligence represents a strong individual difference, it is not necessarily a universally positive or negative one. Like any other ability, individuals with their unique motives, experiences and situations, may utilize the ability toward both ethical and/or unethical behavior (e.g., Howell & Avolio 1992), *regardless* of whom or how ethical behavior is determined. To that extent, emotional intelligence is neutral and can enhance or detract from a person's desire to be good. For example, under a principle-based or "rights" view of ethical criteria, individuals, not societies dictate ethical and unethical behavior. Emotional intelligence could be used to manipulate others toward freedoms (e.g., choosing smoking) that could be justified from a principle-based perspective.

Below we discuss multiple ways in which emotional intelligence may influence individuals, groups and organizations' ethical/unethical decision making process and outcomes. Specifically, we purport that three elements of emotional intelligence have a particularly significant impact: (1) appraisal and expression of emotion, (2) empathy, and (3) regulation of emotion. Below we provide a detailed discussion of each and finish our discussion with some potential implications.

Appraising and expressing emotion in ethical decision making. Mark Twain once remarked, "... emotions are among the toughest things in the world to manufacture out of whole cloth; it is easier to manufacture seven facts than one emotion." If Twain is correct, then those who can interpret emotion accurately in others possess a critical skill in understanding peoples' authentic needs. As mentioned above, accurate appraisal of emotion is significantly tied to successful interpersonal interactions. Further, this ability to be interpersonally sensitive has a number of important consequences for ethics.

First, people who are highly interpersonally sensitive are more likely to engender safe climates for making decisions. As Janis's (1982) classic research on groupthink demonstrated, intimidating work group climates and stressful decision situations can discourage open and frank discussion. Similarly, Argyris (1994) notes that people in organizations are not skillful in surfacing underlying assumptions behind proposed actions. This often results in the stated agreement of one philosophical position, and the behavioral enactment of a very different position. Thus, the ability to understand when people are behaving incongruously with their true feelings would seemingly be a great benefit. Ekman and Friesen (1974) argue that emotions are primarily communicated through facial expressions. Therefore, surfacing people's feelings about a particular issue starts by accurately appraising peoples' emotions through facial expressions and other nonverbal expression. This type of skill is likely to lead to more authentic interpersonal discussion that could produce more informed decisions.

Second, emotionally intelligent individuals who take stands on ethical issues are more likely to be heard and develop a following. This is particularly true for organizational leaders who lead from personal conviction and a set of nonnegotiable values (Bass, 1985, 1998) and also have the legitimacy of a held office. For example, Huy (1999) argues that leaders attempt to evoke change by appealing to followers' emotional states to motivate personal adaptation. Similarly, Fox and Amichai-Hamburger (2001) argue that persuasion of employees to support organizational change is most effective through affective rather than cognitive appeals. Broadly speaking, employees who possess skills in emotional expression are more likely to persuade others toward change or particular courses of action.

When it comes to the emotional appeal of charismatic leaders, several authors have noted the "dark side" of charisma—unethical leaders who use emotions to rouse followers to do their bidding, or leaders who develop unhealthy, overly dependent emotional bonds with followers (Conger, 1990; House & Howell, 1992). Followers can play an important part in resisting the efforts of these types of leaders by using their own emotional intelligence as a "gut check" to determine if the leader's passionate message "feels right" ethically. Conversely, leader-member-exchange research has demonstrated that when leaders and followers engage in high quality exchanges, there is likely to be mutual influence in the relationship (Graen & Uhl-Bien, 1995). Thus, highly charismatic followers can also have significant influence on leaders' ability to resist unethical influences from below.

Empathy. When former president Bill Clinton remarked to the nation, "I feel your pain," his empathic response to the American people showed that he was a leader who was "in touch," emotionally with his constituents. This ability plays a central role in helping people understand how their decisions and ultimately their actions impact the lives of others. In fact, previous research has shown that empathy contributes to people's wanting to engage in helping and prosocial behaviors (Davis et al., 1999). In particular, Davis (1983, 1994) views empathy as taking three important forms labeled as perspective taking, empathic concern and personal distress.

Engaging in *perspective taking* leads people to anticipate the behavior and reactions of others. Further, it focuses individuals on another's behavior which reinforces the notion that the other exists within a framework of a larger community. *Empathic concern* is a reactive emotional response of sympathy for others. *Personal distress* is also a reactive emotional response, but leads to feelings of personal discomfort or anxiety (i.e., actually "feeling another's pain"). Davis, Conklin, Smith, and Luce (1996) assert that when people take on the perspective of others, they are more likely to have feelings of sympathy and consideration as well as experience personal discomfort or distress. This ability may endow empathetic individuals perceived leadership qualities and could play an important role in influencing others toward ethical behavior. Recently, Wolf, Pescosolido, and Druskat (2002) showed that individuals who displayed a high degree of empathy were more likely to emerge as leaders in self-managed teams.

When examining alternatives in a decision making situation, people who have the ability to be empathic may more fully examine their alternatives taking into account the potential for harm to others. In particular, empathy represents a powerful combination of feeling compassion for others and simultaneously activating a discomfort that signals avoidance. More critically, this ability allows decision makers to feel these emotions well *before* any action is taken (Davis, 1999) by reacting to the potential consequences of an action. Thus, empathy acts as a sort of emotional "canary in the coal mine" quickly providing emotionally intelligent people with strong information that informs their cognitive processing about what feels right versus wrong.

Emotion regulation. Anecdotally, those who have spent time in organizational settings know that peoples' moods (emotional states) greatly impact individual and group productivity and performance. Thus, it should not be surprising that years of research in this area have found significant links between emotional states and judgment (Forgas, 1995). Recall that emotion regulation involves the ability to monitor and control one's emotional states. If emotional states are related to judgment and emotion regulation is the capacity to direct emotional states, it follows that emotion regulation should be an important factor in judgment. This raises questions such as "can people regulate their emotional states to make better decisions" and "do positive or negative emotional states differ in their judgment outcomes?" Luckily, a great deal of research has examined these very questions.

Pertinent to this discussion are the emotional states known as positive affect (PA) and negative affect (NA). People who are experiencing PA can be described as excited and enthusiastic whereas people experiencing NA described as sluggish and dull (Watson, Clark, & Tellegan, 1988). According to Watson (2001), "affective traits/temperaments provide a 'set point' that is characteristic for each individual but differs across individuals. Mood varies around this set point" (p. 18). In other words, while people's moods often fluctuate, they seem to fluctuate within a defined range. In general, individuals will attempt to curtail their negative moods or remain in positive moods. For many organizational situations, this natural tendency seems to provide a great deal of benefit. For instance, PA has been associated with people's inclination to be more helpful, self-assured, perform at high levels and be more creative in problem solving (Brief & Weiss, 2002; Isen, Daubman, & Nowicki, 1987).

However, when it comes to decision making, the relationship between mood and decision making is a bit more complex such that different moods can lead to drastically different outcomes. Specifically, PA has been associated with faster decision processes (Isen & Means, 1983), more creative decisions, and greater issue flexibility (Isen & Daubman, 1984) than NA. Further, individuals in positive mood states are more likely to believe good things will happen and less likely to believe bad things will happen (Mayer & Salovey, 1993). In contrast, NA has been linked to more deliberate evaluations of decision criteria. In general, this line of research has shown that people in negative emotional states engage in more systematic processing (i.e., careful review of data) whereas positive emotional states produce heuristic (i.e., relying on "rules of thumb," or shortcuts) processing (Keltner, Ellsworth, & Edwards, 1993).

Thus, despite the long-held notion that emotionally devoid decisions are optimal, the best decision outcomes may, in part, be the result of the decision maker's mood. That is, for complex, ambiguous decisions, NA may be more productive in providing a thorough examination of information whereas PA may lead to better outcomes for tasks requiring creativity or speed (Forgas, 1995). As George (2000) explains, ". . . feelings are necessary to make good decisions" (p. 1030).

Based on the above premise, our belief is that individuals who can effectively regulate their emotional states to optimize the decision situation are more likely to make better decisions. These people have the ability to recognize the need to alter their emotional response in order to produce behaviors that will be most effective. Take for example an employee who is trying to decide whether or not to help another employee examine documents that are somewhat proprietary or confidential in nature. Previous research would suggest that if she can regulate her mood toward NA, she may engage in a more thorough cost-benefit analysis of the situation (Schaller & Cialdini, 1990). In a group situation, when a team is grappling with an ethical dilemma, individuals with the ability to regulate mood in others, could move people away from overly optimistic emotional states, toward ones that would slow people down and allow them to more fully examine alternatives.

Just as critical is the relationship between emotional states and risk orientation. Some research suggests that in nonthreatening contexts, PA may lead to more risk seeking behavior (Nygren, 1998). In light of arguments that suggest managers and employees are socialized to suppress negative feelings and employ "rationality," organizations may reinforce risk seeking behavior among employees. That is, "In the name of positive thinking . . . managers often censor what everyone needs to say and hear" (Argyris, 1994, p. 79). Here again, the ability to understand implicitly that one's mood may lead to overestimating success rates could factor heavily in the decision to engage in behavior. Given the situational pressures and differences in individual dispositions toward mood, regulation is not simple. Hence, those that have a strong ability to regulate may be more likely to put themselves in a position to perceive and confront decisions of an ethical nature more skillfully.

DISCUSSION

The review above suggests that there are indeed likely links between components of emotional intelligence and ethical decision making. In general, we have taken an approach which mostly implies direct or moderating relationships. That is, we believe that emotional intelligence is likely to both

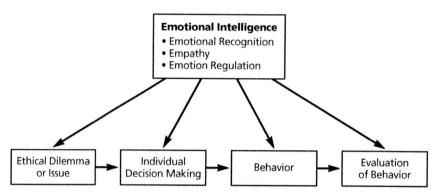

Figure 10.1.   The moderating role of emotional intelligence on common business ethics issues. Adapted from Ferrell and Gresham (1985).

directly influence perception of ethical dilemmas and behavior as well as strengthen the relationship between the dilemma and behavior. Using an adapted version of Ferrell and Gresham's (1989) ethical decision making model, we present a pictorial of this moderating role in Figure 10.1.

In Table 10.1, we provide some examples of ethical dilemmas and ways in which emotional intelligence might influence that issue. For example, dishonest behavior (e.g., lying, stealing) triggers emotional reactions, such as guilt and fear of getting caught, which are then appraised. Based on the individual's ability to appraise and understand the emotions accompanying a potential act of dishonesty, this will inform and affect the individual's emotional reactions to the event, triggering a consideration of the ethical implications, and inform subsequent behavior (e.g., further dishonesty or a confession).

Whistleblowing involves an intrapersonal conflict—an internal struggle of conflicting emotions that need to be recognized and regulated. Empathy may also play a part when the whistleblower identifies with potential victims of corporate misbehavior. More common ethical dilemmas involve interpersonal conflict, such as blaming others, discriminating against them, and generally attempting to avoid personal accountability or blame. In these cases, emotions come into play either through a sort of "gut check"—recognizing one's feelings of guilt—or via empathy when an individual anticipates or feels the victim's emotional reactions.

Research Implications.   How can the growing literature on emotions and emotional intelligence be applied to inform ethical decision making at work, and what are the implications for future research in this area? First, it is clear that emotion plays a critical role in both effective decision making and in making ethical decisions. It is hard to imagine that ethical decision making is a purely cognitive, rational process. Decisions are made with

**Table 10.1.   Common Ethical Issues
and the Role of Emotional Intelligence**

Ethical Issue	Examples	The Role of Emotional Intelligence
Honesty in Communications and Procedures	Layoffs, downsizing, accounting, lying with statistics	*Emotion recognition*—Evaluating the consistency between the communicated message and the nonverbal display.
Conflicts of interest	Bribes, kickbacks	*Empathy*—Identifying with the emotional reactions of recipients of the message; Feeling and anticipating emotions that one might incur from attempting to deceive and the consequences of getting caught
		Emotion regulation—Controlling and concealing feelings of guilt or emotions contradictory to the message
Intrapersonal Conflict	Whistle-blowing	*Emotion recognition*—Recognizing and understanding the conflicting emotions one feels (e.g., fear, anger, sense of justice/injustice)
		Empathy—Identifying with victims' emotions
		Emotion regulation—Controlling emotions that might overwhelm (e.g., fear)
Interpersonal Conflict	Deflecting personal accountability (e.g., scapegoating; blaming others) Discrimination	*Emotion recognition*—Understanding feelings of guilt
		Empathy—Feeling and anticipating others' emotional reactions
		Emotion regulation—Attempting to regulate others' emotions

both the head and the heart. We receive critical information via our emotional "gut" reactions to decision making situations. This is not to say that our gut emotional reactions will always lead us to make good decisions because they "feel right." Certain individuals may derive great pleasure from decisions that lead to the exploitation, duping, cheating, or harming of others. That is why a better understanding of individual differences— including both individual differences in cognitive *and* emotional processing—will help inform our understanding of ethical and unethical decision making. However, there is much research to be done before we can truly inform practitioners about the role that emotions play in causing people to behave ethically and responsibly. But here is what we know so far:

- Emotions help inform decisions by allowing the decision maker to anticipate the positive and negative emotional consequences of a particular decision on the decision maker and on others. The ability to "read" others' emotions, or, in its more "trait like" term, empathy, is critical in both responding to others' feelings and needs and in putting oneself in another's perspective. This is important for workplace supervisors, and has been noted as core component of effective leadership by numerous researchers (Bass, 1990; Hogan & Hogan, 2002; Kellett, Humphrey, & Sleeth, 2002).

- On balance, more empathic individuals should make more ethical decisions because they take into consideration the reactions and feelings of those impacted by the decision. However, it is important to learn from the work on different forms of empathy (e.g., Davis, 1983, 1994), because the tendency to "feel another's pain" may prevent the decisionmaker from making the hard, but necessary (and perhaps ethical), decision that may have negative consequences for others.

- Ability to regulate emotion helps a decision maker monitor his/her own emotional state, and serves to inform about whether a particular decision "feels" good or bad. This ability could be used to regulate emotions productively toward more methodical review of data and situations. Negatively speaking, emotional regulation could also be used to dampen feelings of guilt, anxiety, or shame associated with unethical and immoral decisions. That is, one could "stuff" important emotional indicators of unethical information or behavior. Recent research suggests that emotion regulation does indeed take different forms (see Gross & John, 2003)—some that may help encourage ethical behavior, others that may discourage it.

- Emotional intelligence may be an important key to distinguishing those more likely to make ethical decisions, but we currently do not understand the complexity of the emotional intelligence construct well enough to make these distinctions. As mentioned earlier, possession of emotional intelligence requires both a certain quantity of skill in expressing, perceiving, understanding and regulating emotions, but there appears to be a delicate balance among these abilities. Being too emotionally sensitive, too emotionally expressive, or exercising too much control over one's own emotions may not be "emotionally intelligent."

In order to better understand the role of emotional intelligence in ethical decision-making, important advances must be made. First and foremost, we need to do a better job of both understanding the complex construct of emotional intelligence and measuring it. At the present time, the measurement of emotional intelligence is in a fairly primitive state, with measures taking one of two forms. Some measures of emotional intelligence are similar to self-report personality instruments. Following the "mixed-model" of emotional intelligence, these instruments assess traditional personality constructs (e.g., self-concept, assertiveness), motives, and interpersonal skills (Bar-On, 1997; Schutte et al., 1998). These are relatively new instruments and it can be argued that the psychometric qualities of these instruments have not been fully explored.

The second approach to measuring emotional intelligence is the use of performance-based measures that assess certain emotional skills or abilities, such as abilities to decode facial expressions of emotion and to understand the emotional content of written scenarios (e.g., Mayer, Salovey, & Caruso, 1999). Although these instruments have been more thoroughly tested, with ongoing improvements made, their scope of measurement of the broad construct of emotional intelligence tends to be fairly narrow. As mentioned, this is still a very new area of research.

Another important, needed area of research is to better understand the nomological net surrounding emotional intelligence and ethical decision making. For example, it seems necessary to begin to relate emotional intelligence to other important individual difference variables such as ethical values, cognitive complexity, moral reasoning, and risk orientation. Ethical decision making has always been considered a very "cognitive" process, so the role of emotions has only recently been given serious attention. Research questions here may include examinations of emotional stimuli that "trigger" feelings of right versus wrong; understanding how personal core values illicit emotional responses and how that response influences behavior; how risk orientation may predispose individuals to use emotional intelligence toward unethical behavior.

Recently, a number of theoretical works suggest that emotional intelligence is a critical factor in leadership success. Given our discussion, research on ethical decision making at the leader level may be augmented nicely by incorporating emotional intelligence constructs. For example, Does emotional intelligence moderate the relationship between leaders' perception of ethical issues and follower influence attempts? What role do leaders play in influencing followers emotional reactions to ethical situations? How does a leader's ability to empathize with others impact his/her decision-making behavior?

Most research to date has considered ethical decision making to be a very "cognitive" process. Although the primary focus of this chapter was on emotional intelligence, we encourage researchers to explore the most basic questions regarding the role of emotions in ethical decision making. Only then will we begin to know more about how emotional intelligence informs ethical decision making, serving as a guide to keeping individuals and organizations on the right path.

REFERENCES

Argyris, C. (1994). Good communication that blocks learning. *Harvard Business Review, 72*(4), 77–85.

Ashforth B.E., & Humphrey, R.H. (1995). Emotion in the workplace: A reappraisal. *Human Relations, 48*(2), 97–126.

Ashkanasy, N.M., & Daus, C.S. (2002). Emotion in the workplace: The new challenge for managers. *Academy of Management Executive, 16*(1), 76–86.

Bar-On, R. (1997). *Bar-On Emotional Quotient Inventory: A measure of emotional intelligence.* Toronto: Multi-Health Systems, Inc.

Bass, B.M. (1985). *Leadership and performance beyond expectations.* New York: Free Press.

Bass, B.M. (1990). *Bass & Stogdill's handbook of leadership: Theory, research, and managerial applications* (3rd ed.). New York: Free Press.

Bass, B.M. (1998). *Transformational leadership: Industrial, military, and educational impact.* Mahwah, NJ: Lawrence Erlbaum Associates.

Berry, D.S., & Pennebaker, J.W. (1998). Nonverbal and verbal emotional expression and health. In G.A. Fava & H. Freyberger (Eds.), *Handbook of psychosomatic medicine.* International Universities Press stress and health series (Monograph 9, pp. 69–83). Madison, CT: International Universities Press.

Bommer, M., Gratto, C. Gravender, J., & Tuttle, M. (1987). A behavioral model of ethical and unethical decision making. *Journal of Business Ethics, 6,* 265–280.

Brief, A.P., & Weiss, H.M. (2002). Organizational behavior: Affect in the workplace. *Annual Review of Psychology, 53,* 279–307.

Brotheridge, C.M., & Grandey, A.A. (2001). Emotional labor and burnout: Comparing two perspectives of "people work." *Journal of Vocational Behavior, 60,* 17–39.

Cantor, N., & Kihlstrom, J.F. (1987). *Personality and social intelligence.* Engelwood Cliffs, NJ: Prentice-Hall.

Ciulla, J.B. (2004). The ethical challenges of nonprofit leaders. In R.E. Riggio & S.S. Orr (Eds.), *Improving leadership in nonprofit organizations* (pp. 63–75). San Francisco: Jossey-Bass.

Conger, J.A. (1990). The dark side of leadership. *Organizational Dynamics, 19,* 44–55.

Cooper, R.K., & Sawaff, A. (1997). *Executive EQ: Emotional intelligence in leadership and organizations.* New York: Perigee Books.

Damasio, A.R. (1994). *Decartes' error.* New York: G.P Putnam's Sons.

Daus, C.S., & Ashkanasy, N.M. (2003). Will the real emotional intelligence please stand up? On deconstructing the emotional intelligence "Debate." *The Industrial-Organizational Psychologist, 41*(2), 60–72.

Davies, M., Stankov, L., & Roberts, R.D. (1998). Emotional intelligence: In search of an elusive construct. *Journal of Personality and Social Psychology, 75*(4), 989–1015.

Davis, M.H. (1983). Measuring individual differences in empathy: Evidence for a multidimensional approach. *Journal of Personality and Social Psychology, 44*(1), 113–126.

Davis, M.H. (1994). *Empathy: A social psychological approach.* Madison, WI: Brown & Benchmark.

Davis, M.H., & Oathout, H.A. (1987). Maintenance of satisfaction in romantic relationship behaviors: Empathy and relational competence. *Journal of Personality and Social Psychology, 53*, 397–410.

Davis, M.H., Conklin, L., Smith, A., & Luce, C. (1996). Effect of perspective taking on cognitive representation of persons: A merging of self and other. *Journal of Personality and Social Psychology, 70*(4), 713–726.

Davis, M.H., Mitchell, K.V., Hall, J.A., Lothert, J., Snapp, T., & Meyer, M. (1999). Empathy, expectations, and situational preferences: Personality influences on the decision to participate in volunteer helping behaviors. *Journal of Personality, 67*(3), 469–503.

Ekman, P., & Friesen, W. V. (1974). Detecting deception from the body or face. *Journal of Personality and Social Psychology, 29*, 288–298.

Ekman, P., Friesen, W.V., & Ancoli, S. (1980). Facial signs of emotional experience. *Journal of Personality and Social Psychology, 39*, 1125–1134.

Ferrell, O.C., & Gresham, L.G. (1985). A contingency framework for understanding ethical decision making in marketing. *Journal of Marketing, 49*, 87–96.

Flannery, B.L., & May, D.R. (2000). Environmental ethical decision making in the U.S. metal-fishing industry, *43*(4), 642–662.

Forgas, J. P. (1995). Mood and judgment: The affect infusion model (AIM). *Psychological Bulletin, 117*, 39–66.

Fox, S., & Amichai-Hamburger, Y. (2001). The power of emotional appeals in promoting organizational change programs. *Academy of Management Executive, 15*(4), 84–95.

George, J.M. (2000). Emotions and leadership: The role of emotional intelligence. *Human Relations, 53*(8), 1027–1055.

Goleman, D. (1995). *Emotional intelligence. Why it can matter more than IQ.* New York: Bantam.

Goleman, D. (1998). *Working with emotional intelligence.* New York: Bantam.

Grandey, A.A. (1999). *The effects of emotional labor: Employee attitudes, stress and performance (customer service).* Unpublished doctoral dissertation, Colorado State University.

Gross, J.J. (1999). The emerging field of emotion regulation: An integrative review. *Review of General Psychology, 2*, 271–299.

Gross, J.J., & John, O.P. (2003). Individual differences in two emotion regulation processes: Implications for affect, relationships, and well-being. *Journal of Personality and Social Psychology, 85*, 348–362.

Gundlach, M.J., Douglas, S.C., & Martinko, M.J. (2003). The decision to blow the whistle: A social information processing framework. *Academy of Management Review, 28*(1), 107–123.

Hogan, J., & Hogan, R. (2002). Leadership and sociopolitical intelligence. In R.E. Riggio, S.E., Murphy, & F.J. Pirozzolo (Eds.), *Multiple intelligences and leadership* (pp. 75–88). Mahwah, NJ: Lawrence Erlbaum Associates.

House, R.J., & Howell, J.M. (1992). Personality and charismatic leadership. *Leadership Quarterly, 3*, 81–108.

Howell J.M., & Avolio, B.J. (1992). The ethics of charismatic leadership. Submission or liberation? *Academy of Management Journal, 36*(1), 43–55.

Huy, Q.N. (1999). Emotional capability, emotional intelligence, and radical change. *Academy of Management Review, 24*(2), 325–345.

Isen, A.M. (1985). The asymmetry of happiness and sadness in effects on memory in normal college students. *Journal of Experimental Psychology: General, 114,* 388–391.

Isen, A.M., & Daubman, K.A. (1984). The influence of affect on categorization. *Journal of Personality and Social Psychology, 47,* 1206–1217.

Isen, A.M., Daubman, K.A., & Nowicki, G.P. (1987). Positive affect facilitates creative problem solving. *Journal of Personality and Social Psychology, 52,* 1122–1131.

Janis, I. (1982). *Groupthink: Psychological studies of policy decisions and fiascoes.* Boston, MA: Houghton Mifflin.

Jones, T.M. (1991). Ethical decision making by individuals in organizations: An issue-contingent model. *Academy of Management Review, 16*(2), 366–95.

Jordan, P.J., Ashkanasy, N.M., & Hartel, C.E.J. (2002). Emotional intelligence as a moderator of emotional and behavioral reactions to job insecurity. *Academy of Management Review, 27*(3), 361–372.

Kellett, J.B., Humphrey, R.H., & Sleeth, R.G. (2002). Empathy and complex task performance: Two routes to leadership. *Leadership Quarterly, 13,* 523–544.

Keltner, D., Ellsworth, P.C., & Edwards, K. (1993). Beyond simple pessimism. Effects of sadness and anger on social perception. *Journal of Personality and Social Psychology, 64*(5), 740–752.

Kohlberg, L. (1969). Stage and sequence: The cognitive-developmental approach to socialization. In D. A. Goslin (Ed.), *Handbook of socialization theory and research* (pp. 347–480). Chicago: Rand McNally.

Kramer, R.M. (2003). The harder they fall. *Harvard Business Review, 81*(10), 58–66.

Lord, R.G., & Kanfer, R. (2002). Emotions and organizational behavior. In R.G. Lord, R.J. Klimoski, & R. Kanfer (Eds). *Emotions in the workplace: Understanding the structure and role of emotions in organizational behavior.* San Francisco, CA: Jossey-Bass.

Mayer, J.D., & Salovey, P. (1990). Emotional intelligence. *Imagination, Cognition, & Personality, 9*(3), 185–211.

Mayer, J.D., & Salovey, P. (1997). What is emotional intelligence? In P. Salovey & D.J. Sluyter (Eds.). *Emotional development and emotional intelligence: Educational implications* (pp. 3–34). New York: Basic Books.

Mayer, J.D., Salovey, P., & Caruso, D. (1999). *The Mayer-Salovey-Caruso Emotional Intelligence Test (MSCEIT).* Toronto: Multi-Health Systems.

Mayer, J.D., Salovey, P., & Caruso, D. (2000). Models of emotional intelligence. In R.J. Sternberg (Ed.), *Handbook of Intelligence* (pp. 396–420). Cambridge: University of Cambridge.

Murphy, K.R. (Ed.). (1996). *Individual differences and behavior in organizations.* San Francisco: Jossey-Bass.

Nowicki, S., Jr., & Duke, M.P. (1994). Individual differences in nonverbal communication of affect: The Diagnostic Analysis of Nonverbal Accuracy Scale. *Journal of Nonverbal Behavior, 18,* 9–35.

Nygren, T.E. (1998). Reacting to perceived high-and low-risk win-lose opportunities in a risky decision-making task: Is it framing or affect or both? *Motivation and Emotion, 22*(1), 73–98.

Pizarro, D.A., & Salovey, P. (2002). Being and becoming a good person: The role of emotional intelligence in moral development and behavior. In J. Aronson (Ed.). *Improving academic achievement: Impact of psychological factors in education* (pp.248–278). New York: Academic Press.

Pugh, S.D. (2001). Service with a smile: emotional contagion in the service encounter. *Academy of Management Journal, 44*(5), 1018–1027.

Riggio, R.E. (1986). Assessment of basic social skills. *Journal of Personality and Social Psychology, 51,* 649–660.

Riggio, R.E., Bass, B.M., & Orr, S.S. (2004). Transformational leadership in nonprofit organzations. In R.E. Riggio & S.S. Orr (Eds.), *Improving leadership in nonprofit organizations* (pp. 49–62). San Francisco: Jossey-Bass.

Riggio, R.E., & Carney D.C. (2003). *Manual for the Social Skills Inventory* (2nd ed.). Redwood City, CA: MindGarden.

Rubin, R.S., Tardino, V.M., Daus, C.S., & Munz, D.C. (2005). A reconceptualization of the emotional labor construct: On the development of an integrated theory of perceived emotional dissonance and emotional labor. In C.E.J. Härtel, W. J. Zerbe, & N. M. Ashkanasy (Eds.), *Emotions in organizational behavior* (pp. 189–211). Mahwah, NJ: Earlbaum.

Schaller, M., & Cialdini, R.B. (1990). Happiness, sadness, and helping: A motivational integration. In T.E. Higgins & R.M. Sorrentino (Eds), *Handbook of motivation and cognition: Foundations of social behavior* (Vol. 2, pp. 265–296). New York: Guilford Press.

Schutte, N.S., Malouff, J.M., Hall, L.E., Haggerty, D.J., Cooper, J.T., Golden, C.J., & Dornehim, L. (1998). Development and validation of a measure of emotional intelligence. *Personality and Individual Differences, 25,* 167–177.

Shaw, J.D. (1999). Job satisfaction and turnover intentions: The moderating role of positive affect. *The Journal of Social Psychology, 139*(2), 242–244.

Sloan, A. (2003). Cleaning up dirty business. *Newsweek, 142*(15), 47.

Staw, B.M., Sutton, R.I., & Pelled, L.H. (1994). Employee positive emotion and favorable outcomes at the workplace. *Organization Science, 5,* 51–71.

Treviño, L.K. (1986). Ethical decision making in organizations: A person-situation interactionist model. *Academy of Management Review, 11,* 601–617.

Treviño, L.K., & Youngblood, S.A. (1990). Bad apples in bad barrels: A causal analysis of ethical decision-making behavior. *Journal of Applied Psychology, 75*(4) 378–385.

Watson, D. (2001). *Mood and temperament* New York: Guildford Press.

Watson, D., Clark, L.A., & Tellegen, A. (1988). Development and validation of brief measures of positive and negative affect: the PANAS scales. *Journal of Personality and Social Psychology, 54*(6), 1063–1070.

Wong, C.S., & Law, K.S. (2002). The effects of leader and follower emotional intelligence on performance and attitude: An exploratory study. *Leadership Quarterly, 13,* 243–274.

CHAPTER 11

SELF-CONTROL AND BUSINESS ETHICS

How Strengthening the Self Benefits the Corporation and the Individual

Matthew T. Gailliot and Roy F. Baumeister

INTRODUCTION

That human beings engage in undesirable acts harmful to the self seems inevitable. Many people smoke, drink, and overeat; some gamble, steal, and fight. To overcome the vast multitude of problems plaguing modern American society, it is necessary to exert self-control. Self-control is the capacity to override habitual responses, alter inner states, and change one's behavior. Exerting self-control is probably the only route to reaching the potential of healthy human functioning. Without this capacity, dire consequences abound: Crime, teen pregnancy, alcoholism, drug addiction, venereal disease, educational underachievement, domestic violence, and numerous other social ills. Applying self-discipline and control in one's life is difficult as it often requires sacrificing immediate, short-term pleasures for more desirable rewards that wait in the future. Even if society at large

Positive Psychology in Business Ethics and Corporate Responsibility, pages 231–247
Copyright © 2005 by Information Age Publishing
All rights of reproduction in any form reserved.

does not experience the effects of poor self-control, the individual often does (e.g., eating binges, spending sprees, procrastination).

But as immensely discouraging as many of these actions can be, their negative impact is dwarfed by the magnitude of the individual's ability to change. Many people do successfully change themselves in positive, constructive ways. They pursue long-term goals successfully and begin to fulfill their individual potentialities.

Many psychologists have theorized about the vast potential of humanity's ability to change and exert greater self-control. Perhaps most optimistic was Abraham Maslow with his ideas of the self-actualizing individual. Maslow recognized human frailties and failures, but he remained brightly optimistic about the human capacity for health, happiness, and self-actualization. At the core of his optimism is the concept of self-control, in the sense of the application of effort to avoid or refrain from acts harmful to the self. (The term self-regulation will be used interchangeably with self-control, although some authors assign different meanings to these terms.)

The self is an active entity that intentionally engages in volitional processes to change, alter, or modify itself. Although failures of self-control are commonplace, such as smoking, compulsive spending, and overeating, large multitudes of people do in fact change their behavior toward more desirable ends. Recent research on self-control reveals that the self's ability to change or alter its behavior is an essential aspect of the human psyche that is highly encouraging. The understanding of self-control should lead to the maximization of the individual's strengths and diminishment of his or her weaknesses, as well as providing knowledge beneficial to most aspects of life, including ethics in business and corporate responsibility.

Self-control is a powerful source of human strength, and hence we think it important that positive psychology recognize it (Baumeister & Vohs, in press). In our view, self-control is an important key to positive and adaptive human functioning. The capacity for self-control is much greater in human beings than in other species, suggesting that human evolution proceeded in part by greatly enhancing this capacity in order to create the distinctively human psyche with its remarkable powers. Enhanced self-control cannot only reduce many personal and societal problems; it can enable people to fulfill their potential in love, work, and leisure. In the world of business, self-control can contribute to achievement, thrift, teamwork, harmony, better decision-making, and other positive outcomes. Exhibiting proper self-control is also imperative to numerous issues vital to ethical behavior in the workplace. By strengthening self-control in the individual worker, the business executive can hope to reduce sexual harassment, employee dishonesty, corruption, and other misbehavior.

Before directly discussing the positive components of self-control and its useful application in the business world, however, it is first necessary to describe what is known about the components of self-control and how it functions. The first part of the chapter will provide an overview of the research program on self-control by one of the authors. Business implications and applications will then be surveyed.

SELF-CONTROL AS A MUSCLE

Research on self-control has revealed several intriguing results: The application of self-control appears to parallel the use of a muscle in several ways. Muscles can become fatigued with use in the short-term. If you were to run up a flight of stairs, you would obviously have less energy to descend back down the same set of stairs. Several studies have suggested that exerting self-control produces a similar depletion of energy. More specifically, it has been found that an initial act of self-control depletes some inner resource that is required for subsequent acts of self-control. For the design of most of these studies, some people engage in an act of self-control (e.g., not eating tempting food, suppressing emotions) and other people do not. Because only the former group should exhibit signs of depletion resulting from the initial task, their performance on an unrelated, subsequent task requiring self-control is impaired relative to that of those who are not depleted. It appears that the inner resource used for acts of self-control is also used for several other functions of the self.

Yet a muscle can also be strengthened in the long run through exercise. Self-control also appears to increase in strength with use. Several studies have shown this pattern, with repeated acts in self-control leading to improvements over time. Individuals exhibit large differences in their ability to exert self-control and improvements through exercise may contribute to these dissimilarities.

Short-term Depletion

As mentioned previously, it appears that applying self-control in one behavior makes it more difficult to do the same later on. Thus, self-control functions akin to a muscle or strength that relies upon a single resource. Research indicates several acts of self-control that rely upon this single resource for strength, including altering emotions, controlling thoughts, stifling impulses, and making decisions.

In a first study, Muraven, Tice, and Baumeister (1998) examined how regulating emotions affected people's ability to apply self-control in a seemingly unrelated subsequent task. Participants initially watched an upsetting film, during which they tried to increase or decrease their emotional reactions. Consequently, these participants performed more poorly on a measure of physical stamina (squeezing a handgrip), as compared to a group of participants who simply watched the film without trying to alter their emotional states. Squeezing a handgrip requires self-control because one must continuously exert effort and override the natural response to give up. Thus, the initial act of self-control (i.e., altering one's emotion) apparently depleted some inner resource that might otherwise have been used for later acts of self-control. Similar effects occurred after thought suppression, such that after trying not to think about a white bear, participants were less able to persist in a subsequent task.

These results were replicated in another study in which Muraven et al. (1998) examined how the same thought suppression procedure would affect people's ability to regulate their emotions. First, some participants avoided thinking about a white bear and others engaged in an equally difficult task (i.e., solving arithmetic problems). Then, they were shown a comedy video clip and were instructed to suppress any emotional reaction they had. Because the thought suppression task required self-control whereas solving math problems did not (because no habitual response had to be overridden), it was expected that only thought regulation would to lead to depletion. And this is exactly what was found: Participants who attempted to control their thoughts were significantly less able to suppress their emotions. They smiled and laughed more and appeared more amused by the video.

It has also been found that resisting temptation by controlling one's impulses is another process that drains self-regulatory strength (Baumeister, Bratslavsky, Muraven, & Tice, 1998). In one study, hungry participants were seated in a room in which delicious cookies were recently baked. These cookies were then placed in front of the participants, along with other chocolates and a bowl of radishes. Some participants were allowed to eat whatever they wanted (and others were not presented with any food). Another group of participants, however, were allowed to eat only from the bowl of radishes. Next, participants attempted to trace a geometric figure without lifting their pencil, an outcome that was impossible with the figures they were given. Because their self-regulatory resources had been depleted, the participants who ate radishes gave up sooner on the impossible tracing task, made fewer attempts at solving the puzzles, and reported being more tired.

Choice and Decision-Making

Several studies also indicate that acts of decision-making lead to depletion (and vice-versa) and that this depletion also leads to lower quality decisions. Thus, the self's resources are not only allocated toward tasks requiring self-control, but are also needed for optimal cognitive functioning. In one study, for instance, college undergraduates were asked to give a speech about increasing tuition (Baumeister et al., 1998). Some participants did not have to decide how they felt about the issue. Instead, they were asked to take a particular stand (e.g., supporting an increase in tuition). Other participants had to decide themselves how they felt about the issue. After making the decision, participants tried to complete unsolvable geometric puzzles (no one actually made a speech). Students who had to choose whether to support increasing tuition gave up sooner on the unsolvable puzzles, as compared to people who were told which speech to make. Thus, the simple act of making a decision apparently depleted the same resource needed for self-control.

These results have also been confirmed by subsequent work. In one study, participants were shown a long list of commercial products and were allowed to choose which products they wished to have (Twenge, Tice, Schmeichel, & Baumeister, 2000). Another group of participants supplied ratings of how frequently they used the same products, but were not required to make any decisions. Thus, only the first group should have exhibited signs of depletion because they were required to engage in active volition. Consequently, participants in the decision-making group were less able to force themselves to drink a bitter tasting beverage, whereas those not depleted drank substantially more.

People also become more passive in their decision-making when their resources are depleted (Baumeister et al., 1998). After an initial act of self-control, participants in one study were shown a boring film that they could stop watching whenever they wished. When the decision to end the film required an active response (i.e., pressing a button to end the film), the depleted participants preferred to remain passive (as demonstrated by their waiting longer to stop the film). Thus, when the self's resources are depleted, decision-making tends to reflect a more passive, easier route.

When people become depleted, their ability to think logically and make appropriate decisions is also impaired. For example, after previously exerting self-control, participants perform relatively poor on tests requiring reasoning and analytical skills (Schmeichel, Vohs, & Baumeister, 2003). When deciding how much a commercial product is worth or how much one is willing to pay for it, depleted participants overestimate the value of the items and are willing to pay more than non-depleted participants. Vohs and Faber (in press) showed that depletion of self-control resources caused people to manage their money less thriftily and less effectively. In one study, participants were asked what was the maximum amount they would spend for a series of products, and depleted participants consistently were willing to spend higher amounts. In another study, participants were given a stake of $10 that they could either keep or spend on an assortment of cheap, low-quality items from the university bookstore. Depleted participants spent over half their money on those items, whereas non-depleted participants averaged less than one dollar. Although these findings focus on consumers rather than sellers and manufacturers, the implications for the business persons are clear: Thrift and careful money management are fostered by high self-control, whereas depleted persons lean toward spending what they have in the present moment.

Evidence from non-experimental studies also supports a model of limited self-control strength. When under stress, for instance, people become increasingly emotional and irritable, smoke more, break diets or overeat, and abuse alcohol or other drugs (Baumeister, Heatherton, & Tice, 1994). They are less able to control their emotions when they are tired, upset, under stress, or experiencing other demands (Muraven et al., 1998). Self-control also seems to be at its weakest later in the day when people are most likely to be depleted. During the night, people are more likely to give in to tempting foods and break their diets, commit regretful sexual acts, smoke cigarettes and drink alcohol, and engage in violent and impulsive crimes. Although other factors probably influence these behavioral patterns (e.g., having more free-time during the afternoon), they nonetheless are consistent with patterns of ego depletion.

It seems the self has one resource that is necessary for myriad tasks. Controlling one's thoughts, emotions, and impulses, thinking logically, and making decisions all become more difficult when one is depleted. Engaging in these acts consumes one's self-control strength. These findings demonstrate how self-control functions like a muscle by becoming fatigued in the short run. Unfortunately, this strength appears to be drastically limited. For example, simply by having people decide which commercial products they would like to own, they were unable to drink an aversive tasting beverage. This suggests that a person can perform optimally in only a few tasks requiring self-control at any given moment. If one task requires a significant portion of the self's resources, then someone could potentially fail at even the simplest of tasks later on.

The severe limitations of this resource suggested by the research seemingly indicate that an individual should fail at most of his or her endeavors. However, this is obviously not the case. Almost everyone is required to make numerous decisions daily, yet people do not always fail to control their behavior. Then how does one manage all of these simultaneous or consecutive depleting tasks? One solution seems to be through exercise.

Long-term Improvements

Consistent with the muscle analogy, self-control also appears to improve with exercise. The more one exerts self-control, the easier it becomes. This property is supported in several ways. For example, one is most likely to be successful quitting drinking or smoking not during the first attempt, but after multiple, successive attempts at quitting (Schacter, 1982). Because each attempt should increase self-control strength, then it is reasonable that later attempts would become easier. Likewise, someone who recovers from an addiction to alcohol stands a greater chance of being able to quit smoking cigarettes (Breslau, Peterson, Schultz, Andreski, & Chilcoat, 1996; Zimmerman, Warheit, Ulbrich, & Auth, 1990).

Experimental evidence also indicates that self-control can improve through repeated exercise. In one study, participants were less able to squeeze a handgrip after a previous exercise in thought suppression (Muraven, Baumeister, & Tice, 1999). Following these activities, some participants engaged in a single self-regulatory task during the course of two weeks, such as improving body posture, avoiding bad moods, or keeping a food diary. The participants then returned to the laboratory once again to complete the handgrip and thought suppression exercises. Relative to those who did not practice self-control, participants who engaged in self-control during the two weeks were able to persist longer in the handgrip exercise. In a similar design, improvements in self-control strength were found after having participants use their non-dominant hand for different tasks (e.g., opening doors) or change how they normally speak (e.g., avoid saying slang words) (Oaten, Cheng, & Baumeister, 2003).

Thus, there is a wide assortment of evidence that self-control functions akin to a strength or muscle. Like a muscle, extensive use can cause depletion in the short-run, but repeated exercise can improve self-regulatory strength over time. This principle has been supported not only through observations of everyday living, but also in laboratory studies where variables are experimentally manipulated and controlled. Hence, the notion that self-control functions like a strength is well founded. Although it is clear that practicing self-control makes overriding a habitual response less depleting, it is not entirely clear as to exactly why this occurs. Consistently exerting self-control for a particular act (e.g., going to the gym) can make that act occur automatically and thus, no longer consume the self's resources. However, the exact mechanisms underlying improvements in self-control strength in general are still unknown.

Conservation

Because the self's resources can become depleted on a short-term basis and may be extremely limited (even though they may improve with exercise), it seems unrealistic that the human organism would deplete itself entirely. Also, individuals lacking in self-control would be at an extreme disadvantage, because their resources would be consumed at a frightening pace. One prospect that would counter such drastic consequences is that of conservation, whereby the self does not entirely deplete its self-regulatory strength, but rather conserves the remainder of it when engaging in multiple depleting exercises. This would help explain how laboratory exercises seemed to severely deplete the self through only minimally difficult tasks (e.g., squeezing a handgrip).

Direct support of such conservation comes from a series of experiments by Muraven and Slessareva (2003). By providing some participants with greater incentives to exert self-control, they found that the effects of depletion could be entirely eliminated. In their first study, for instance, participants depleted from a thought suppression exercise persisted in their attempts to trace a geometric figure (which was impossible) for an equal amount of time as non-depleted subjects, but only when they believed the tracing task could be useful in the study of Alzheimer's. In the other two experiments, participants were able to muster their self-control strength despite previous depleting exercises when they were more highly motivated and when they believed their self-control efforts would lead to later success. Muraven and Slessareva concluded that depletion does not necessarily indicate that an individual cannot expend additional resources, but rather that one is not willing to do so without sufficient motivation. In other words, a depleted individual will conserve his or her resources for more important endeavors.

Replenishment

Despite the self's resources being conserved for more important uses, self-regulatory strength can still become depleted. How is this stock of energy replenished? It obviously is restored at some point, especially because self-control can improve with repeated exercise. But by what process does this occur? There appear to be two answers to this question so far. One means is through rest and the other is through experiencing positive affect.

An extensive examination into self-control failure by Baumeister et al. (1994) indicated that self-control is restored with proper amounts of rest. First, people usually do not fail at self-regulation early in the morning when they are well rested. It would be unusual to be on a diet and begin devouring cupcakes as soon as one awakes. Instead, a person is more likely to fail at self-regulation later in the day when fatigue is likely to set in. As mentioned previously, fatigue is related to several self-regulatory failures.

Positive emotions are another means through which the self may replenish its strength. Tice, Dale, and Baumeister (2000) found that people being put into a positive mood in between consecutive self-control exercises demonstrated less depletion than those who did not experience the positive emotional state. This finding meshes nicely with other studies finding that bad moods lead to self-regulatory failures (Baumeister et al., 1994), because negative affect should have the opposite effect on self-control. Even though more research would again be desirable in replicating these findings, it does appear that positive affect serves to replenish the self.

Individual Differences

Because the self's resources are augmented through exercise and replenishment, the idea arises that self-regulatory strength should vary between different individuals. Because some people would engage in self-control exercises more frequently than others or be better rested, this is a logical assumption. The comparison to a muscle further highlights the differences that exist between different people. Some people have a stronger self-control muscle than others and this provides them with several advantages. Several studies have found that one's ability to delay gratification is a stable trait (Mischel, Shoda, & Peake, 1988; Shoda, Mischel, & Peake, 1990). People low in self-control tend to exhibit deficits in several different areas of their lives. For instance, they more frequently engage in criminal acts, drink and use illegal substances, smoke, are absent at work or school, experience unwanted pregnancies, spend impulsively, and become divorced. They also receive lower grades (Tangney, Baumeister, & Boone, in press) and are more likely to engage in fighting, vandalism, and petty theft (Engels, Finkenauer, den Exter Blokland, & Baumeister, 2000). Because self-control relates to so many important aspects of life, self-control can be viewed as a pervasive component of the self. Much of an individual's character is influenced by his or her capacity for self-control.

Acquiescence and Overriding

The notion of self-control strength parallels the view that an impulse has a strength of its own, and that one must overpower it through self-control to avoid giving in to temptation. If an impulse is to be stifled, then self-control must exert a stronger force. For example, the alcoholic's ability to refrain from drinking must be stronger than his or her impulse to drink. Thus, when one fails to exert proper self-control (e.g., drinking alcohol), it is more a matter of being unable to overcome one's impulses, rather than being overpowered by an irresistible urge. It is not that it is impossible to resist, but rather is difficult and exhausting to do so.

Indirect support for this viewpoint comes from one study by Hursh and Winger (1995) who investigated drug addicts' consumption of illegal substances. They found that addicts consumed more drugs when prices decreased and less when prices increased. Although it is not surprising that addicts use more drugs when they are cheaper, their buying less drugs when prices rise suggests that they have some control over their addiction. If they did not, then the price of the substance should be irrelevant.

POSITIVE ASPECTS OF SELF-CONTROL

The idea that one gives in to temptation through acquiescence leads to how self-control is actually a positive phenomenon of psychology. It is the individual's decision to yield to temptation that leads to self-control failure, not the utter strength of the impulse. This view of self-control emphasizes the power of the individual to control his or her fate, as opposed to being at the mercy of temptations and other environmental factors. Indeed, the greater an individual's self-control, the less he or she is driven by external factors.

To be sure, many individuals demonstrate low levels of self-control, which leads to failures in multiple domains in their lives; the self can become depleted quickly and when it is, self-regulatory failure seems certain; a single resource is required for numerous self-regulatory tasks, such as altering emotions and stifling impulses. Even the essential gist of self-control seems negative: A highly appealing activity is currently available, but one must choose to deny this immediate, pleasurable opportunity in the hopes of receiving greater rewards in the future.

However, the topic of self-control is actually a refreshing, positive arena of the human psyche. First and foremost, every individual has the ability to control his or her own behavior. Even though it is sometimes tempting to engage in behaviors that might harm oneself or others, the individual has the ability to refrain from such behaviors in most situations. When an individual consistently does choose to delay gratification he or she is greatly rewarded, performing better intellectually, socially, and emotionally (Mischel et al., 1988). The choice to submit to temptation is made by the individual, even though environmental and other factors may make that decision the more difficult one. Even so, self-control should be able to increase through regular exercise. This aspect alone is highly encouraging, for even though individual differences exist in self-regulatory strength, they need not be permanent. If an individual feels his or her self is weak and too quickly depleted, then he or she may work to strengthen it. The strength of the self appears to only be limited (relatively) by the individual's willingness to work to improve it.

Another positive aspect of self-control is that the individual chooses how and when to expend the self's resources. Even though the particular application of this muscle is draining to the self, it is the individual's choice as to when it should be used. Thus, an individual low in self-control is not entirely disadvantaged provided that he or she is able to select a specific number of self-regulatory spheres (e.g., procrastination, physical exercise) that are the most important, albeit a relatively smaller number than those with higher self-control. Yet if one makes this choice poorly and expends the self's energy in domains less beneficial to the self, the natural process of conservation exists to serve as a safety net. The individual apparently cannot or does not expend all of his or her energy during a single task, thereby becoming highly vulnerable to danger should that energy be needed, but rather is protected by the mechanism of conservation. Also, with increased motivation, the effects of depletion can be minimized, if not entirely eliminated (Muraven & Slessareva, 2003).

Despite the unavoidable downside to short-term depletion, it is highly reassuring that the effects are only temporary. By obtaining a sufficient amount of rest and experiencing positive emotions, the self should be able to replenish itself. The exploration of this avenue of research is particularly exciting, for it should provide the antidote for depletion. The prospect of knowing accurately how to mitigate the effects of depletion can only prove extremely useful. Thus, the self may not need to be weak or limited at all, provided it can be improved immediately and sufficiently. Ultimately, this will allow current behaviors to be molded into ones more advantageous to one's pursuits and avoid the negative, self-defeating behaviors in which individuals sometimes engage. This will enable the individual to procure the more desirable, long-term outcomes and successfully endure the momentary displeasures that render them less obtainable. With the advancement of the current understanding of self-control, this should become all the easier by learning how to replenish and strengthen the self's resources, what pitfalls to avoid that weaken it, and how to avoid yielding to temptation.

Another point about self-control is that the majority of the acts it encompasses are controlled, conscious processes. For example, making decisions, thought suppression, and the like predominantly require one's active attention. Yet the bulk of human behavior is not controlled or conscious, it is automatic. Tritely put, humans are creatures of habit, which is perhaps due to a reliance upon automaticity. Because so much of human behavior is automatic, it is possible that what once required active intervention by the self (and thus was depleting) can become automatic. This would be highly beneficial, as it would conserve the valuable resources of the self and save them for other, more controlled tasks. By practicing self-control, it may be that self-regulatory acts are made automatic easier and quicker.

SELF-CONTROL APPLIED TO THE BUSINESS WORLD

The power of self-control can potentially provide great benefits for businesses and corporations. Allowing employees to function optimally in regard to self-control permits both the individual and company to prosper. But in order for this to occur, managers must first be aware of the multiple sources by which the individual may become depleted, and they must then take the appropriate measures to curb its effects. There are several ways in which depletion may occur from working demands, such as tasks being structured consecutively with little time for rest. Uncontrollable stress, looming deadlines, and other pressures should also lead to depletion. When these factors exist, the individual often struggles in dealing with the negative emotions they create (e.g., anxiety) and in avoiding the unpleasant thoughts they elicit.

Decision-making is perhaps the most important source of workplace depletion, due to its necessity and prevalence. Any decision that is important or not part of a standard routine should be depleting. This could include determining what course of action to pursue, where to stand on a particular issue, and any purchasing considerations. As indicated by Schmeichel et al.'s (2003) study, any cognitive process requiring logical reasoning or comprehension will most likely impair self-regulatory functioning.

The business executive should be aware that factors outside the workplace also can deplete the individual, which would carry over into workplace performance. In today's society these are numerous, although typical causes are stress in the home, marital problems, conflicts with friends and relatives, economic worries, even difficulties in one's leisurely pursuits. There are several avenues managers can take to minimize depletion and thus maximize the health and productivity of their workers. First, because concurrent and consecutive acts can deplete the self, it is necessary to avoid burdening employees with too many tasks requiring self-control or decision-making. Because exerting proper self-control is more difficult with fatigue, productivity and decision-making should be at their best when workers are refreshed. Developing regularity and routine whenever possible should allow employees to conserve the self's limited resources for more novel tasks. If an employee does become depleted, a greater incentive to work (e.g., reminders of bonuses, raises, or promotions) should lessen his or her tendency to conserve.

Failing to consider the effects of self-regulatory depletion can have high costs for any business; properly incorporating the nature of self-control into the business model should be highly profitable. A depleted worker would exhibit cognitive detriments drastic to any company's success: An inability to reason effectively, poor logical deduction, and a lack of comprehension. With depletion, the individual often chooses the more passive route, which is not necessarily the best course of action. Workers would also become less productive and have difficulty persisting in many tasks. A lack of self-control results in myopic preferences, thereby inhibiting the successful setting and reaching of long-term goals.

SELF-CONTROL AND ETHICS IN BUSINESS

The ability to exert self-control is oftentimes crucial to enacting ethical behavior. The desires of the individual sometimes diverge from what ethical considerations mandate and thus, the individual must exert self-control to override his or her inner desires. To be sure, lapses of ethics cannot always be attributed to a lack of self-control. Sometimes, people might not consider whether they are behaving ethically and they will simply proceed to behave as they wish. Other times, a person refrains from unethical behavior because of external demands (e.g., being watched by the boss). When the external demands are removed (e.g., the boss leaves), the person no longer behaves ethically. In this case, the lapse in ethics does not arise from a lack of inner resources. However, a lack of self-control can contribute to unethical behavior when the constraints are internal in nature. For example, an employee who resists the temptation to steal because being honest is important to his self-concept may no longer be able to resist the temptation when he is depleted. When self-control failure results in a lapse of ethics it is probably because the unethical behavior was more desirable (e.g., more rewarding, more habitual) than any available alternative and the individual could no longer pursue any of the alternative courses of action.

Because depletion impairs reasoning skills, depleted employees might not effectively consider the costs and benefits associated with ethical and unethical behavior. After an initial act of self-control, people might focus on the present moment and ignore future consequences (Vohs & Schmeichel, 2003). Consequently, ethical decision making might suffer when employees lack self-control because they fail to consider the ramifications of their actions and possibly ignore the benefits of their other options. To illustrate, consider sexual harassment in the context of self-regulatory failure. Perhaps an upper-level manager is physically attracted to a subordinate. He is accustomed to being flirtatious and constantly must stifle this impulse when he encounters the subordinate. When his self-control strength has been depleted, he may no longer acknowledge that behaving lasciviously is inappropriate. Instead, he may focus only on his current desires and be unable to refrain from acting upon them. Other possible examples of how self-control might relate to ethical behaviors are provided in Table 11.1.

Table 11.1.

Behavior	Components of self-control failure
Theft	• Desire to possess an item belonging to the company
	• Increased focus on that desire
	• Less consideration of costs (e.g., getting caught, harming others)
	• Inability to refrain from stealing
Environmental disregard	• Desire to engage in or promote an activity that directly or indirectly harms the environment
	• Inability to follow environmental guidelines
Discrimination	• Impaired cognition leading to an increased reliance on stereotypes (i.e., automatic cognitions)
	• Biased perception of outgroup members
	• Increased habitual tendency to favor ingroup members
Privacy violations	• Habitual curiosity conflicts with the need to respect others
	• Ability to refrain from violating the rights of others abates
Child and immigration labor	• Conflicting desires to increase profits and respect needs of others
	• Negation of potential costs
	• Hiring children and immigrants becomes increasingly appealing
Employee destructiveness	• Pre-existent desire to neglect or destroy company property (e.g., due to laziness or anger)
	• Inability to control emotions
	• Inability to follow appropriate rules
Executive compensation	• Desire to reward oneself (versus one's subordinates)
	• Increased selfishness

Of course, these possibilities warrant further investigation, but they would not be difficult to test empirically. For instance, one would predict that after engaging in an initial act of self-control (e.g., making decisions), participants would be less able to distinguish between ethical and unethical behavior and their behavior would probably reflect a lack of ethical considerations (e.g., by stealing). When competing demands on behavior exist, depletion should cause one to engage in the most appealing or habitual course of action, regardless of how ethical that behavior is. In some cases, people's inner desires can be selfish and unethical. However, it is possible that depletion could contribute to ethical behavior if a person wants to behave ethically, but has been refraining from doing so. In the case of "whistle-blowing," for instance, a worker might actively refrain from divulging to others the unethical behavior of her superiors, but can no longer do so when she is depleted.

Yet the negative effects of depletion can be countered through replenishment. Creating the most desirable working environment for employees within a successful company is one cornerstone of corporate responsibility and ethics. Allowing proper rest and providing for positive emotions in the workplace are two means toward this end, and they are also vital to high self-control. Replenishment can take several forms in the business environment. On a short-term basis, companies can provide breaks, games, and enjoyable social interactions. For more long-term benefits, individuals should demonstrate greater self-control when they are provided with more vacations, less demanding schedules, and frequent opportunities to improve their moods (e.g., through exercising).

Businesses can also seek to improve their employees' self-control through long-term exercise, which would again benefit the corporation. This could be accomplished by assigning or encouraging tasks that are somewhat draining to the self, but would ultimately serve to strengthen an individual's self-control. Some examples of such exercises could be employees working out at the gym or attending self-help seminars. Even the most minor activities requiring self-control may create longitudinal improvements, such as Muraven et al. (1999) found when participants tried to improve their posture. These tasks should be the least depleting as possible, so as to avoid short-term depletion, but as demanding as is necessary to ultimately increase self-regulatory strength.

CONCLUSION

In closing, the study of self-control is an exciting area of psychology that holds the promise of enabling people to fulfill their potential and live more satisfying, productive lives. Exerting proper self-control in life is essential should one wish to enjoy one's physical, mental, and social capabilities to the fullest extent. Self-control is one essential aspect of the human psyche that is superior to that of other social creatures, yet it is not without its flaws. Research shows that the self can become depleted on a short-term basis, which results in impairments in several different spheres, including decision-making, resisting temptation, and thought and emotion regulation. Yet this negative outcome is not necessarily unavoidable, as there are means for restoration and longitudinal improvement.

Applying the current findings to settings outside the laboratory is useful for obtaining the full benefits from the current stock of knowledge, and the world of business is an ideal setting to begin. There are several avenues companies may pursue to profit fully from an understanding of self-control, which will ultimately improve not only the corporation, but also each individual employee. More specifically, successful self-regulation can lead to enhanced worker productivity through greater persistence and hard work, improved decision-making, and a reduction in the amount of unethical behavior, such as sexual harassment, dishonesty, and corruption. Ironically, the actions needed in the world of business are an example of self-control in itself: The company's short-term gains in productivity must be sacrificed (e.g., by providing breaks and vacations) for more desirable long-term outcomes (e.g., productive employees making better decisions). The ability to work toward the future, even when sacrifices in the present are called for, is probably one crucial reason that self-control evolved in the human psyche, and it continues to confer benefits both to individuals and companies.

REFERENCES

Baumeister, R.F., Bratslavsky, E., Muraven, M., & Tice, D.M. (1998). Ego depletion: Is the active self a limited resource? *Journal of Personality and Social Psychology*, 74, 1252–1265.

Baumeister, R.F., Heatherton, T.F., & Tice, D.M. (1994). *Losing control: How and why people fail at self-regulation.* San Diego, CA: Academic Press.

Baumeister, R.F., & Vohs, K.D. (in press). Self-regulation and self-control. To appear in C. Peterson & M.E.P. Seligman (Eds.), *The VIA Manual of Strengths.* Cincinnati, OH: Values in Action Institute.

Breslau, N., Peterson, E., Schultz, L., Andreski, P., & Chilcoat, H. (1996). Are smokers with alcohol disorders less likely to quit? *American Journal of Public Health*, 86, 985–990.

Engels, R., Finkenauer, C., den Exter Blokland, E.A.W., & Baumeister, R. F. (2000). *Parental influences on self-control and juvenile delinquency.* Manuscript in preparation, Utrecht University, Netherlands.

Hursh, S.R., & Winger, G. (1995) Normalized demand for drugs and other reinforcers. *Journal of Experimental Analysis of Behavior*, 64, 373–384.

Maslow, A.H. (1968). *Toward a psychology of being.* New York: John Wiley and Sons.

Mischel, W., Shoda, Y., & Peake, P.K. (1988). The nature of adolescent competencies predicted by preschool delay of gratification. *Journal of Personality and Social Psychology, 54,* 687–696.

Muraven, M., & Slessareva, E. (2003). Mechanisms of self-control failure: Motivation and Limited Resources. *Personality and Social Psychology Bulletin, 29,* 894–906.

Muraven, M., Baumeister, R.F., & Tice, D.M. (1999). Longitudinal improvement of self-regulation through practice: Building self-control through repeated exercise. *Journal of Social Psychology, 139,* 446–457.

Muraven, M., Tice, D.M., & Baumeister, R.F. (1998). Self-control as limited resource: Regulatory depletion patterns. *Journal of Personality and Social Psychology, 74,* 774–789.

Oaten, M., Cheng, K., & Baumeister, R.F. (2003). *Strengthening the regulatory muscle: The longitudinal benefits of exercising self-control.* Manuscript in preparation, Macquarie University.

Schacter, S. (1982). Recidivism and self-cure of smoking and obesity. *American Psychologist, 37,* 436–444.

Schmeichel, B.J., Vohs, K.D., & Baumeister, R.F. (2003). Intellectual performance and ego depletion: Role of the self in logical reasoning and other information processing. *Journal of Personality and Social Psychology, 85,* 33–46.

Shoda, Y., Mischel, W., & Peake, P.K. (1990). Predicting adolescent cognitive and self-regulatory competencies from preschool delay of gratification: Identifying diagnostic conditions. *Developmental Psychology, 26,* 978–986.

Tangney, J.P., Baumeister, R.F., & Boone, A.L. (in press). High self-control predicts good adjustment, less pathology, better grades, and interpersonal success. *Journal of Personality.*

Tice, D.M., Dale, K.P., & Baumeister, R.F. (2000). *Replenishing the self: Positive emotions offset the effects of ego depletion.* Manuscript in preparation, Case Western Reserve University.

Twenge, J.M., Tice, D.M., Schmeichel, B., & Baumeister, R.F. (2000). *Decision fatigue: Making multiple personal decisions depletes the self's resources.* Manuscript submitted for publication.

Vohs, K.D., & Faber, R. (in press). Self-regulation and impulsive spending patterns. To appear in P.A. Keller & D.W. Rook (Eds.), *Advances in consumer research.*

Vohs, K.D., & Schmeichel, B.J. (2003). Self-regulation and the extended now: Controlling the self alters the subjective experience of time. *Journal of Personality and Social Psychology, 85,* 217–230.

Zimmerman, R.S., Warheit, G.J., Ulbrich, P.M., & Auth, J.B. (1990). The relationship between alcohol use and attempts and success at smoking cessation. *Addictive Behaviors, 15,* 197–207.

CHAPTER 12

THE ETHICS OF HOPE

A Guide for Social Responsibility in Contemporary Business

Hal S. Shorey, Kevin L. Rand, and C. R. Snyder

INTRODUCTION

Although there was a move toward greater accountability in businesses prior to recent high-profile scandals, such large-scale failures of the social trust have increased the perceived societal need for corporate social responsibility and ramped up the debate on regulation versus deregulation (see Sridharan, Dickes, & Caines, 2002). Although these regulatory strategies (including ethics codes) may lead to some changed business behaviors, they are unlikely to succeed because they emphasize avoidance goals that focus on avoiding losses or negative outcomes. Such avoidance goals do not motivate or promote pro-social conduct (Margolis, 2001; Natale, 1983) because they are not positively reinforced. That is to say, when an avoidance goal is attained, the recipient receives no sense of having gained anything.

The limited effectiveness of regulatory strategies for instilling cultures of social responsibility in contemporary business highlights the need to incor-

Positive Psychology in Business Ethics and Corporate Responsibility, pages 249–264
Copyright © 2005 by Information Age Publishing

249

porate psychological research on motivation into models of business ethics (Vidaver-Cohen, 2001). It is in this spirit that we presently introduce *hope theory* (Snyder, 2002; Snyder, Harris et al., 1991) and demonstrate how hope can be applied to shape socially responsible attitudes and their associated behaviors. We will begin by defining hope. Using examples from the last decade of hope research, we then will describe how hope contributes to positive performance outcomes, mental health, and adaptive decision-making. Finally, after tying hope findings to theory and research on social responsibility and business ethics, we will conclude by outlining what we call the *ethics of hope*. In this context, ethics is a system of accepted beliefs that control behavior. Through applying this hopeful thinking and beliefs-system to real-world settings, we derive a set of workable guidelines for ethical decision-making in contemporary business.

HOPE: THEORY AND RESEARCH

Hope (Snyder, 2002; Snyder, Harris et al., 1991) reflects a motivational thought process composed of: (1) well-defined goals; (2) the perceived ability to identify strategies to achieve those goals (pathways); and (3) the perceived motivation (agency) to utilize those pathways to pursue desired outcomes. Each of these three components, goals, pathways, and agency, must be present for hopeful thinking to occur. For example, without goals as targets for guiding behaviors, strategies and motivations are irrelevant. Likewise, when a goal is present, failure to identify pathways or a lack of mental agency to implement those pathways will prevent goal attainments.

Hopeful thinking develops in the context of secure childhood relationships with adult role models who are consistent in their availability and responsiveness (Shorey, Snyder, Yang, & Lewin, 2003; Snyder, 1994). Accordingly, hope becomes a stable trait-like disposition through prolonged childhood interactions with such adults, or "coaches" (Snyder, 1994). These coaches promote children's exploratory behaviors by providing secure bases of support to which children can retreat for comfort and reenergization before launching into their next goal pursuits. The developing child gradually internalizes this secure-base relationship. Moreover, the subsequently developed roadmaps (i.e., cognitive schema) for pursuing goals and understanding how others and surrounding environments will support those goals, instill a sense of trust in the reliability of cause and effect relationships (see Shorey, Snyder, Rand, Hockemeyer, & Feldman, 2002; Snyder, 1994). Thus, when developed properly, these schemas impart a sense of hope.

As we will elucidate shortly, this hope-filled developmental trajectory has important implications for the goals that people and organizations choose, as well as their conduct in pursuit of those goals. Perhaps most important, this developmental model also shows that hope is a learned pattern of goal-directed thought.

Those people who have learned to think with high rather than low hope: (1) perform better; (2) derive greater satisfaction from their performances; (3) become happier; (4) derive physical and mental-health benefits; and, (5) work more closely with others for the greater common good (Snyder, 2002). Furthermore, not only do high- relative to low-hope people experience less depression, less generalized anxiety (Shorey et al., 2003; Shorey, Snyder, Etchison, Hilleary, & Little, 2003; Snyder, Harris et al., 1991), and greater positive affect (Snyder, Harris et al., 1991), but they also retain their positive thoughts and feelings even after failure experiences (Shorey, 2003).

In addition to the aforementioned hope-related benefits, other high-hope characteristics have far-reaching implications—particularly for business settings. As will be elaborated shortly, these characteristics translate into the leadership abilities and socially responsible behaviors that lead to greater long-term business profitability. Accordingly, high- as compared to low-hope people have: (1) more goals; (2) goals that are more challenging (stretch goals); (3) better skills in clearly conceptualizing their goals; and, (4) higher probabilities of reaching their goals (Snyder, 2002; Snyder, Cheavens, & Sympson, 1997; Snyder, Harris et al., 1991). Similarly, high- relative to low-hope students have higher grade point averages throughout their educational careers and have lower dropout rates and correspondingly higher graduation rates in college (Chang, 1998; Curry, Snyder, Cook, Ruby, & Rehm, 1997; Snyder, Shorey et al., 2002; Snyder, Hoza et al., 1997).

In relation to low-hope persons, the superior achievements of high-hope persons reflect their lower performance anxieties (Snyder, 1999), along with their abilities to use feedback from failure experiences to improve future performances (Snyder, 2002; Snyder, Shorey et al., 2002). These high-hope persons are able to use feedback adaptively because they take failures to mean that they did not try hard enough or use the right strategies (Shorey, 2003; Snyder, 1994). In contrast, when low-hope people receive negative feedback about their performances, they are likely to have negative and excessive failure ruminations that further interfere with clear goal-directed thinking (Snyder, 1999; Snyder, Lopez, Shorey, Rand, & Feldman, 2003; Snyder & Pulvers, 2001).

At first glance, it makes sense that in anticipation of poor performances and failures, the low-hopers would choose goals where they could succeed easily. Nevertheless, there also are cases where low-hope persons choose extremely difficult, even obviously unobtainable goals (Snyder, 1994). This is because failures at such goals can be attributed to how difficult those goals were rather than to a lack of personal (or business) resources. As such, these low-hope people are using the difficulty of their high goals as anticipatory excuses (Snyder, Higgins, & Stucky, 1983).

In fact, personal resources are what low-hope people lack. They are bereft of abilities to adequately develop new, alternative pathways. Thus, they become rigid in their problem solving and keep using the same strategies and attempting the same goals even after repeated failures (Zander, 1971). The resulting negative self-fulfilling prophecies unfortunately increase the probabilities of future failures as well.

In contrast to the rigid low-hope pattern, high-hope people are flexible in their choices. They choose stretch goals that are challenging, but not so difficult as to be impossible (Snyder, 2002). They also are more likely than low-hope people to develop alternative pathways to go around obstacles when their goal routes are impeded. Likewise, high-hopers seem to understand that when obstacles are truly insurmountable, the best strategy sometimes is to let go of that particular goal (Snyder et al., 1997) and to re-goal (see Snyder, Feldman, Shorey, & Rand, 2002). Because goals in business (e.g., securing a production contract) usually are sub-goals to even larger goals (increasing profits), re-goaling itself can be conceived as the ability to find new and innovative pathways.

HOPE AS PRO-SOCIAL MOTIVATION

In today's highly technical and diverse business environments, no one person can possess all the information needed to achieve the goals of the organization. Accordingly, successful companies must learn to effectively manage their human and social capital as valuable resources (Luthans & Youssef, in press). Thus, people become some important pathways to successfully attain organizational goals. Companies that do not value their social capital (i.e., their employees) deplete this scarce resource and suffer long-term negative consequences. High-hope people and companies, in contrast, do not have this difficulty because they are invested socially (Snyder, Cheavens et al., 1997). They: (1) take pleasure in seeing other people succeed (Snyder, Cheavens et al., 1997); (2) have greater secure attachments to others (Shorey, Snyder, Yang, & Lewin, 2003); (3) perceive high levels of social support (Vaux et al., 1986); (4) are able to take others' perspectives (Rieger, 1993); and, (5) have trust in their abilities to predict future outcomes (Shorey et al., 2002). Therefore, as high-hope people achieve their goals and accordingly are promoted to leadership positions, they are likely to express their pro-social motivations by taking on roles of "coaches" and acting as mentors for others (see Snyder, 1994; Snyder & Shorey, in press).

Having been imbued with senses of security and trust by working with such supportive "coaches," employees' increasingly high levels of hope become valuable assets to companies. As an example, consider the following characteristics of high-hope employees reported in a recent survey of hope in American businesses (Snyder, 2003). High-hope employees were: (1) courteous to fellow workers and customers, especially during difficult discussions or interactions; (2) good sports about fellow workers getting rewards (raises, advancement, recognition, etc.); (3) not blaming of fellow workers, management, or customers when difficulties arose; and (4) willing to help other workers and to assist in their local communities.

High-hope people's prosocial motivations also are reflected in their having important goals in domains outside of work and career (i.e., social, family, romance: Snyder, Cheavens et al., 1997; Sympson, 1999). High-hope people are able to use their social goals to maintain high levels of hope when they encounter impediments in other life arenas (Snyder, Cheavens et al., 1997). Low-hope people, on the other hand, seem to lack such abilities. Having generally fewer goals, they tend to invest heavily in specific life arenas—a prime one being their careers. Accordingly, when experiencing difficulties at work, low hopers do not have the external interests to replenish their hopes. Thus, low- as compared to high-hope people should be more prone to job burnout (Snyder, 1994). Finally, because hope operates at the group as well as at the individual level (see Shorey, Snyder, Warner, & Myren, 2003; Snyder, Cheavens et al., 1997), companies also may become too narrowly focused in their goals and lose motivation during economic downturns. This is a major reason that companies should diversify and develop socially responsible goals.

When Problems Arise: The Role of Goals in Decision Making

Goals, the first and anchoring component of hopeful thinking, direct and determine the majority of human behaviors (Adler, as cited in Ansbacher & Ansbacher, 1956). Goals are so powerful that they influence how people act, even when those people are unaware that they have such goals (Bargh & Chartrand, 1999). After all, if we had to think about each of our many daily goal pursuits, our cognitive processes would be overwhelmed and, as a result, we would be far less likely to take action. Thus, non-conscious, unarticulated goal pursuits are adaptive. They also can be problematic, however. For example, a goal for personal (or corporate) financial security could be achieved by either working cooperatively and seeking social inclusion, or behaving competitively and treating other people or organizations as threats. Indeed, this latter case is a prime source of unethical conduct. It often involves persons or groups with high levels of agency thinking who are pursuing non-conscious, competitive goals, and leaving wakes of destruction behind them.

Although society invests heavily in imparting prosocial values and goals to its children, there is a minority of persons for whom hopeful thinking becomes directed at non-socially sanctioned goals (see Shorey et al., 2002; Snyder, 1994). For example, some corporate managers may be high in hope in that they are able to: (1) set goals (e.g., maximize stock valuation for short-term profit taking); (2) identify strategies for achieving those goals (e.g., inflate earnings reports by creating "dummy companies" and hiding losses); and (3) motivate themselves and their followers to pursue goals (e.g., "we all will get wealthy"). Such hope is adaptive to the extent that it enables these managers and their "inside" groups to attain senses of security in highly competitive or even hostile business environments. Thus, these people are pursuing specific goals that are congruent with the values of their unique social subgroups. This is not so different from the phenomena of "group think," in which groups that are isolated from outside influences establish a set of values and disregard all alternatives (Janis, 1971). In this same way, cultures within business organizations may create value systems that promote the pursuit of goals that are outside of acceptable societal norms.

In addition to the true high-hope people who are socially invested (at least within their groups), there is a subset of persons whose "apparent" hope is an avoidant defense against "perceived" inferiorities. People with this *defensive achievement orientation* strive for perceived superiority through achievements in areas such as work or academics where successes can be realized and, at the same time, where close interpersonal relationships can be avoided. The self-worth of a person, however, is not derived in a social vacuum, but rather in relation to others (see Leary & Baumeister, 2000). Thus, the goals pursued by people with high defensive achievement orientations may appear to be approach goals in content (e.g., to gain promotions), when in fact these underlying goals are aimed at avoiding feelings of inferiority (i.e., avoidance goals). Because success in achieving avoidance goals yields little in the way of psychological benefits, people with defensive achievement orientations do not benefit fully from their goal-directed cognitions (Shorey et al., 2003). It follows, therefore, that success never is enough for a person with a defensive achievement orientation.

Furthermore, success never is enough for rogue companies or despot dictators. A corporate CEO, for example, may appear to have high hope when striving to gain power within the organization, or when strengthening the economic position of his or her organization in the marketplace. Having achieved such a position, however, goals usually shift to ones of maintaining market position, avoiding losses, and retaining power. Once again, because avoidance goals are not psychologically reinforcing, agency thinking begins to wane and accordingly it becomes more difficult to develop pathways. When the inevitable goal blockages then are encountered, a sense of desperation may lead to the adoption of unethical pathways (sub-goals) that previously had not been considered. To compound the problems, if the executive in such a position has a defensive achievement orientation, then the competitors and followers alike may be trampled or sacrificed in the interest of that executive's goal attainments. Thus, the combination of avoidance goals and a lack of prosocial motivation may lead to extreme unethical behaviors.

The aforementioned unethical behaviors contribute to employees losing trust in their organizations and their leaders. Such trust is the most important ingredient of effective leadership (Fairholm, 1997), and its absence can bring about the demise of hope in employees (Shorey & Snyder, 2004). Moreover, the recent rise in employee turnover has created climates where businesses are reluctant to share too much information with employees who may not be with the organization in the future (Adams III et al., 2003). Thus, important information is withheld from employees and distributed only on a need-to-know basis. Consequently, employees do not know what to expect and they then lose their abilities to predict future outcomes. Hope, or the ability to accurately predict probabilities of future goal attainments, is lost in such environments. Lacking clear goals to anchor hopeful thinking, having lost trust in their own abilities, and distrusting company motives, employees in such circumstances are likely to experience heightened stress, depression, and job burnout, along with lowered on-the-job efficiencies.

GOAL CHOICE PERSPECTIVES IN BUSINESS

Historically, there have been two dominant perspectives about the goals that businesses should pursue. The first of these positions, classical economic theory, holds that the primary goal of business should be to maximize profits (Friedman, 1970; Marcoux, 2003). Within this perspective, other socially responsible goals may be secondary. Taken to an extreme, some have even argued that "doing good" is wasteful in that the socially conscious, ethical organization is inefficient and thus will be driven out of the competitive marketplace (see Peterson, 2002).

The alternative to classical economic theory proposes that corporations have responsibilities to others (i.e., the "stakeholders," including consumers, employees, and the environment) that go beyond the interests of corporate boards and shareholders (see Clarkson Centre for Business Ethics, 1999; Freeman, 1984). This is because businesses operate within and have an impact upon their environments. Thus, companies are indebted to and owe services to their surrounding environments. We agree with this socially responsible perspective and believe that this approach provides the only viable means whereby businesses can be profitably sustained over time. This is not to say that we prefer social objectives to economic ones. Indeed, the first supports the latter. We do propose, however, that when businesses lack long-term socially responsible perspectives, they often contribute to their own downfalls by failing to protect the surrounding environments that sustain them.

As suggested previously in our discussion of non-consciously-held goals, the perspectives of profit maximization versus social responsibility yield differing goals and divergent models of what constitutes acceptable behaviors. We are aware that profit maximization and social responsibility are not polar opposites and that there is a healthy balance where profitability and social responsibility coexist. Indeed, describing how this can be done is one of our purposes in this chapter. Adherence to socially responsible behavior is, however, a rate-limiting step beyond which making more money becomes ethically problematic. For example, when corporations have the maximization of profits as their *only* priorities, unethical behaviors that make money to the detriments of social interests may become acceptable. These higher-order profit-maximizing goals also lead to the generation of congruent sub-goals. For example, a pharmaceutical company wishing to maximize profits by rushing a new drug to market might adopt a sub-goal (pathway) of suppressing non-supportive research findings. The resulting cascade of increasingly discrete supporting sub-goals and their pathways then could proliferate unethical conduct throughout the organizational hierarchy—from the upper corporate echelons to the filing clerks. Those in the lower echelons may not take personal responsibility for their supporting roles by deferring responsibility to superiors (similar to World War II concentration camp guards who were "just following orders") (Snyder et al., 1983). Thus, over time, the guiding profit maximization goal of the organization infiltrates the personal (un)ethical conduct of everyday workers.

BUILDING SOCIALLY RESPONSIBLE ENVIRONMENTS: THE ETHICS OF HOPE

Although classical economic theory emphasized profit maximization as the primary goal of the business enterprise (see Natale, 1983), the present interdependence of world financial markets make it unrealistic for companies to view themselves as isolated (individualistic) entities on the economic stage. In addition, proactive consumers and investors increasingly are applying the "power of the purse" to pressure companies to act in accordance with more socially conscious societal norms (Ruf, Krishna-murty, & Paul, 1996). Thus, the "me first" attitude that previously has characterized Western business cultures no longer may be appropriate. As the *tragedy of the commons* (Hardin, 1968) powerfully illustrates, when individuals (or companies) act in the interest of short-term personal gains, scarce resources are depleted and everyone, including those who realized the short-term gains, is harmed (Edney, 1979). Thus, the only way to sustain a healthy, profitable business is to consider the social interests of others, including the environment (Natale, 1983). For this reason, Natale (1983) proposed a systems approach in which "... each business will need to discover for itself (1) what its goals are, (2) if the goals 'fit' today's economy, and (3) how to achieve those goals" (Natale, 1983, p. 60). In short, because hope is a system of thinking that involves (1) having clear, well-defined goals, (2) identifying the pathways, or the "how" of achieving those goals, along with (3) the motivation of creating sustained profitability, Natale was issuing a call for hope in the business world.

We have suggested elsewhere that organizational change must begin at the top, with the high hopes of effective leaders (Shorey & Snyder, 2004; Snyder & Shorey, in press). Such leaders understand that authoritarian leadership, no matter how benign, does not produce happy, healthy, and productive workplaces. Thus, effective leaders must work hard to engender reciprocal respect and trust within their organizations. Trust and security are absolutely essential for the development of hope, and one way to build such trust is through open, strong communications, from corporate news-letters to mini-meetings in the hall that encourage independent thought and discourse.

Communications are vital for the high-hope organization's goal attainments because hope in organizations operates similarly to hope in individuals. Within organizations, however, the components of hope, goals, agency, and pathways, may reside in multiple individuals as opposed to residing within one person. For example, although the goal-setting component of hope may rest with top leadership, the pathways component may belong to smaller work groups further down in the organizational structure. The agency component, in turn, may reside within rank-and-file employees, as their positive morale feeds back up the organizational hierarchy to fuel the goal-pursuit machine.

Open communications also lead to organizational transparency in that the objectively stated goals are open to debate and public scrutiny, thereby discouraging unethical conduct. On this point, it is important for employees to know that their companies adhere to ethical, people-oriented business practices because this knowledge increases employees' trust in how their companies will treat them. Employees also are less likely to feel taken advantage of if companies share their financial information internally. Such disclosures and progress reports give everyone an idea of how the company is doing. As such, people know where the company stands, what its goals are, and what happens when those goals are or are not met. When there are no secrets, everyone can share in the goals and successes of the company.

Having established an environment of trust and security, the next phase in fostering the *ethics of hope* is to anchor hope to concrete goals. In order for goals to be effective, they must be: (1) clearly defined; (2) challenging (but achievable); and (3) measurable according to preestablished criteria. This last point is particularly important because success cannot be experienced if there are no concrete ways of telling when goals have been achieved. Successes are important for agency thinking because the positive emotions from those experiences feed back, energize, and keep people moving toward their goals. For this same reason, setting measurable sub-goals to the higher order goal is important so that success can be experienced along the way. Lastly, to increase the reinforcing properties of successful goal achievements, goals should be framed in terms of approaching positive as opposed to avoiding negative outcomes (see Tversky & Kahneman, 1981).

Although sub-goals may be achieved in close temporal proximity, such short-term goals should not be ends unto themselves. We have found that high-hope individuals and companies have long-term goals—visions—for their futures. Such long-term goals are important for social responsibility in business because they are the beacons that guide ethical behaviors. Put another way, when freestanding short-term goals are adopted, there is no higher order framework in which to judge how goals fit with the values of the company. For example, many publicly held companies have freestanding, short-term goals of showing maximal profit performances on quarterly balance sheets in order to please investors and raise stock prices (Peterson, 2002; also see Soros, 1998). Because many corporate executives are compensated with stock options, these executives also have personal stakes in the reporting of short-term company profits. Behaviors are guided accordingly, with the possibility of unethical activities increasing in such atmospheres.

The pattern just described can be seen in the ways that for-profit HMO's, seeking short-term performance outcomes, have instituted policies that encourage prescribing antidepressants as the primary treatment for depression. Although this treatment is more cost-effective in the short term (good for the balance sheet), in the long run, treating patients with antidepressants without accompanying psychotherapy translates into higher relapse rates (bad for long-term profitability) (Gloaguen, Cottrauz, Cucherat, & Blackburn, 1998; Simons, Murphy, Levine, & Wetzel, 1986). If companies knew that depressed patients still would be customers in the long run, they may be inclined to pursue this latter course. Given that such patients may be customers of different companies at that future time, however, from a short-term financial perspective, it may make more sense to stick with the least expensive treatment. As this example illustrates, the short-term profit maximization goals can be incongruent with long-term goals for customer health (as the name Health Maintenance Organization implies), or even inconsistent with long-term corporate financial successes.

This antidepressant case illustrates the importance of: (1) publicly articulating goals—goals that can be overtly stated without negative consequences (e.g., when there is nothing to hide); (2) setting higher-order "guiding" goals; and (3) making sure that short-term goals (including incentives, e.g., stock options) actually are sub-goals that are congruent with the company's guiding principles. Accordingly, our HMO must draw a distinction to determine if the guiding goal is one that could be problematic when publicly articulated: "short-term profit maximization and the raising of stock prices," or, if the goal is congruent with societal values: "to promote the health of customers while generating sustainable long-term profitability." In the first case, all stakeholders—customers, employees, and stockholders—are disadvantaged over time. Furthermore, company managers and employees may engage in unethical conduct or generate damaging pathways in their attempts to support the short-term, profit-maximization goal. In contrast, if the second, socially responsible guiding goal is adopted, the interests of all stakeholders are likely to be upheld. Thus, without resorting to punishing poor behaviors (the goal of regulatory strategies), the tenets of non-malevolence (do no harm) and benevolence (do good for all concerned) will be upheld. Indeed, these are the primary tenets of many ethics codes (e.g., American Psychological Association, 2002).

BUILDING HOPE IN EMPLOYEES

Motivational theorists have long proposed the creation of environments in which people are able to meet their personal goals by performing their jobs in ways that will lead to the organization attaining its goals (see Natale, 1983). People also must have the necessary educations and training to succeed at their jobs. It follows that it is important to teach people hope pathways as part of a socially responsible approach to creating a healthy business.

This pro-employee attitude has been shown to benefit the company. For example, Lawler (1986) found that companies in which employees were allowed to pursue self-improving educational goals were more productive than companies where such personal growth was discouraged. Such pro-employee policies also engender increased trust among employees for their organizations, and there is strong empirical evidence that such trust results in superior employee on-the-job performances (Lloyd, 1990). Thus, being kind to employees has distinct benefits, with "nice" companies out-performing "nasty" companies by an average of 86%. These "nice" firms also showed higher returns on investments and grew faster than their "nasty" counterparts (Lloyd, 1990).

As the economy shifts from a production base to service, technology, and information bases, people will become increasingly important as valuable resources (Jaffe, 1995). Accordingly, some have argued that healthy companies in today's marketplace are the ones that are concerned with workers' personal values, including their creativity and individuality (Maccoby, 1988). Part of fostering creativity and individuality is to give people control over their work. By having control, employees are able to see the complete set of cause-and-effect mechanisms that are operating in their on-the-job goal pursuits. Just as understanding causal connections helps children to develop hope, so too does witnessing such causal relationships engender hope among employees. Lastly, the ability to generate multiple, new, and innovative pathways often requires acquiring new skills. Hence, a company environment that encourages skill building, even if the benefits are not immediate, engenders employee hope.

As employees experience more on-the-job successes as a result of their increasingly high-hope thinking, their pro-social orientations will contribute to the overall climate of social responsibility within a company. The sub-goals and pathways then created by these high-hope employees will be congruent with and promote the companies' guiding pro-social visions. These pro-social visions may take the form of pursuing goals in the community that do not necessarily benefit the company in the short term. Even so, the involvements of businesses in community-based projects can yield payoffs beyond improved public relations through such programs as internships, job shadowing, and on-the-job training (Schwartz & Post, 2002).

As should be evident in the previous discussion, hope and socially responsible behavior reciprocally determine each other. By engaging in pro-employee activities, an organization increases the individual hope levels of its members. In turn, this increased hope results in more benefits not only to the organization, but also to the larger community.

SUMMARY AND CONCLUSIONS

Our thesis has been that hope, both at the individual and at the company levels, engenders social responsibility in the ways that businesses conduct themselves. Using a hope-based systems approach to guide organizations in how to conceptualize and structure their goals also encourages ethical, people-oriented decision-making. Lastly, we have specified ways through which businesses can create environments where hopeful thinking can flourish.

Consistent with our theoretical expectations, in the Snyder (2003) survey of American businesses, the highest-hope organizations exhibited the following characteristics:

- No one, including management, is greatly feared by employees.
- There is a "level playing field" where everyone has an equal chance to succeed.
- Advancement and benefits are linked to effort expended.
- The "lowest" person in the organization is treated with respect.
- Managements' priority is to help employees do the best jobs possible.
- There is open two-way communication between employees and management.
- Employee feedback is solicited and listened to.
- Decisions are given to employees who are doing the particular work.
- Employees are included in making company goals.
- Employees are given responsibility for finding solutions to problems.
- Employees are the ones who carry out solutions.
- Enduring relationships with customers (long-term goals) are encouraged rather than given sales objectives (short-term goals).

As can be seen, the high-hope company is one that values and implements inclusive, socially oriented business policies. High-hope companies also build hope in their host communities and in society at large by investing in social and environmental causes. They realize that healthier natural environments and healthier communities pay back such investments in the form of healthy and happy workers, *along with increased demand for their products*. Thus, high-hope companies enrich the contextual environments in which their businesses grow.

Workers, managers, members of corporate boards, and CEO's alike may wish to seriously consider our *ethics of hope* in order to improve their business climates. In a similar fashion, students, researchers, and consultants in business ethics and practices should look for additional ways to implement these ethics of hope and use them to further engender ethical conduct in the workplace. Our take-home message, therefore, is that the tenets of hope theory can be applied not only to produce and sustain healthy financial profits, but also to contribute to ethical people-oriented conduct and to the greater social good. Thus, even the most avid proponent of the "bottom line" financial profit approach may be drawn to the ethics of hope because they offer "win-win" business opportunities.

REFERENCES

Adams III, V.H., Snyder, C.R., Rand, K.L., King. E., Sigmon, D., & Pulvers, K. (2003). Hope in the work place. In R. Giacalone & C. Jurkiewicz (Eds.), *Workplace spirituality and organizational performance* (pp. 367–377). Armonk, New York: Sharpe.

American Psychological Association. (2002). Ethical principles of psychologists and code of conduct. *American Psychologist, 57,* 1060–1073.

Ansbacher, H.L., & Ansbacher, R.R. (Eds.). (1956). *The individual psychology of Alfred Adler: A systematic presentation in selections from his writings.* Oxford: Basic Books.

Bargh, J.A., & Chartrand, T.L. (1999). The unbearable automaticity of being. *American Psychologist, 54,* 462–479.

Chang, E.C. (1998). Hope, problem-solving ability, and coping in a college student population: Some implications for theory and practice. *Journal of Clinical Psychology, 20,* 498–520.

Clarkson Centre for Business Ethics. (1999). *Principles of stakeholder management.* Toronto: CCBE.

Curry, L.A., Snyder, C.R., Cook, D.L., Ruby, B.C., & Rehm, M. (1997). The role of hope in student-athlete academic and sport achievement. *Journal of Personality and Social Psychology, 73,* 1257–1267.

Edney, J.J. (1979). The nuts game: A concise common dilemma analog. *Environmental Psychology and Nonverbal Behavior, 3,* 252–254.

Fairholm, G.W. (1997). *Leadership and the culture of trust.* Westport, CT: Praeger Publishers.

Freeman, R.E. (1984). *Strategic management: A stakeholder approach.* Boston: Pitman.

Friedman, M. (1970, September 13). The social responsibility of business is to increase its profits. *The New York Times,* p. SM17.

Gloaguen, V., Cottraux, J., Cucherat, M., & Blackburn, I.M. (1998). A meta-analysis of the effects of cognitive therapy in depressed patients. *Journal of Affective Disorders, 49,* 59–72.

Hardin, G. (1968). The tragedy of the commons. *Science, 162,* 1243–1248.

Jaffe, D.T. (1995). The healthy company: Research paradigms for organizational and personal health. In S. L. Sauter & L.R. Murphy (Eds.), *Organizational risk factors for job stress* (pp. 13–39). Washington, DC: American Psychological Association.

Janis, I.L. (1971, November). Groupthink. *Psychology Today,* pp. 43–46. New York: Basic Books.

Lawler, E.E., III (1986). *High-involvement management.* San Francisco: Jossey-Bass.

Leary, M.R., & Baumeister, R.F. (2000). The nature and function of self-esteem: Sociometer theory. In M.P. Zanna (Ed.), *Advances in experimental social psychology* (Vol. 32, pp. 1–62). San Diego, CA: Academic Press.

Lloyd, T. (1990). *The nice company.* London: Bloomsbury.

Luthans, F., & Youssef, C. M. (in press). Human, social, and now positive psychological capital management: Investing in people for competitive advantage. *Organizational Dynamics.*

Maccoby, M. (1988). *Why work? Leading the new generation.* New York: Simon & Schuster.

Marcoux, A.M. (2003). A fiduciary argument against stakeholder theory. *Business Ethics Quarterly, 13,* 1–24.

Margolis, J.D. (2001). Psychological pragmatism and the imperative of aims: A new approach for business ethics. In J. Dienhart, D. Moberg, & R. Duska (Eds.), *The next phase of business ethics, Vol. 3: Integrating psychology and ethics* (pp. 27–50). New York: Elsevier Science Ltd.

Natale, S.M. (1983). *Ethics and morals in business.* Birmingham, AL: REP.

Peterson, V.C. (2002). *Beyond rules in society and business.* Cheltenham: Edward Elgar.

Rieger, E. (1993). *Correlates of adult hope, including high- and low-hope young adults' recollections of parents.* Honor's thesis, University of Kansas, Department of Psychology, Lawrence, Kansas.

Ruf, B., Krishnamurti, M., & Paul, K. (1996). Corporate social monitoring: A comparison of the relative values of religious activists and public affairs officers. *Personal and Professional Ethics Journal, 15*(2), 51–67.

Schwartz, R.H., & Post, F.R. (2002). The unexplored potential of hope to level the playing field. *Journal of Business Ethics, 37,* 135–143.

Shorey, H.S. (2003). *Theories of intelligence, academic hope, and persistence after a failure experience.* Unpublished Master's Thesis. University of Kansas, Lawrence.

Shorey, H.S., & Snyder, C.R. (2004, June). *Hope as a common process in effective leadership.* Paper presented at the inaugural Gallup Institute Leadership Summit, Omaha, Nebraska.

Shorey, H.S., Snyder, C.R., Etchison, S., Hilleary, S.M., & Little, T. (2003). *Hope: Adaptive and maladaptive patterns as a function of attachment style.* Poster presented at the American Psychological Association Convention, Toronto, Canada.

Shorey, H.S., Snyder, C.R., Rand, K.L., Hockemeyer, J., & Feldman, D. (2002). Somewhere over the rainbow: Hope theory weathers its first decade. *Psychological Inquiry, 13,* 322–331.

Shorey, H.S., Snyder, C.R., Warner, T., & Myren, J. R. (2003). *Hope and perceived discrimination among African-Americans, Hispanics, and Caucasians.* Poster presented at the annual meeting of the Midwestern Psychological Association, Chicago, Illinois.

Shorey, H.S., Snyder, C.R., Yang, X., & Lewin, M.R. (2003). The role of hope as a mediator in recollected parenting, adult attachment, and mental health. *Journal of Social and Clinical Psychology, 22,* 685–715.

Simons, A.D., Murphy, G.D., Levine, J.L., & Wetzel, R.D. (1986). Cognitive therapy and pharmacotherapy for depression: Sustained improvements over 1 year. *Archives of General Psychiatry, 43,* 43–48.

Snyder, C.R. (1994). *The psychology of hope: You can get there from here.* New York: Free Press.

Snyder, C.R. (1999). Hope, goal-blocking thoughts, and test-related anxieties. *Psychological Reports, 84,* 206–208.

Snyder, C.R. (2002). Hope theory: Rainbows in the mind. *Psychological Inquiry, 13,* 249–275.

Snyder, C.R. (2003). *Hope in American business.* Unpublished survey data, University of Kansas, Lawrence.

Snyder, C.R., Cheavens, J., & Sympson, S.C. (1997). Hope: An individual motive for social commerce. *Group Dynamics: Theory, Research, and Practice, 1,* 107–118.

Snyder, C.R., Feldman, D., Shorey, H.S., & Rand, K.L. (2002). Hopeful choices: A school counselor's guide to hope theory. *Professional School Counseling, 5,* 298–307.

Snyder, C.R., Harris, C., Anderson, J.R., Holleran, S.A., Irving, L.M., Sigmon, S.T., et al. (1991). The will and the ways: Development and validation of an individual-differences measure of hope. *Journal of Personality and Social Psychology, 60,* 570–585.

Snyder, C.R., Higgins, R.L., & Stucky, R. (1983). *Excuses: Masquerades in search of grace.* New York: Wiley Interscience.

Snyder, C.R., Hoza, B., Pelham, W.E., Rapoff, M., Ware, L., Danovsky, M., Highberger, L., Rubinstein, H., & Stahl, K.J. (1997). The development and validation of the Children's Hope Scale. *Journal of Pediatric Psychology, 22,* 399–421.

Snyder, C.R., Lopez, S., Shorey, H.S., Rand, K.L., & Feldman, D.B. (2003) Hope theory, measurements, and applications to school psychology. *School Psychology Quarterly, 18,* 122–139.

Snyder, C.R., & Pulvers, K.M. (2001). Dr. Seuss, the coping machine, and "Oh, the places you'll go." In C.R. Snyder (Ed.), *Coping with stress: Effective people and places* (pp. 3–29). New York: Oxford University Press.

Snyder, C.R., & Shorey, H.S. (in press). The role of hope in effective leadership. In K. Christensen (Ed.), *Encyclopedia of leadership.* Harrison, NY: Berkshire Publishers.

Snyder, C.R., Shorey, H.S., Cheavens, J., Pulvers, K.M., Adams III, V.H., & Wiklund, C. (2002). Hope and academic success in college. *Journal of Educational Psychology, 94,* 820–826.

Soros, G. (1998). *The crisis of global capitalism: Open society endangered.* London: Little, Brown and Company.

Sridharan, U.V., Dickes, L., Caines, W.R. (2002). The social impact of business failure: Enron. *Mid-American Journal of Business, 17*(2), 11–21.

Sympson, S. (1999). *Validation of the Domain Specific Hope Scale.* Unpublished doctoral dissertation, Department of Psychology, University of Kansas, Lawrence.

Tversky, A., & Kahneman, D. (1981). The framing of decisions and the psychology of choice. *Science, 211,* 453–458.

Vaux, A., Phillips, J., Hooly, L., Thompson, B., Williams, D., & Stewart, D. (1986). The Social Support Appraisals (SSA) Scale: Studies of reliability and validity. *American Journal of Community Psychology, 14,* 195–219.

Vidaver-Cohen, D. (2001). Motivational appeal in normative theories of enterprise. In J. Dienhart, D. Moberg, & R. Duska (Eds.), *The next phase of business ethics: Integrating psychology and ethics.* New York: Elsevier Science Ltd.

Zander, A. (1971). *Motives and goals in groups.* New York: Academic Press.

CHAPTER 13

FORGIVENESS AND POSITIVE PSYCHOLOGY IN BUSINESS ETHICS AND CORPORATE SOCIAL RESPONSIBILITY

Everett L. Worthington Jr., Jack W. Berry, Victoria A. Shivy, and Evan Browstein

INTRODUCTION

To live is to experience transgressions, both those we inflict and those inflicted on us. Most adults spend about one-third of their waking hours in a business environment, so how they cope with transgressions in the business environment can affect their quality of life. Hart (1999) recently challenged occupational researchers to more carefully examine work experiences that are not only positive or beneficial to well-being, but also those that are negative or harmful to well-being. He found that between 3% and 13% of the variability in life satisfaction was accounted for by job satisfaction, a figure comparable to the results of other studies (e.g., Adams, King, & King, 1996). Businesses are attending more often to the affective side of work (Barsade, Brief, & Spataro, 2003; Brief & Weiss, 1992; Frederickson, 2000).

Positive Psychology in Business Ethics and Corporate Responsibility, pages 265–284
Copyright © 2005 by Information Age Publishing
All rights of reproduction in any form reserved.

Business ethics is concerned with how businesses deal with society. Businesses transact publicly with customers, shareholders, and people in the broader social arena. Business ethics also deals with how people treat each other within the workplace. In the present chapter, we address three issues. First, we define transgressions and discuss how people deal with them, especially through justice and forgiveness. Second, we explore the relationship of forgiveness to positive psychology, business ethics, and corporate responsibility. Third, we describe some implications of our reasoning for managers, administrators, corporate decision-makers, and society.

We propose a hypothesis: businesses deal ethically with transgressions in the public arena (e.g., with customers, larger communities, shareholders, and policy) differently from the way workers deal ethically with workplace transgressions. We term these an *ethics of the mind* versus an *ethics of the heart*, respectively (see Table 13.1). We offer tentative evidence supporting this hypothesis, and apply our reasoning about forgiveness and these two approaches to ethics within the business context.

Table 13.1. Ethics of the Mind and Ethics of the Heart

Type of Ethics	Ethics of the Mind	Ethics of the Heart
Characteristics	Rational analysis; principle-driven; abstract; emotionally detached; global	Context-sensitive; people-oriented; personal; community-oriented; emotionally connected; local
Motivation	Justice	Mercy
Motivated Actions	Reasoning about what is fair or just	Decisional forgiveness; Emotional forgiveness
Implications	Mechanistic, value-free, behavioral or cognitive neuroscience, the decade of the brain	Life-sciences, value-informed virtues, emotional, the neuroscience of emotion, positive psychology and multiculturalism

TRANSGRESSIONS, INJUSTICE, UNFORGIVENESS, JUSTICE, AND FORGIVENESS

Forgiveness and Unforgiveness

There are many way of defining forgiveness. Some scholars define it as an act of the will (DiBlaiso, 1998), as an interpersonal process between parties (Baumeister, Exline, & Sommer, 1998), as cognitive change from negative, vengeful rumination to positive thoughts about the transgressor (Flanigan, 1992), or as motivational change in which people give up the motivations either to exact vengeance or to avoid the perpetrator, and to replace those motivations with more neutral or even conciliatory motivations (McCullough, Fincham, & Tsang, 2003; McCullough et al., 1998). We distinguish two types of forgiveness (Exline et al., 2003; Worthington, 2003). *Decisional forgiveness* is willfully granting that one will not seek revenge against or avoid (unless contact is dangerous) a transgressor and will release the person from the interpersonal debt incurred by transgressing. It is an intention statement that is meant to govern one's future behavior toward the transgressor. *Emotional forgiveness* is the juxtaposition of other-oriented positive emotions against negative, unforgiving emotions (Worthington & Wade, 1999). We believe that changes in emotion, will, cognition, motivation, decision-making, interpersonal behaviors, and interactions signifying behavioral forgiveness all occur when people forgive emotionally, but we argue that emotional transformation is the key.

Transgressions

Transgressions are violations of boundaries, which can be divided into two primary types—*hurts* and *offenses.* Hurts are violations of physical or psychological boundaries. Offenses are violations of moral boundaries (Worthington & Wade, 1999). Transgressions vary in severity. People rarely experience a transgression simply as a hurt or an offense. Offenses and hurts are tied together in most people's phenomenal experience. Some people experience almost every transgression as a hurt; others experience almost every one as an offense.

Workplace transgressions have been studied under several different names. Robinson and Bennett (1995) studied employee deviance. Workers transgress through property deviance (e.g., theft, fraud, embezzlement, sabotage, or vandalism) and production deviance (e.g., wasting organizational resources, underperforming, wasting company time). Robinson and Bennett (1995) also identify two other types of employee behaviors that violate organizational norms and threaten organizational well-being: political deviance (e.g., gossiping, showing favoritism) and personal aggression (e.g., physical or verbal abuse, sexual harassment).

Problems in on-the-job social exchanges and violations of workplace psychological contracts have been examined mostly in the context of the organizational justice literature (Cropanzano, Byrne, Bobocel, & Rupp, 2001; Elovainio, Kivimaki, Vahtera, Virtanen, & Keltikangas-Jarvinen, 2003) under the umbrella terms of *interactional justice* or of *relational justice.* These forms of organizational justice both focus on the quality of interpersonal interactions at work (Cropanzano, Prehar, & Chen, 2002). Writers are often concerned with managers' violations of either distributive or procedural justice, or both. Distributive justice involves equitable distribution of resources. Procedural justice involves following stated processes.

In a recent study of abusive supervision, Tepper (2000) argued that the voluntary turnover of workers seems better predicted by violations of interactional justice than by violations of procedural or distributive justice. This highlights the importance of interpersonal relationships on the job. Tepper (2000) speculated that subordinates of abusive supervisors may respond to transgressions by actively engaging in organizational anti-citizenship behaviors such as revenge (Bies & Tripp, 1996) or retaliation (Skarlicki & Folger, 1997)—that is, by transgressing themselves. Thus, the costs of workplace transgressions may escalate over time.

Leymann (1990) suggested that workplace "mobbing" was sometimes used to harm targeted workers. Mobbing is an escalated conflict that unfolds over time, with frequent harassing actions that are carried out systematically to stress a target person (Zapf, 1999). Workplace mobbing behaviors are more sophisticated, nonphysical forms of the bullying behaviors observed at schools. The prevalence of mobbing is estimated at 16% in the U.S. workplace and 11% in Europe (Vandekerckhove & Commers, 2003), and the organizational costs of mobbing are being recognized by organizational researchers.

Emotional and Cognitive Responses to Transgressions

People respond to transgressions with anger (Berry et al., 2001; McCullough et al., 2001), fear (of being hurt again), or both (Worthington, 1998). People may later ruminate about transgressions (Berry et al., 2001; McCullough et al., 2001). Rumination can be vengeful (Berry et al., 2001), fearful, or depressive (Brooks et al., 2003). Type of rumination has been shown to mediate between transgressions and emotions and between transgressions and forgiveness (Berry et al., 2005). In addition, rumination may be perceived as voluntary (or at least controllable), or it may be perceived as uncontrollable and intrusive (McCullough et al., 2003). In the workplace, rumination occupies worker attention. In addition, rumination has been linked to impairment through a variety of psychological disorders—depression, anxiety, anger, posttraumatic stress disorder, and obsessive-compulsive disorders. Thus, both performance and production might be compromised.

Offenses and hurts usually are perceived as unjust. People hope that injustices will be made right again. Making an injustice right involves putting the relationship back into balance. The *injustice gap* (Exline et al., 2003) involves the perceptual difference between the way a person would like a situation to be resolved and the current state of affairs. Events that influence a person's optimal expectations can reduce or increase the injustice gap. For example, if an abused worker finds that the CEO demotes the worker's boss, the injustice gap is narrowed. Similarly, if the current status changes, that too can affect the injustice gap. For example, if mobbing escalates, an injustice gap will widen.

The emotions that people experience in response to a transgression are proportional to the size of the injustice gap (Worthington & Scherer, 2004). When the gap is large, the emotions tend toward bitterness, resentment, hostility, hatred, anger and fear. We have defined *unforgiveness* as the complex emotion made up of those emotions (Worthington & Wade, 1999). Worthington and Scherer (2004) hypothesized that the amount of unforgiveness people experience will determine the motivation to eliminate unforgiving emotions. The relationship between the degree of unforgiveness and the motivation to rid oneself of unforgiveness does not always manifest itself immediately. Rather, unforgiveness often takes a toll on a person's physical, mental, relational, and sometimes spiritual well-being. Often, perceiving these negative effects of unforgiveness on well-being heightens the motivation to reduce unforgiveness.

Elovainio et al. (2003) reported a ($N = 4076$) longitudinal study on perceptions of organizational justice among hospital employees. They hypothesized that perceived violations of organizational justice would create stress, which would affect health. Relational injustices by managers did predict illness-related absence from work.

Not all relational discord in the workplace is due to transgressions by managers. Coworkers and subordinates inflict transgressions. Coworker transgressions, and the unpleasant and stressful work environment they engender, also contribute to missed work, decreased productivity, relationship stress, and problems in mental and physical health (see Brownstein, Worthington, Berry, & Shivy, 2005).

Reviewers agree that more research should focus on the nature, antecedents, and consequences of negative affective events in the workplace (Beis & Tripp, 2001; Weiss & Cropanzano, 1996). When interpersonal transgressions occur in the workplace, employees may respond to negative emotions by withdrawing from organizational life, reducing cooperative behaviors, seeking revenge, or by exhibiting aggressive behaviors (Bies & Tripp, 2001; Skarlicki & Folger, 1997). These reactions may be conceptualized broadly as an effort to "right" perceived injustice (Cropanzano et al., 2001). Others might simply avoid a stressful situation. Still others may focus on controlling their negative emotions within the unjust situation.

Lowering Emotional Unforgiveness

There are numerous ways that the negative emotions caused by transgressions can be lowered (Worthington, 2003). For example, a person can seek to bring about or can passively observe justice and thereby reduce the perceived injustice gap. This might involve institutional penalties or shame enacted on a perpetrator. Or injustice could be redressed (and emotional unforgiveness reduced) if an employee were forced to apologize or make restitution for a mistake. This could occur even at the corporate level. Punitive damages levied against negligent companies are a salient example. Individuals might also reduce the magnitude of the perceived injustice gap by spiritual acts, such as praying for divine justice or appealing to *karma* (i.e., universal justice).

Beyond seeing justice occur, workers can reduce the perceived injustice gap by constructing different narratives about the situation, which might excuse or even justify the perpetrator's action. The injustice gap can be narrowed by lowering the standard one expects when one narrates a different story. The worker might also simply decide to accept or ignore the transgression and move on with his or her life. Such acceptance lowers the expectation for the eventual resolution of the injustice and thereby reduces the injustice gap. Forgetting injustices, especially those that are unimportant, certainly reduces unforgiveness. Workers reduce their sense of injustice and unforgiveness by numerous other ways as well (see Worthington, 2003).

Each of these ways of reducing unforgiveness involves the elimination of negative emotional states. None, however, result in a positive emotional state. Enter positive psychology (Frederickson, 2000; Turner, Barling, & Zacharatos, 2000) and forgiveness (Bradfield & Aquino, 1999). Emotional forgiveness, in which negative emotions are replaced by positive other-oriented emotions (i.e., empathy, sympathy, compassion, or love), provides the only coping strategy that can reduce unforgiveness and move beyond the neutral state to yield net positive emotion. Two uncommon possible exceptions occur. First, one might exact revenge and thus feel positively. The problem with revenge, though it might produce an immediate increase in positive affect, is that it can lead to an escalation of conflict, which can bring about long-term negative consequences for all parties. Even if one successfully retaliates against a coworker, the retaliator will likely get a reputation for being vengeful. This can provoke *other people* to launch preemptive strikes. Thus, in the end, retaliation and revenge are usually counterproductive. Second, one might observe some negative event befall the transgressor, such as seeing a worker against whom one held a minor grudge fired. While such events reduce a worker's unforgiveness, the events are uncontrollable and not reliable coping mechanisms.

We note that forgiveness might promote positive well-being rather than merely reducing risks for negative well-being. Positive Psychology is the focus on conditions that stimulate human flourishing. The alternatives to forgiveness indeed reduce negative emotions and thereby might allow a person to expend more energy in flourishing. However, actions such as seeking justice, acceptance, or re-narrating an event do not promote flourishing directly. Other actions are needed to promote flourishing.

Reconciliation

Reconciliation is the restoration of trust in a relationship in which trust has been violated or impaired (Worthington, 2003). Forgiveness is either decisional or emotional. It is experienced within an individual's body. Reconciliation is relational. It is important not to confuse the two. A worker might forgive but still not trust a manager. Forgiveness might stimulate people to reconcile, but it is not necessarily connected with reconciliation. In fact, people may forgive others who are dead, but can never restore trust in the relationship. On the other hand, reconciliation might occur without forgiveness. In business settings, people might restore trust after a transgression through working together on common tasks. However, they might hold a grudge for years as a result of a past transgression. Ideally, forgiveness stimulates reconciliation, but it doesn't have to.

Consequences of Unforgiveness to Individuals and Businesses

For individuals, unforgiveness has health consequences. These tend to manifest in the later years of life (Tossaint et al., 2001). Short-term effects of unforgiveness can also be experienced. In the business setting, unforgiving people can feel angry, depressed, and fearful, and thus might miss work or be unproductive (Berry et al., 2005; Elovainio et al., 2003). In addition, people who experience many or large transgressions in the workplace might change jobs, introducing other costs to businesses. New workers must be recruited and trained, requiring a period of adjustment during which they are less productive than they later will be. Unforgiveness in consumers can also affect businesses. Unforgiveness can keep people from using a product, stimulate them to criticize the business, or result in boycotts or lawsuits. Unforgiveness is costly.

Forgiveness is an act of mercy and grace (to appropriate some terms often employed in theological contexts). When a person transgresses, he or she builds up a social and perhaps economic debt. The injustice gap probably cannot be eliminated through justice alone, as we have shown in a series of studies that use both self-report and physiological methods (Witvliet, Wade, Worthington, & Berry, 2004; Witvliet, Worthington, Root, Sato, Ludwig, & Exline, 2003). Forgiveness, as an act of mercy, is not giving someone what he or she deserves (i.e., mercy), but is also giving someone something he or she does not deserve (i.e., grace).

THE NATURE OF BUSINESS ETHICS
AND CORPORATE SOCIAL RESPONSIBILITY

With this understanding of people's reactions to transgressions–whether inflicted by a corporation or co-worker—we turn to specific cases within the work setting that raise ethical issues. As we examine six cases, we will see that different types of cases arouse different responses in the people involved. We will thus argue that principle-driven ethics might not be the best way to approach all ethical violations or issues.

Case Examples about Business and the Public

Case # 1: Violations of public trust.   At the corporate level, malpractice in business can result in transgressions against the public, customers, or clients. These transgressions violate public trust (Meyer, 2000). For example, the Firestone Corporation made defective products; Enron violated public trust in shady accounting; and Martha Stewart was convicted of insider-trading. The injury inflicted goes beyond just injury to people affected by defective tires or lost money. It also involves damage to the reputations of the Firestone Corporation, Enron, and K-Mart. Ways to repair physical, economic, and reputational damages are needed.

Case # 2: Apology in medical mistakes.   Medical malpractice results annually in up to 98,000 deaths plus numerous other physical injuries or worsened medical conditions (Institute of Medicine, 1999). A typical response to malpractice in medicine is for people to sue the medical practitioner and then settle disputes through litigation. This strategy results in many negative social consequences, such as increased medical malpractice cost, which are passed along to government through Medicare and Medicaid, and to customers through increased insurance premiums. Studies have suggested that medical malpractice suits could be drastically reduced if physicians apologized for their malpractice behavior (e.g., Vincent et al., 1994). An apology involves an admission of guilt; therefore, more cases might be settled in favor of the plaintiff. But it might also reduce the number of cases that are brought to trial. The studies estimated that at least

15% of all suits lodged would not have been pursued had the physician admitted a mistake and apologized (see Cohen, 2000).

Case #3. Immediate admission of wrongdoing and restitution in medical mistakes.   The Lexington Kentucky Veteran's Administration Medical Center (VAMC) lost two large lawsuits in the 1980s (see Cohen, 2002, for a discussion). The VAMC paid $1.5 M for those settlements. Afterward, they made a policy decision to admit to errors immediately and try to settle fairly with patients who were injured by malpractice. The result has been documented in studies of the economics of that decision (Cohen, 2002). The VAMC has paid only $1.8 M over the subsequent decade. In this case, apologizing and seeking justice after medical errors made good economic sense as well as upholding high ethics.

Case # 4. Drug screening in the workplace.   Consider drug screening in the workplace. The management of a company decides that drug screening is conducive to a positive work environment. Furthermore, they reason that drug screening is socially responsible; it prevents potential crime and violence in society by detecting people who are using drugs. Issues of individual autonomy and freedom bump up against a paternalistic approach to controlling morality within the company. Furthermore, the drug screening might detect drugs that are used recreationally and not infringe directly on the work situation. To what degree does a company, in the name of social responsibility and corporate morale, have the right to intrude on people's non-work behavior?

Case # 5. Differential treatment of employees in the workplace.   A personnel committee evaluates the annual performance of workers using reports from the workers. A deadline is set to review the performance reports. All workers but one submit reports by the deadline. How should the personnel committee proceed? That worker was allowed more time to construct the report, and the personnel committee was allowed less time to review the report. To what degree should their anger enter into the evaluation? To what degree should justice dictate that higher standards be employed to balance the advantage of the worker who had more time to construct the report?

Case # 6. Power differentials.   Let us assume that a work unit has been cohesive in the past. Then the two most senior people in the unit become involved in a power struggle. They hurt and offend each other, act negatively toward each other, and triangulate junior members of the unit. Overall, the productivity of the unit is compromised. How do the supervisor, the senior members, and the junior members deal with the ethical responsibilities toward each other, the company, and the public?

Ethical Dilemmas in Business

There are commonalties across the cases. The categories of ethical dilemmas tend to involve (1) *how businesses interact with their customers or stockholders* (cases 1–3) and (2) *how individuals within businesses tend to treat each other* (cases 4–6). Within businesses, transgressions occur across roles. Subordinates might offend their superiors. Workers might offend each other. Managers might hurt or offend their subordinates. In all the cases, transgressions were perceived, and it is likely that unforgiveness was experienced by some of the participants.

Traditionally, in such cases, ethics has been approached in a rational, principle-driven, and abstract way. The ethical issues have typically been treated as problems to be solved, and the solution has been thought of in terms of applying ethical principles to the problem, such as the principle of doing no harm (i.e., non-malfeasance), doing good (i.e., benevolence), fairness or equal treatment (i.e., justice), and balancing autonomy and choice against duty and responsibility. Thus most business ethics has involved discourses about principles. Some debates have been consequentialist. That is, the dilemma is discussed in terms of net benefit versus harm to various people. Decisions are made on the basis of the most positive or least negative net consequences. In contrast, some ethical theory has approached ethical discourse as de-ontological. In such theories, people do their duty or do what is right according to a set of guiding principles, regardless of the consequences to others. Ethical discourse is primarily an activity of theorizing philosophically about dilemmas, rationally analyzing ethical principles, and expecting that people can and will apply these principles when they face difficult decisions. To assist, ethics casebooks consider real-life examples that presumably help people apply ethical principles rationally.

In an alternative approach, ethical decisions might be made in the context of habitual decisions within a community. This distinction was made in a classic book by Oakenshott (1962). He argued that people acquire habits by living with people who habitually behave in a certain manner. We acquire habits in the same way that we acquire our native language. He argues, then, that one way of understanding ethical behavior is to understand the habits that are derived from living for years in a community. These might be called habits of the heart (Bellah et al., 1985). Such an approach to ethics is contrasted with ethical abstract principles that are used to make individual decisions that guide our behavior.

The fundamental question we wish to raise about the practice of business ethics in day-to-day business communities boils down to this. Is ethical discourse and analysis, which is largely principle-focused, actually the way that people make ethical decisions? Or do people make ethical decisions differently? Furthermore, *should* ethical decision-making be primarily rational? Or *should* it be contextualized by community?

We thus put forward a tentative hypothesis. We suggest that there is an *ethics of the mind* that involves rational, principle-driven analysis and the application of those principles (like non-malfeasance or beneficence) through (1) recognizing that the case at hand requires an ethical decision, (2) recognizing the principles that are applicable, and (3) reasoning about which principles should be applied if principles compete. We suggest, too, that there is an *ethics of the heart.* An ethics of the heart involves sensitivity to interpersonal and emotional context (though it is not completely divorced from principles).

We suspect that the ethics of the mind was born in the industrial revolution, which encouraged people to develop mechanistic metaphors for life. The computer spawned a metaphor for mind that generated the cognitive revolution and led to the flourishing of cognitive neuroscience. The ethics of the heart was born more recently. Biological developments across the life sciences have redirected public attention toward life, complex environments, and emergence of patterns and new systems. These changes have spawned new metaphors and fueled the move toward positive psychology, virtues and values, multiculturalism, and a neurobiology of emotion—especially positive emotion.

An Experiment to Support This Reasoning

Some recent studies address our hypothesis. Greene et al. (2001), in Cohen's laboratory, posed a moral dilemma to people using the "footbridge problem." Imagine that you are standing on a footbridge high above a railroad track. You see a train barreling down the track at five strangers who will be killed. However, by your hand is a switch that can divert the train into a sidetrack where only one stranger is standing. Do you pull the switch? The moral problem boils down to whether you will act purposefully to allow one death or will passively allow five people to die. In Greene et al.'s experiment, 90% of people said they would pull the switch.

Here is a second similar dilemma. A train approaches, which will kill five strangers, but this time the switch is far below where you are standing. If the switch is tripped, it will divert the train to a sidetrack where there are no people. You consider throwing yourself from the footbridge to trip the switch. But you realize that you do not weigh enough to trip the switch. However, an overweight stranger is sitting on a nearby banister. You can easily tip that stranger over the banister to trip the switch, but he will die. Would you push the person? Morally, this is virtually an identical problem.

Yet Greene et al. found that this time only about 10% said they would push the stranger to trip the switch.

All participants were in functional MRI units as the footbridge problem was described. During the first footbridge problem, brain areas associated with logical reasoning in the prefrontal cortex were most active. In the second problem, the same areas were activated during in the initial description of the dilemma, but as soon as the mention that a person would have to be actively pushed to his death, cortical activity decreased markedly. Limbic (emotional) activity became most pronounced.

Greene et al.'s study suggests that personal ethical decision-making is not always analyzed abstractly and rationally. Instead, emotion can override reason. Not only does brain functioning differ, but also the decisions differed dramatically. This suggests that the decisions from rational, principle-driven ethical decision-making exercises might differ in brain-processes and in actual outcomes from emotion-driven hands-on decisions.

More Evidence

This has been shown previously in Milgram's (1974) classic studies on obedience. People were urged by an experimenter to give what they thought were painful and dangerous electric shocks (no shocks were actually given) to a learner (actually a confederate). People to whom the study was described applied principle-driven ethics. Almost all said they would administer no shocks. In the actual situation, most people gave shocks. People responded more strongly to their *personal closeness* to the experimenter (a nearby experimenter elicited more obedience) or to the learner (a more distant learner elicited more obedience). Personal ethics and principled ethics differed.

At Manchester University (England), Tom Farrow and his colleagues (Farrow et al., 2001) have used functional MRIs to scan people's brains while they reasoned about transgressions. Farrow et al. found that when people reasoned about the fairness and justice of transgressions, much of the neural activity occurred in the prefrontal cortex. However, when people reasoned about whether they might forgive the transgressions, neural activity involved less cortical activity and more limbic system activity.

We conclude that, when dealing with transgressions, two types of thinking are involved. One type of thinking involves rational analysis and judgment about whether events are fair or just. Our review of these few studies suggests that ethical reasoning might be helped by logical, philosophical discourse. People benefit by having thought through difficult decisions and by examining cases that could be pivotal in helping make a general decision. However, we also find that the more personal the transgression, the more likely it is to be responded to using emotional processes rather than applying rational, principle-driven analysis. Reasoning is involved, but primarily it is limbic system activity that *conditions* how people respond. In the same way that Okenshott has argued about ethics, the way people make personal decisions has much to do with habits of the heart rather than with habits of the mind.

These experiments are suggestive, not definitive. They support our hypothesis that individuals might gravitate toward one of two modes of acting—an ethics of the mind or of the heart—*under different circumstances.* Both are prevalent in our culture. Different situations bring out each.

APPLICATION TO BUSINESS ETHICS

Forgiveness, Justice, and Ethics of the Mind in Public Interaction

Earlier we described two types of business situations in which forgiveness might be considered. In one instance (cases 1–3), businesses had to deal with customers. Rarely do business decision-makers need to forgive customers. However, customers often consider whether they will forgive businesses. This is true of biomedical, healthcare, information-technology, and product-driven businesses. Companies make mistakes that affect customers. Customers must wrestle with how they will respond emotionally and cognitively to the business. The literature on service failure explores ways that businesses redress their "transgressions" to promote forgiveness in dissatisfied customers (Smith, Bolton, & Wenger, 1999; Kelly, Hoffman, & Davis, 1993).

Forgiveness, Justice, and Ethics of the Heart in Ways People Treat Each Other at Work

In the other instance, many transgressions take place within work-a-day business environments. These might be between boards of directors and management, between management and workers, and among workers. These transgressions are up-close and personal. They thus engage people's emotions. Rather than trying to provide case studies that illustrate ways we categorize and analyze transgressions within businesses (i.e., an ethics of the mind), we suggest that ethical behavior in the workplace might better be shaped by an ethics of the heart.

The task of management is to provide a means of shaping corporate culture such that an ethic of responding with empathy, altruism, forbearance and forgiveness might be promoted. The role of the manager in modeling such behavior is crucial. A manager who advocates an ethic of forbearance, tolerance, and forgiveness, yet who vindictively punishes his or her workers for transgressions, or allows such interactions to occur will likely not produce a community that values positive responses to transgressions. People are highly attuned to situational cues. The behaviors of executives and the behaviors of middle managers are extremely important. In fact, the middle manager might be the key person in establishing such a culture. Upper management formulates policies, makes personnel decisions, and directs the business. Middle managers deal with subordinates daily, directly influencing the way workers treat each other. Certainly upper management interacts personally with middle managers, and their values will be transmitted to middle managers. But the most pivotal position seems to be the middle manager or line supervisor.

A Boundary Issue: Ethics and Forgiveness in "Right-sizing"

Case Study.   Brandon was 59 years old. One year before he would be eligible for retirement, the company hit an economic downturn. They severed Brandon from employment and left him with two weeks pay and no retirement. His 24 years of loyal service meant nothing. Since that time, Brandon has been living on Social Security.

Historical context.   Cultural historian Jackson Lears (2003) has observed that, in the last one-third of the 20th century, the business climate changed dramatically. From the end of the 19th century through the late 1960s, business enterprise was characterized by stability and loyalty. In capital-intensive industries, businesses did not often lay its workers off. Workers and companies were loyal to each other. People believed that workers and businesses could control their destiny through hard work and meritorious performance. Lears argues that this is no longer the case.

In the late 1960s, computers and communication technologies changed the nature of industry. The major resource of companies became, not machines and complicated industrial processes, but workers. As business cycles shifted, companies shifted resources. They added workers just in time or laid them off. Lears argued that this shift in business dynamics has led to a culture of contingency; that is, few people now believe that their employer will reward their prolonged efforts. Instead, they feel that chance events or arbitrary decisions might eliminate them from the workforce or might cause them to be hired back into the workforce.

Loyalty, commitment, and betrayal in the modern business.   This raises a question for business ethics in the early 21st century. The virtues of loyalty and commitment, which dominated business for years, no longer dominate. Neither businesses nor workers are loyal. Workers fluidly leave jobs to take a better position. Companies lay off workers with little justification.

"Commitment" seems now to be understood as serial loyalty (i.e., an employee gives fidelity to a single employer but does not feel that commitment implies loyalty over time). Despite this shifting societal understanding of commitment, business managers often feel betrayed when a worker changes jobs, and workers often feel betrayed when they are laid off or downsized away from their job. These transgressions trigger negative emotions of resentment, anger, and bitterness toward the other side. Because downsizing and job-hopping occur more frequently than in the past, people are ambivalent about working in a corporate climate. On one hand, people do not value their own loyalty and commitment. On the other hand, they feel that an injustice is done when they are on the receiving end of lack of loyalty or commitment.

In coping with such lack of job loyalty—by companies or by employees—emotional forgiveness might be called for by workers and managers. If a worker becomes resentful, bitter, and hostile toward an employer because of being downsized out of a job after 15 years of loyal service, then the worker can be impaired in his or her attitude toward other future employers. This might result in personnel managers detecting a negative attitude and being reluctant to hire the person. And if managers develop resentment and bitterness because they see the employees as fickle and disloyal, then that attitude will likely be transmitted to the workers. Such an attitude would inevitably create a poor interpersonal environment that does not attract excellent workers to the company.

The implications for business ethics are numerous. First, informed consent is crucial in helping people understand the relative stability of a job. Businesses might inform people of past turnover rates to allow people to formulate reasonable expectations of company loyalty versus responsiveness to market conditions. Second, the principle of non-malfeasance dictates that companies responsibly act to minimize the harm that their actions might cause. Traditional HR-sponsored separation programs—such as resume writing, job-seeking skills and the like—might be supplemented with discussions of alternative ways to deal with job loss. Programs might discuss forgiveness as well as other ways of dealing with perceived transgressions or misunderstandings (such as acceptance, moving on with one's life, looking at ways to re-narrate the accounts of events that might provide some justification for downsizing, and other ways of responding to transgressions). Third, the principle of beneficence dictates that a business should strive to provide benefits to the severed employee. Businesses recognize that companies have a presence in the community, and simply downsizing people without providing compensatory benefits will, in the end, result in poor public image and possibly (because of public reaction) additional economic cost.

Because of changes in work and common culture (i.e., Lears, 2003), downsizing and job-hopping provide cases on the border between dealing with workers and the public. They require both ethics of the mind and the heart to deal with effectively.

Benefits of Forgiveness at the Workgroup, Organizational, and Societal Levels

In business settings, most people think almost exclusively in terms of justice. Injustices are seen as the source of negative affect, and thus redressing and preventing injustices are seen as the solutions for negative affect. However, not all injustices are preventable. And even when injustices are dealt with fairly, negative affect can still poison work relationships, affect productivity of workers (even those not directly involved in the injustice), and contribute to workplace stress and ill health. Forgiveness can help people avoid or resolve such problems. The work group and organization can be more affectively positive more often and can thus be a place that fosters more productivity when more workers are more forgiving. Turnover might also be lessened.

We have suggested that forgiveness is not the only way to deal with injustice and unforgiveness. Importantly, individuals and work groups should not feel that they must forgive if they are philosophically or religiously opposed to forgiving (Worthington, 2003). Many alternatives exist.

Furthermore, justice in its variety of work-related applications, is still the *sine qua non* for excellence in the work environment. However, justice and forgiveness are not mortal enemies—as they are sometimes presumed to be. Witvliet and her colleagues and others (Karremans & Van Lange, 2004; Witvliet et al., 2004; Witvliet et al., 2003) have shown that receiving justice can narrow the injustice gap and thus make forgiving easier.

At the societal level, forgiveness is one option that may be employed in response to injustices. Worthington and Berry (2004) have outlined the societal costs and benefits of forgiving—including economic benefits to businesses and the economy, physical health benefits, and mental health benefits. Postmodernism seems to be an increasingly more influential social philosophy. The ethics of the heart, which we have described, is certainly matched well with postmodernism.

In the present chapter, we have unashamedly touted the benefits of forgiveness. Perhaps the reader wonders how much we are willing to claim. Can forgiveness transform entire social systems? While we would not say "never," we believe that widespread social reform is not likely due to adopting a more widespread ethic of forgiveness. Forgiveness is not for everyone, and not everyone should be stretched or sawed into that Procrustean bed. Forgiveness can be misapplied. People can confuse it with reconciliation and conclude that, if they forgive a wrong, they necessarily should reconcile. Sometimes it is dangerous, unwise, or impossible to reconcile. Forgiveness, while not opposed to seeking justice, can erode the justice motive if people allow it. Weakening the drive for social justice would be unfortunate if it led to perpetuation or widening of social or economic inequities. Forgiveness is not a panacea. It is a tool for widening our ethical options from primarily an ethics of the mind to also include an ethics of the heart.

SUMMARY

We have argued throughout this chapter that businesses must deal with transgressions because transgressions are a part of being human and because we spend much of our lives at work. We also argued that ethical discourse, an ethics of the mind, has a role in shaping ways that people deal with ethical decisions. However, we have not been content to treat that ethical discourse as the *sine qua non* of ethics. Instead, we have argued for a relationship ethic, an ethics of the heart, which sets the communal tone for ways that people deal with personal transgressions. Emotional forgiveness is primarily associated with the ethics of the heart and with ways managers and workers treat each other. Some issues straddle the fence—such as issues of loyalty. Our modern *Zeitgeist* makes consideration of forgiveness timely, but the issues are far from simple. Thoughtful managers, however, will benefit from applying these ideas in human relations outside of and within the business setting.

NOTE

1. This is a complex moral problem when it is fully analyzed. It does not necessarily boil down to the harm of five versus one. It involves issues such as whether murder is involved if one actively diverts a train to kill a person. The social implications of doing such as act could be argued as harmful to more people in society than the one.

REFERENCES

Adams, G.A., King, L.A., & King, D.W. (1996). Relationships of job and family involvement, family social support, and work-family conflict with job and life satisfaction. *Journal of Applied Psychology, 81,* 411–420.

Barsade, S.G., Brief, A.P., & Spataro, S.E. (2003). The affective revolution in organizational behavior: The emergence of a paradigm. In J. Greenberg (Ed.), *Organizational behavior: The state of the science* (2nd ed., pp. 3–52). Mahwah, NJ: Lawrence Erlbaum.

Baumeister, R.F., Exline, J.J., & Sommer, K.L. (1998). The victim role, grudge theory, and two dimensions of forgiveness. In E.L. Worthington, Jr. (Ed.), *Dimensions of forgiveness: Psychological research and theological perspectives* (pp. 79–104). Philadelphia: Templeton Foundation Press.

Bellah, R.N, Madsen, R., Sullivan, W.M., Swidler, A., & Tipton, S.M. (1985). *Habits of the heart: Individualism and commitment in American life.* New York: Harper & Row.

Berry, J.W., Worthington, E.L., Jr., O'Connor, L., Parrott, L. III, & Wade, N.G. (2005). Forgiveness, vengeful rumination, and affective traits. *Journal of Personality, 73,* 1–43.

Berry, J.W., Worthington, E.L., Jr., Parrott, L. III, O'Connor, L., & Wade, N.G. (2001). Dispositional forgivingness: Development and construct validity of the Transgression Narrative Test of Forgivingness (TNTF). *Personality and Social Psychology Bulletin, 27,* 1277–1290.

Bies, R.J., & Tripp, T.M. (2001). A passion for justice: The rationality and morality of revenge. In R. Cropanzano (Ed.), *Justice in the workplace: From theory to practice* (Vol. 2, pp. 197–226). Mahwah, NJ: Lawrence Erlbaum.

Bradfield, M., & Aquino, K. (1999). The effects of blame attributions and offender likeableness on forgiveness and revenge in the workplace. *Journal of Management, 25,* 607–631.

Brief, A.P., & Weiss, H.M. (2002). Organizational behavior: Affect in the workplace. *Annual Review of Psychology, 53,* 279–307.

Brooks, C.W., Toussaint, L., & Worthington, E.L. Jr. (2003). *The relationship between forgiveness and depression: Rumination as a link.* Unpublished manuscript, Idaho State University.

Brownstein, E., Worthington, E.L., Jr., Berry, J.W., & Shivy, V. (2005). *Transgressions in the workplace: Associations with worker personality, productivity, physical health, and mental health.* Manuscript under editorial review.

Cohen, J.R. (2002). Apology and organizations: Exploring an example from medical practice. *Fordham Urban Law Journal, 27,* 1447–1482.

Cropanzano, R., Byrne, Z.S., Bobocel, D.R., & Rupp, D.E. (2001). Moral virtues, fairness heuristics, social entities, and other denizens of organizational justice. *Journal of Vocational Behavior, 58,* 164–209.

Cropanzano, R., Prehar, C.A., & Chen, P.Y. (2002). Using social exchange theory to distinguish procedural from interactional justice. *Group & Organization Management, 27,* 324–351.

DiBlasio, F. (1998). The use of decision-based forgiveness intervention within intergenerational family therapy. *Journal of Family Therapy, 20,* 77–94.

Elovainio, M., Kivimaki, M., Vahtera, J., Virtanen, M., & Keltikangas-Jarvinen, L. (2003). Personality as a moderator in the relations between perceptions of organizational justice and sickness absence. *Journal of Vocational Behavior, 63,* 379–395.

Exline, J.J., Worthington, E.L., Jr., Hill, P.C., & McCullough, M.E. (2003). Forgiveness and justice: A research agenda for social and personality psychology. *Personality and Social Psychology Review, 337–348.*

Farrow, T.F.D., Zheng, Y., Wilkinson, I.D., Spence, S.A., Deakin, J.F.W., Tarrier, N., Griffiths, P.D., & Woodruff, P.W.R. (2001). Investigating the functional anatomy of empathy and forgiveness. *Neuroreport, 12,* 2433–2438.

Flanigan, B. (1992). *Forgiving the unforgivable.* New York: Macmillan.

Frederickson, B.L. (2000). Why positive emotions matter in organizations: Lessons from the Broaden-and-Build model. *Psychologist-Manager Journal, 4,* 131–142.

Greene, J.D., Sommerville, R.B., Nystrom, L.E., Darley, J.M., & Cohen, J.D. (2001). An fMRI investigation of emotional engagement in moral judgment. *Science, 293,* 2105–2108.

Hart, P.M. (1999). Predicting employee life satisfaction: A coherent model of personality, work and nonwork experiences, and domain satisfactions. *Journal of Applied Psychology, 84,* 564–584.

Institute of Medicine. (1999). *To err is human.* Washington, DC: Author.

Karremans, J.C., & Van Lange, P.A.M. (January 2004). *Does activating justice help or hurt in promoting forgiveness?* Presented at the 5th Annual Meeting of the Society for Personality and Social Psychology, Austin, TX.

Kelly, W., Hoffman, D.K., & Davis, M.A. (1993). A typology of retail failures and recoveries. *Journal of Retailing, 69,* 429–452.

Lears, J. (2003). *Something for nothing: Luck in America.* New York: Viking Press.

Leymann, H. (1990). Mobbing and psychological terror at workplaces. *Violence and Victims, 5,* 119–126.

McCullough, M.E., Fincham, F.D., & Tsang, J. (2003). Forgiveness, forbearance, and time: The temporal unfolding of transgression-related interpersonal motivations. *Journal of Personality and Social Psychology, 84,* 540–557.

McCullough, M.E., Worthington, E.L. Jr., & Rachal, K.C. (1997). Interpersonal forgiving in close relationships. *Journal of Personality and Social Psychology, 73,* 321–336.

McCullough, M.E., Bellah, C.G., Kilpatrick, S.D., & Johnson, J.L. (2001). Vengefulness: Relationships with forgiveness, rumination, well-being, and the Big Five. *Personality and Social Psychology Bulletin, 27,* 601–610.

McCullough, M.F., Rachal, K.C., Sandage, S.J., Worthington, E.L., Jr., Brown, S.W., & Hight, T.L. (1998). Interpersonal forgiving in close relationships II: Theoretical elaboration and measurement. *Journal of Personality and Social Psychology, 75,* 1586–1603.

Meyer, L.R. (2000). Forgiveness and public trust. *Fordham Urban Law Journal, 27,* 1515–1540.

Milgram, S. (1974). *Obedience to authority.* New York: Harper & Row.

Oakenshott, M. (1962). *Rationalism in politics and other essays.* Washington, DC: Liberty Fund.

Robinson, S.L., & Bennett, R.J. (1995). A typology of deviant workplace behaviors: A multidimensional scaling study. *Academy of Management Journal, 38,* 555–572.

Skarlicki, D.P., & Folger, R. (1997). Retaliation in the workplace: The roles of distributive, procedural, and interactional justice. *Journal of Applied Psychology, 82,* 434–443.

Smith, A.K., Bolton, R.N., & Wagner, J. (1999). A model of customer satisfaction with service encounters involving failure and recovery. *Journal of Marketing Research, 36,* 356–372.

Tepper, B.J. (2000). Consequences of abusive supervision. *Academy of Management Journal, 43,* 178–190.

Toussaint, L.L., Williams, D.R., Musick, M.A., & Everson, S.A. (2001). Forgiveness and health: Age differences in a U.S. probability sample. *Journal of Adult Development, 8,* 249–257.

Turner, N., Barling, J., & Zacharatos, A. (2000). Positive psychology at work. In C.R. Snyder & S.J. Lopez (Eds.), *Handbook of positive psychology* (pp. 715–728). London: Oxford University Press.

Vandekerckhove, W., & Commers, M.S.R. (2003). Downward workplace mobbing: A sign of the times? *Journal of Business Ethics, 45,* 41–50.

Vincent C., Young, M., & Phillips, A. (1994). Why do people sue doctors? A study of patients and their relatives taking legal action. *Lancet, 343,* 1609–1613.

Weiss, H.M., & Cropanzano, R. (1996). Affective events theory: A theoretical discussion of the structure, causes and consequences of affective experiences at work. In B.M. Staw & L.L. Cummings (Eds.), *Research in organizational behavior* (Vo. 18, pp. 1–74). Greenwich, CT: JAI Press.

Witvliet, C.V.O., Wade, N.G., Worthington, E.L., Jr., & Berry, J.W. (2004). *Effects of apology and restitution on victims' unforgiveness, empathy, forgiveness, and psychophysiology: Words can speak as loudly as actions.* Under editorial review, Holland, MI, Hope College.

Witvliet, C.V.O., Worthington, E.L., Jr., Root, L.M., Sato, A.F., Ludwig, T.E., & Exline, J.J. (2003). *Justice, forgiveness, and emotion: A psychophysiological analysis.* Under editorial review, Holland, MI, Hope College.

Worthington, E.L., Jr. (2003). *Forgiving and reconciling: Bridges to wholeness and hope.* Downers Grove, IL: InterVarsity Press.

Worthington, E.L., Jr., & Berry, J.W. (2004). Can society afford not to promote forgiveness and reconciliation? In R.L. Hampton & T.P. Gullotta (Eds.), *Promoting social, ethnic, and religious understanding and reconciliation* (pp. 159–192). Washington, DC: Child Welfare League of America.

Worthington, E.L., Jr., & Scherer, M. (2004). Forgiveness is an emotion-focused coping strategy that can reduce health risks and promote health resilience: Theory, review, and hypotheses. *Psychology and Health, 19,* 385–405.

Worthington, E.L., Jr., & Wade, N.G. (1999). The social psychology of unforgiveness and forgiveness and implications for clinical practice. *Journal of Social and Clinical Psychology, 18,* 385–418.

Zapf, D. (1999). Organizational, work group related and personal causes of mobbing/bullying at work. *International Journal of Manpower, 20,* 70–85.

Printed in the United States
48782LVS00001B/218

9 781593 113223